Class, Codes and Control

Primary Socialization, Language and Education
Edited by Basil Bernstein
University of London Institute of Education
Sociological Research Unit

I *Social Class, Language and Communication*
W. Brandis & D. Henderson

II *A Linguistic Description and Computer Program for Children's Speech*
G. J. Turner & B. A. Mohan

III *Talk Reform*
D. M. & G. A. Gahagan

IV *Class, Codes and Control*
Volume 1 *Theoretical Studies towards a Sociology of Language*
Volume 2 *Applied Studies towards a Sociology of Language*
B. Bernstein

V *A Question of Answers (2 vols)*
W. P. Robinson & S. J. Rackstraw

VI *Social Control and Socialization*
J. Cook

A catalogue of other series of Social Science books published by Routledge will be found at the end of this volume.

Class, Codes and Control

Volume 2
Applied Studies towards a Sociology of Language

edited by

Basil Bernstein

Professor in the Sociology of Education
Head of the Sociological Research Unit
University of London Institute of Education

ROUTLEDGE & KEGAN PAUL

London and Boston

First published 1973
by Routledge & Kegan Paul Ltd
Broadway House,
68–74 Carter Lane,
London EC4V 5EL and
9 Park Street,
Boston, Mass. 02108, U.S.A.
Printed in Great Britain by
Clarke, Doble & Brendon Ltd, Plymouth
and set in 10 on 11 pt Times Roman

ISBN 0 7100 7396 8

Contents

Contributors

B. Bernstein	Head of the S.R.U., Professor of the Sociology of Education, University of London Institute of Education.
J. A. Cook	University of California, Berkeley; formerly Research Officer, S.R.U.
C. D. Creed	Lecturer in Psychology, University of Aberdeen; formerly Research Assistant, S.R.U.
M. A. K. Halliday	Fellow of the Center for Advanced Study and Research, Palo Alto, Stanford, 1972–3; formerly Professor of Linguistics, University College, London.
R. Hasan	Formerly Research Officer, S.R.U.
P. R. Hawkins	Lecturer in English, Victoria University of Wellington, New Zealand; formerly Assistant Research Officer, S.R.U.
D. Henderson	Research Officer, S.R.U.
R. E. Pickvance	Formerly Research Assistant, S.R.U.
W. P. Robinson	Senior Lecturer in Psychology, University of Southampton; formerly Deputy Head of the S.R.U.
G. J. Turner	Research Officer, S.R.U.
D. Young	Senior Lecturer in Sociology, North-East London Polytechnic; formerly Research Officer, S.R.U.

Acknowledgments

The publishers and Professor Bernstein would like to thank the following for permission to reprint material in this volume:

Sociology and the Clarendon Press, Oxford, for

'Social class differences in conceptions of the uses of toys' by Basil Bernstein and Douglas Young, from *Sociology*, vol. 1, no. 2, 1967.

'Social class differences in the relevance of language to socialization' by Basil Bernstein and Dorothy Henderson from *Sociology*, vol. 3, no. 1, January 1969.

'Contextual specificity, discretion and cognitive socialization' by Dorothy Henderson from *Sociology*, vol. 4, no. 3, September 1971.

Language and Speech for

'Perceptual and verbal discriminations of "elaborated" and "restricted" code users' by W. P. Robinson and C. D. Creed from *Language and Speech*, vol. 11, part 3, July–September 1968.
'Social class, the nominal group and reference' by Peter Hawkins, from *Language and Speech*, vol. 12, part 2, April–June 1969.
'Social class differences in the expression of uncertainty in five-year-old children' by Geoffrey Turner and Richard Pickvance, from *Language and Speech*, vol. 14, part 4, October–December 1971.

The S.R.U. acknowledges with gratitude the co-operation of teachers, parents and children. We should like to take this opportunity of thanking the two L.E.A.s who played an important part in the creation of the sample of schools. We should also like to thank the Department of Education and Science, the Ford Foundation, the Nuffield Foundation and the Social Science Research Council for the grants which made the research possible.

Foreword

M. A. K. Halliday

The work of Professor Basil Bernstein has sometimes been referred to as 'a theory of educational failure'. This seems to me misleading; the truth is both more, and less, than this implies. More, because Bernstein's theory is a theory about society, how a society persists and how it changes; it is a theory of the nature and processes of cultural transmission, and of the essential part that is played by language therein. Education is one of the forms taken by the transmission process, and must inevitably be a major channel for persistence and change; but there are other channels—and the education system itself is shaped by the social structure. Less, because Bernstein does not claim to be providing a total explanation of the causes of educational failure; he is offering an interpretation of one aspect of it, the fact that the distribution of failure is not random but follows certain known and sadly predictable patterns—by and large, it is a problem which faces children of the lower working class in large urban areas. Even here Bernstein is not trying to tell the whole story; what he is doing is to supply the essential link that was missing from the chain of relevant factors.

Nevertheless, it is perhaps inevitable that Bernstein's work should be best known through its application to educational problems, since these are the most striking and the most public of the issues with which he is concerned. After the relative confidence of fifteen post-war years, the 1960s were marked by growing awareness of a crisis in education, a realization that it was not enough to ensure that all children were adequately nourished and spent a certain number of years receiving formal education in school. The 'crisis' consists in the discovery that large numbers of children of normal intelligence, who have always had enough to eat, pass through the school system and come out as failures. We say, 'society has given them the opportunity, and they have failed to respond to it'; we feel hurt, and we want to know the reason why. (The formulation is not intended to imply a lack of genuine concern.)

Many people are aware of the existence of a hypothesis that educational failure is in some sense to be explained as linguistic failure. Something has gone wrong, it is suggested, with the language. This notion is in the air, so to speak; and the source of it is to be found in Bernstein's work—even though the various forms in which it is mooted often bear little relation to Bernstein's ideas. The terms that have become most widely current are Bernstein's 'elaborated code' and 'restricted code'; and in spite of the care which Bernstein has taken to emphasize that neither is more highly valued than the other, and that the hypothesis is that both are necessary for successful living—though the processes of formal education may demand the elaborated code—there is a widespread impression that Bernstein is saying (1) that some children speak elaborated code and some children speak restricted code, and (2) that the latter is an inferior form of speech, and therefore children who speak it are likely to fail. With these is sometimes compounded a further distortion according to which elaborated code is somehow equated with standard language and restricted code with non-standard. And the confusion is complete.

But if there is confusion, it is because there is something to be confused about. The difficulty is a very real one, and it is this. If language is the key factor, the primary channel, in socialization, and if the form taken by the socialization process is (in part) responsible for educational failure, then language is to blame; there must be something wrong about the language of the children who fail in school. So the reasoning goes. Either their language is deficient in some way, or, if not, then it is so different from the 'received' language of the school (and, by implication, of the community) that it is *as if* it was deficient—it acts as a barrier to successful learning and teaching. So we find two main versions of the 'language failure' theory, a 'deficit' version and a 'difference' version; and these have been discussed at length in the context of 'Black English' in the United States, where the problem of educational failure tends to be posed in ethnic rather than in social class terms. The language failure theory is sometimes referred to Bernstein's work, and he has even been held responsible for the deficit version of the theory, although nothing could be further removed from his own thinking. The fact that language failure is offered both as an interpretation of Bernstein's theories and as an alternative to them shows how complex the issues are and how easily they become clouded.

Let us consider the notion of language failure. According to the deficit version of the theory, the child who fails in school fails because he has not got enough language. It then becomes necessary to say where, in his language, the deficiency lies; and according to linguistic theory there are four possibilities, although these are combinable—the deficiency might lie in more than one: sounds, words, constructions and meanings.

Probably few people nowadays would diagnose the trouble as deficiency in sounds, although the 'our job is to teach them to talk properly' view of education is still with us, and might be taken to imply some such judgment of the case. If we leave this aside, there are two, and possibly a third, variants of the theory: not enough vocabulary, not enough grammar (or 'structures', in contemporary jargon), and a rarer and rather sophisticated alternative, not enough meanings. (Perhaps we should recognize another variant, according to which the child has no language at all. This cannot seriously be called a theory; but some people who would vigorously deny it if it was put to them in that form behave as if they held this view—'they have been exposed to good English, so obviously they have not the resources with which to absorb it.') We have to take these views seriously; they are held by serious-minded people of good faith who have thought about the problem and are anxious to find a solution. At the same time it needs to be said quite firmly that they are wrong.

There is no convincing evidence that children who fail in school have a smaller available vocabulary, or a less rich grammatical system, than those who succeed. Studies measuring the extent of the vocabulary used by children in the performance of specific tasks, though very valuable, do not tell us about their total resources; and formulations of the overall size of a child's vocabulary tend to conceal some doubtful assumptions about the nature of language. In the first place, one cannot really separate vocabulary from grammar; the two form a single component in the linguistic system, and measuring one without the other is misleading. It may well be that one individual extends his potential more by enlarging his grammatical resources, while another, or the same individual at a different time, does so by building up a larger vocabulary; and different varieties of a language, for example its spoken and written forms, tend to exploit these resources differentially. Second, there are so many problems in counting—how do we decide what a person *could* have said, or whether two things he *did* say were the same or different?—that it is hardly possible to assess an individual's linguistic resources accurately in quantitative terms. Finally, even if we could do so, it would tell us very little about his linguistic potential, which depends only in the last resort on the size of inventory. One does not count the gestures in order to evaluate the qualities of an actor, or judge a composer by the number of different chords and phrases he uses; it is only necessary to think of the immense variation, among writers, in the extent of the linguistic resources they typically deploy. In other words, there is no reliable way of saying 'this child has a smaller linguistic inventory (than that one, or than some presumed standard)'; and it would not help us much if we could.

But there are more serious weaknesses in the deficit theory. If there is a deficit, we have to ask: is it that the child has not got enough language, or that he does not know how to use what he has? But this question is meaningless. There is no sense in which we can maintain that he knows a linguistic form but cannot use it. (Of course one may get the meaning of a word or a construction wrong, but that is not what the question is about; in that case one does not know it.) The fact that we are led to pose the question in this way is an indication of the basic fallacy in the theory, a fallacy the nature of which we can see even more clearly when we pose another awkward question: is the presumed deficit an individual matter, or is it sub-cultural? Here we must assume the second, since the former would not offer any explanation of the pattern of educational failure. In other words the supposition is that there are groups of people—social class groups, ethnic groups, family types or some other—whose language is deficient; in linguistic terms, that there are deficient social dialects. As soon as we put it like that, the fallacy becomes obvious. Unfortunately, as Joan Baratz pointed out in a similar context, the idea of a deficient dialect is so patently self-contradictory and absurd that no linguist has ever taken the trouble to deny it. Perhaps the time has come to make an explicit denial.

We are left with the 'difference' version of the theory. This holds that some children's language is different from others'; this is undeniable, so the question is whether it is relevant. If one child's language differs from another's, but neither is deficient relative to the other, why is one of the children at a disadvantage?

The answer comes in two forms, one being a stronger variant of the other. We assume that the difference is that between a dialect and the standard language (in linguistic terms, between non-standard and standard dialects). Then, in the weaker variant, the child who speaks the non-standard dialect is at a disadvantage because certain factors demand the use of the standard. Many such factors could be cited, but they tend to fall under three headings: the teacher, the subject-matter, and the system. The child who speaks non-standard may be penalized by the teacher for doing so; he has to handle material presented in the standard language, for example in textbooks; and he has to adjust to an educational process and a way of life that is largely or entirely conducted in the standard language. This already raises the odds against him; and they are raised still higher if we now take the stronger variant of the difference theory, which adds the further explanation that non-standard dialects are discriminated against by society. In other words, the standard language is required not only by specific factors in the child's education but also by social pressures and prejudices, which have the effect that the child's own mother tongue is downgraded and he is stereotyped as likely to fail.

Now all this is certainly true. Moreover, as Frederick Williams found in testing the 'stereotype hypothesis' in the United States, the teacher's expectations of a pupil's performance tend to correspond rather closely to the extent to which that pupil's dialect diverges from the standard—and children, like adults, tend to act out their stereotypes: if you have decided in advance that a child will fail, he probably will. Many of the assumptions of the difference theory are justified, and these undoubtedly play some part in educational failure.

But there is still one question unanswered. If children are suffering because of their dialect, why do they not learn another one? Children have no difficulty in doing this; in many parts of the world it is quite common for a child to learn three or even four varieties of his mother tongue. Rural dialects in Britain differ from the standard much more widely than the urban dialects do, either in Britain or in America; yet rural children do not have the problem, which is well known to be an urban one. Moreover there is considerable evidence that these children who, it is claimed, are failing because they cannot handle the standard language can imitate it perfectly well outside the classroom, and often do. Perhaps then the problem lies in the written language: has the dialect-speaking child a special difficulty in learning to read in the standard? But here we are on even weaker ground, because the English writing system is splendidly neutral with regard to dialect. It is as well adapted to Glaswegian or Harlem speech as it is to standard British or American; that is its great strength. There are no special *linguistic* problems involved in learning to read just because one happens to speak a non-standard variety of English.

In other words, the 'difference' version of the language failure theory does not explain why dialect-speaking children come off badly—for the very good reason that the child who speaks a non-standard dialect is not under any linguistic disadvantage at all. His disadvantage is a social one. This does not mean that it is not real; but it means that it is misleading to treat it as if it was linguistic and to seek to apply linguistic remedies. Part of the social disadvantage lies in society's attitudes to language and to dialect—including those of the teacher, who may interpose false notions about language which *create* problems of a linguistic nature. But these are only manifestations of patterns in the social structure; they do not add up to a linguistic explanation of the facts.

So the language failure theory, in both its versions, stands rejected. We have removed all linguistic content from the hypothesis about educational failure. The fault rests neither with language as a system (the deficit version) nor with language as an institution (the difference version); the explanation is a social one (and, in Bernstein's words, 'education cannot compensate for society'). And here, in my own thinking, the matter rested, for a considerable time; I did not accept that there was any essentially linguistic element in the situation.

But, reconsidering in the light of Bernstein's work, especially his more recent thinking, we can see that the question 'deficit or difference?' is the wrong question. It is not what the issue is about. If we look at the results of investigations carried out by Bernstein and his colleagues, as reported in the present volume, and in other monographs in the series, we find that these studies reveal certain differences which correlate significantly with social class; these differences are there, and they are in some sense linguistic—they have to do with language. But the differences do not usually appear undisguised in the linguistic forms, the grammar and vocabulary, of the children's speech. They are, rather, differences of interpretation, evaluation, orientation, on the part of the children and of their mothers. Even where the primary data are drawn from samples of children's spontaneous speech, and this is analysed in linguistic terms, the focus of attention is always on the principles of the social functioning of language. Two features of the research stand out in this connection. One is the emphasis on 'critical social contexts', as Bernstein has defined and identified them: generalized situation types which have greatest significance for the child's socialization and for his interpretation of experience. The other is the focus on the variable *function* of language within these contexts, and on the functional meaning potential that is available to, and typically exhibited by, the child who is participating.

What Bernstein's work suggests is that there may be differences in the relative orientation of different social groups towards the various functions of language in given contexts and towards the different areas of meaning that may be explored within a given function. Now if this is so, then when these differences manifest themselves in the contexts that are critical for the socialization process they may have a profound effect on the child's social learning; and therefore on his response to education, because built in to the educational process are a number of assumptions and practices that reflect differentially not only the values but also the communication patterns and learning styles of different sub-cultures. As Bernstein has pointed out, not only does this tend to favour certain modes of learning over others, but it also creates for some children a continuity of culture between home and school which it largely denies to others.

This puts the question of the role of language in a different light. We can interpret the codes, from a linguistic point of view, as differences of orientation within the total semiotic potential. There is evidence in Bernstein's work that different social groups or sub-cultures place a high value on different orders of meaning. Hence differences arise in the prominence accorded to one or another socio-semantic 'set', or meaning potential within a given context. For any particular sub-culture, certain functions of language, or areas of meaning within a given function, may receive relatively greater emphasis; these will often reflect values which are implicit and submerged, but in other instances the values might be explicitly recognized—such different concepts as 'fellowship', 'soul', 'blarney', 'brow' (highbrow, lowbrow), suggest certain functional orientations which might well be examined from this standpoint. And there will be other orders of meaning, and other functions of language, that are relatively less highly valued and receive less emphasis. In general this does not matter. But let us now suppose that the semiotic modes that are relatively stressed by one group are *positive* with respect to the school—they are favoured and extended in the educational process, either inherently or because this is how education has come to be actualized—while those that are relatively stressed by another group are largely irrelevant, or even *negative*, in the educational context. We then have a plausible interpretation of the role of language in educational failure. It is, certainly, much over-simplified, as we have stated it here. But it places language in a perspective that is relevant to education—namely as the key factor in cultural transmission—instead of isolating it as something on its own.

This is somewhat removed from the notion of 'language failure', in either the deficit or the difference versions. We have had to direct attention beyond the forms of language, beyond accent and dialect and the morphological and syntactic particulars of this or that variety of English, on to meaning and social function. Of course, there are myths and misconceptions about, and attitudes towards, the forms of language, and these enter into and complicate the picture. It is important to make it clear that speakers of English who have no initial *h* or no postvocalic *r*, no verbal substitute or no definite article or no *–s* on the third person singular present tense, are not verbal defectives (if they are, then we all are, since any such list could always be made up—as this one was—of standard as well as non-standard features); nor is the underlying logic of one group any different from that of another. But just as the language element in educational failure cannot be reduced to a question of linguistic forms, so also it cannot be wholly reduced to one of attitudes to those forms and the stereotypes that result from them. It cannot be reduced to a concept of linguistic failure at all.

However, if we reject the equation 'educational failure = linguistic failure', this does not mean that we reject any interpretation of the problem in linguistic terms. Language is central to Bernstein's theory; but in order to understand the place that it occupies, it is necessary to think of language as meaning rather than of language as structure. The problem can then be seen to be one of linguistic success rather than linguistic failure. Every normal child has a fully functional linguistic system; the difficulty is that of reconciling one functional orientation with another. The remedy will not lie in the administration of concentrated doses of linguistic structure. It *may* lie, in part, in the broadening of the functional perspective—that of the school, as much as that of the individual pupil. This, in turn, demands a broadening of our own conceptions, especially our conceptions of meaning and of language. Not the least of Bernstein's contributions is the part that his work, and that of his colleagues, has played in bringing this about.

Introduction

In this second volume I have put together a series of papers written by members of the University of London Institute of Education Sociological Research Unit. Six of these papers are appearing in print for the first time. It is also unlikely that these papers will appear in future monographs in the form they take in this volume. In essence the papers represent work in progress where particular ideas were tested and coding procedures worked out which, we thought, would orientate us in future analyses. The papers cover a time period from 1966 to 1971, and involve nine members of the Sociological Research Unit. Although W. Brandis is not represented by a specific paper, he has played a major part in advising on methodological problems involved in both the collection and analysis of the data.

The papers are grouped together under four headings: 'Maternal orientations to communication'; 'Aspects of the speech of five-year-old children'; 'Aspects of the speech of seven-year-old children'; and 'Two theoretical issues'. There is also an appendix containing a new paper by Professor Michael Halliday. The authors of the papers have commented on the guiding theory and have interpreted and modified it according to their particular research problem. The size of the sample used varies with the problems and the technique of analysis. In a number of cases, however, as in Henderson and Turner's two studies, the samples used are respectively the same. Each paper provides an isolated glimpse of the overall work, and it is hoped that collectively they will provide a means of obtaining some perspective on the total work. In part I the three papers are almost wholly concerned with aspects of maternal communication, as this relates to regulative and instructional contexts. The first paper, (Bernstein and Young), is based upon data obtained from the first interview with the mother, before her child went to school for the first time. We wanted to obtain some ideas of the mother's conception of the use of toys, for we thought this might reflect her cognitive orientation. There were other questions put to the mother in this interview about play and toys, and so it was possible to check the priority the mother gave to certain uses of toys against later open-ended questions in the same areas (see Jones, 1966; Bernstein, 1967). We also were interested to see the relationships between a measure of maternal communication and the ranking of various uses of toys. The evidence shows that in the working class, scores on this simple measure of communication are associated with a higher ranking of the explorative function of toys.

The second and third papers which complete part I are based upon the communication section of the second interview with the mothers which took place two years after the first. Both these papers use the same sample. In the second interview we repeated some of the communication schedules which the mothers answered in the first interview. We improved on the earlier 'avoidance of questions' schedule (see Bernstein and Young). This earlier schedule was much too general. The second version specified a range of hypothetical questions which a child might ask. We obtained results with the repeated and modified schedules which were very similar to the results we obtained two years earlier. Bernstein and Henderson's paper takes its theoretical starting point from the distinction drawn between object and person relationships (see volume 1, chapter 8). This paper opens up the question of possible cultural differences in the relevance of language in the socialization of the child into object and person relationships. Henderson's paper covers a greater range of contexts, e.g. inter-personal, regulative, instructional. Henderson shows that when mothers were given a choice of four ways of explaining the meaning of a word to their child, middle-class mothers chose more frequently as their first choice 'abstract' or context-independent definitions, whilst working-class mothers chose more frequently 'concrete' or context-dependent definitions. The mothers were offered a choice of two types of 'concrete' definitions: implicit and explicit. The working-class mothers chose more frequently than the middle-class mothers the implicit type. We can compare this finding obtained through the use of an insensitive technique, the questionnaire, with the findings of Hawkins and Turner (see chapters 4 and 7) and Cook (1971, 1972). Both Turner and Hawkins suggest that the children of the working-class mothers have a preference for implicit (context-dependent) forms of speech, and Cook repeats a similar preference in the mothers' speech. Henderson interprets her findings in the light of the model offered in chapter 10 of volume 1. In forthcoming work we hope to show in some detail the interrelationships between social class, types of family structures, and forms of communication.

In part II there are three papers concerned with aspects of the speech of five-year-old children. The first paper by Hawkins examines the choices within the nominal group made by the children (263) when they told a simple story based upon four pictures and when they described picture cards. Hawkins used a form of cohesion analysis developed by Dr Hasan (see chapter 10). His findings suggest that, given the eliciting contexts, working-class children have a somewhat greater preference for exophoric language use; that is, where the referents are in the context rather than explicitly realized in the speech. He also shows that middle-class children exploit rather more than working-class children the possibilities within the nominal group. Hawkins's paper is a great advance on the work I had done earlier on pronominal usage. It paved the way to the distinction between context-dependent and context-independent meanings, which in turn enabled more precise definitions to be given to the universalistic/particularistic distinction initially developed in 1962 (see volume 1, chapter 5). It is a matter of some interest that two researchers in Hungary who used the Sociological Research Unit eliciting material, found that Hungarian working-class children also used, more often than middle-class children, implicit forms of speech. The paper by Turner and Pickvance examines expressions of uncertainty and tentativeness in the speech of five-year-old children. Whilst the linguistic usage of such expressions are not necessarily indicators of 'cognitive flexibility', they may well be indicators of the child's *verbal* realization that there is a discrepancy between his verbal coding and what is potentially available to be coded. Turner and Pickvance's analysis reveals social class differences between the children in their use of such expressions. They also show that middle-class five-year-old children have a greater preference for ego-centric sequences. Such sequences have been interpreted by Bernstein (1962), Lawton (1968) and Cook (1971) as markers of an individualized role and therefore more likely, given the context, to be associated with an elaborated code. On the other hand socio-centric sequences, have been interpreted as markers of a communalized role and as such are more likely to be associated with a restricted code. Turner and Pickvance compared the five-year-old children's use of ego-centric sequences with the analysis made by Cook (1971) of the speech of the mothers of the children. Cook found that the middle-class mothers made more use of ego-centric sequences, expressions of tentativeness and conditional statements in a regulative context than working-class mothers. Turner and

Pickvance suggest a possible relationship between mothers and their children in the relative use of such expressions. As no correlational analysis on the basis of a mother and her child has yet been made, we can only say that their results are suggestive. It is a matter of interest that the relative use of these expressions is only very weakly related to the measured ability of the children.

The reader might consider that the inclusion of the paper by Robinson and Creed in part II is somewhat out of keeping with the rest of the papers. I have decided to include it for a number of reasons. The paper describes an experiment to test the effects of the language programme designed by D. and G. Gahagan, published under the title of *Talk Reform: an exploratory language programme for infant school children*, Routledge & Kegan Paul, 1970. The experiment required children to indicate in what way pairs of pictures were different. The children who took part in this study were matched for various criteria, one of which was based upon linguistic measures of the children's speech at five years of age; one and a half years *before* the experiment. These linguistic measures were not only very crude, but they were drawn from the children's speech across a range of contexts. These measures were not specific to any context, *and* the eliciting contexts in no way resembled the experimental task the children were offered one and a half years later. Robinson and Creed found that there was a relationship between these linguistic measures and the extent to which the children were able to indicate differences between the pairs of pictures.

The second reason for the inclusion of this paper is to make the reader aware of some of the problems of 'matching' groups. One of the criteria used for 'matching' the children was the social-class position of the parents. The social-class scale was based upon the education and occupation of *both* parents. Robinson and Creed found that one child's speech and discriminative behaviour was very much at odds with his parents' social-class position; so much so that the removal of this child from the sample would have raised considerably the level of statistically significant differences between the groups under comparison. Robinson and Creed then examined more closely the social-class position of the parents, as indexed by our procedures of measurement. They found that the mother of this child had been to a grammar school, and that she did not leave school until seventeen. However, the father had been to a non-selective school, had left school at fourteen and had been continuously employed in an unskilled position; according to our social-class scale, this would indicate working class. If we had been in a position to match the children on the index of *maternal* communication and control, which we developed later, it is possible that we might have discovered this discrepancy, as we would have noted that the mother's score on the index was at variance with the social-class position of the family. Such an inconsistency is perhaps not so critical where the sample is very large, but as Robinson and Creed's sample is very small, it did have a major effect. The lesson seems to be that, when we 'match' groups, we should be careful to ensure that we 'match' for the relevant parameters. In this case, the global social-class index masked a relevant parameter—the education of the mother.

In part III there are three papers which examine aspects of the speech of seven-year-old children. The first paper by Hawkins is an inquiry into social class differences in the use of hesitation in speech. In 1962 (see volume 1) I applied Professor Goldman-Eisler's technique of hesitation analysis. Hawkins's analysis is a far more sophisticated study. Hawkins shows the relationship between hesitation and clause and group structures. His research suggests that working-class boys spent a greater amount of time pausing at clause boundaries; whereas middle-class children used more often what Hawkins calls the longest 'genuine' hesitation pause, many of which were located *within* the clause. Hawkins considers that this is an indication of *within* clause lexical planning. Robinson's paper, which follows, analyses the answering behaviour of mothers and children, and shows the inter-relationship between their styles. This paper attempts to examine the strength of the relationship between the types of explanation offered by mothers and the types of explanations offered by their children. Robinson developed a complex set of categories for his analysis to which only brief reference is made in the paper. The category system is fully set out in the Sociological Research Unit monograph entitled *A Question of Answers*, by W. P. Robinson and S. J. Rackstraw, Routledge & Kegan Paul, 1972. Robinson does show that there are significant differences between the answering styles of middle-class and working-class mothers and children. Of more interest is the suggestion that the answering styles of mothers and children in the working class are more similar than the answering styles of mothers and children in the middle class. Another important finding is that there was *little* relationship between the linguistic measures used to assess the mothers' speech and the social-class position of the family. It may well be that the more delicate analysis which has been recently developed by Hasan and Turner would have given a more sensitive description of the speech. I am inclined to think that if the semantic styles differ we might reasonably expect differences in their linguistic realization.

It is the case, however, that the analysis used by Robinson does not show class differences in the speech. One of the major difficulties of the research has been the problem of working out in detail code realization of *different* contexts. Code indicators of one context are not necessarily the same for another. We probably have been most successful in working out code realizations of the regulative context. I am fairly sure this is because the sociological side of the theory is particularly strong (or less weak) in its ability to specify the underlying semantic structure of the different forms of control realized by elaborated and restricted codes.

Turner's paper which completes part III compares the speech of five-year-old children with the same children's speech at seven years of age. Turner analyses the strategies of control used by middle-class and working-class children elicited by a context which contained a property offence (a ball breaking a window). The reader will notice that there has been a change in the method of linguistic analysis. Turner applied Halliday's recent network theory to a grid for the study of strategies of social control (Bernstein and Cook, 1965). The context of control (the regulative context) contains from this point of view a number of sub-systems. Each sub-system opens out as a network of polar choices which can become increasingly delicate as one moves from the left to the right of the network. The semantic structure of each sub-system derives from the theory of codes (see Cook, chapter 11 for an extensive account of this derivation). Each choice in the network can in principle be given a grammatical characterization. In this way sociology can provide the semantic structure of the choice system and linguistics provides for its grammatical realization. This approach is a great step forward in the integration of sociological and linguistic elements of the theory. I believe that Halliday's network theory could provide an exciting approach to sociolinguistic studies given that the sociological theory is sufficiently strong to realize the semantic structure of the network. Given the young age of the children and the contextual constraints, only three sub-systems of the total grid were applicable: choices within the punishment system, simple choices within the positional component of the appeals system and simple choices within the reparative system. What is of unusual interest is that Turner compares the strategies and speech of five-year-old children with the speech and strategies of the same children at seven years of age, when they were offered the *same* eliciting context. Turner shows a clear pattern of class related differences which are maintained at seven years of age. He also shows that the children's strategies are only very weakly related to their measured intelligence. We have some check on the reliability of Turner's study. During the first interview of the mothers before the sample child went to school, the mothers were asked questions about what they would do if the child committed a number of misdemeanours. When the children were seven years of age, the same questions, with minor modifications, were put to them. We thus have some knowledge of the mothers' reported control styles and speech, and those of the children, independently of Turner's study (Cook 1971, 1972). On the whole, Turner's results agree with Cook's findings. It is a matter of interest that although Cook's study revealed class differences between the children in their choices within the punishment system, it did not reveal any class differences in the children's choices within the positional system. Turner's analysis does. *This shows the importance of developing very delicate, but theoretically relevant categories where the eliciting context is strongly framed and focused and where the age of the children sharply reduces their range of choices.*

Part IV contains two very substantial essays by Dr Hasan and Dr Cook. Dr Hasan's essay, 'Code, register and social dialect', deals essentially with the problem of distinguishing between these different concepts. Dr Hasan is well-equipped for such a problem as she has worked very closely with Halliday's theory and in her own right Dr Hasan has developed a theory of the cohesive elements in speech. Dr Hasan uses Durkheim's concepts of mechanical and organic solidarity to set up a model for the exposition of ideal types of restricted and elaborated codes. I also believe that Durkheim's analysis of modes of social integration underlies the concept of codes. Although Dr Hasan limits herself to exposition, it would be wrong to believe that she does not have major reservations about the socio-linguistic theory and the problems of its empirical exploration (see Hasan, 1972). The discussion of register in her paper is deceptive, as it, in its own right, advances the theory of register. I take the major point of her paper to be that the three concepts, codes, register and dialect, despite a superficial similarity, focus upon quite different problems and inhabit quite distinct logical levels of analysis. Dr Cook reviews critically a range of studies in sociology and social psychology, which focus upon the study of social control and socialization within the family. She shows the omission in such research of the study of speech and the lack (until recently) of a socio-linguistic perspective. The major point of Dr Cook's paper is a plea to take as the focus of study the natural language of everyday encounters, in order to reveal the sequencing principles and indexical properties implicit in the negotiation of everyday meanings. Dr Cook argues that such an approach would reduce the violation, by the reconstructed logic of the researcher, of the meanings spontaneously generated in family inter-actions. At the same time, such an approach would provide a sharper focus upon the assumptions underlying the creation of social order. In this way, studies of socialization could be greatly enhanced by the ethnomethodological perspective of Garfinkel and Cicourel. Dr Cook's approach is also an implicit and welcome critique of the theory and methods used by the Sociological Research Unit. The perennial problem remains however, of showing the relationships between the wider institutional structure and the sequencing rules and indexical properties of everyday talk.

Finally, the appendix contains a new paper by Professor Michael Halliday. Professor Halliday is one of the small group of linguists who are changing our perspective on language through the integration of linguistics with semantics. Through such integration we can see the relationships between language and society. 'The social functions which language is serving in the life of the child determine both the options which he creates for himself and their realization in structure . . . The internal organization of natural language can best be explained in the light of the social functions which language has evolved to serve' (Halliday). Professor Halliday's paper provides us with an excellent opportunity to explore his approach to the child's initial acquisition of the functions of language. It is a matter of great personal regret that my own work until recently was insufficiently developed, was insufficiently explicit, to take full advantage of Halliday's researches. I have always found his ideas a constant source of encouragement, stimulation and development. I regard it as a great privilege to be able to include in this volume his introduction and paper.

I hope that the collection of research papers written by members of the Sociological Research Unit will give some overall impression of the range of work we have carried out. It may well be that in the last analysis its importance lies in the questions which have been opened up and the procedures used, rather than in the findings. For the latter will undoubtedly cease to hold as the transmission principles of socialization change. It is the case that the studies in this volume all use social class as the major background variable. However, some of the studies here do point the way to future analyses in which we hope to show how the effect of social class is mediated through types of family structures which in turn create different forms of communication. One of the major difficulties in exploring the theory which has guided our work is the problem of constructing eliciting contexts which would be applicable to children of different ages, sex, measured ability and, of critical significance, very different social backgrounds. The same problem, of course, applies to the interviewing of the mothers. There is also the irony of working with a theory which suggests a relationship between the different social structuring of meaning and the form of its linguistic realization *and* then designing 'common' experimental contexts for its empirical study. This raises immediately the question of the relationships between a theory and the *procedures* used for its empirical exploration; for the procedures used may create data which are inappropriate to such exploration. The procedures themselves are often governed by the size of the sample, the research budget and wider policy issues. It may well be that the fundamental research problem is the initial study of the *procedures* necessary for creating an appropriate relationship between a theory and what counts as data relevant to it. It would be interesting to apply to a grant-giving body for the large sum of money such a study would require. Ironically, one is much more likely to obtain such a grant *after* this vital research step. It is not unusual in the natural sciences for large sums of money to be given for the express purpose of developing the procedures of observation. Why not in the social sciences?

The major advantage of the procedures we have used is that they enable a mapping of the problem and they suggest further areas of more delicate enquiry.

Finally, there may be a group of purists who take issue with the sub-title of these volumes. Many of our studies appear to be concerned with micro aspects of the behaviour of children, or limited aspects of the inter-actions within the families. I am of the opinion that what makes something sociological has nothing to do with the phenomena, but everything to do with the conceptual system to which the phenomena is referred. There is no one particular which is unworthy of sociological study: what gives it its worth is an imaginative transformation which allows us a view of the latent and changing structure of society.

As the research reported in this volume has not focused upon the school, it is possible to interpret our findings as offering support for the thesis which maintains that educational failure is primarily a function of processes of communication within the family. I do not hold such a thesis (see chapters 10 and 11 of *Class Codes and Control* Vol. 1). However, it is clearly the case that the class structure influences the distribution of what counts as privileged resources in *both* the home and the school. It is also the case that the social assumptions underlying the form and content of public education also have their bases in the same class structure. Our research provides some evidence that there are *differences* in the social functions of communication which have their origin in the class structure. Whether these differences confer relative advantages, that is, whether these differences are transformed into inequalities, depends, primarily and fundamentally, upon the assumptions underlying educational practice.

References

BERNSTEIN, B. (1962), 'Linguistic codes, hesitation phenomena and intelligence', *Language and Speech*, 5.

BERNSTEIN, B. and COOK, J. (1965), 'Social Control Grid', in Cook, J., (1972) *Socialization and Social Control*, London, Routledge & Kegan Paul.

BERNSTEIN, B. (1967), 'Play and the infant school', *Where*, Supplement 11, *Toys*.

BERNSTEIN, B. (1971), *Class, Codes and Control: Theoretical Studies Towards a Sociology of Language*, London, Routledge & Kegan Paul.

COOK, J. (1971), 'An enquiry into patterns of communication and control between mothers and their children in different social classes', Ph.D. Thesis, University of London. Published as *Socialization and Social Control: A Study of the Language of Mothers and Their Children*, London, Routledge & Kegan Paul, 1972.

GAHAGAN, D. and GAHAGAN, G. (1970), *Talk Reform: an Exploratory Language Programme for Infant School Children*, London, Routledge & Kegan Paul.

HASAN, R. (1972), 'Codes and their realization' (manuscript).

JONES, J. (1966), 'Social class and the under fives', *New Society*, 22 December.

LAWTON, D. (1968), *Social Class, Language and Education*, London, Routledge & Kegan Paul.

ROBINSON, P. and RACKSTRAW, S. (1972), *A Question of Answers*, vols I and II, London, Routledge & Kegan Paul.

Part I Maternal orientations to communication

Chapter I Social class differences in conceptions of the uses of toys

B. Bernstein and D. Young

Introduction

The Sociological Research Unit of the Institute of Education, University of London, is currently undertaking an inquiry into: (1) the origins of social class differences in the responsiveness of parents to education; (2) the linguistic development of children aged five years through to seven years: and (3) the influence of patterns of communication and control in the home on (1) and (2).

The sample under discussion consists of 351 families drawn from two areas, one of which is mainly working-class and the other mainly middle-class (as assessed in terms of occupation and education of both parents). The middle-class area, however, shows a slight bias towards the higher social class groups whilst the working-class area shows a corresponding bias towards the lower social class groups. In each area the school was the initial sampling unit. The Unit obtained from the schools the names and addresses of the parents who had a five-year-old child going to school for the first time in September 1964 in the working-class area, and in 1965 for the middle-class area. In the middle-class area five schools were chosen in order to give as wide a range of middle-class families as was possible in terms of the resources of the Research Unit.

A similar procedure was adopted in the working-class area. However, experimental work undertaken by the Unit in the infant school was a major influence upon the selection of schools, and thirteen schools were chosen altogether.[1]

A tape-recorded interview was arranged with the mothers in the summer preceding the child's commencing school. The interviews covered such topics as the range and type of preparation of the child for school, the mother's concepts of play, toys, brightness, learning, how she conceptualized the boundaries between herself and the school, her patterns of communication with (and control over) the child, and her factual knowledge of the school system. In this report we shall present findings bearing upon social class differences in the mother's conception of the uses of toys.

It seems important to examine the significance of toys for at least the following two reasons:

(1) The cognitive, social and fantasy development of children is said to be enhanced through the use of toys and the medium of play (Moore, 1964).

(2) The infant school offers, as a medium of education, a controlled form of play environment. It emphasizes a view of the child as a spontaneous seeker and explorer of relevance and relations (Gardner, 1956, 1966).

Thus, differences between social class groups in their attitude to toys might affect the child within the home, and also the child's chances of profiting from the controlled play environment at the infant school.

Method

The interview with the mother included open and closed questions about play and toys. A closed schedule concerned with the various uses of toys was inserted between a series of open questions on aspects of play and toys. The closed schedule was a simple ranking task, and took the following form:

Here are some ideas about what toys are for. Please put 1 for the use which you think is most important, a 2 for the next most important, and so on until 6 for the least important.

A. To keep children amused by themselves.
B. So that they can play with other children.
C. So that they can find out about things.
D. To free the mother so that she can do other things.
E. To help them when they go to school.
F. To show that mother cares when she has been away.

Hypotheses

The following hypotheses were derived from the conceptual framework underlying previous papers (Bernstein, 1961, 1964).

(1) That there would be social class differences in consensus concerning the mothers' conceptions of the uses of toys.

(2) That statement E would be a less important choice for the middle-class and more clearly distinguished from C in the rank order than for other class groups, as C represents a more general

conception than E. (This hypothesis can be regarded as a more explicit formulation of the first hypothesis. The choices thought to be important in the schedule were C and E as positive choices, and D and F as negative, lower order choices.)
(3) *Within* social class there would be differences in the mothers' conceptions of the uses of toys, due to intra-class differences in maternal patterns of communication with children.
(4) That there would be a correlation between the mothers' conceptions of the uses of toys and the measured intelligence of their children.

In order to test these hypotheses two previously constructed indices were used, one concerned with social class and the other with patterns of mother–child communication.

(*a*) *Social class index* (Brandis)
An index of social class was derived from a factor analysis of the mother's and father's occupational and educational experience. From the resultant standardized scores of the factor analysis, five social class groups were distinguished: two clearly middle-class, one marginal class (having some middle-class and some working-class characteristics), and two clearly working-class.

(*b*) *Communication index* (Brandis)
This index was based upon the combined scores from two closed schedules concerned with aspects of communication between mother and child.[2] The first schedule assessed the willingness of the mother to take up her child's attempts at verbal inter-action across a range of behavioural settings. The second schedule assessed the extent to which the mother would avoid or evade answering difficult questions put to her by the child. A factor analysis was carried out which justified the scoring procedures used. Thus a high score on this index represented a mother who indicated that she would take up the child's attempts at verbal inter-action in a range of contexts, and who would explain rather than avoid answering difficult questions put to her by her child.

Analysis: statistical method

Application of the social class index revealed that the 351 mothers were distributed, over five social class categories, in the following way:

middle class: 110 lower middle class: 56
marginal social class: 65
upper working class: 62 lower working class: 58

For each social class grouping, Kendall's (1948) coefficient of concordance was calculated, as a gross measure of consensus within the groupings concerned. In order to see how individual statements fared within each grouping, their average rank positions were also calculated. Finally, the rankings for each social grouping were cross-classified with respect to the communication index variable. This was done in order to see whether mothers scoring high on the communication index also showed higher concordance, and more emphatic tendencies to accept or reject particular statements.

Results

Hypothesis 1 That there would be social class differences in the mothers' conceptions of the uses of toys.

TABLE 1.1 *Coefficients of concordance by social class and average rank of each item on toy schedule*

Social class	*Coefficients of concordance*	*Statements* A	*B*	*C*	*D*	*E*	*F*	*N*
Middle class	0·58	2·8	3·1	1·5	5·1	3·4	5·2	110
Lower middle class	0·46	3·3	3·3	1·6	5·2	2·9	4·6	56
Marginal social class	0·30	3·4	3·6	2·0	5·0	2·8	4·2	65
Upper working class	0·22	3·4	3·4	2·5	5·0	2·8	3·7	62
Lower working class	0·09	3·4	3·4	2·9	4·3	3·0	4·0	58

Table 1.1 reveals a coefficient of concordance of 0·58 in the highest social class grouping. This is followed by progressively smaller coefficients (0·46, 0·30, 0·22) until, in the lowest social class, the coefficient falls to 0·09.

Discussion

It is natural to ask whether there is a general conception in our society about the uses of toys which is most explicit in the middle classes and which grows vaguer as one moves down the social class scale, or whether the decreasing concordance is due to the fact that the lower classes 'fragment' into distinct sub-groups.

This question may be partly answered if we examine the extent to which the various choices show signs of differentiation from each other. One possible way of showing this is to take an *arbitrary* deviation of ±1·5 in average rank from the mean rank of 3·5, as an indication of clear rejection or acceptance of a particular choice. When this criterion is used as an index of differentiation among the choices, the following picture emerges:

(1) No choices meet this criterion in the lower working-class group.
(2) In the upper working classes and all classes above this group, statement D (to free the mother so that she can do other things) is clearly rejected.
(3) In the marginal social class and all classes above this group statement C (to find out about things) is clearly accepted.
(4) In the middle classes, and only in the middle classes, a *third* statement is differentiated. This is statement F (to show that mother cares when she has been away) which, like statement D, is clearly rejected.

Thus the middle class shows three differentiated choices, the lower middle class and marginal class two differentiated choices, the upper working class only one differentiated choice and the lower working class not one. There is, therefore, evidence, if the criterion for inferring structure is accepted, of a clear social class gradient in the differentiation of the choices, with the middle class possessing the most uniformly differentiated set of choices.

Hypothesis 2 That statement E would be a less important choice for the middle class and more clearly distinguished from C in the rank order than for other class groups.

It can be seen that the distance in rank order between C (to find out about things) and E (to help them when they go to school) is greater for the middle-class group than for any other group. (Middle class = 1·9, lower middle class = 1·3, marginal class = 0·8, upper working class = 0·3 and lower working class = 0·1). In addition, the middle class give statement E a lower ranking (and statement C a higher ranking) than do any of the four lower social classes. Hypothesis 2 can, therefore, be regarded as well supported.

Hypothesis 3 Within social class there would be differences in the mothers' conceptions of the uses of toys as a result of intra-class differences in maternal patterns of communication to children.

TABLE 1.2 *Coefficients of concordance within communication index scores for lower working class*

Lower working class	*Coefficients of concordance*	*Statements* A	*B*	*C*	*D*	*E*	*F*	*N*
High communication index	0·30	3·8	3·2	2·1	5·1	3·0	3·8	14
Low communication index	0·05	3·3	3·4	3·1	4·0	3·0	4·0	44

TABLE 1.3 *Coefficients of concordance within communication index scores for upper working class*

Upper working class	*Coefficients of concordance*	*A*	*B*	*C*	*D*	*E*	*F*	*N*
		Statements						
High communication index	0·44	3·5	3·4	1·9	5·7	2·8	3·7	15
Medium communication index	0·27	3·3	3·4	2·5	5·5	2·7	3·9	23
Low communication index	0·09	3·5	3·5	2·9	4·5	3·0	3·6	24

TABLE 1.4 *Coefficients of concordance within communication index scores for marginal social class*

Marginal social class	*Coefficients of concordance*	*A*	*B*	*C*	*D*	*E*	*F*	*N*
		Statements						
High communication index	0·39	3·8	3·7	1·6	5·0	2·8	4·2	17
Medium communication index	0·32	3·3	3·6	2·1	5·2	2·8	4·0	31
Low communication index	0·22	3·2	3·6	2·4	4·5	2·8	4·5	17

It is clear from Tables 1.2, 1.3 and 1.4 that the communication index score (the measure of mother–child communication mentioned earlier) within each of the lower working, upper working and marginal classes, powerfully affects the coefficient of concordance. The higher the level of the communication index the higher the coefficient of concordance. This effect does not, however, extend to the lower middle and middle classes, so no tables are given for these two groups.

Discussion

If we look at the relationship between the degree of differentiation of the rankings and the score on the communication index (using the $\pm 1{\cdot}5$ criterion mentioned earlier) then the following tendencies emerge:

(1) In the lower working class, statement D (to free the mother so that she can do other things) is the only item rejected.

(2) In the upper working class, statement D is even more strongly rejected and statement C (to find out about things) becomes a more favoured choice.

(3) In the marginal social class, statement C rises still further in rank order.

Thus, holding social class constant, differences in the score on the communication index affect the coefficient of concordance, and there is a tendency for choices C and D to show greater differentiation from the other choices. The communication index does not produce any change in either the coefficient of concordance or in the degree of differentiation of choices in the lower middle- and middle-class groups. However, it is thought that measures of more complex communications (which are currently being worked out) may reveal such differences within these two classes. Hypothesis 3 is therefore confirmed only in respect of the lower three classes. It is worth noting that the effect of high or low communication index score on the coefficient of concordance is:

(1) To raise the coefficient for the lower working-class group to the level exhibited by the (overall) marginal class group when the index is high, and to depress the coefficient to that below the (overall) lower working-class group when the index is low.
(2) To raise the coefficient for the upper working-class group to the level of the lower middle-class group when the index is high, and to depress the coefficient to the level of the lower working-class group when the index is low.
(3) To raise the coefficient for the marginal social class group half-way towards the lower middle-class group when the index is high and to depress the coefficient to the level of the upper working class when the index is low.

Also of interest is the fact that when the concordance coefficient rises as a consequence of high communication index score, the rank orders become more similar to those shown by the corresponding higher social class group. Conversely, when the coefficient falls as a consequence of low communication index score, the rank orders become more similar to those exhibited by the corresponding lower social class group. It is possible that the degree of communication (as measured by the index) facilitates mobility between social class groups through the agency of education.

Hypothesis 4 That there is a relationship between the mother's conception of the use of toys and measured intelligence.

When the children (n = 174) in the working-class area were six years old the Wechsler Intelligence Scale for Children was administered. (The WISC will be given to the middle class when they are six.) An analysis was made of the mothers who ranked statement C *first* and who ranked statement D *last*, in order to see if there was a correlation between such ranking and ability test scores.[3]

The results are given below:

	Correlation	*Significance*
WISC (verbal)	r = 0·17	$p < 0{\cdot}05$
WISC (performance)	r = 0·28	$p < 0{\cdot}001$
WISC (full-scale)	r = 0·25	$p < 0.001$

These results indicated that hypothesis 4, relating conceptions of the use of toys to measured ability of children, has received some measure of support.

In the absence of this result, it might be argued that the mothers' conceptions of the uses of toys simply reflected what the mothers took to be socially acceptable or desirable responses. However, as there is a correlation between the mothers' priorities over the uses of toys and the ability of the child (as indexed by the WISC test), there is reasonable ground for believing that mothers' reported beliefs *do* in fact have behavioural consequences for their children. It is important to note that the mothers' conceptions of the uses of toys are more highly correlated with the *performance* scale than with the verbal scale of the WISC. This would seem to suggest that ability on the relatively less verbally loaded sections of the WISC may be affected by the cultural or sub-cultural definition of the significance of toys. It is worth emphasizing that the mothers were interviewed when the children were four years six months and the WISC was given to the children when they were six years.

Conclusion

It is of interest that although the interview with the mother was clearly about education, and had been in progress for some time before the 'toy' schedule was given, the highest average rank given to statement E (to help them when they go to school) was only 2·80. This choice, one might have thought, would have been the socially approved response for those with no clear views about toys. However, this does not appear to have been the case.

In view of the support obtained for the four hypotheses, the research can be said to have demonstrated a social class differentiation in mothers' conceptions of the uses of toys. It is not suggested for one moment that the middle-class mother always sees or uses toys for their cognitive or 'fantasy' possibilities. Nor is it suggested that the average middle-class conception is in some sense the only possible or 'best' conception. It is equally important to point out that it is *not* held that the working class have *no* conception of the use of toys—only that collectively they do not share the middle-class conception. However, the middle-class conception is harmonious with the conception held in the infant school. Indeed, the Unit has independent evidence (to widen the issue) that many working-class mothers do not see play in the infant school as of educational significance, whereas many middle-class mothers *do* see play in this light.

The significance of a toy depends more on the mother's interpretation of the toy to the child than on any intrinsic property of the toy. The mother's interpretation of the toy is, in turn, probably a reflection of the general guidance and control procedures that she employs in her dealings with the child.[4] Of some significance here is the expected relation between the score on the communication index and the conception of the uses of toys. The score on this index gives some indication of the range and quality of the mother's communications to the child. Verbal inter-action indices of this kind seem potentially capable of making relatively fine discriminations within a social class group, and of accounting for variations within the class concerned. This matter is still under investigation.

Of some importance is the finding that there is a correlation between the mothers' ranked choices in the 'toy' schedule and the intelligence of their children. If it is true that many members of the working class do not share certain priorities (and the concept upon which they are based), then their children are foregoing the behavioural consequences of the presence of such a concept, namely, a possible increase in measured ability score. Thus for the working-class child a whole order of potential learning may not be available. By a similar argument, it can be said that inasmuch as the middle-class mother's concept of the use of toys is in harmony with that of the infant school, then the middle-class child is more likely than the working-class child to explore profitably the potentiality of the infant class. Moreover, such exploration will occur *earlier* in his infant school career, as there is a continuity between the home and the infant school. The working-class child may have to learn what for the middle-class child is given by his primary socialization. It would seem that, even at the age of five years, there is differential access to processes which facilitate the development of ability and the opportunity to benefit from school, in terms of the current definitions of the form and contents of education.

Summary

Different conceptions of the uses of toys were analysed in a sample of 351 families. The following hypotheses were tested:

(1) That there would be social class differences in consensus concerning the mothers' conceptions of the uses of toys.
(2) That statement E would be a less important choice for the middle class and more clearly distinguished from statement C in the rank order than for other class groups, as statement C represents a more general conception than statement E.
(3) *Within* social class there would be differences in the mothers' conceptions of the uses of toys due to intra-class differences in maternal patterns of communication with children.
(4) That there would be a correlation between the mothers' conceptions of the uses of toys and the measured intelligence of their children.

The results secured a good measure of support for all four hypotheses. However, a closer analysis is required in order to understand variations within social class in the degree of concordance, and this is currently being undertaken.

It is hypothesized that class-determined differences in the conception of the uses of toys have a bearing upon both the development of measured intelligence and on the ability of the child to adjust to and profit from the current infant school experience.

References

BERNSTEIN, B. (1961), 'Social class and linguistic development: a theory of social learning', in *Education, Economy and Society* (eds) A. H. Halsey, J. Floud, and C. A. Anderson. New York: Free Press.

BERNSTEIN, B. (1964), 'Family role systems, socialization and Communication', paper given at the Conference on Cross-Cultural Research into Childhood and Adolescence, University of Chicago.

BRANDIS, W. (1966), 'Indices of social class, communication and control: research memoranda', Sociological Research Unit, University of London, Institute of Education.

GARDNER, D. (1956), *Education of Young Children*. London: Methuen.

GARDNER, D. (1966), *Experiment and Tradition in Primary Schools*. London: Methuen.

MOORE, T. (1964), 'Realism and fantasy in children's play', *Journal of Child Psychology and Psychiatry*, 5, pp. 15–36.

Notes

1 A detailed account of the sample is given in Brandis, W. and Henderson, D., *Social Class, Language and Communication*, London: Routledge & Kegan Paul, 1970.

2 One schedule presented the mother with seven inter-actional contexts with her child (when she was working around the house, when she was trying to relax, when she was in the 'bus or tube, at mealtimes, when she was talking to her husband, when she was in a shop, when she was in the street). For each context the following choices were offered; tell him to stop, tell him to wait, answer him quickly, chat to him. The mother was asked what she normally did in each context when she was with her child. In the second schedule the mother was asked to indicate how she dealt with questions put to her by her child which were difficult to explain to a child. She was given five statements each of which was scaled, never, sometimes, or often. The statements were: try and change the subject, make up something till he's older, tell him a little bit until he asks again, tell him all you can, tell him to ask daddy.

3 Whilst it is true that this ranking pattern is highly correlated with social class and social class is correlated with the WISC score, it is also the case that when social class is partialled out a significant correlation remains above the 0.01 level of confidence between the above ranking pattern and WISC scores.

4 What is true for toys may equally well be true for television and the mass media; the content may be less important than the way the content is represented to the child.

Chapter 2 Social class differences in the relevance of language to socialization

B. Bernstein and D. Henderson

Introduction

One of the most important movements in behavioural science since the war is the convergence of interest upon the study of basic processes of communication and their regulative functions. The one discipline which appears so far least affected is sociology. However, from different quarters there are now signs of growing interest (Grimshaw, 1972; Fishman, 1966; Cicourel, 1964; Garfinkel, 1967; Hymes, 1966). The study of the educationally disadvantaged has also led to a concentration of research into the process of language acquisition, into the relationships between language and cognition and into the social antecedents and regulative consequences of forms of language use.

The Sociological Research Unit at the University of London is engaged upon an exploratory study of forms of familial socialization which affect orientations towards the use of language. We shall present here the results of a closed schedule designed to reveal the relative emphasis which members of social class groups place upon the use of language in different areas of the socialization of the preschool child. Although this report is confined to a study only of the mothers' *orientation* towards the relevance of language, as this group of mothers have been interviewed twice within a three-year period and because two speech samples have been collected from their children when aged five years and seven years, it should prove to be possible to obtain some measure of both the reliability and validity of the mothers' reports.[1]

This report is the first step in the analysis of the section of the second questionnaire given to the mothers which enquired into the orientation of the mother towards various uses of language. As the other sections were concerned with the decision-making within the family, its kinship and community relationships, the procedures of control and role definition, the relationships between home and school, we can relate the orientation towards various uses of language to a range of variables.

In the discussion section of the paper we present a model which gives a sociological explanation of social learning in terms of the mediation of the linguistic process in socialization.

Hypotheses

The following hypothese (derived from Bernstein 1966 and 1972*) are to be tested:

(1) Both middle class and working class would place greater emphasis upon the use of language in inter-personal aspects of socialization than the emphasis placed upon language in the socialization into basic skills.

(2) The shift in emphasis in the use of language from the skill to the person area would be much greater for the middle-class group.

(3) Within the skill area the middle-class group would place a greater emphasis upon language in the transmission of principles.

Description of the sample

The total sample consists of 312 mothers drawn from two areas: one a working-class area and the other a middle-class area. The *r* between area and social class of the parents is 0·74. The index of social class was constructed by W. Brandis of the Sociological Research Unit and is based upon the terminal education and occupation of husband and wife. A full description of the index will be found in Brandis and Henderson (1970). Social class is measured on a ten-point scale 0–9. The sample used in this paper consists of 50 mothers randomly selected from the middle-class area and 50 mothers randomly selected from the working-class area. It was necessary to limit the sample of this study in order that a detailed analysis could be carried out, and to examine possible social class differences in response to the schedule. In terms of the ten-point scale, the mean social class position of the middle-class group is 2·8 and the mean social class position of the working-class group is 6·9.

* This paper was written in 1968.

The closed schedule[2]

The closed schedule consisted of a list of eleven statements which covered the major aspects of socialization. As the schedule was presented, the interviewer put to each mother the question which was printed above the list of statements: 'If parents could not speak, how much *more* difficult do you think it would be for them to do the following things with young children who had not yet started school?' The mother's attention was then directed to the statements and she was asked to assess the difficulty she thought dumb parents would experience in dealing with each situation. A six-point scale was provided: very much more difficult, much more difficult, more difficult, not too difficult, fairly easy, easy. The statements are listed below in the order in which they were presented on the schedule (We are thinking here of early childhood):

(1)	Teaching them everyday tasks like dressing, and using a knife and fork.	(Motor skill)
(2)	Helping them to make things.	(Constructional skill)
(3)	Drawing their attention to different shapes.	(Perceptual skill)
(4)	Playing games with them.	(Dummy)
(5)	Showing them what is right and wrong.	(Moral principles)
(6)	Letting them know what you are feeling.	(Mother-oriented affective)
(7)	Showing them how things work.	(Cognitive)
(8)	Helping them to work things out for themselves.	(Independent-cognitive)
(9)	Disciplining them.	(Control)
(10)	Showing them how pleased you are with their progress.	(Dummy)
(11)	Dealing with them when they are unhappy.	(Child-oriented affective)

Statements 4 and 10 were deliberately inserted as dummy statements designed to move the mother's responses across to 'fairly easy' and 'easy' and thus mitigate the emphasis placed on 'difficulty' in the initial question. In fact, these statements elicited the responses 'fairly easy' or 'easy' from 72 per cent of the middle-class mothers and from 76 per cent of the working-class mothers. No other statements shifted both groups to the 'easy' points of the scale to this extent. Four of the statements—1, 2, 3 and 7—were concerned with the transmission of skills. Five of the statements—5, 6, 8, 9, and 11—were concerned with aspects of social control. Statements 1, 2, 3 and 7 will be referred to as the *skill* area of statements, and statements 5, 6, 8, 9 and 11 will be referred to as the *person* area of statements. The points of the scale 'very much more difficult', 'much more difficult' and 'more difficult' will be referred to as the 'difficult' points of the scale, whilst 'fairly easy' and 'easy' will be referred to as the 'easy' points of the scale. 'Not too difficult' will be referred to as the mid-point of the scale.

It will be remembered that the aim of the schedule was to examine the effect of the social class position of the mothers on their perception of the role of language as a socializing process.[3] In order to obtain such information it was necessary to focus the mother's attention upon the relevance of language across a number of different areas. It was thought that mothers would experience great difficulty if they were simply asked to what extent they relied upon language when dealing with their children. We constructed a general situation such that each mother was faced with a problem of comparison. She also had to assess the difficulty of transmitting skills and dealing with inter-personal processes without language. This focused her attention upon the relevance of the linguistic component of the inter-action. At the same time, it was necessary to ensure, as far as possible, that the mother should not feel that the problem was a challenge to her own extra-verbal ingenuity with her child, and so the problem was presented with the general referents *parents* and *young children*. It was equally necessary to preclude the possible use of other linguistic alternatives and therefore we stated the problem in terms of young children who had *not yet started school* and were thus unlikely to be able to read written instructions or explanations.

Method

The analysis was carried out in three stages. In the first stage we examined the population scores, in the second stage we examined the responses of individual mothers within each social class to each statement, and in the third stage analyses of variance were carried out in order to examine the inter-action between the social class position of the mothers and their responses within and between the *skill* and *person* areas of statements.

First stage

The population scores enabled us:

(*a*) to examine the distribution of maternal responses across the scale for each statement.
(*b*) to examine the total number of responses across the scale within each area of statements.
(*c*) to compare the total population scores within each area of statements in terms of 'difficult' and 'easy' responses.

We were then in a position to compare differences in patterns of response in relation to the statements.

Second stage

The difference between the number of 'difficult' responses and the number of 'easy' responses to each statement was examined in terms of the social class of the mothers. This procedure also enabled us to compare the 'difficult' to 'easy' responses for each statement with reference to social class.

Third stage

(*a*) A 2×2 analysis of variance on repeated measures was carried out. This type of analysis enabled us to control for within-person variance as well as for between-people variance and residual variance. Each point on the scale was assigned a score as follows:

Very much more difficult	+3
Much more difficult	+2
More difficult	+1
Not too difficult	0
Fairly easy	−1
Easy	−2

The basic unit of the analysis here was the individual mother's mean response score to the four *skill* statements. This was compared to the mother's mean response score to the five *person* statements. The analysis enabled us to test for significance the differential emphasis upon difficulty in response to each area of statements and its relationship with social class.
(*b*) A 2×5 analysis of variance on repeated measures was carried out on the maternal responses to each of the statements within the *person* area, in order to find out whether there was a significant

inter-action effect between the social class of the mothers and the individual statements.

(*c*) For the same reason a 2×4 analysis was carried out on the maternal responses to the individual statements within the *skill* area.

Results

First, we will deal briefly with the results which were found when the population scores were examined. It must be emphasized that the main justification for this stage of the analysis was to discover whether differences between the responses to the statements, as well as differences between the social class groups, were sufficiently large to justify carrying out a more sensitive analysis on the data. We will then deal at greater length with the results of the second and third stages of the analysis.

1 The population responses

The distribution of the population responses across the scale show that the patterns of distributions differ markedly between the *person* statements and the *skill* statements (Table 2.1). The responses cluster at the 'difficult' points of the scale in response to the *person* statements, whereas the distribution is normal, with 'not too difficult' operating as the mid-point, in response to the *skill* statements. Since the two areas of statements were clearly eliciting quite different patterns of response, we decided to compare the summed scores across all the statements within each area for each point of the scale. We then found that although both middle-class and working-class mothers showed a marked move to 'difficult' responses within the *person* area in comparison with their responses within the *skill* area, the relative shift was greater in the case of the middle-class responses (Table 2.1). In order to make a more stringent comparison the responses 'very much more difficult' and 'much more difficult' were summed within each social class and compared with the summed responses 'fairly easy' and 'easy'. We found that the social class differences in response within each area of statements were very great. In particular, the shift of middle-class responses from the *skill* area to the *person* area in terms of the emphasis upon difficulty was just over 5 to 1, whereas the shift of working-class responses from the *skill* area to the *person* area was just under 2 to 1 (Table 2.2).

TABLE 2.1 *Distributions of population responses to statements*

*The scale**		*Skill statements*				*Person statements*				
		1	2	3	7	5	6	8	9	11
Middle-class responses	0	0	1	1	3	12	12	13	19	11
	1	0	4	5	9	12	12	12	8	11
	2	7	12	11	13	19	12	18	14	15
	3	20	21	16	17	5	11	4	8	9
	4	15	7	12	7	2	2	3	0	2
	5	8	5	5	1	0	1	0	1	2
Working-class responses	0	9	4	4	4	4	10	11	11	10
	1	5	5	5	6	13	4	9	7	4
	2	3	7	6	8	11	12	14	13	11
	3	23	23	27	20	14	10	11	8	10
	4	5	7	6	10	4	8	4	9	8
	5	5	4	2	2	4	6	1	2	7

* 0 — Very much more difficult
1 — Much more difficult
2 — More difficult
3 — Not too difficult
4 — Fairly easy
5 — Easy

TABLE 2.2 *Percentages of summed difficult/easy responses in each area*

		% Difficult (0, 1)	*% Easy (4, 5)*	*Total no. responses*
MC	*Person* statements	48·8	5·2	250
	Skill statements	11·5	30·0	200
WC	*Person* statements	33·2	21·2	250
	Skill statements	21·0	20·4	200

2 Individual responses to statements

In the next stage of the analysis we examined the *individual* responses within each social class to each statement, in terms of the ratios of 'difficult' to 'easy' responses. Again we found that both middle-class and working-class mothers had shifted to the 'difficult' points of the scale in response to the *person* statements. But *within* the *person* area, middle-class mothers placed greater emphasis upon difficulty than did working-class mothers (Table 2.1). Within the *skill* area we found a reversal in the pattern of response on the part of middle-class mothers. Middle-class mothers were less likely to give an 'easy' response to the statement 'Showing them how things work' than the working-class mothers. Table 2.1 also shows that more working-class mothers than middle-class mothers gave a 'difficult' response to the statement 'Teaching them everyday tasks like dressing, and using a knife and fork'.

3 The analysis of variance

(*a*) The results of the 2×2 analysis of variance on repeated measures show that the differential emphasis on difficulty between the two areas is highly significant ($F_{1,98} = 294{\cdot}53$, $p > 0{\cdot}001$). Very much greater emphasis was placed upon difficulty within the *person* area of statements than within the *skill* area of statements. However, the analysis also showed that, although greater emphasis was placed on the difficulty of dealing with the situations described in the *person* area by *all* the mothers, the difference between the responses of the middle-class mothers in relation to the two areas of statements was significantly greater than the difference between the responses of the working-class mothers ($F_{1,98} = 73{\cdot}60$, $p > 0{\cdot}001$). Middle-class mothers placed much *greater* emphasis upon the difficulty of doing the things described in the *person* area than the working-class mothers, but they placed much *less* emphasis upon the difficulty of doing the things described in the *skill* area than the working-class mothers. This highly significant inter-action effect illustrates the polarization of the responses of middle-class mothers in relation to the two areas of statements.

We will now turn to the results of the analyses of maternal responses *within* each area.

(*b*) Within the *skill* area the results show that middle-class mothers placed very much less emphasis on language than working-class mothers on the difficulty of doing the things described in these statements, and that this difference in response was highly significant ($F_{1,98} = 228{\cdot}78$, $p > 0{\cdot}001$). This finding replicates the result found by the previous analysis. However, a highly significant interaction effect between the social class of the mothers and responses to individual *skill* statements was revealed by this analysis. Working-class mothers placed significantly greater emphasis on difficulty in response to the statement 'Teaching them everyday tasks like dressing and using a knife and fork', than did middle-class mothers; middle-class mothers, on the other hand, placed significantly greater emphasis on difficulty in response to the statement 'Showing them

TABLE 2.3 *Summary table of mean scores*

	Statements		
	Skill area	*Person area*	*Total $\bar{x}$*
$\bar{x}$ Middle Class:	0·07	1·49	0·78
$\bar{x}$ Working class:	0·33	0·80	0·56
Sample $\bar{x}$	0·20	1·14	

TABLE 2.4 *Summary table of mean scores*

	Skill statements				
	1	*2*	*3*	*7*	*Total $\bar{x}$*
$\bar{x}$ Middle class:	−0·48	0·12	0·04	0·62	0·30
$\bar{x}$ Working class:	0·48	0·28	0·36	0·36	1·50
Sample $\bar{x}$	0·01	0·20	0·20	0·49	

how things work' than did working-class mothers ($F_{3,294} = 74{\cdot}88$, $p > 0{\cdot}001$).

(*c*) The 2×5 analysis of maternal responses to the five *person* statements shows that middle-class mothers considered that these situations would be more difficult to deal with without language than did working-class mothers. This differential emphasis on difficulty in relation to the *person* statements is highly significant ($F_{1,98} = 14{\cdot}25$, $p > 0{\cdot}001$). A highly significant main order effect, *irrespective* of the social class position of the mothers, arose out of differences in response to individual statements ($F_{4,392} = 6{\cdot}49$, $p > 0{\cdot}001$).

This result shows that individual statements within the *person* area had elicited very different responses from both middle-class and working-class mothers. We were therefore interested to know how the responses differed *between* the *person* statements. In other words, how were the *person* statements *ranked* in difficulty? The mean scores are presented below as they were ranked in order of difficulty by *all* the mothers in the sample.

	Person statements	*Mean scores*
(8)	Helping them to work things out for themselves	1·37
(9)	Disciplining them	1·32
(5)	Showing them what is right and wrong	1·14
(6)	Letting them know what you are feeling	0·98
(11)	Dealing with them when they are unhappy	0·91

Summary of results

Differences in response were shown to be due to (*a*) the statements within each area (*b*) the social class of the mothers, and (*c*) the interaction between social class and individual statements. We find that middle-class mothers consider language less relevant to the situations described by the *skill* statements than do working-class mothers. There is one exception. Middle-class mothers considered that 'Showing them how things work', would be *more* difficult to deal with without language than working-class mothers. Conversely, middle-class mothers place greater emphasis upon language than working-class mothers in response to the *person* statements. However, *all* the mothers considered the *person* situations more difficult to cope with than the *skill* situations.

TABLE 2.5 *Summary table of mean scores*

	Person statements					
	5	*6*	*8*	*9*	*11*	*Total* $\bar{x}$
$\bar{x}$ Middle class:	1·54	1·36	1·56	1·70	1·28	7·44
$\bar{x}$ Working class:	0·74	0·60	1·18	0·94	0·54	4·00
Sample $\bar{x}$	1·14	0·98	1·37	1·32	0·91	

Methodological criticisms of the schedule[4]

The rationale for the construction of the schedule has been given earlier in this paper, nevertheless, a number of methodological issues are raised by the design.

Let us examine the points one by one, and see to what extent each issue is resolved in the light of the analysis.

1. The definition of the problem is lengthy and contains three items of information which the mother has to bear in mind throughout her responses to *all* the statements if the results are to be a reliable measure of her orientation to language in relation to major aspects of socialization.

Very great differences in response were found between the statements which described skills and the statements which described aspects of inter-personal processes, irrespective of the social class of the mothers in the sample. It can reasonably be argued that such differences in the emphasis upon difficulty would not have been found if the mothers had merely assessed each statement without reference to the role of speech and its absence. We can assume then that the question, despite its complexity, was borne in mind by the mothers throughout their responses. It focused their attention on the linguistic aspect of their own behaviour with their children.

2. In order to assess the difficulty for dumb parents when doing a number of things with young children, the mother can only refer to her *own* experience in each situation and try to imagine how difficult she herself would find each situation if *she* could not speak. Such an assessment involves an internal three-stage experiment, and this may have been quite difficult for some mothers. However, this point is clearly related to the first point, since it can reasonably be assumed that if the mother bears the problem in mind *throughout* her responses then she is forced to focus upon her *own* reliance upon language.

3. The mother is asked to discriminate *between* degrees of difficulty on a six-point scale, two points of which do not refer to difficulty but to ease. It may be that some mothers found it difficult to use the six-point scale. They had either to keep all the points in mind in response to each statement, or they had frequently to refer back to the scale. If they failed to do this then their responses would be unreliable.

The 2×5 analysis of the mother's responses to the five *person* statements has shown that, although all mothers emphasized difficulty in response to these statements rather than to the *skill* statements, there were significant differences in the emphasis upon difficulty *between* the statements. The fact that the problem emphasized difficulty—'how much *more* difficult do you think it would be?'—may have given rise to greater discrimination between degrees of difficulty. This result strongly suggested that the mothers, irrespective of social class, were indeed discriminating between the 'difficult' points of the scale. We decided to examine the data in order to find out whether the percentage of mothers within each social class using *more than one 'difficult' point* in response to the control statements and *more than one 'easy' point* in response to the *skill* statements differed. We found that there was no difference in the percentage of mothers within each social class using *all three* 'difficult' points in response to the *person* statements, and that *all* the percentage differences were minimal in response to the *skill* statements. The major differences between the social class groups occurs in the relative use of only *one* 'difficult' point in response to the *person* statements. Eighteen per cent of the middle-class mothers used only one 'difficult' point in response to these statements whereas 40 per cent of the working-class mothers used only one 'difficult' point. This could well argue a lack of discrimination between degrees of difficulty as set out in the scale on the part of nearly half the working-class sub-sample. One final point should be made in regard to discrimination. Discrimination between the 'difficult' points did not relate to the *number* of *person* statements which elicited a 'difficult' response, nor to the *number* of *skill* statements which elicited an 'easy' response. It is important to stress this point since we suspected that there may have been a greater likelihood of discrimination if a mother was confining herself to the 'difficult' part of the scale across all five *person* statements.

We were also interested in the extent of movement *across* the scale. We considered that this, together with the discrimination *within* the scale might justify a six-point scale, since this would reveal the extent to which mothers limited their responses to adjacent points. Seventy-eight per cent of the middle-class mothers and 62 per cent of the working-class mothers distributed their responses across at least four points of the scale. Examination of the data showed that mothers who moved across four or more points of the scale when responding to the statements were much more likely to use one of the extreme points, 'very much more difficult', and 'easy', than were mothers who moved across less than four points.

We then examined the number of mothers who moved across five or six points of the scale, since this clearly involved the use of one or both extreme points. We found that 48 per cent of the middle-class mothers, but only 28 per cent of the working-class mothers, moved across five or six points. This may be an indication that the middle-class mothers in our sample were better able to use a six-point scale, either because of their ability to bear the six points in mind, or because of their greater readiness to refer back to the scale frequently.

4. There was inadequate randomization of the statements. This is particularly relevant to the close proximity of the statements 'Helping them to work things out for themselves' and 'Showing them how things work'. It was thought that the lexical similarity of these two statements might have prevented the mothers from discriminating between them, despite the fact that they describe rather different activities and orientations. Surprisingly, the analysis of the mothers' responses showed that more working-class mothers than middle-class mothers discriminated between these two statements. The implication of this finding will be taken up later in the discussion. At present it is sufficient to point out that the social class group which one may have least expected to discriminate

between two very similar statements did, in fact, do so. Finally, the fact that the mothers did discriminate between the statements—that they did not exhibit response sets—is shown by the pattern of their responses across the scale. Statements 1, 2, 3 and 4 elicited 'easy' responses; statements 5 and 6 elicited 'difficult' responses; statement 7 elicited 'easy' responses; statements 8 and 9 elicited 'difficult' responses; statement 10 elicited 'easy' responses; and statement 11 elicited 'difficult' responses. This pattern was consistent for both middle-class and working-class mothers.

Summary of criticisms

It is clear that movement from 'difficult' responses to 'easy' responses was triggered by the two main areas. Discrimination between degrees of difficulty was dependent upon individual statements: there were significant differences in the ranking of the *person* statements in order of difficulty, and the order was the same for both social class groups. Movement across four points of the scale was found to involve the use of one of the extreme points, and there was very little difference in the number of middle-class and working-class mothers who used the scale in this way. However, more of the middle-class mothers moved across five or six points of the scale than did the working-class mothers. This raises the substantive question as to the orientation of the working-class group; they may not have required such a sensitive scale. We might add that few researchers have carried out such a close examination of their results in terms of their scaling procedures. Our experience suggests that, although on balance our scaling procedure was justified, the following recommendation might provide a more reliable measure. We suggest that in order to overcome some of the scaling difficulties for the mother it is recommended first to ask the general question and then, for each statement, ask the mother whether she thought it on the whole difficult or on the whole easy. We could then present the mother with a three-point scale for degrees of difficulty or a three-point scale for relative ease, depending upon her general response.

Discussion

The results show that the middle class, relative to the working class, place a greater emphasis upon the use of language in dealing with situations within the person area. The working class, relative to the middle class, place a greater emphasis upon the use of language in the transmission of various skills. However, within the skill area the middle class place a greater emphasis upon the use of language in their response to the statement, 'Showing them how things work', whereas within the same area the working class place a greater emphasis upon the use of language in response to the statement, 'Teaching them everyday tasks like dressing, and using a knife and fork'.

Can these differences in emphasis be accounted for in terms of differences in the relevance of these two *areas* for the social classes? In other words, does the move to language simply reflect the relevance of the area? Or is it the case that both areas respectively have equal relevance to the social classes but their verbal realization is different? It is unlikely that the middle class relative to the working class value basic skills less and yet it is this group which places a reduced emphasis upon language in the skill area. It would be just as difficult to maintain that socialization into relationships between persons is not of *equal* relevance to every sub-cultural group, although the *form* of that socialization may well vary. On the other hand, the very marked shift by *both* groups towards language in the person area and away from language in the skill area may well reflect the greater importance of control over persons rather than control over the development of skills in the socialization of the very young child. It is therefore unlikely that the shifts in emphasis placed upon the use of language in each of the two areas respectively, by the two social class groups can be explained in terms of the difference in the relevance of the skill area and the person area. It might be that middle-class mothers can conceive of a variety of ways, other than linguistic, for the acquisition of skills and for this reason these mothers place less emphasis upon language. Whereas the working-class mothers can conceive of fewer alternatives to language for the acquisition of skills. This might seem to be a plausible explanation, but we think that it by no means accounts for the differences between the social classes.

We shall argue that the explanation is to be found in the nature of the social relationship when skills and person relationships are transmitted. If it is the case that in the working class knowledge is transmitted through a social relationship in which the receiver is relatively passive and if, in the middle class, knowledge is transmitted through a social relationship in which the receiver is active, then we might expect the distribution of responses which have been revealed. It may be that motor, perceptual and manipulative skills are acquired by the child in the middle class by his exposure to varied and attractive stimuli which the child explores on his *own* terms. In other words, in the acquisition of motor, perceptual and manipulative skills, the child regulates his own learning in a carefully controlled environment. It is of significance that despite the relatively greater emphasis placed upon language in the skill area by the working-class group, the middle class place greater emphasis upon language in response to the statement, 'Showing them how things work'. It is likely that this statement, for the middle class, raises questions of the transmission of principles, whereas the other three statements within the same area *do not*. If this is the case, then the situation for the middle-class child is particularly fortunate. For, on the one hand, he is socialized into elementary skill learning through role relationships which emphasize autonomy *and* he has access to principles.

In the working-class group, the concept of learning may well be different and, therefore, the form the social relationship takes when skills are acquired would be of a different order. The concept of learning here seems to be less one of self-regulated learning in an arranged environment and more a concept of a didactic theory of learning implying a passive receiver, in which a mother has little alternative but to tell or instruct a child. Although the emphasis in the working-class group, relative to the middle class, is upon language, presumably upon *telling* or instructing, the child is much less likely to receive explanations of principles. Thus it may be that the working-class child learns skills in terms only of an understanding of the operations they entail, whereas the middle-class child learns both the operations and principles.

Other work of the Sociological Research Unit can be referred to here in support of these hypotheses. Two years prior to the interview in which the present schedule was administered, a sample of 351 middle-class and working-class mothers (of which the sample used in this paper is a sub-sample) were given a questionnaire in which the mothers were invited to give their views upon a range of experiences relevant to their child's behaviour in the infant school. We found that when middle-class mothers were asked to rank in order of importance six possible uses of toys, they ranked more highly than did the working-class mothers 'To find out about things' (Bernstein and Young, 1967; see chapter 1). Further, middle-class mothers saw the role of the infant-school child as an active role, whereas the working-class mothers tended to see this role as a passive one (Jones, 1966). Middle-class mothers, relative to working-class mothers, indicated that 'play' in the infant school had educational significance (Bernstein, 1967).

It would appear then that the difference in the response of middle-class and working-class mothers to the relevance of language in the acquisition of various skills is more likely to arise out of differences in the concept of learning than out of differences between the social classes in terms of the value placed upon the learning of such skills. The socialization of the middle-class child into the acquisition of skills is into both operations and principles which are learned in a social context which emphasizes *autonomy*. In the case of the working-class child, his socialization into skills emphasizes operations rather than principles learned in a social context where the child is accorded *reduced autonomy* by the mother.

We will now turn to discuss the differences between the social classes in their emphasis upon the use of language in inter-personal contexts. The results are very clear. Where the context is inter-personal, the middle class, relative to the working class, move markedly towards the use of language. Further, the shift in the emphasis upon language from the skill area to the person area is very much greater in the middle class than in the working class. Thus, the verbal realization of affects, moral principles, and their application to behaviour, and independence in cognitive functioning, is much more likely to be linguistically elaborated in the middle class than in the working class. This is *not* to say that these aspects of socialization do not have the same significance in the working class, only that (according to the mothers' responses) language is of less relevance in the form of the socialization.

Indeed, *both* classes rank the statements (in the person area) in the same order of difficulty.

It is not possible to infer from the mothers' responses what they actually would say to the child, but again we can refer to evidence obtained from the first interview with the mothers two years earlier. This evidence strongly suggests that:

(1) The middle-class mothers are more likely than working-class mothers to take up the child's attempts to inter-act verbally with the mother in a range of contexts.
(2) The middle-class mothers are less likely to avoid or evade answering difficult questions put to them by their children.
(3) The middle-class mothers are less likely to use coercive methods of control.
(4) The middle-class mothers are more likely to explain to the child why they want a change in his behaviour. (Bernstein and Brandis, 1970).

Thus, we have good reasons for believing that not only is there a difference between the social classes in their emphasis upon language in contexts of inter-personal control, but there is a difference in the meanings which are verbally realized. It would seem that the internalizing of the principles of the moral order, the relating of this order to the specifics of the child's behaviour, the communication of feeling, is realized far more through language in the middle class than in the working class. The social is made explicit in one group, whereas the social is rendered less explicit in the other. Where the social is made explicit through language then that which is internalized can itself become an object (Mead, 1934). Perhaps here we can begin to see that the form of control over persons in the middle class induces a reflexive relation to the social order, whereas, in the working class, the form of control over persons induces a relatively less reflexive relation to the social order (See Note).

The question of the relatively greater emphasis upon the use of language in the inter-personal area raises fundamental questions about the nature of middle-class forms of socialization which would take us beyond the confines of an empirical research report. In Bernstein (1965 and particularly 1972) there is an extensive discussion of the social antecedents of forms of language use and socialization. The view taken in these and other papers is that linguistic codes are realizations of social structure, and both shape the contents of social roles and the process by which they are learned. In short, it has been suggested that the use of elaborated codes renders the implicit explicit, whereas the use of restricted codes reduces the possibility of such explicitness. Thus the codes and their variants regulate the cultural meanings which are rendered both explicit and individuated through the use of language. Whilst there is no evidence in this paper that middle-class mothers use forms of an elaborated code and working-class mothers use forms of a restricted code, Robinson and Rackstraw's analysis (1967) of the answering behaviour of mothers in the main sample indicates grounds for believing that these coding orientations are likely to be found. Further, the works of Bernstein and Brandis (1970) and Cook (1972) show that the forms of control used by the middle class and the working class are consonant with the predictions derived from the socio-linguistic theory.

We have suggested that in the middle class skills are acquired in such a way that the child has access both to operations and principles. He tends to regulate his own learning in an arranged environment which encourages autonomy in skill acquisition. For this reason the middle-class mothers place less emphasis upon the use of language in the statements within the skill area. In the case of the working-class child, we have argued that he is socialized more into the acquisition of operations than into principles through a social relationship which encourages passivity in the learner and so reduces autonomy in skill acquisition.[5] Thus the working-class mothers, relative to middle-class mothers, place greater emphasis upon the use of language when responding to the statements in the skill area. In the case of control over persons, we have suggested that the forms of such control in the middle class arise out of a social structure which is realized through the use of elaborated codes, whereas the forms of control in the sub-group of the working class under examination arise out of a social structure which is realized through forms of a restricted code. As a result, the form of control in the middle class induces a reflexive relation upon the part of the child towards the social order, whereas in the working class the forms of control induce a much less reflexive relation to the social order.

We should point out that a developed reflexive relation to the social order does not necessarily imply role-distancing behaviour. In the same way, reduced reflexiveness to a particularistic social order does not necessarily imply that role-distancing behaviour will *not* occur in relation to members of a society holding universalistic status.

We can best summarize our interpretation of the results of this analysis and the more general explanation given in this paper, by the use of the following model:

			Social structure ↓ Emphasis on language	
Orientation	*Role/self-concept*		M.C.	W.C.
Persons	Reflexiveness:	→	High	Low
Skills	Autonomy:	→	Low	High
Implicit theory of learning:			Self-regulating	Didactic

The model should be read *horizontally* in relation to the areas of orientation and consequent emphasis on language, and *vertically* in relation to implicit theories of learning and emphasis upon language. For example, if there is a *high* emphasis upon the use of language in terms of orientation to *persons* then this will tend to generate high *reflexiveness* of the self-concept; if the emphasis on the use of language is *low* then this will generate *reduced reflexiveness* of the self-concept. In terms of the orientation to *skills*, a *low* emphasis on language will generate *autonomy* in the self-concept, whilst a *high* emphasis on language in this area will *reduce autonomy* in the self-concept. At the same time, the relative emphasis upon the use of language in these two areas perhaps implies different implicit theories of learning. Where the emphasis upon the use of language is *high* in terms of orientation to persons or *low* in terms of orientation to skills, then the implicit theory of learning is *self-regulating*. Where the emphasis on the use of language is *low* in terms of orientation to persons or *high* in terms of orientation to skills, then the implicit theory of learning is *didactic*.[6] It is important to add that, in this paper, because of the small sample, we have treated the middle class and working class as homogeneous groups. When the total sample is analysed it may be possible to show that there are sub-groups within each social class group who respond differently in relation to these two areas. It is quite possible that differential emphasis upon the use of language in terms of the acquisition of skills or inter-personal control is related to differences in the form of the social relationships. A sub-culture may give rise to an implicit theory of learning which is self-regulating in terms of orientation to persons and didactic in terms of orientation to skills, or *vice versa*. The relationship between culture, linguistic codes, implicit theories of learning and differential emphasis upon the use of language is a matter of investigation. An extensive discussion in Bernstein (1972) deals with the relationship between social structure, forms of social relationship, linguistic codes, and different orders of meaning. The hypotheses on which our model is based are derived from this paper.

We can now develop our discussion in regard to possible discontinuities between implicit theories of learning in the home and explicit theories of learning in the school. It is suggested that there may be, for the working-class child in the primary school, two sources of discontinuity; one in the area of skill acquisition and the other in the area of inter-personal relations. If, for example, the school emphasizes autonomy in the acquisition of skills but the implicit concept of learning in the home is didactic in relation to skills, this will be a major source of discontinuity. Similarly, if the school is concerned with the development of reflexive relations in the area of inter-personal relations but the implicit concept of social learning in the home operates to reduce reflexiveness in this area, then this will be another source of discontinuity. It may be unreasonable to expect children exposed to such discontinuities to respond initially to forms of control which presuppose a culture and socialization very different from their own.

Earlier in this discussion we referred to the fortunate situation of the middle-class child in terms of the results of our analysis. His role relationships emphasize autonomy in the acquisition of skills and reflexiveness in the area of inter-personal relations. He is accorded discretion to *achieve* his social role. On the other hand, the role relationships of the working-class child, in terms of our analysis, reduce his autonomy in the skill area and reduce reflexiveness in the inter-personal area. He has much less discretion—his social role is *assigned* in the *home*.

In this paper we have shown that maternal definitions of the role of language as a socializing process are dependent upon the area of orientation, and that this differential emphasis on the use of language is related to different forms of social relationship within the social structure. Further, we have argued that the differential emphasis on the use of language in relation to certain areas of orientation may reflect different implicit theories of learning which affect the self-concept of the child. We have suggested that these different implicit theories of learning in the home may conflict with the theories of learning in the school, and in this way give rise to major sources of discontinuity between the home and the school.

This analysis has enabled us to construct a model which gives a sociological explanation of social learning through the mediation of the linguistic process of socialization.

Conclusion

We must emphasize that our data consists of mothers' reports not of their actual behaviour, and that these reports have been obtained through the use of a closed schedule. The analysis of the degree and type of discrimination on the part of the middle-class and working-class mothers gives us reasonable grounds for believing that the scaling procedures and the statements were appropriate. We also believe that the situation constructed was such that the 'right' or conventional response was not obvious to the mothers. We have shown that both groups ranked the statements in the person area according to the same gradient of difficult. However, we cannot present at the moment an analysis of possible differences between the social classes in their interpretation of the statements. We may be able to throw some light on social class differences in the interpretation of the statements when the responses of the mothers to the closed schedule are related to their responses to the other schedules within the language section of the second questionnaire *and* to the results of the analysis of the initial questionnaire.

The findings presented here indicate very clear differences between the social class groups in their relative emphasis upon language. We hope to be able to utilize the model offered in the conclusion of the discussion to show, when the total sample is analysed, *intra-class* differences in the orientation to the use of language in these two areas of socialization. Perhaps the most important conclusion of this paper is to stress the need for small scale naturalistic and experimental studies of the channels, codes and contexts which control the process of socialization.

In conclusion, it is the case that the three hypotheses given in the introduction have been confirmed. The findings have also revealed that working-class mothers relative to middle-class mothers place a greater emphasis upon language in the acquisition of basic skills. The inferential structure developed in the discussion makes explicit the relationships between macro aspects of social structure and micro aspects of socialization.

Note

The diagram below sets out the different relationships between reflexiveness and autonomy which may arise as a result of the cultural meanings realized through language.

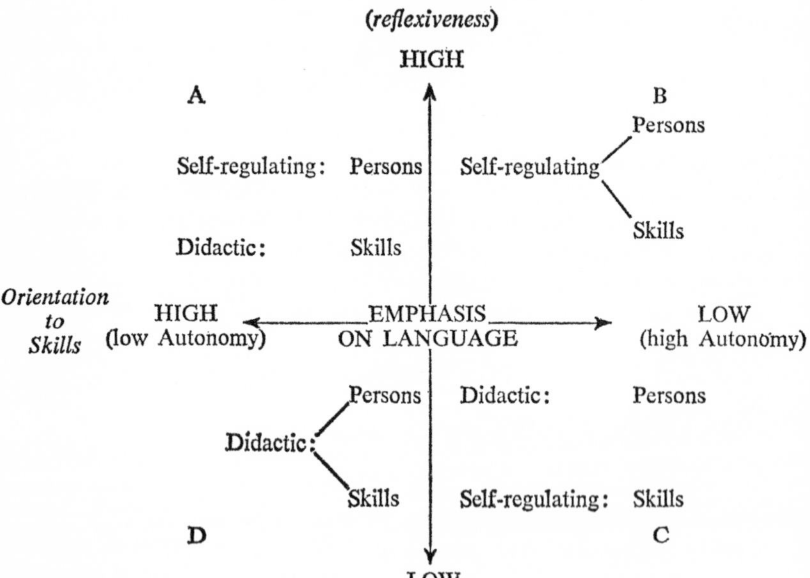

The diagram should be read as follows. The vertical and horizontal axes are scaled in terms of the emphasis upon language. The vertical axis refers to degrees of reflexiveness in socialization into relationships with persons and the horizontal axis refers to degrees of autonomy in the acquisition of skills. The four quadrants contain similarities and differences between implicit theories of learning. These control the forms of the socialization into the two basic areas of socialization. Whilst quadrants 'B' and 'D' would apply to sections of the middle class and working class respectively, the model indicates the probability of intra-class variance both at one point and over time.

The model only permits statements about the emphasis upon language; no inferences can be drawn which refer to the nature of the information. In order to examine the latter it would be necessary to know the dominant linguistic code used in each area of socialization. Whilst it is unlikely that individuals limited to restricted codes would hold self-regulating theories of learning (except embryonically) didactic theories of learning may well be held by users of *both* elaborated and restricted codes. The hypothetical relationships between social structure, family role systems, linguistic codes and person and object verbally realized meanings are set out in Bernstein (1972).

The concept of reflexiveness[7]

It is useful to distinguish between two aspects of reflexiveness; a role and an ideational aspect.

Ideational aspects:
Reflexiveness here refers to the degree to which an individual is able to make explicit verbally the principles underlying object and person relationships. Thus we could have high or low reflexiveness towards objects and/or persons.

Role aspects:
Within role Reflexiveness here refers to the range of alternatives or options which are accorded to any given role. Thus we could have high or low reflexiveness in terms of the range of alternatives made available.

Between role Reflexiveness here would refer to the degree of insulation among the *meanings* made available through role relationships. Roles may be more or less insulated from each other and so may the meanings to which the roles give access.

Where the meanings made available through different roles are highly insulated we could say that there is low reflexiveness; where the meanings made available through different roles *reverberate* against each other (low insulation) we could say there is high reflexiveness.

This formulation indicates that the relationship between language and reflexiveness and the cultural and the institutional order is indeed complex.

Notes

1 The work reported in this paper was supported by grants from the Department of Education and Science and the Ford Foundation to whom, gratefully, acknowledgment is made. Thanks are also given to the Local Education Authorities for their close help and co-operation in the research.

2 The schedule was designed by Marian Bernstein and Basil Bernstein.

3 This schedule was one of a series which made up the communication section of the second interview. See chapter 3 for total findings. All sample children were seven years of age.

4 We are not here elaborating upon the more complex issues of sub-cultural differences in the interpretation of statements within closed schedules.

5 The peer group rather than the home may constitute for the working-class child an explorative and imaginative context.

6 On implicit theories of learning, see J. Klein, *Samples of British Culture,* vol. II, Routledge & Kegan Paul, 1965; G. Trasler (ed.), *The Formative Years*, BBC Publication, 1968; R. D. Hess and V. C. Shipman, 'Early experience and the socialisation of cognitive modes in children', *Child Development*, 1965, 36, no. 4, pp. 869–86.

7 We are very grateful to Mr Michael Young, Lecturer in the Sociology of Education, University of London, Institute of Education, for his comments upon this formulation.

References

BERNSTEIN, B. (1965), 'A socio-linguistic approach to social learning', *Social Science Survey* (ed.) Julius Gould. London: Penguin.

BERNSTEIN, B. (1967), 'Play and the infant school', *Where*, Supplement 11, *Toys*.

BERNSTEIN, B. (1972), 'A socio-linguistic approach to socialization', *Directions in Sociolinguistics* (eds) J. Gumperz and D. Hymes. Holt, Rinehart & Winston.

BERNSTEIN, B. and YOUNG, D. (1967), 'Social class differences in conceptions of the uses of toys', *Sociology*, 1, no. 2, May and reprinted in the present volume.

BERNSTEIN, B. and BRANDIS, W. (1970), 'Social class differences in communication and control', in W. Brandis and D. Henderson.

BRANDIS, W. and HENDERSON, D. (1970), *Social Class, Language and Communication*. London: Routledge & Kegan Paul.

CICOUREL, A. V. (1964), *Methods and Measurement in Sociology*. New York: Free Press.

COOK, J. (1972), *Social Control and Socialization*. London: Routledge & Kegan Paul (in press).

FISHMAN, J. (1966), *Language Loyalty in the United States*. The Hague: Mouton.

GARFINKEL, H. (1967), *Studies in Ethnomethodology*. Prentice-Hall.

GRIMSHAW, A. D. (1972), 'Socio-linguistics', in *Handbook of Communication* (eds) W. Schramm, I. Pool, N. Maccob, E. Parker, L. Fein. Rand McNally. In press.

HYMES, D. (1966), 'On communicative competence'. This paper is revised from the one presented at the *Research Planning Conference on Language Development Among Disadvantaged Children*, held under the sponsorship of the Department of Educational Psychology and Guidance, Ferkauf Graduate School, Yeshiva University, 1966. The paper is available from Department of Social Anthropology, University of Pennsylvania, Philadelphia.

JONES, J. (1966), 'Social class and the under-fives', *New Society*, December.

LOEVINGER, J. (1959), 'Patterns of parenthood as theories of learning', *J. Soc. and Ab. Psychol.*, pp. 148–50.

MEAD, G. H. (1934), *Mind, Self and Society*. University of Chicago Press.

ROBINSON, W. P. and RACKSTRAW, S. J. (1967), 'Variations in mothers' answers to children's questions, as a function of social class, verbal intelligence test scores and sex', *Sociology*, 1, no. 3.

WINER, B. J. (1962), *Statistical Principles in Experimental Design*. McGraw-Hill, chapters 4 and 8.

Chapter 3 Contextual specificity, discretion and cognitive socialization: with special reference to language

D. Henderson

The Sociological Research Unit of the Department of Sociology, University of London Institute of Education has been engaged, for the past five years, upon a study of variations between and within social class in familial patterns of communication and control. These have been examined in relation to the socialization of the child considering particularly his response to school. The theory which initially guided this research is set out in Bernstein (1962, 1964, 1972). This paper is concerned to examine social class differences in reported orientations in the emphasis on, and the contextual usage of, language in the socialization of the child.

The sample under discussion consists of 100 mothers who form a randomly selected sub-sample of 312 mothers who were interviewed when their children who are also part of the enquiry, were seven years of age.[1] These mothers were originally interviewed three months before the sample children went to school for the first time. The second interview with the mothers was concerned to examine:

(1) The nature of the familial role system.
(2) The degree to which the family is embedded in its kinship system and in the community.
(3) The orientation to various usages of language in the socialization of the child.
(4) The socialization of the child into the school.

We shall report here those findings which relate to the mother's orientation to various usages of language during socialization. Schedules were prepared (see Appendix) which we hoped would illuminate social class differences across a range of communication contexts involving both the mother with other adults *and* the mother and her child.

The major purpose of this paper is to show:

(1) The relationship between social class and the contextual specificity of maternal communication.
(2) The relationship between maternal communication and the range of discretion accorded to the child.
(3) The relationship between communication and the cognitive socialization of the child.

As we have said, the sample with which we are concerned consists of 100 mothers, randomly selected from a sub-sample of 312 mothers. One hundred and twenty of the mothers live in a MC (middle-class) area of London and 192 live in a WC (working-class) area. The variation between area and social class of the parents is 0·74. The index of social class was constructed by Walter Brandis of the Sociological Research Unit; it is based upon the terminal education and occupation of husband and wife. A full description of the index will be found in Brandis and Henderson (1970). Social class is measured on a ten-point scale, 0–9. In terms of the ten-point scale, the mean social class position of the MC group is 2·8, and the mean social class position of the WC group is 6·9. It was necessary to limit the sample of this study in order that a detailed analysis could be carried out, and in order to explore the data in depth. Before discussing the results of the analysis we shall state initially our expectation of the findings.

Mother–adult communication

The following hypotheses (derived from Bernstein, 1962, 1964, and 1972) were to be tested:

(1) There would be social class differences in the frequency with which mothers talked to others for various reasons:
   (*a*) MC mothers would talk more frequently, for cognitive reasons.
   (*b*) MC mothers would talk more frequently, for interpersonal reasons.
   (*c*) WC mothers would talk more frequently, for purely social reasons.
(2) There would be social class differences in the assessment of the relative helpfulness of words as against actions. MC mothers would find *words* most helpful, whilst WC mothers would find *actions* most helpful.

Two schedules were designed in order to find out about the mothers' orientation towards the use of language in inter-action with other adults. In one case mothers were asked how frequently they talked to other people for various reasons. The reasons given fell into three broad areas of discourse: the cognitive, the inter-personal/affective, and the purely social. Here the mother was asked to report on her actual behaviour. In the second case the mothers were asked to give their assessment of the relative helpfulness of words as against actions across a range of situations. All the situations given in this schedule were inter-personal or affective in character, and so would constitute a check on the responses to the inter-personal/affective statements in the other schedule.

Results

Schedule A. The first of these schedules was designed in order to find out how frequently the mother talked to other people for various reasons. Twelve reasons were given and a three-point scale was provided: 'I *hardly ever* find myself talking'; 'I *sometimes* find myself talking'; 'I *often* find myself talking'. The mothers were asked to place a tick in the appropriate box for each of the reasons (see Appendix: Schedule A). This scale was scored 0, 1, and 2, from *hardly ever* to *often*.

The responses were then analysed in two parts. The primary analysis was concerned with (a) the differences between the two social class groups in terms of the overall frequency with which they talked to other adults and (b) with the relationships between the social class of the mother and her response to each of the twelve reasons. It was considered that the most appropriate statistical test of these differences was an analysis of variance with repeated measures. This analysis takes account of three sources of variance: variance *between* groups, variance *within* groups, and variance in response across a range of measures by the same subject. Thus each mother acts as her own control across a range of experimental conditions. The conditions in this case were the twelve reasons. (In fact, this type of analysis was considered to be the most appropriate for nearly all of the closed schedules with which we will be concerned, and whenever possible an experimental plan on repeated measures was carried out.)

The analysis of the mothers' responses revealed a significant overall difference between MC and WC in reported frequency of talking with other people. MC mothers talked more frequently than WC mothers ($F_{1,98} = 274{\cdot}40$, $p = 0{\cdot}001$). Nevertheless, the mothers varied in the frequency with which they talked for particular reasons, and this was due to an inter-action between the social class of the mother and the reasons for talking ($F_{11,1078} = 69{\cdot}72$, $p = 0{\cdot}001$).

In order to elucidate these results further, it was decided to group the reasons in terms of the areas of discourse to which they referred. The twelve items covered three broad areas of discourse. Four reasons referred to the generally *social* areas: 'To be friendly'; 'About what I have seen on television'; 'To increase the number of people I know'; 'About my children'. None of these reasons as stated reflected either an overt affective or cognitive component, as did the other reasons. Four of the other reasons *did* have a strong *cognitive* component and these were grouped together: 'To exchange ideas'; 'To question the world around me'; 'To find out more about people'; 'To increase my knowledge of the world'. This left four further reasons for talking. However, one of these reasons—'To find out what other people think of me'—elicited an almost total negative response from all the mothers in the sample, irrespective of social class, so it was dropped from further analysis. The remaining three reasons all have an *affective or inter-personal* component. These were 'To decide what is right and wrong'; 'To show my feelings to others'; 'So that those close to me can understand me better'. Thus we were left with our three areas of discourse—the *social*, the *cognitive*, and the *inter-personal/affective*. Since a second analysis of variance on repeated measures was to be carried out, this time treating areas of discourse as the measures, the mean score obtained by each mother in each area was found. It was necessary to use this scoring procedure since two of the areas with which we were concerned contained four reasons, and one only three. The results of this second analysis of mothers' reasons for talking to other people revealed that, when the responses to the three areas of discourse were combined, there was *no* significant social class difference in the overall frequency with which mothers talked to other people. However, a second order inter-action effect showed that this lack of difference in *overall* frequency was due to the relationship between the social class of the mother and the frequency with which they talked in *particular* areas ($F_{2,196} = 14{\cdot}18$, $p = 0{\cdot}001$). An analysis of simple main effects to test the direction of this inter-action revealed that WC mothers talked to other people significantly more frequently than MC mothers for *inter-personal/affective* reasons ($F_{1,294} = 10{\cdot}65$, $p = 0{\cdot}01$). On the other hand, MC mothers talked significantly more frequently than WC mothers for cognitive reasons ($F_{1,294} = 11{\cdot}12$, $p = 0{\cdot}01$). There was no significant difference between the social classes in the frequency with which mothers talked for purely social reasons.

We shall now consider the degree to which the mothers positively discriminated *between* areas of discourse as measured by the differential frequency with which they talked in each area. To this end a further analysis of the simple main effects was carried out. The results showed that although both MC and WC mothers discriminated between areas of discourse, MC mothers revealed discrimination at a higher level of significance ($F_{2,196} = 12{\cdot}69$, $p = 0{\cdot}01$) than WC mothers ($F_{2,196} = 3{\cdot}78$, $p = 0{\cdot}05$). The total mean scores for each social class within each area are shown in the following table:

TABLE 3.1

	Inter-personal/ affective	*Cognitive*	*Social*
Middle class	48·52	68·00	61·25
Working class	63·45	52·75	60·25

It can clearly be seen, that, on the whole, MC mothers talked much less frequently for inter-personal/affective reasons in comparison with the frequency with which they talked for cognitive or purely social reasons. The differences in emphasis are not so great within the WC, but the table shows the WC mothers talked least frequently for cognitive reasons.

Schedule B. The second of the schedules which deal with adult communication was designed in order to examine the differential emphasis which mothers placed on language when dealing with other people. It was suggested to the mothers that there are many ways of letting other people know what one is thinking or feeling, and that some people think that words may not always help. They were then asked to look at a list of six situations and say for each which they would find *more* helpful, words or actions.

Again, the mothers' responses were analysed with a 2×6 experimental plan on repeated measures—treating the situations as the different measures. A score of 1 was assigned to a response which indicated that *words* were found more helpful, and a score of 0 to a response which indicated that *actions* were found more helpful.

A significant main order difference between the two social class groups was found in terms of the frequency with which *words* were found more helpful. Unexpectedly, WC mothers showed significantly greater preference for *words* than MC mothers ($F_{1,98} = 5{\cdot}66$, $p = 0{\cdot}025$). At the same time, there was a highly significant difference between the situations stated and the preference for words ($F_{5,490} = 24{\cdot}94$, $p = 0{\cdot}001$). A second order inter-action effect showed that there was a significant relationship between the social class of the mother and the statements most likely to elicit a preference for *words* rather than actions ($F_{5,490} = 8{\cdot}18$, $p = 0{\cdot}001$). An analysis of simple main effects of social class on each of the situations showed that *two* of the six situations appeared to be mainly responsible for the major differences between the MC and WC mothers. WC mothers showed a marked preference for *words* when responding to the statements 'Comforting friends when they are in distress' ($F_{1,588} = 22{\cdot}05$, $p = 0{\cdot}001$) and 'Stopping myself feeling angry' ($F_{1,588} = 20{\cdot}00$, $p = 0{\cdot}001$).

Comment

When we consider the mothers' orientation to language in relation to other adults, we find that, on the whole, MC mothers discriminated more sharply between various areas of discourse than WC mothers in terms of the frequency with which they reported talking in each area. Further, MC mothers were more likely to explore verbally the *cognitive* area, whereas WC mothers were more likely to explore the inter-personal/affective area. Whilst the exploration of the cognitive area by MC mothers was not unexpected, the emphasis on language in the inter-personal/affective area on the part of the WC mothers was both unexpected and intriguing. In order to understand this finding, we must turn to the relative preference of MC and WC mothers for *words* as against *actions*. It will be remembered that we found an overall preference for *words* on the part of WC mothers, and an overall preference for *actions* on the part of MC mothers. This again was an unexpected finding: we had expected quite the reverse. However, when the data was more closely examined, it was found that *two* statements accounted for the overall preference of the WC for words and the MC for actions—'Comforting others when they are in distress' and 'Stopping myself feeling angry'. An examination of the schedule in question will show that these were the most affectively loaded of all the statements, and it seems that it was this affective loading which polarized the responses of MC and WC mothers. If we hypothesize that WC mothers are more likely than MC mothers, in such situations, to spontaneously talk about their feelings, we can perhaps begin to understand why WC mothers reported that they talked with *most* frequency for inter-personal/affective reasons. We should also remember that it is this area of discourse which was most likely to be avoided verbally by the MC mothers in our sample. It would seem as if the inter-personal/affective area of experience is of some concern for both groups of mothers, but that they handle it very differently in inter-action with other adults. The WC mothers put no brake on the verbalization of strong affect, nor do they manifest any inhibition about verbalizing their own inter-personal concerns. The MC mothers, on the other hand, may only talk about the inter-personal or verbally realize strong affect to a special category of persons, i.e. friends. The questions put to mothers in the two schedules referred to non-determinate other adults. We are suggesting that the MC mothers make a sharp differentiation between various classes of social relationship. The referents of the questions in these two schedules, i.e. the 'other', may well have been different for the two social classes.[2] This points to a weakness in the schedules; the 'other' ought to have been more determinate. It is still the case that the MC mothers move to actions rather than words in powerfully affective contexts. It is difficult to interpret the significance of this choice. Minimally, it appears as if the MC place the emphasis upon *doing* something in such contexts. If we take the stated choices at their face value, it seems that the MC may be more concerned to bring about, actively, a *change* in the situation. It may be that the WC move to words is indicative of a spontaneous verbal response to painful situations. We have already stated that (*a*) the MC mothers discriminated more sharply between the inter-personal and the cognitive areas of discourse than the WC mothers and (*b*) the MC mothers discriminated more sharply between the two *most* powerfully affective contexts and the *less* powerfully affective contexts than the WC mothers.

To summarize, MC mothers clearly differentiate more sharply in terms of areas of discourse and the *context* of inter-action than do the WC mothers in this sample. The only hypothesis supported refers to the MC preference for talking more than the WC in the cognitive area.

Later work has shown that there is *within* the WC group a significant negative correlation between mothers who choose words rather than actions and the child's WISC scores at six years of age. This fact offers slight support for the interpretation that the preference for *actions* may contain a cognitive component.

Mother–child communication

The following hypotheses were to be tested:

(1) Both MC and WC would place greater emphasis upon the use of language in inter-personal aspects of socialization

than the emphasis placed upon language in the socialization into basic skills.

(2) The shift in emphasis in the use of language from the skill to the person area would be much greater in the MC group.

(3) Within the skill area the MC group would place a greater emphasis upon language in the transmission of principles.

(4) MC mothers would be more likely than WC mothers to take up the child's attempts to initiate verbal inter-action.

(5) There would be social class differences in the frequency with which questions were avoided or evaded. MC mothers would avoid answering less frequently than WC mothers.

(6) There would be differences in response *between* types of questions. Some questions would elicit greater avoidance than others.

(7) MC mothers would choose general definitions when explaining things to children more frequently than WC mothers.

(8) MC mothers would choose exact, explicit concrete examples more frequently than WC mothers.

(9) WC mothers would be more likely to choose concrete examples than MC mothers.

Four of the schedules were designed in order to examine the mother's orientation towards the use of language with children, and to examine three aspects of the mother's pattern of verbal communication with her seven-year-old child.

Results

Schedule A. This schedule was designed to examine differences in the emphasis placed on the use of language in two areas of the socialization of pre-school children: inter-person relationships and the acquisition of basic skills. As these results have been extensively discussed in Bernstein and Henderson (1969) we shall only briefly summarize them here. This schedule was an attempt to discover the relative emphasis placed upon language in the socialization of the child into inter-person relationships and into elementary skill acquisition. Questions 5, 6, 8, 9, and 11 refer to the person area, questions 1, 2, 3, and 7 refer to the skill area, and questions 4 and 10 are dummy questions designed to move the mothers' responses towards the 'easy' point of the scale.

The overall difference in emphasis between the two areas, irrespective of the social class of the mothers, is highly significant ($F_{1,98} = 294{\cdot}53$, $p = 0{\cdot}001$). However, although greater emphasis was placed upon difficulty in the *person* area by *all* the mothers, the difference between the mean responses of the MC mothers, in relation to the two areas, was significantly greater than the difference between the mean responses of the WC mothers ($F_{1,98} = 73{\cdot}60$, $p = 0{\cdot}001$). MC mothers placed much *greater* emphasis upon the difficulty of doing the things described in the *person* area than the WC mothers, but much *less* emphasis upon the difficulty of doing the things described in the *skill* area. This highly significant interaction effect illustrates the polarization of the MC mothers' responses in relation to the two areas.

TABLE 3.2

	Statements		
	Skill areas	*Person areas*	*Total $\bar{x}$*
$\bar{x}$ Middle class	0·03	1·49	0·78
$\bar{x}$ Working class	0·33	0·80	0·56
Sample $\bar{x}$	0·20	1·14	

Table 3.2 sets out the mean scores for each social class within each area. The higher the score the greater the emphasis and the lower the score the less the emphasis. At the same time a highly significant inter-action effect between the social class of the mothers and responses to the individual skill statements was found. MC mothers placed significantly greater emphasis on difficulty than the WC mothers in response to the statement 'Showing them how things work' ($F_{3,294} = 74{\cdot}88$, $p = 0{\cdot}001$). Table 3.3 shows the mean score of each social class for each of the statements in the skill area. Again, the higher the score the greater the emphasis, the lower the score the less the emphasis.

TABLE 3.3

Statement	*1*	2	*3*	*7*	*Total $\bar{x}$*
$\bar{x}$ Middle class	−0·48	0·12	0·04	0·62	0·30
$\bar{x}$ Working class	0·48	0·28	0·36	0·36	1·50
Sample $\bar{x}$	0·01	0·20	0·20	0·49	

We can summarize the results as follows:

(1) MC mothers, relative to WC mothers, placed a greater emphasis upon the use of language in the socialization of the child into inter- and intra-personal relationships, whereas the WC placed a relatively greater emphasis upon language in the socialization of the child into elementary skills.

(2) Without prejudice to the above, MC mothers placed greater emphasis on the use of language in the transmission of principles, i.e. 'Showing them how things work'. Here the MC, relative to the WC, appeared to find it necessary to explicate the principles *verbally*.

(3) The MC mothers, relative to the WC mothers, more *sharply* discriminated between the skill and person areas, as this is evidenced by the differential emphasis on the use of language.

Schedule B. This schedule was constructed in order to find out how the mother responded to her child's attempts to chat to her across a range of seven fairly typical contexts. Four different strategies were provided, and the mother was asked to place a tick against the one she was most likely to take up for each of the seven situations. The strategies were:

(*a*) 'Tell him to stop', which was scored 1.
(*b*) 'Tell him to wait', which was scored 2.
(*c*) 'Answer him quickly', which was scored 3.
(*d*) 'Chat to him', which was scored 4.

A preliminary examination of the data revealed that there were minimal differences in response to particular contexts, so it was decided to analyse the differential frequency with which particular strategies were taken up. A 2×4 experimental plan on repeated measures was therefore undertaken. The analysis revealed that MC mothers had significantly higher scores than WC mothers, thus showing that they were more likely to respond by chatting to the child ($F_{1,98} = 24{\cdot}07$, $p = 0{\cdot}001$). There was also a significant difference overall in the choice of strategies taken up ($F_{3,294} = 235{\cdot}17$, $p = 0{\cdot}001$). A second order inter-action effect due to the relationship between the social class of the mother and the strategy most frequently taken up was also significant ($F_{3,294} = 12{\cdot}20$, $p = 0{\cdot}001$). A further analysis of the simple main effects of social class on each of the strategies showed that there was a significant difference between the two social class groups on one strategy only—'Chat to him'. MC mothers were more likely to take up this strategy than WC mothers ($F_{1,392} = 682{\cdot}22$, $p = 0{\cdot}01$). The analysis of simple main effects was extended to the differential choice of strategies *within* each social class. Both MC ($F_{3,294} = 166{\cdot}42$, $p = 0{\cdot}01$), and WC mothers ($F_{3,294} = 80{\cdot}95$, $p = 0{\cdot}01$) discriminated significantly between the frequency with which certain strategies were taken up. In both cases the strategy most frequently avoided was 'Tell him to stop', and in both cases the most frequent strategy was 'Chat to him'. There was little discrimination between 'Tell him to wait' and 'Answer him quickly', although discrimination between these two strategies tended to be greater in the WC than in the MC.

Schedule C. Here the mothers were presented with eight questions which a child was likely to ask, and they were invited to choose their initial response to each question from among six possible responses. Four of these responses indicated avoidance or evasion of the question on the part of the mother, whilst two were positive responses—'Take the opportunity to discuss the matter with him' and 'Give him a brief answer and see if he's satisfied'. It was considered that the latter response allowed the child greater discretion in regulating the mother's flow of information than the former, and for this reason it was assigned the highest score—2. 'Take the opportunity to discuss the matter with him' was assigned a score of 1, and any avoidance response was given a score of 0. The method of analysis was a 2×8 experimental plan, on repeated measures, the measures being the questions.

A significant main order difference was found due to the social class of the mothers. WC mothers more frequently avoided or evaded answering questions than MC mothers ($F_{1,98} = 38{\cdot}40$, $p = 0{\cdot}001$). There was also a significant second order difference due to an inter-action effect between the social class of the mother and the particular question to which she responded ($F_{7,686} = 2{\cdot}92$, $p = 0{\cdot}01$). An analysis of the simple main effects of social class on the questions showed that there were significant differences in response *between* the questions within the WC but *not* within the MC ($F_{7,686} = 3{\cdot}74$, $p = 0{\cdot}01$). In other words, WC mothers were much more likely to avoid answering *particular* questions. A further analysis of simple main effects of social class on *each* of the questions was carried out, and we found that the questions which elicited the greatest incidence of avoidance among the mothers were:

(*a*) Why there are wars.
(*b*) Why boys are different from girls.
(*c*) Why some people are mentally disturbed.
(*d*) Daddy's part in making babies.

We then decided to carry out a secondary analysis of the data, because, not only were we interested in the relative incidence of avoidance responses, but also in the relative frequencies of the two positive responses within each social class. The percentage distributions of the total scores were examined, and are presented in Table 3.4.

We can clearly see from Table 3.4 that the maximum difference between MC and WC mothers is in the incidence of avoidance, despite the fact that for both classes it is the most infrequent type of response. However, within the WC there is a very much greater incidence of 'discussion' responses relative to 'brief answer' responses, whilst the difference between these two types of response is minimal within the MC. Thus we find that when WC mothers do not avoid answering a question they are much more likely to take up the 'discussion' option than the 'brief answer' option. In order to test for the significance of these differences between the social class groups, t-tests were carried out. As we would expect, there was no significant difference between the two groups in the frequency with which the 'discussion' option was taken up. And, as we might expect, on the basis of the results of the initial analysis, WC mothers avoided answering questions more frequently than MC mothers ($t = 11{\cdot}97$, df 98, $p = 0{\cdot}001$). At the same time, MC mothers differed significantly from WC mothers in the frequency with which they took up the 'brief answers' option ($t = 61{\cdot}56$, df 98, $p = 0{\cdot}001$). However, we can see from the percentage distribution in the following table that this was almost entirely due to the relative avoidance of 'brief answer' responses on the part of WC mothers in favour of 'discussion'.

TABLE 3.4

	Percentage distribution of total scores			
	Avoidance	*Discussion*	*Brief answer*	*Total*
MC ($N = 400$)	4·25	48·25	47·50	100·00
WC ($N = 400$)	23·00	55·75	21·25	100·00

TABLE 3.5

	Numbers of mothers					
	Avoidance		*'Discussion'*		*'Brief answers'*	
Questions	*MC*	*WC*	*MC*	*WC*	*MC*	*WC*
1	0	7	30	28	20	15
2	3	18	19	18	28	14
3*	2	13	26	29	22	8
4*	3	12	19	29	28	9
5	1	6	29	33	20	11
6	0	6	33	35	17	9
7*	7	24	13	17	30	9
8	1	6	24	34	25	10

*'Why boys are different from girls', 'Daddy's part in making babies' and 'Why some people are mentally disturbed', respectively.

Now, our findings showed that WC mothers discriminated between the questions in terms of avoidance–discussion responses on the whole. Examination of our data suggested that, whilst MC mothers did not discriminate in terms of avoidance, they might well be discriminating between the questions in terms of the *type* of positive response. The above table shows that MC mothers tended to respond with 'brief answers' to those statements which elicited avoidance responses from WC mothers.

Comment

In Bernstein and Henderson (1969; see chapter 2) discussion was offered of the found differences in the use of language in the socialization of the pre-school child, inter-personal relationships and the acquisition of basic skills. Briefly, it was suggested that the MC are more concerned to make verbally explicit for the child the whole inter-personal area. Such explicitness provides for a greater reflexiveness on the part of the MC towards this area of experience. We note that MC mothers are more likely to take up attempts of the child to talk in a range of contexts. Further, that they report that they are less likely to avoid answering the child's questions in the inter-personal area. The MC mothers are more likely to give the response 'Give him a brief answer and see if he is satisfied' to what might be considered three very difficult questions to answer; whereas the WC tend to give 'avoidance' responses to the same questions. These results confirm all the hypotheses which relate to the schedules. The findings on the 'chat' and the 'avoidance' schedules repeat the results obtained from similar but less specific schedules put to the mother two years earlier (Brandis and Henderson, 1970).

We will now consider in rather more detail the analysis of schedule C (the 'avoidance' schedule). We find that not only do MC mothers avoid or evade answering difficult questions *less* than the WC mothers, but also that the MC mothers discriminated between the questions. Within the WC discrimination only took the form of avoidance versus non-avoidance, whereas within the MC discrimination took the form of choosing between *different types of non-avoidance responses*. Questions which dealt with critical aspects of inter- or intra-personal relationships elicited the greatest avoidance among the WC mothers. These same questions elicited a particular type of response from MC mothers: they were more likely to elicit the response 'Give him a brief answer and see if he's satisfied' than 'Take the opportunity to discuss the matter with him'. It might be thought that such a response in the MC may have operated in lieu of an avoidance response. When this schedule was designed, it was considered that giving the child a brief answer and waiting to see if he was satisfied allowed the child greater discretion to regulate the amount of information.

It is a matter of considerable interest that the questions which called out the child-regulating strategy on the part of the MC mothers are all questions which on the whole elicit *avoidance* strategies from the WC mothers. These questions 'Why boys are different from girls', 'Daddy's part in making babies' and 'Why some people are mentally disturbed' were originally asked because it was thought that they refer to highly critical areas of experience which may form a taboo area. The MC mother's response indicates that (1) she is prepared to offer an explanation and (2) she may be conscious of not wanting to overload the child and so *gives* the child the initiative in seeking more information. We regard this as an important example of how these mothers will take into account the relationship between the explanatory style *and* the particular needs of the child. The MC mothers' explanatory styles appear to be *contingent* upon the problem, her explanations appear to be *context-specific*.

Whereas we feel confident in our interpretation of the contextual switch upon the part of the MC to 'Give him a brief answer and see if he's satisfied', we are not able to make strong inferences from the WC overall preference, when they do *not* avoid, for 'Take the opportunity to discuss it with him'. If the WC mother did not avoid the question, she was forced to choose one of the two explanatory strategies. It is conceivable that the *meaning* of the 'brief answer' strategy is *different* for the two social classes. We have some evidence to suggest that this is indeed likely to be the case. When we examined, *within* the WC sample, the inter-correlation between mothers who choose 'Give him a brief answer etc.', and the mothers who opt for the 'Chat to him' strategy, we find that the correlation is significantly negative ($r = 0{\cdot}29$, $p = 0{\cdot}05$). On the other hand, the correlation between the 'discussion' response and the 'Chat to him' strategy is significantly positive ($r = 0{\cdot}43$, $p = 0{\cdot}01$). Therefore, within the WC sample the strategy 'Give him a brief answer etc.', is unlikely to be an index of a self-regulatory teaching style. It is more likely to be a minimal information strategy on the 'avoidance' dimension. We can strengthen this inference by giving the inter-correlation between the choice of the 'discussion' strategy and the frequency with which questions are avoided by the mother, which is significantly negative ($r = -0{\cdot}28$, $p = 0{\cdot}05$). The more verbally responsive the WC mother reports she is to her child, the more likely she is to give a 'discussion' response. We find *no* relationship between the choice of 'Give him a brief answer, etc.', and the choice of the 'Chat to him' strategy *within* the MC sample. Similarly, within the MC sample there is *no* relationship between 'Give him a brief answer' and avoidance of questions. Thus, MC mothers who choose 'Give him a brief answer' are not necessarily verbally unresponsive to their children. Minimally, we can say that 'Give him a brief answer' is an alternative response to 'discussion' in the MC. The MC mother's response is dependent upon the *question*, not upon the mother's *general* orientation to her child.

Schedule D results

This schedule was constructed in order to find out how mothers explained the meanings of words to their children. We were particularly interested in finding out what *types* of definitions mothers were most likely to give. Four words were presented to the mother —'cool', 'mix', 'dangerous', and 'flexible'—and they were asked to choose *two* of four possible types of response for each of these words. The choices had to be ranked in terms of the *first* statement the mother would be most likely to choose and then the statement which she thought *second* best. Since there were four different types of statement given for each word, there was a possibility of the mother choosing any one of *six* possible combinations of statements in response to any one item. Thus it can be seen that, at first sight, the mothers' responses to this schedule promised to be rather difficult to analyse.

The four statements offered for each word were presented in the form of (*a*) a general definition, (*b*) an antonym, (*c*) a highly specific concrete example, and (*d*) a much less specific concrete example. The various possible combinations of first and second choices, then, were as follows:

(1) General definition and highly specific concrete example.
(2) General definition and an antonym.
(3) General definition and least specific concrete example.
(4) Highly specific concrete example and least specific concrete example.
(5) Highly specific concrete example and antonym.
(6) Least specific concrete example and antonym.

The various responses were not scored in any way, because this would have involved putting differential values on each of the combined choices. It was considered that this was unjustified. For example, how should one choose between the differential values of a general definition combined with a highly specific concrete example, and an antonym combined with a highly specific concrete example? Finally, it was decided to find:

(*a*) the total number of each possible combination for *each* word within each social class;

(*b*) the total number of each possible combination *across* the four words within each social class;
(*c*) the *first* choice responses for *each* word within each social class;
(*d*) the *first* choice responses *across* the four words within each social class.

First, a 2×4 chi-square was carried out in order to find out whether there was a significant social class difference in the incidence of *different* combined choices given across the four words. It was therefore possible for a mother to give one type of combined response for all four items, or for her to vary her response with each word, thus giving four different combinations. The result of this chi-square test showed that there was indeed a significant difference between the two social class groups on this measure. WC mothers were most likely to use only one or two different combinations across the four words, whilst MC mothers were most likely to use three or four different combinations across the words ($\chi^2 = 9{\cdot}94$, *df* 3, $p = 0{\cdot}02$). We then tested for the significance of differences in the number of *first* choice responses across all four words, in a similar fashion, but no significant differences were found. It is important to stress that here we were concerned to examine *variation* in first choice response across the four words, *not* incidence of particular first choice responses.

Next, we were interested in differences between the social class groups in terms of the *first* choice response to *each* word. Four 2×4 chi-squares were carried out. This analysis revealed that there were significant differences in response to three of the words, as follows:

Mix: MC mothers were most likely to choose the highly specific concrete example first, whereas WC mothers were most likely to choose the least specific concrete example first ($\chi^2 = 21{\cdot}28$, *df* 3, $p = 0{\cdot}001$).

Dangerous: MC mothers were most likely to choose the general definition first, whereas WC mothers were most likely to choose the least specific concrete example first ($\chi^2 = 20{\cdot}32$, *df* 3, $p = 0{\cdot}001$).

Flexible: MC mothers were most likely to choose the general definition first, whereas WC mothers were more likely to choose the highly specific concrete example first ($\chi^2 = 14{\cdot}14$, *df* 3, $p = 0{\cdot}01$).

To summarize briefly, MC mothers were found to be more likely than WC mothers to choose a general definition *first* in response to two of the words, 'dangerous' and 'flexible'. WC mothers were found to be more likely than MC mothers to choose the least specific concrete example *first* in response to two of the words, 'mix' and 'dangerous'.

The differences between MC and WC mothers in terms of the *combined* responses to each word were then examined. Four 2×6 chi-squares were carried out. Significant social class differences were found in relation to *two* of the words:

Dangerous: MC mothers were more likely to choose the general definition and the antonym, *or* the general definition and the highly specific concrete example, whereas WC mothers were more likely to choose the highly specific concrete example and the least specific concrete example ($\chi^2 = 20{\cdot}02$, *df* 5, $p = 0{\cdot}01$).

Flexible: MC mothers were more likely to choose both the general definition and the highly specific concrete example, whereas WC mothers were more likely to choose both the highly specific and the least specific concrete examples ($\chi^2 = 11{\cdot}06$, *df* 5, $p = 0{\cdot}05$).

Again, we can briefly summarize these results. For both of the words which elicited significant differences in response, MC mothers were more likely to choose general definitions with highly specific concrete examples, whilst WC mothers, on the other hand, were more orientated to *both* varieties of concrete examples.

We can now examine the results of four 2×4 chi-squares which tested for significant differences in the *incidence* of particular *first* choices across the four words. No significant differences in the overall incidence of general definitions or least specific concrete examples were found. But there were significant differences in the incidence of highly specific concrete examples and in the incidence of antonyms.

Highly specific concrete examples: MC mothers were more likely than WC mothers to choose this type of statement when defining 'cool' and 'mix', and they were least likely to do this when defining 'dangerous' and 'flexible'. On the other hand, WC mothers were more likely than MC mothers to choose this type of statement when defining 'dangerous' and 'flexible' but least likely to do this when defining 'cool' and 'mix' ($\chi^2 = 13{\cdot}43$, *df* 3, $p = 0{\cdot}01$).

Antonyms: The overall incidence of the use of antonyms as first choices was low, but MC mothers were more likely to choose this type of statement than WC mothers. Antonyms were most likely to occur as first choices in the definition of 'cool' ($\chi^2 = 15{\cdot}99$, *df* 3, $p = 0{\cdot}01$).

Although these findings were extremely interesting, we found them somewhat difficult to summarize succinctly. It was therefore decided to examine the responses to each word in terms *only* of the *first* choices and these were to be summarized as either *abstract* in orientation (*e.g.* general definitions or antonyms) or *concrete* in orientation (*e.g.* highly specific and least specific concrete examples). Four 2×2 chi-squares were then carried out.

The MC and the WC mothers did not differ significantly when defining 'cool' and 'mix', although there was a tendency in both cases for MC mothers to be more abstract in orientation. There were significant differences in the cases of 'dangerous' and 'flexible':

Dangerous: MC mothers were most likely to give abstract definitions, whilst WC mothers were most likely to give concrete definitions ($\chi^2 = 13{\cdot}10$, *df* 1, $p = 0{\cdot}001$).

Flexible: MC mothers were again most likely to give abstract definitions, whilst WC mothers were most likely to give concrete definitions ($\chi^2 = 10{\cdot}20$, *df* 1, $p = 0{\cdot}01$).

Let us now summarize the findings of the analysis of this schedule, with the help of appropriate tables. MC mothers were found to be more consistent across the words than WC mothers in the type of statement which they chose first, as the following table clearly shows:

TABLE 3.6

Number of different first choices used	*MC*	*WC*
1 or 2	36	24
3 or 4	14	26

The relevant first choice was most likely to be a general definition. However, despite the consistency shown by the MC mothers in the type of first choices, there was greater variation within the MC in the number of different combinations used across the four words. This logically indicates that their second choice of definition was more likely to be contingent upon the particular word than was the case in the WC.

TABLE 3.7
Incidence of first choice definitions across words

	MC	*WC*
General definition	118	76
Antonym	12	8
Highly specific concrete	51	60
Least specific concrete	19	56
Total	200	200

TABLE 3.8

Number of different combined responses	*MC*	*WC*
1 or 2	18	28
3 or 4	32	22

Next, MC mothers were more likely than WC mothers to choose an abstract definition first, whereas WC mothers were more likely to choose a concrete definition first, overall.

TABLE 3.9

	MC	*WC*
Abstract	130	84
Concrete	70	116
Total	200	200

Finally, there were differences in the incidence of different types of combined first and second choice responses. MC mothers were more likely than WC mothers to choose a general definition with an antonym. WC mothers, on the other hand, were more likely than MC mothers to choose both a highly specific with a least specific concrete example, overall.

TABLE 3.10

Combined choices	*MC*	*WC*
General definition + highly specific concrete	87	74
General definition + antonym	30	17
General definition + least specific concrete	38	36
Highly specific concrete + antonym	12	10
Highly specific concrete + least specific concrete	30	50
Least specific concrete + antonym	3	13

Comment

We find that MC mothers were not only more likely to aim primarily at a higher level of generality or abstraction when defining words for their children, but also that when they considered it necessary to give a concrete example, the example chosen was more *explicit* and *precise* than the examples chosen by WC mothers. MC mothers, at the same time, discriminated more frequently *between* the words requiring definition in terms of the response chosen as second-best. We find that, despite the relatively infrequent use of antonyms by all mothers, MC mothers were more likely to use them than WC mothers, but their use of antonyms was *totally* avoided when defining 'mix', whilst their use was equally distributed when defining 'cool', 'dangerous', and 'flexible'. In other words, MC mothers were more likely to employ antonyms when defining *states* whereas the use of antonyms was avoided when defining a *process*. The WC mothers did not discriminate between the words in this way.

Whilst the data at our disposal from this schedule does not allow us to make any firm interpretation in terms of maternal teaching styles, we think the results here may reflect a tendency towards a *deductive* teaching style on the part of the MC mothers, and an *inductive* teaching style on the part of the WC mothers. Minimally, our justification for this hypothesis is based upon the overwhelming number of general definitions chosen by MC mothers as their primary response, and upon the much greater incidence of concrete examples among the primary responses of WC mothers. This is not to say that MC mothers do *not* give concrete examples, and that WC mothers do *not* give general definitions. MC mothers move from the general to the specific, whereas the WC mothers, when they use a general definition, rank it below a concrete example. They move from the specific to the general.[3]

General discussion

First let us consider the questions of the contextual specificity of the verbal communications of the mothers *and* the emphasis upon language in different contexts. Contextual specificity of the communications refers to the extent that the mothers discriminate between contexts or to discrimination betwen verbal strategies within the *same* context. Emphasis refers to the extent to which a context evokes verbal communication.

Emphasis

Mother–adult communication

(1) When we analysed the 'words/action' schedule (B), we found that it was two statements 'Comforting others when they were in distress' and 'Stopping myself from feeling angry' which were responsible for the social class differences in the choice.

WC mothers preferred *words* and MC mothers preferred actions.

(2) MC mothers reported that they talked more frequently to other adults than did the WC mothers. The analysis of variance on repeated measures showed that the MC mothers reported that they talked more frequently in the cognitive area, whereas the WC mothers reported that they talked more frequently in the *inter-personal* area. We have commented in the paper about these unexpected findings.

Mother–child communication

(3) MC mothers reported that they were more likely to chat to the child across a range of contexts. However, the most common strategies for *both* social classes were 'Tell him to stop' and 'Chat to him'.

(4) MC mothers reported that they placed a relatively greater emphasis than did WC mothers upon the use of language in the socialization of the child into person relationships, whereas WC mothers reported that they placed a greater emphasis upon the use of language than did the MC mothers in the socialization of the child into elementary skills. However, the MC mothers emphasized language within the skill area in response to the question 'Showing him how things work'.

Contextual specificity

Mother–adult communication

(1) The analysis of schedule A (talking to adults) revealed that MC mothers discriminated *more* sharply *among the three areas of discourse* social, inter-personal, and cognitive in terms of frequency of talking than did the WC mothers.

Mother–child communication

(2) The analysis of schedule C (answering or evading questions put by the child to the mother) showed that the MC mothers alternated between *two* information-giving responses 'Take the opportunity to discuss the matter with him' and 'Give him a brief answer and see if he's satisfied', whereas the WC were more confined to the discussion strategy. We showed that in the WC, the 'brief answer' strategy was related to the avoidance dimension and also to mothers who were much less likely to take up the child's attempts to chat to the mother.

Of more significance, the MC used the strategy 'Give him a brief answer and see if he's satisfied' in response to the statements 'Why boys are different from girls', 'Daddy's part in making babies' and 'Why some people are mentally disturbed'. Thus the explanatory style of the MC mother appears to be contingent upon the problem: her explanations appear to be contextually specific.

(3) The analysis of the schedule concerned with word defining strategies showed that despite the infrequent use of antonyms by all mothers, MC mothers *totally* avoided their use when defining 'mix' but they distributed the use of this strategy across the other three words. They avoided the use of the antonym when defining *processes*. The WC mothers did not discriminate between the words in this way. MC mothers discriminated more between the words in terms of their second best choice of definitions.

(4) The analysis of schedule A showed that although all mothers reported that they placed a greater emphasis upon the use of language in socializing the pre-school child into person-relationships rather than into elementary skills, the shift was five times as great in the MC from one area to the other, but only two and a half times in the case of the WC. It would appear then that the MC mothers made a much clearer differentiation between the use of language in the skill and person area than did the WC mothers. The MC mothers' responses were more context specific.

(5) There is an interesting difference between the mother of different social class background in the verbal realization of the inter-personal area of discourse. (On the one hand we have the MC mothers who seem to be unwilling to talk to unspecified adults for inter-personal reasons but who place a positive emphasis on talking to their children in this area.) They also do not avoid or evade answering critical questions put by their children in the same area. On the other hand the WC mothers, who seem to be most willing to talk to other adults for inter-personal reasons, place less emphasis upon the use of language in this area when talking to their children, relative to the MC mothers. The WC also positively avoid answering critical questions in this area. This class difference in the contextual constraint upon talking in the inter-personal area may simply have arisen out of the *classification* we have introduced. On the other hand, it could point to the need for further enquiry into the relationships between role and topic as this is affected by social class.

Discretion

We will now go on to consider the discretion accorded to the child by the mother. By discretion we mean the range of alternatives the mother makes available to the child in different contexts. The data we have presented here does not allow us much room for comment. Other data the Sociological Research Unit has collected bears rather more pertinently on this area (Bernstein and Young, 1967; Jones, 1966; Bernstein and Brandis, 1970). However, we can here point to the finding that MC mothers are more likely to take up their child's attempts to *initiate* verbal inter-action in a range of contexts. Further, that the MC relative to the WC use an information giving strategy which, if we interpret it correctly, permits the child to regulate the amount of information he receives ('Give him a brief answer and see if he's satisfied').

Cognitive socialization

We have shown that according to the mothers' reports, MC mothers, relative to WC mothers

(1) Favour abstract definitions—the class defining principle.
(2) Favour *explicit* rather than implicit 'concrete' definitions.
(3) Favour information giving strategies in answer to children's questions. They avoid or evade answering questions much less.
(4) Favour emphasizing language in the transmission of moral principles and the recognition of feeling.
(5) Favour emphasizing language in the transmission of principles as these relate to objects. ('Showing him how things work').
(6) Favour talking frequently to unspecified other adults in the cognitive area. This leads us to assume that the MC mothers' cognitive world, relative to the WC mothers' cognitive world, is expanding, and the *consequences feed back to her child*.

We can summarize by suggesting that the MC child not only has access to a greater range of educationally relevant knowledge but that relative to the WC child he is orientated through language to *principles* as these relate to objects and persons. The MC child through the form of his linguistic socialization, relative to the WC child, is made aware of the meta-languages through which a certain form of knowledge is acquired. Our data strongly suggests that this is much less the case for the WC child.

It should be apparent that the linguistic socialization of the MC child is critically relevant to his ability to profit from the educational experience as this is *currently* defined. There is little discontinuity between the symbolic orders of the school and those to which he has been socialized through his family. Whereas for the working-class child there is a hiatus between the symbolic orders of the school and those of his family. He is less oriented towards the meta-languages of control and innovation and the pattern of social relationships through which they are transmitted. *The genesis of educational failure, according to our findings, may well be found in the patterns of communication and control which are realizations and thus transmitters of specific sub-cultures.*[4]

It is important to emphasize and re-emphasize that these reported social class differences in forms of communication do *not* justify the inference that the WC communication forms are impoverished. Neither does it indicate that this group is linguistically deprived. It simply reveals that sub-cultures or, indeed, cultures, place a differential emphasis upon *language* in the context of socialization. The differences we have reported point to differences in the *social function* of linguistic communication. It is clearly the case that all cultures or sub-cultures are realized through communication forms which contain their own unique, imaginative and aesthetic possibilities. Our schedules were *not* designed to reveal such possibilities. It must be borne in mind that this indicates that we have studied only a narrow range of competence and a narrow range of social relationships.

In conclusion, all but two of the hypotheses given in the introduction have been confirmed. The findings have also revealed certain unexpected fluctuations in patterns of communication within each social class, as well as directing our attention to differences in the degree of contextual-specificity. Thus, the analysis has enabled us to show that the patterning of verbal communication and, therefore, maternal definitions of the role of language in the socializing process, are dependent on, and must be examined within, contexts of use. The behavioural setting and the topic under discussion are major determinants of *what* is said and *how* it is said (Hymes, 1962, 1967; Gumperz, 1972; Williams and Naremore, 1969; Ervin-Tripp, 1964). In later publications we hope to be able to show that these different forms of communication arise out of different orderings of roles within the family. We also hope to be able to show not only the variation in forms of communication *between* sub-cultural groups, but also the variations which are found *within* sub-cultural groups, together with their social antecedents. The communication system is itself a reflection and transmitter, of the underlying boundary maintenance procedures within the family. Perhaps the most important conclusion is one which has been stressed before: the need for small-scale naturalistic and experimental studies of the channels, codes and contexts which control processes of socialization.

Appendix 1

Socialization, context, and communication

We shall discuss here further the three components we have distinguished in the text.

1. *Contextual-specificity*

This refers to differences in communication elicited by different contexts. A context can be described as the behavioural relevant setting in which role relationships are embedded. Thus as contexts change, so does role and setting. The degree of contextual-specificity of communication can only be measured in terms of differences across a *range* of contexts. There may well be some underlying structure which patterns the differences across a range of contexts (elaborated and restricted codes).

2. *Cognitive orientations*

These may be evaluated upon a Universalistic/Particularistic (Parsons and Shils, 1951) dimension. Universalistic orders of meaning arise when principles and operations are made verbally explicit and are elaborated; particularistic orders of meaning arise when principles and operations are rendered implicit and less elaborated. Thus universalistic orders of meaning are less tied to a given context, whereas particularistic orders of meaning are clearly tied to a given context and receive their significance essentially in terms of that context.

3. *Discretion*

Discretion refers to the range of alternatives open to the communicant occupying the lowest status, *i.e.* the socialized. Thus when discretion is high, the socialized is able to modify, extend and initiate communications. Where it is low, such possibilities are made less available.

A number of combinations are possible on the basis of these three elements which may stand in an orthogonal relationship to each other. Their particular relationship to each other may affect the relative strength of boundary maintenance *in the area under discussion.*

Let us take as one example the area of explanation. For the purpose of illustration only two sets of relationships will be selected.

Discourse explanatory	1	2
Contextual-specificity	High	Low
Discretion	High	Low
Cognitive orientations	Universalistic	Particularistic

1. Contextual-specificity high, discretion high, universalistic meanings. This will give rise to a dynamic cognitive orientation in which learning is achieved, and access is given to the meta-language of control and innovation. This will generate a weak boundary maintaining system which is open to exploration at the level of principles *and* operations.

2. Contextual-specificity low, discretion low, particularistic meanings. This will give rise to a static cognitive orientation in which learning is assigned, and there is no access to the meta-languages of control and innovation. Thus the boundary maintaining system will be strong as there is little exploration at the level of principles *and* operations.

We should point out that the relationship between these three elements—contextual-specificity, discretion and cognitive ordering—may vary not only with the different cultural groups in any *common* area of discourse, but also with age, sex, and age-relation status. They may vary also according to the topic and nature of the discourse.

Appendix 2

Note to schedule D

Schedule D was a particularly difficult schedule to design as it called for four distinct types of explanations which could be offered to a child of *seven years of age.* On the whole, we felt reasonably confident about the general definitions and antonyms.

	General	Antonyms
Cool	It's a little bit warmer than cold.	It's the opposite of warm.
Mix	To put things together.	It's the opposite of separate.
Dangerous	It's when you might get hurt.	It's the opposite of safe.
Flexible	Something that will bend without breaking.	It's the opposite of rigid or stiff.

The major problem in the design was separating the concrete *explicit* from the concrete *implicit.*

Cool	It's when something is no longer warm to touch.	It's what you feel when the sun goes in
Mix	It's what you do when you put different paints together to make different colours.	When I make a stew the food is all mixed up.
Dangerous	A road where there are lots of accidents.	It's dangerous to play with fire.
Flexible	Rubber is flexible.	Your shoes are flexible.

We think that when one considers *all* the 'explicit' statements and *all* the 'implicit' statements then one can see a difference in the type of explanation. Three of the 'implicit' statements mention the word to be defined in the explanation. The fourth contrasts 'it's what you feel when the sun goes in' (implicit) where the state is left open, with 'it's when something is no longer hot to touch' (explicit). In one case (the word 'flexible') the choice is between two explanations, both using the word 'flexible' in the statements: 'shoes are flexible' (implicit) and 'rubber is flexible' (explicit). We considered that the latter statement was a less limiting example than the former.

We found that despite the difficulty in clearly separating the concrete explanations into two unambiguous classes, there was a greater incidence of implicit concrete choices within the WC and a greater incidence of explicit concrete choices within the MC. We feel that this is a potentially useful approach which is worthy of greater development.

Mother-adult communication

Schedule A

Here is a short list of reasons for talking to other people.
Please tick how much you find yourself talking:

	I *hardly ever* find myself talking	I *sometimes* find myself talking	I *often* find myself talking
1. To be friendly			
2. To exchange ideas			
3. About what I have seen on television			
4. To increase the number of people I know			
5. To find out what other people think of me			
6. About my children			
7. To question the world around me			
8. To find out more about people			
9. To decide what is right and wrong			
10. To show my feelings to others			
11. To increase my knowledge about the world			
12. So that those close to me can understand me better			

Mother-adult communication

Schedule B

There are many ways of letting people know what you are thinking or feeling. Some people think that words may not always help. Would you look at the following list and say for each situation which you find *more* helpful—words or actions.

	I find words more helpful	I find actions more helpful
a. Comforting friends when they are in distress		
b. Stopping myself feeling angry		
c. Coping with personal doubts and anxieties		

d. Letting others know how much I care for them	
e. Letting others know just what I really mean	
f. To find out whether other people are sincere or genuine	

Mother-child communication

Schedule A

If parents could not speak, how much *more* difficult do you think it would be for them to do the followings things with young children who had not yet started school?

	Very much more difficult	Much more difficult	More difficult	Not too difficult	Fairly easy	Easy
Teaching them everyday tasks, like dressing, and using a knife and fork						
Helping them to make things						
Drawing their attention to different shapes						
Playing games with them						
Showing them what is right and wrong						
Letting them know what you are feeling						
Showing them how things work						
Helping them to work things out for themselves						
Disciplining them						
Showing them how pleased you are with their progress						
Dealing with them when they are unhappy						

Mother-child communication

Schedule B

Children often chatter quite a lot. Please say what you usually do if . . . starts chattering:	Tell him to stop	Tell him to wait	Answer him quickly	Chat with him
1. When you are working around the house				
2. When you are walking along the street				
3. When you are trying to relax				
4. When you are talking to your husband				
5. When you are in a shop				
6. When you are in a bus or tube				
7. At meal-times				

Mother-child communication

Schedule C

Here are some more questions that . . . might ask. For each question, please say what you would be most likely to do *first.*

Question
1. Why we have rules
2. Why there are wars
3. Why boys are different from girls
4. Why some people are mentally disturbed
5. Why some people are rich and others poor
6. Why some people are physically disabled
7. Daddy's part in making babies
8. Why people die

Strategies
a. Make up something until he is older
b. Tell him to ask Daddy
c. Try and change the subject
d. Take the opportunity to discuss the matter with him
e. Tell him he's not old enough to understand
f. Give him a brief answer and see if he's satisfied

Mother-child communication

Schedule D

If you were explaining the meaning of the following words to your child . . . which *two* of the four statements would you choose? Please put the figure 1 by the statement you would be most likely to choose, and a figure 2 by the statement you think is second best.

'COOL'

1. It's when something is no longer hot to touch
2. It's the opposite of warm
3. It's what you feel when the sun goes in
4. It's a little bit warmer than 'cold'

'MIX'

1. To put things together
2. When I make a stew the food is all mixed up
3. It's what you do when you put different paints together to make different colours
4. It's the opposite of separate

'DANGEROUS'

1. It's when you might get hurt
2. A road where there are lots of accidents
3. It's dangerous to play with fire
4. It's the opposite of safe

'FLEXIBLE'

1. Rubber is flexible
2. It's the opposite of rigid or stiff
3. Your shoes are flexible
4. Something that will bend without breaking

Notes

1 This is the same sample as in the previous chapter.

2 The 'other adults' for the WC may well have been people they know well in the neighbourhood. The WC may not formalize categories of inter-personal relations in the same way as the MC.

3 This does not mean that the MC adopts a more efficient teaching style.

4 Clearly this statement holds only in relation to a *particular* definition of the form, content and context of education.

References

BERNSTEIN, B. (1962), 'Family role systems, communication and socialization', S.R.U. manuscript.

BERNSTEIN, B. (1964), 'Family role systems, socialization and communication', paper given at the Conference on Cross-Cultural Research into Childhood and Adolescence, University of Chicago, 1964.

BERNSTEIN, B. (1972), 'A socio-linguistic approach to socialization: with some references to educability', *Directions in Sociolinguistics* (eds) J. Gumperz and D. Hymes. New York: Holt, Rinehart & Winston.

BERNSTEIN, B. and HENDERSON, D. (1969), 'Social class differences in the relevance of language to socialization', *Sociology*, 3.

BERNSTEIN, B. and BRANDIS, W. (1970), 'Social class differences in communication and control', in W. Brandis and D. Henderson, *Social Class, Language and Communication*. London: Routledge & Kegan Paul.

BERNSTEIN, B. and YOUNG, D. (1967), 'Social class differences in conceptions of the uses of toys', *Sociology* 1, no. 2, May, and reprinted in the present volume.

BRANDIS, W. and HENDERSON, D. (1970), *Social Class, Language and Communication*. London: Routledge & Kegan Paul.

ERVIN-TRIPP, S. (1964), 'An analysis of the interaction of language, topic and listener', *The Ethnography of Communication*, (eds) J. Gumperz and D. Hymes, special publication of *American Anthropologist*, 66, 2, no. 6.

GUMPERZ, J. (1972), 'On the ethnology of linguistic change', *Directions in Sociolinguistics* (eds) J. Gumperz and J. Hymes. New York: Holt, Rinehart & Winston.

HENDERSON, D. (1970), 'Social class differences in form-class usage among five-year-old children', in W. Brandis and D. Henderson, *Social Class, Language and Communication*.

HYMES. D. (1962), 'The ethnography of speaking', in *Anthropology and Human Behaviour* (eds) Gladwin and Sturtevand, Washington D.C.: Anthropology Society of Washington.

HYMES, D. (1967), 'Models of the inter-action of language and social setting', *Journal of Social Issues*, 23.

JONES, J. (1966), 'Social class and the under-fives', *New Society*, December.

PARSONS, T. and SHILS, E. (1951), *Towards a General Theory of Action*. Harvard University Press (chapter 1).

WILLIAMS, F. and NAREMORE, R. C. (1969), 'On the functional analysis of social class differences in modes of speech', *Speech Monographs*, xxxvi, no. 2.

WINER, B. (1962), *Statistical Principles in Experimental Design*. McGraw-Hill (chapters 4 and 8).

Part II Aspects of the speech of five-year-old children

Chapter 4 Social class, the nominal group and reference

P. R. Hawkins

Introduction

In this paper we intend to show how the speech of five-year-old children of middle-class and working-class parents differs in the choices they take up within the nominal group. This investigation is part of the general research of the Sociological Research Unit into the relationships between the social background of children and their uses of language.

The sample of children was chosen from two geographically separate areas of London, one containing a predominantly working-class population, the other middle-class. The children were interviewed individually after they had been at school for three weeks. Their mothers had also been interviewed in the summer before the children went to school. We determined the social position of the family in terms of the educational and occupational status of the mother and of the father (Brandis, 1970). The total sample consists of 291 working-class children and 148 middle-class. Each interview with the children lasted about half an hour, during which they were asked to perform six different 'tasks', each designed to elicit different kinds of speech and to involve language in a variety of situations. In this paper we shall present some results obtained from the two 'tasks' which produced the greatest quantity of speech.

Bernstein (1962) and Lawton (1964) had already shown, in studies of adolescents of similar measured ability, aged between twelve and fifteen, that social class differences occur in the use of a number of grammatical categories, including adjectives, 'uncommon' adjectives, and the personal pronoun *I*, which are used more frequently by the middle class, and the personal pronouns *you* and *they* which are preferred by the working class. Bernstein hypothesized that the use of these pronouns indicated a 'lack of specification', which 'also implies that there is possibly some implicit agreement about the referent such that the elaboration is redundant'. Henderson (1970) has found that the five-year-old middle-class children of similar measured ability to the working class use significantly more adjectives, different adjectives, nouns, and different nouns, than the working class, over three 'tasks' in the speech schedule, including the two tasks which are discussed below. Since nouns, adjectives, and pronouns (as they are known in 'traditional' grammar) can be conveniently brought together under the concept of the 'nominal group', it was thought that a detailed grammatical study of this element might produce interesting results.

The nominal group is a feature of Halliday's 'scale and category grammar', and it was in terms of this grammar that the speech of the five-year-old children was analysed. A coding frame was prepared by a member of the Unit, G. J. Turner, and a computer program was written to count the frequency of occurrence of each grammatical category, and of certain combinations. This program was applied to a carefully controlled sub-sample of 110 children, and this enabled us to make comparisons between middle-class and working-class children, children of high, medium, and low verbal ability, and so on.

The results of this analysis, so far as the nominal group was concerned, indicated that, independent of the measured ability of the children, there was a broad tendency for the middle-class children to use the noun and its associated forms more frequently, while the working-class children made greater use of the pronoun and forms associated with it. These results were consonant with the predictions obtained from Bernstein's theory of restricted and elaborated codes, in terms of which one would expect the middle-class children to show relatively greater flexibility in their choices within the nominal group, and their groups to be more elaborated. Details of the results will be given in a monograph by the author, to be published later this year.

As a consequence of these initial findings, it was decided to extend the investigation of the nominal group, to look at certain grammatical categories within it in more detail, and to apply the analysis to a larger sample of 312 children. A correlation programme is now being run, to compare 43 linguistic variables connected with the nominal group, with certain sociological indices of the child's background, and with his intelligence as measured by tests of verbal ability. Some of the major findings which have already emerged from this analysis will be presented here. It is first necessary, however, to give details of the sample, the two 'tasks' of the speech schedule, and the structure of the nominal group.

The sample

The sample consists of all the 148 children from the middle-class area who were interviewed, and 180 of the 291 from the working-class area. These 180 children are representative of the total 291 in terms of social class and ability. From the sample, seven children (four working class, three middle class) have been excluded because their quantity of speech does not reach a required minimum, and nine (four working class, five middle class) have been excluded because relevant information about their social background or IQ is missing. This reduces the sample to 140 and 172 children respectively. Since the results to be presented here, however, are based on χ^2 tests, we wished to make each of the two groups as homogeneous as possible in their social class composition. We therefore excluded any middle-class (or marginally middle-class) children who happened to live in the working-class area, and working-class or marginally working-class children in the middle-class area. (The correlation between each area and social class is 0·74.) Our sample then consisted of 124 middle-class children and 139 working-class children.

The tasks

Of the two tasks to be considered, the first was designed to elicit narrative speech, and consists of a series of 4 picture cards which, together, tell a little story, rather like a strip-cartoon without captions. There are three series, of which one is reproduced below as an example. The children were asked to look at the cards and tell the story.

The second task is concerned with descriptive speech, and again has three parts. Postcard-size reproductions of paintings by the early twentieth-century Belgian 'primitive' artist, Hector Trotin, were given to the children, who were asked to describe what was going on in the picture, what the people were doing, and what the picture was all about. The paintings are highly colourful, and depict scenes of activity, for example the departure of a train from a railway station. Each of the three postcards was presented to the child separately.

Speech-eliciting situation

The nominal group

The nominal group, as defined within 'scale and category grammar', usually operates as subject or complement within the clause, and contains three parts: first, the 'head', which is obligatory, and usually consists of a 'noun' or a 'pronoun', though other parts of speech may occur there; second, any word or words occurring within the group and *before* the 'head' are known as 'modifiers', while (third) those occurring *after* the 'head' are called 'qualifiers'. 'Modifiers' are again sub-classified into categories defined according to their position of occurrence, for example, 'deictics' (words like *the, a, some, no*), 'ordinatives' (*two, three, first, next*), 'epithets' (*little, red, naughty*), and 'nominals' (roughly the traditional 'noun adjective' like *stone* in *a stone wall*). 'Qualifiers' may also be sub-classified, basically into one-word qualifiers (e.g. *all, else, both*) or group-qualifiers (the dog *in the window*) or clause-qualifiers (the man *who owned the house*).

The terms used are thus defined structurally, in contra-distinction to the traditional terms, which are defined by a rather imprecise mixture of semantic and structural criteria. A few examples may help to show how the nominal group is built up:

modifier (optional)	*head* (obligatory)	*qualifier* (optional)
a naughty	boy	
two black	cats	
a railway	train	
	they	all
	something	else
the	lady	in the carriage
	some	of them
very	hungry	

Note that a nominal group may appear at any position within the clause, except as a 'predicator' (or 'verb'). The clause 'they broke the window with a ball' contains three nominal groups, *they, the window, a ball*. Note, too, that within this structure an epithet may occur at 'head' modified by an 'intensifier', as in the last example above. The 'head' is therefore not always a noun or pronoun, as the penultimate example also shows.

The modifiers in the above examples were chosen to represent some of the sub-categories possible; we have, for example, two deictics, *a, the*; one ordinative, *two*; two epithets, *naughty, black*;

one nominal, *railway*; and one intensifier, *very*. It is possible for all these sub-categories to occur in one single group, e.g.

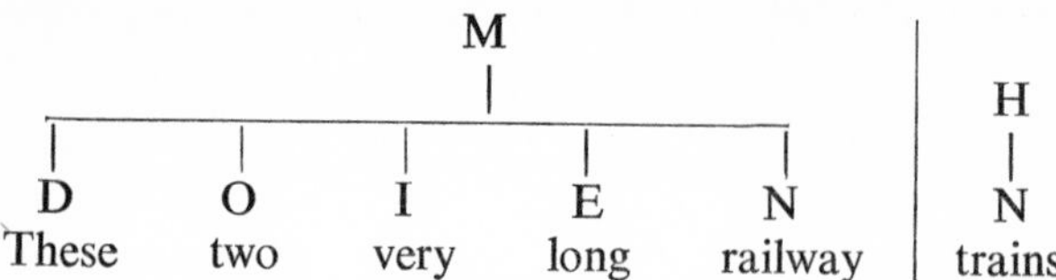

Clearly, it is when we have a noun at 'head' that the widest range of modification becomes possible. Indeed, modification is almost impossible in front of a pronoun, since we do not allow constructions such as *the he, two they*, etc. Pronouns may be *qualified* but the range is limited. The most frequent qualification is the word *all*, as in *they all* in the example above. The trend of the middle-class children towards the noun, therefore, and that of the working-class children towards the pronoun, is an important finding, since it means that the middle-class children are opening up for themselves the possibility of expansion on a much wider scale, whereas for the working-class children who use the pronoun the opportunities are very much more restricted.

We needed more information than this, however, to illuminate the real meaning of this finding. It was necessary to know how and where the pronouns or nouns were being used. It might have been the case, for example, that the middle-class children were producing sentences like 'The boy kicked the ball and the ball broke the window', whereas the working-class children would substitute *it* for the second occurrence of *the ball* and thereby convey exactly the same meaning more concisely. Compare, on the other hand, the two (somewhat exaggerated) versions of the same story below, parallel in clause structure, but the one using nouns, the other pronouns.

(1) Three boys are playing football and one boy kicks the ball and it goes through the window the ball breaks the window and the boys are looking at it and a man comes out and shouts at them because they've broken the window so they run away and then that lady looks out of her window and she tells the boys off.

(no. of nouns 13 no. of pronouns 6)

(2) They're playing football and he kicks it and it goes through there it breaks the window and they're looking at it and he comes out and shouts at them because they've broken it so they run away and then she looks out and she tells them off.

(no. of nouns 2 no. of pronouns 14)

There is a difference here, not only in the amount of elaboration, actual or potential, of the nominal group, but also in the amount of information communicated. The former version explicitly states *who* performed the various actions and *what* objects or persons were affected by them. It is a version which can be immediately understood and interpreted, even without reference to the pictures themselves.

The second of the versions makes enormous demands on the listener. It means that the context (in this case the series of pictures) must be present if the listener is to understand who and what is being referred to. It assumes that the listener can *see* the pictures the speaker is describing, or knows enough about them not to need the relevant information about the characters and objects involved. If we can show that this is the kind of language associated with working-class children, whereas the former is more typical of the middle class, then we have further strong evidence of a linguistic nature in support of Bernstein's 'restricted code' and 'elaborated code'. If the working class are indeed confined to a 'restricted code', then it ought to be possible to show that the second version of the story above, with its extensive use of pronouns, is typical of the kind of speech working-class children use. How is it possible to demonstrate that their pronouns, of which we know they use more, are employed in this way?

The concept of reference

A recent paper by a colleague of Halliday's, Dr Ruqaiya Hasan (1968), is concerned with the concept of reference and cohesion within and between clauses and sentences in English. Briefly, narrative cohesion is usually achieved by the use of grammatical items which refer either backwards (to something already mentioned) or forwards (to something about to be mentioned). 'Backwards' reference is known as anaphoric reference, 'forwards' as cataphoric. Examples of their use are:

(1) Anaphoric: The boy kicked the ball and it broke the window (where *it* refers backwards to *the ball*).
(2) Cataphoric: It was the ball that broke the window (where *it* refers forwards to *that broke the window*).

Anaphoric reference is much more common than cataphoric, and may be applied to a variety of grammatical categories, principally to pronouns, but also to deictics like *this, that*. There is, however, a third possibility open to reference, and that is the reference known as 'exophoric', or reference 'outwards' to the 'context of situation'. In this case, the pronoun or other grammatical item refers not to something already or about to be *mentioned*, but to something in the environment of the speaker. If, for example, one is standing on the edge of a football field and the players are clustered round the goal, one might say 'they've scored!' and there would be no doubt who *they* referred to.

If we apply these reference categories 'anaphoric' and 'exophoric' to the two versions of the story given above, we can clearly see that the six pronouns in the first all have referents within the text itself—they refer backwards to things or people already mentioned, such as the ball, the window, the boys; they are therefore *anaphoric* in reference. Most of the pronouns in the second version, however, are quite different. They refer 'outwards' to items in the pictures which the listener is supposed to be aware of. The first 'they', for example, refers to 'the three boys you can [presumably] see in Card 1'; 'he' refers to 'the boy in the picture with his foot raised'; 'it' refers to 'the football there'; and so on. This kind of reference is *exophoric* in nature. If, then, we can show that the working-class children not only use more pronouns, but use more exophoric pronouns, than the middle class, then we can show that they are using pronouns in a different kind of way, for a different purpose.

This, then, is the basis of our present examination of the nominal group. We divided pronouns into anaphoric (including the occasional cataphoric) and exophoric, and counted them separately. We also included in the analysis a number of other grammatical items where this choice of reference is possible; these are:

(1) *this, that* occurring at 'head',
e.g. anaphoric: 'Go away' *that's* what she said
exophoric: *That's* a little boy

(2) *this, that* occurring at 'modifier',
e.g. anaphoric (rare): The boy broke the window . . . so the lady told that boy off
exophoric: These boys were playing football

(3) *Here, there* occurring at 'head' after a preposition,
e.g. on *here*, up *there*, along *there* (always exophoric)

Results

Where the linguistic variables mentioned above are not used by all the children, we can compare the two social class groups by means of χ^2 tests. These tests are based on the number of children in each group who use the category, compared with the number who do not.

The category 'anaphoric pronoun' was used at least once by all the children, and cannot therefore be compared by a χ^2 test. Instead, the average number used by each child will be given.

In the Tables below, a probability of less than 0·05 (i.e. less than 1 in 20) is considered statistically significant. A probability of 0·01 is regarded as a highly significant result. The results for each task are given separately.

total N = 263 middle class = 124 working class = 139

TABLE 4.1 *Picture stories (narrative)*

Category	*Position in nominal group*	*Reference*	*Used by more children in*	*Value of* χ^2	*P*
pronoun	head	exophoric	working class	2·05	0·16
this, that	head	exophoric	working class	5·61	0·02
this, that	modifier	exophoric	working class	6·24	0·01
here, there	head	exophoric	working class	6·24	0·01
this, that	head	anaphoric	middle class	8·03	0·005

TABLE 4.2 *Trotin cards (descriptive)*

Category	*Position in nominal group*	*Reference*	*Used by more children in*	*Value of* χ^2	*P*
pronoun	head	exophoric	working class	4·21	0·04
this, that	head	exophoric	—	0·02	n.s.
this, that	modifier	exophoric	working class	7·91	0·007
here, there	head	exophoric	working class	8·33	0·004
this, that	head	anaphoric	—	0·02	n.s.

TABLE 4.3 *Frequency of use of anaphoric and exophoric pronouns*

	Anaphoric pronouns (average number per child)		*Exophoric pronouns (average number per child)*	
	W.C.	M.C.	W.C.	M.C.
Picture stories	16·0	14·3	4·12	2·84
Trotin cards	9·6	5·9	4·59	2·44

We can see from Table 4.3 that, in narrating the picture stories, the frequency with which the average child uses *anaphoric* pronouns differs very little between middle class and working class. But in the use of *exophoric* pronouns the two classes differ enormously. The average middle-class child uses 2·84, the average working class child 4·12—half as many again. Since most children in both classes use at least one, the difference shown by χ^2 does not quite reach the level of significance. Yet for the other categories which involve exophoric reference, the results of χ^2 are all significant; more working-class children use these categories than middle class. When we look at *anaphoric this, that*, on the other hand, we find that it is the middle class who use it more.

The same pattern is followed in the descriptive speech (Trotin cards). Again, more working-class than middle-class children used the exophoric categories—the pronouns, *this, that* as modifier, and *here, there*, and the difference reaches a high level of significance. Only one category failed to show a significant difference.

If we look now at the noun and the linguistic variables associated with it, we find evidence that more middle-class children use these categories, and they use them more frequently. There is no space here to go into detail, but we have found that, on the picture stories, more middle-class children use the following categories:

(1) Epithets at 'head'—$\chi^2 = 15{\cdot}2$, $p < 0{\cdot}001$ (very highly significant). Used for 'evaluative' statements like *the boy was hungry, Mummy was cross, the girl was frightened.*

(2) Epithets other than *little, big* at 'modifier'—$\chi^2 = 18{\cdot}45$, $p < 0{\cdot}001$ (very highly significant).[1] Used for description or the ascription of attitude, e.g. *a huge whale, the naughty cat.*

(3) Two or more ordinatives—$\chi^2 = 6{\cdot}36$, $p < 0{\cdot}01$. Not just '*three* boys playing football' (most children mentioned *three* here) but also a further specification of number, e.g. '*three* boys running away', '*two* boys in a boat', etc.

(4) Intensifiers before epithets—$\chi^2 = 21{\cdot}55$, $p < 0{\cdot}001$. Words like *very, so, too*, e.g. the fish was *too heavy* for him.

(5) 'Rankshifted' clauses at 'head' (roughly equal to the traditional noun-clause)—$\chi^2 = 5{\cdot}67$, $p < 0{\cdot}02$. Clauses which 'replace' a noun or pronoun, e.g. she saw *them running away*. He thought *it was a fish*.

Discussion

These results provide substantial evidence that the working-class children in our sample are using not just more pronouns, but more pronouns of the exophoric kind, which rely heavily for their interpretation on the surrounding context. Furthermore, all the other exophoric categories lend support to this finding, and the pattern of differences appears both in narrative and in descriptive speech, more especially in the former. In the picture stories, we also find that the difference in the use of anaphoric pronouns is very small, which indicates that children of both classes are using them to establish cohesion from one clause to the next.

It is not the case, therefore, that the middle class are merely repeating a noun or noun-phrase while the working class are substituting an anaphoric pronoun for it. What seems to be happening, on the contrary, is that the middle class are being more specific, and more elaborate. They are referring to the objects, and the characters, by name, not by the vague *he, she, it, they.*

This difference is important for two reasons: first, because it enables the middle-class child to elaborate—he can talk about *three big* boys but he cannot talk about *three big* they; and second, and more important, the middle-class child can be understood outside the immediate context, without reference to the 'here and now'. His speech can be interpreted on its own without the pictures if necessary, and he makes no assumption that the listener can see the pictures in front of him and knows implicitly who is meant by *he, she, it, they.* The working-class child, on the other hand, does make these assumptions, and his speech is therefore tied to the context in which it occurs.

We should point out that these results do not take into account the measured intelligence of the children, which is one of the variables in our correlation programme. On the other hand, although differences in measured ability between the middle-class and working-class groups do exist, our previous research indicates that the choice between noun and pronoun at 'head' is more closely associated with the index of the social class of the parents than with measures of the verbal ability of the children.

Conclusion

With this evidence we have shown very considerable differences between the type of speech produced by middle-class children and that of working-class children, which may well have important cognitive consequences. Middle-class children do not simply use more nouns, they also exploit the possibilities of elaborating the nominal group more widely. Their speech is, in Bernstein's terms, more differentiated. The working-class children, on the other hand, tend to use pronouns instead of nouns as 'heads', which reduces the possibilities of both modification and qualification, and they rely on the listener's awareness of the situation to achieve comprehension. These findings substantiate the predictions derived from Bernstein's theory of restricted and elaborated codes, which was used to provide the framework for the research.

Summary

In a sample of 124 middle-class children and 139 working-class children, it has been shown that significantly more working-class children use items of exophoric reference, particularly third-person pronouns, while significantly more middle-class children use parts of speech associated with the noun. The conclusions support Bernstein's theory of 'restricted' and 'elaborated' codes.

Notes

1 The epithets *little*, *big*, being the commonest epithets, and frequently used like a formula, without real meaning, were counted separately.

References

BERNSTEIN, B. (1962), 'Social class linguistic codes and grammatical elements', *Language and Speech,* October–December.

BERNSTEIN, B. (1965), 'A socio-linguistic approach to social learning', in J. Gould (ed.) *Social Science Survey*. London: Penguin.

BRANDIS, W. (1970), Memoranda available from the Sociological Research Unit, also in *Social Class, Language and Communication*, W. Brandis and D. Henderson. London: Routledge & Kegan Paul.

HALLIDAY, M. A. K. (1966), 'Grammar, society and the noun', Inaugural lecture delivered at University College, London, November.

HASAN, R. (1968), *Grammatical Cohesion in Spoken and Written English*, part I, Nuffield Programme in Linguistics and English teaching, Paper no. 7. London: Longmans.

HENDERSON, D. (1970), 'Social class differences in form-class usage and form-class switching among 5-year-old children', *Social Class, Language and Communication*, W. Brandis and D. Henderson. London: Routledge & Kegan Paul.

LAWTON, D. (1964), 'Social class language differences in group discussions', *Language and Speech*, July–September.

MOHAN, B. and TURNER, G. J. (1970), 'Grammatical analysis, its computer program, and application', *Social Class and the Speech of Five-year-old Children*, I. London: Routledge & Kegan Paul.

Chapter 5 Social class differences in the expression of uncertainty in five-year-old children

G. J. Turner and R. E. Pickvance

Introduction

The value of examining the linguistic devices[1] employed in the expression of uncertainty has been suggested mainly by two studies —Bernstein (1962) and Loban (1966). Bernstein reported social class differences in the use of the ego-centric sequence 'I think' and the socio-centric sequences 'you know', 'you see' and 'isn't it?', etc.: the middle-class subjects (sixteen-year-old boys) used the ego-centric sequence more and the working class used the socio-centric sequences more. This difference held even for the sub-groups that were matched for verbal ability and non-verbal ability. Bernstein suggested that both types of sequence are indicators of uncertainty —that they are functional equivalents—but that they have different effects on the flow of communication. The socio-centric sequences, by inviting the listener to affirm what the speaker has said, 'tend to close communication in a particular area rather than facilitate its development and elaboration'. The ego-centric sequence, by contrast, 'allows the listener far more degrees of freedom and may be regarded as an invitation to develop communication on his own terms'. Expressed in another way, the socio-centric sequences are associated with communalized roles and the ego-centric sequence with individualized roles. Loban compared two groups of subjects, those ranked extremely high in language proficiency and those ranked extremely low (on the basis of teachers' ratings), and found that 'those subjects who proved to have the greatest power over language—by every measure that could be applied, not just the combined Teachers' Rating Scale and Vocabulary Test—were the subjects who most frequently used language to express tentativeness'. Loban commented that 'the child with less power over language appears to be less flexible in his thinking, is not often capable of seeing more than one alternative, and apparently summons up all his linguistic resources merely to make a flat dogmatic statement'. Loban's study demonstrated a relationship between verbal ability and the use of tentative statements, but there is a complication, since the high group proved to be drawn from those with a higher socio-economic status than the low group.

From the point of view of Bernstein's theory of elaborated and restricted codes, it is important to control for both social class differences and differences in intelligence. This is relevant to the present study since Bernstein (1962) associates the ego-centric sequence with an elaborated code and the socio-centric sequences with a restricted code. Bernstein (1965) expresses the relationship between the codes and social structure *and* intelligence as follows:

> The orientation towards these codes . . . may be independent of the psychology of the child, independent of his native ability, although the *level* at which the code is used will undoubtedly reflect purely psychological attributes. The orientation towards these codes may be governed entirely by the form of social relation, or more generally by the quality of the social structure.

The present study tests the hypothesis that the orientation towards the use of expressions of uncertainty is more strongly related to social class than to verbal ability.

Method

Subjects

The total sample collected by the Sociological Research Unit consisted of 439 children at age five. If we sub-sample this population according to a factorial design, one with a two-way division on sex, social class and verbal intelligence test scores, it is possible to obtain a factorial sample, comprising 160 subjects, with 20 subjects per cell. If we introduce a fourth variable with a two-way division, the communication index (a measure of the degree of verbal interaction between the mother and child), the size of the sample is greatly reduced. In fact, a sample comprising 80 subjects, with 5 subjects per cell, has proved practical. Previous work has been performed on this latter sample (Rackstraw and Robinson, 1967; Henderson, 1970). As the present work involves the examination of infrequently occurring linguistic phenomena, it was desirable to use the larger factorial sample because of the increase in reliability.

The diagram below is a pictorial representation of the factorial design. The number of children in each cell is indicated.

	MC[2]		WC	
	MIQ	HIQ	MIQ	HIQ
B	20	20	20	20
G	20	20	20	20

Indices

Social class was measured in terms of the occupation and education of each parent, according to a procedure worked out by Brandis (1970). Briefly, occupational status was defined in terms of the Hall-Jones scale (with a range of 1–7 points) and educational status was measured in terms of a two-point scale (non-minimal education scoring 1 and minimal education scoring 2). The educational items were given three times the weight of occupational status and the summed scores were compressed into a ten-point scale, 0–9, such that 0–2 is 'totally MC', 3 is 'predominantly MC', . . . 7 is 'predominantly WC' and 8–9 is 'totally WC'.

The means for social class for the eight groups of children are given below:

TABLE 5.1 *Means for social class*

	MC		*WC*	
	Mean	*s.d.*	*Mean*	*s.d.*
MIQ B	2·40	1·67	7·35	0·75
MIQ G	2·90	1·25	7·30	0·73
HIQ B	1·85	1·04	7·10	1·07
HIQ G	2·10	0·72	6·85	0·93

The intelligence test score categories defined high as being at the 90th percentile or higher on the Crichton vocabulary scale and medium as 50th to 75th (the mean for the high group was 90·83 and the mean for the medium group 63·84). Sixteen children in the sample (10 per cent) deviated from this criterion but made appropriate scores on a second test: the English picture vocabulary test.

Materials

The children were interviewed individually during their first three weeks at school. Each interview lasted about half an hour, during which they were required to perform six tasks, designed to elicit different kinds of speech, such as narrative, descriptive and explanatory speech. Two tasks elicited the greatest amount of speech and so far these tasks have received the most intensive investigation. The present study focuses on these two tasks.

Both tasks involved the use of cards (as none of the other four tasks did): one employed picture story cards and the other coloured picture cards. There were three sets of picture story cards, each set comprising four cards, which the interviewer laid down in the correct sequence. In the other task, there were three coloured picture cards, postcard-size reproductions of detailed paintings by Trotin, and each of these was presented to the child separately.

The instructions for administering the first set of picture story cards and the Trotin coloured picture cards are reproduced below. The instructions for the other two picture stories were slightly briefer.

PICTURE STORY CARDS

(i) Football

'Now we are going to play another game. I've got some pictures that tell a story. I'm going to show them to you and I want you to tell me the story. This one, and this one . . . and this one tell a story' (laying cards down fairly slowly, but not so slowly that a child interrupts).

'This is a story about some boys playing football. The ball breaks a window (point to card 2). The story starts here (point to card 1).'

If child stops after the first card, say:

'What happens next?' pointing to card 2. Repeat this for all cards if necessary. When the child has told his story:

Point to picture 3: 'What's the man saying?'

Point to picture 4: 'What about the lady?'

Probe: (if child says 'I don't know').

'What do you think he *might* be saying?'

TROTIN COLOURED PICTURE CARDS

Give the child only one picture at a time. Give him time to look at the picture and make unsolicited comments. Then say:

'What's going on in this picture?'

'What's happening?'

If the child says very little, add:

'Tell me what you can see.'
'What are they doing?'
'What else is going on?'

Final question:
'What shall we call this picture? What name shall we give it?'

Coding frame

The coding frame is essentially based on Bernstein's 'ego-centric sequence' and 'socio-centric sequence' categories and Loban's 'tentative statement' category. Bernstein's categories were taken over intact and then further sub-divisions were made. Instead of Loban's general category 'tentative statements', several more specific categories were established, most of which could be illustrated with examples taken from Loban. Loban's general category was not adopted partly because its exact limits were not known and partly because it overlapped with Bernstein's 'ego-centric sequence' category (Loban gives the example 'That, I *think*, is in Africa').

There are many ways of making tentative statements: we established categories which covered the main ways *used* by the children in our sample; other categories such as 'disjunctive statements' (e.g. There's a house or a church), 'conditional statements' (e.g. If it's got a hole in there, it's a guitar) and 'suppositions' (e.g. I suppose/bet/expect/guess, etc.) were considered but it was found that the subjects made statements such as these very rarely, if at all.

We defined expressions of uncertainty in such a way as to include 'questions' and 'refusals'. Loban examined 'questions' as a separate category and, interestingly, the category did not reveal the same pattern of results as the 'tentative statement' category. 'Refusals' were not examined by Loban.

The categories we used were defined as far as possible in formal linguistic terms, employing a mode of description based on 'Systemic Grammar' (see Halliday, 1967a, 1967b and 1968). Many of the syntactic options we were concerned with are handled in the 'speech-functional' or 'inter-personal' component of the grammar by the clause systems of mood and modality; others are handled in the 'experiental' component by the clause system of transitivity.

A. *EGO-CENTRIC SEQUENCE*

Two types of this sequence were distinguished, the criterion being phonological—whether the tonic fell on 'think' or on 'I' (for 'tonic', see Halliday, 1963): (1) Tentative, the tonic on 'think' (e.g. I *think* it's a man selling bottles); (2) Self-differentiating, the tonic on 'I' (e.g. *I* think some of the men'll have to sit in there). Three structural positions were distinguished for the sequence: initial (e.g. I think we'll call it a station); medial (e.g. That's wrong 'cos we should have that I think indoors); and final (e.g. That's a squirrel, I think).

B. *SOCIO-CENTRIC SEQUENCES*

These were sub-divided into two types: (1) 'You know/see' (e.g. Well he's fishing, you see); (2) Tags (e.g. He falls in the water, doesn't he?). Tags were differentiated into two further types: (*a*) Constant polarity tags (e.g. It's a dog, isn't it?); (*b*) Reversed polarity tags (e.g. They can't climb up a roof without a ladder, can they?; It's William, isn't it?). In the case of reversed polarity tags, if the verbal group in the first clause is positive, the verbal group in the tag clause is negative, and vice-versa, but in the case of constant polarity tags the polarity of the verbal groups is the same in both clauses (for 'polarity' and 'reversed polarity tag', see Sinclair, 1965).

C. *QUESTIONS*

Two main types of question were recognized: (1) Direct (e.g. What's that?); (2) Indirect (e.g. I wonder what that is). Indirect questions contain the preface, 'I wonder', 'I can't think', 'I don't know', etc., the actual query being given in a reported clause. Both types of questions were sub-divided into two further types: (*a*) Polar or Yes/No (e.g. Aren't those naughty cats?; I wonder if I can see a letter); (*b*) Wh- (e.g. What's that thing?; I wonder what they are). The characteristic features of clauses such as 'I wonder ——' may be described mainly with reference to the transitivity system (Halliday, 1968); the differences between polar and wh-questions are handled in the mood system (Huddleston *et al*., 1968).

D. *REFUSALS*

These are explicit refusals to answer the interviewer's questions; for example, in response to the interviewer's 'What's the man saying?' a child may give 'I don't know', 'I can't think', 'I can't say'; 'I don't know what'; 'I don't know what the man's saying', etc. A refusal may be distinguished from an indirect question on two main grounds: one, a refusal always refers to a question put by the interviewer, whereas an indirect question never does—the query is the child's own; and two, because the refusal refers to a preceding question, it may be elliptical in form pre-supposing the preceding question either partially or totally (e.g. I don't know what, I don't know); an indirect question, as defined here, may not presuppose a question put by the interviewer (for 'ellipsis' and 'presupposition', see Hasan, 1968).

E. *ASSESSMENTS OF POSSIBILITY AND PROBABILITY*

These assessments may be made by two means: (1) modal adjuncts (e.g. They're eating carrots perhaps or cake; Maybe she's saying . . .); (2) verbal auxiliaries (e.g. Might be a tunnel actually might; Could be a funny aeroplane). Modal adjuncts and verbal auxiliaries are the principal ways of expressing 'modality' (Halliday, 1969); some modalities have a personalized form—'I *think*' is an example, but we have treated this under A.

F. *SUPPOSITIONS BASED ON PERCEPTION*

These are statements with 'look as if/as though/like' (e.g. They look as if they're bridesmaids; Looks as though it's going; It looks like it's going to be flooded; It looks like a stream).

In order to characterize precisely the speech texts with which this paper is concerned, it is necessary to consider three distinctions:

1. *Task-oriented speech v. other speech.* Task-oriented speech is speech about the content of the cards, mainly as focused on by the interviewer's questions (e.g. What are the people doing?), but not necessarily so; questions from the child (e.g. What's that there?) may be task-oriented. Other speech includes: (*a*) speech before and after the administration of the task (e.g. What are we going to do next?); (*b*) speech about the administration of the tasks (e.g. Is that tape-recorder working?; Is this the last picture?); and (*c*) personal interjections (e.g. We went on a train when we were going on our holidays; Have you got a table as big as that at your house?).
2. *Role-play speech v. non-role-play speech.* Task-oriented speech is sub-divided into these two types. Role-play speech occurs when the child purports to give the *speech of others*, either directly or indirectly (e.g. The lady said: 'You are very naughty boys'; The lady said they were very naughty boys). Non-role-play speech is any other task-oriented speech.

3. *Elicited speech v. non-elicited speech.* This distinction pertains to non-role-play speech. Elicited speech is scored when a child as it were takes over part of the interviewer's speech in the first sentence he utters after receiving a question (e.g. Interviewer: 'What do you think he might be saying?'—Child: 'I think he might be saying . . .'). If the child's immediate reply does not take over part of the interviewer's speech, his speech is non-elicited. Also, if he displays expressions used by the interviewer in contexts other than that of immediate reply, this speech is regarded as non-elicited.

Unless otherwise stated, this study is concerned with task-oriented speech which is of the non-role-play speech kind and which is non-elicited.

No controls for amount of speech were made: most analyses were confined to dividing children into users and non-users of the categories and the reduction of scores to proportions would not have affected such classifications. We might add that other researchers in the Sociological Research Unit, Henderson (1970) and Hawkins (1969), using sub-samples (80 children and 263 children respectively) from the same main sample of children, have reported no significant differences in length of output.

Treatment of results

Initially a three-way comparison was made, contrasting social class, intelligence test scores and sex. Lancaster's partition of χ^2 was used,[3] a test which yielded first-order, second-order and third-order inter-actions. It was found that the second-order and third-order inter-actions were generally small and insignificant, whilst the first-order inter-actions yielded much sharper differences. The first-order inter-actions are, of course, equivalent to 2×2 χ^2 tests: they differ from Yates's χ^2 tests, however, in that they do not incorporate the correction factor.

For reasons of space, it was desirable to limit the number of individual results reported. The second-order and third-order inter-actions could be ignored. As we were concentrating on the 2×2 χ^2's, it seemed desirable to make use of the greater accuracy afforded by Yates's χ^2 test. Yates's test was applied[4] and it is the results of Yates's test, not Lancaster's, that are presented in this paper. Comparisons yielding no significant differences are either ignored or only mentioned briefly.

In case of one measure 'refusals' the scores were such as to permit the use of analyses of variance.

Results

A. *EGO-CENTRIC SEQUENCE*

TABLE 5.2 *Ego-centric sequence*

	MC	*WC*	χ^2	*p*
(i) Picture story	8[5]	0	6·45	0·01
(ii) Trotin	22	9	5·76	0·02
(iii) Picture story and Trotin	27[6]	9	10·36	0·01

Social class differences in the use of the ego-centric sequence were found. The sequence was used by more middle-class children in both the picture story task ($\chi^2 = 6{\cdot}45$, $p < 0{\cdot}01$) and the Trotin task ($\chi^2 = 5{\cdot}76$, $p < 0{\cdot}02$). In all, 34 per cent of the middle-class children employed the sequence, as compared with 11 per cent of the working-class children.

The ego-centric sequence may occur initially, medially or finally in the sentence. There were only two instances of it occurring medially. It was most commonly used in the initial position: in all 23 middle-class children as compared with 6 working-class used it in this position ($\chi^2 = 10{\cdot}78$, $p < 0{\cdot}01$), and 10 middle-class children as compared with 2 working-class used it in the final position ($\chi^2 = 4{\cdot}41$, $p < 0{\cdot}05$).

The sequence was sub-divided into two types: '*I* think' (self-differentiating) and 'I *think*' (tentative). Only 3 children, all middle-class, used '*I* think', whereas 35 children used 'I *think*'.

The clauses with which the ego-centric sequence was associated were differentiated into classes. The ascriptive clause (e.g. It's a parachute, I think; I think that's a child) discriminated between the social classes: 10 middle-class children used this clause as compared with 2 working-class children ($\chi^2 = 4{\cdot}41$, $p < 0{\cdot}05$).

B. *SOCIO-CENTRIC SEQUENCES*

TABLE 5.3 *Socio-centric sequences: reversed polarity tag type*

	MIQ	*HIQ*	χ^2	*p*
(i) Picture story	16	8		
(ii) Trotin	33	20	4·06	0·05
(iii) Picture story and Trotin	36	23	3·87	0·05

Socio-centric sequences of the 'you know/see' type were extremely rare, whilst those of the tag type were relatively common. Only 4 children (2 MC and 2 WC) used 'you know/see'. By contrast, approximately two-fifths of the total sample used at least one socio-centric sequence of the tag type. Most of these tags were reversed polarity tags. More medium-ability children used these tags, the difference being significant on the Trotin task ($\chi^2 = 4{\cdot}06$, $p < 0{\cdot}05$) and on the two tasks combined ($\chi^2 = 3{\cdot}87$, $p < 0{\cdot}05$). In all, 45 per cent of the medium-ability children as compared with 29 per cent of the high-ability children used socio-centric sequences of the reversed polarity tag type.

C. *QUESTIONS*

TABLE 5.4a *Direct questions*

	MIQ	*HIQ*	χ^2	*p*
(i) Picture story	11	9		
(ii) Trotin	43	28	4·96	0·05
(iii) Picture story and Trotin	45	30	5·36	0·05

TABLE 5.4b *Indirect questions*

	MC	*WC*	χ^2	*p*
(i) Picture story	1	2		
(ii) Trotin	17	5	6·38	0·02
(iii) Picture story and Trotin	17	7	3·97	0·05

No significant social class or ability differences emerged for the use of questions when the questions were undifferentiated. But a division of the questions into direct and indirect did reveal significant differences.

The results for direct questions follow a similar pattern to those for the reversed polarity tags. It is verbal ability, not social class, that is important. More children of medium ability asked direct questions on the Trotin task ($\chi^2 = 4{\cdot}96$, $p < 0{\cdot}05$) and this difference is maintained when the two tasks are considered together ($\chi^2 = 5{\cdot}36$, $p < 0{\cdot}05$). As many as 56 per cent of the children of medium ability used direct questions, whereas only 37 per cent of those of high ability used them.

The results for indirect questions reveal a different pattern: social class is important. Significantly more middle-class children asked indirect questions on the Trotin task ($\chi^2 = 6{\cdot}38$, $p < 0{\cdot}02$) and a similar, though less significant, result is obtained when both tasks are combined ($\chi^2 = 3{\cdot}97$, $p < 0{\cdot}05$). In all, 21 per cent of the middle-class children and 9 per cent of the working-class used this type of construction.

Both types of questions, direct and indirect, were sub-divided into polar and wh- questions. More children used the wh- type than used the polar, 38 per cent as opposed to 24 per cent of the sample. Verbal ability and social class differences were associated with the wh- type only. Significantly more medium-ability children used direct wh- questions on the Trotin task ($\chi^2 = 3{\cdot}99$, $p < 0{\cdot}05$): 34 medium-ability children *v.* 21 high-ability children. By contrast, significantly more middle-class children used indirect wh- questions on this task ($\chi^2 = 6{\cdot}38$, $p < 0{\cdot}02$): 17 middle-class children *v.* 5 working-class children. These differences were maintained when the two tasks were considered together.

The question arises: did the children who used the indirect form avoid the direct form or did they use both? The answer is that they tended to use both: 13 out of 17 middle-class children did so and 5 out of 7 working-class. This result in turn raises the question: did the middle-class children tend to have more wh- questions per child? To answer this question, we calculated (*a*) how many children had two or more occurrences of wh- questions and (*b*) how many had three or more occurrences of these questions. A significant difference emerged in each case: 23 middle-class children as compared with 11 working-class had two or more occurrences ($\chi^2 = 4{\cdot}52$, $p < 0{\cdot}05$) and 15 middle-class as compared with 5 working-class had three or more occurrences ($\chi^2 = 4{\cdot}63$, $p < 0{\cdot}05$).

The wh- questions were sub-divided according to the wh- item used. In most instances the wh- item was *what:* 53 of the 60 children who used direct wh- questions and 20 of the 24 who used indirect wh- questions had at least one occurrence of a question with *what.* Other wh- items were relatively rare. Only one significant difference emerged from this sub-classification: in all, 10 medium-ability children asked questions with *why* or *what . . . for* whereas only 1 high-ability child did so ($\chi^2 = 6{\cdot}25$, $p < 0{\cdot}02$).

Most of the questions with *what* were of the type illustrated by 'What's that?' and 'What's that thing?'. By examining the answers the children gave to these questions, either spontaneously or when prompted by the interviewer, we were able to discover what the children were asking about. Various entities were referred to by the children, but two items, the airships on the Trotin cards, were referred to relatively often. Of the 15 working-class children who asked (and answered) a question of the 'What's that?' type, 12 (that is, 80 per cent) made reference to the airships in their answers, whereas of the 17 comparable middle-class children 8 (47 per cent) did so. Moreover, in the case of the working-class there was a sex difference: 10 working-class boys asked a question about these items whereas only 2 girls did so ($\chi^2 = 4{\cdot}80$, $p < 0{\cdot}05$).

D. *REFUSALS*

TABLE 5.5 *Refusals*

	MC	*WC*	χ^2	*p*
(i) Picture story	39	29	8·70	0·01
(ii) Trotin	35	26		
(iii) Picture story and Trotin	52	35	6·45	0·02

More middle-class children gave refusals: the class difference attains significance on the picture story task ($\chi^2 = 8{\cdot}70$, $p < 0{\cdot}01$) and when the two tasks are combined ($\chi^2 = 6{\cdot}45$, $p < 0{\cdot}02$). In all, 65 per cent of the middle-class children gave at least one refusal whilst 44 per cent of the working class did so.

The elliptical form of refusal, 'I don't know', occurred relatively frequently and it was appropriate to perform analyses of variance on this measure. The results of these tests follow a similar pattern to those obtained on the χ^2 tests. Again, it is social class, not sex or verbal ability, that is related to the use of these expressions. The class difference is significant on the picture story task ($F_{1,152} = 6{\cdot}86$, $p < 0{\cdot}01$), and on the two tasks combined ($F_{1,152} = 6{\cdot}64$, $p < 0{\cdot}01$).

Each question in the interview schedule was considered individually and the number of children giving refusal responses to it noted, in order to ascertain which questions or types of question gave the children most difficulty. The main differences observed are given in Table 5.6.

TABLE 5.6 *Refusals related to interviewer's questions*

	MC	*WC*	χ^2	*p*
Refusal to:				
Any role-play speech question	32	16	6·70	0·01
1st role-play speech question on 1st picture story	22	7	8·25	0·01
'What's happening?' on Trotin	10	1	6·25	0·02

The questions most associated with refusals were the role-play speech questions on the picture story task. Significantly more middle-class children refused to answer these questions ($\chi^2 = 6{\cdot}70$, $p < 0{\cdot}01$), especially the first one ($\chi^2 = 8{\cdot}25$, $p < 0{\cdot}01$).

In general, when a child refused to answer a role-play speech question (e.g. 'What's the man saying?'), an additional (more tentative) question was put (e.g. 'What do you think he *might* be saying?'). Relatively few children had difficulty with the questions formulated in this way. For example, 22 middle-class children refused to answer the first role-play speech question, but only 3 out of the 20 who were given the additional probe still refused to answer.

On the Trotin task, significantly more middle-class children gave refusals to 'What's happening?', that is, the second question on each section of the task ($\chi^2 = 6{\cdot}25$, $p < 0{\cdot}02$). There was also a tendency for middle-class children to give refusals to 'What are they doing?' ($\chi^2 = 3{\cdot}28$, $p < 0{\cdot}10$) and 'What else is going on?' ($\chi^2 = 3{\cdot}01$, $p < 0{\cdot}10$). These questions have obvious similarities, and contrast with 'Tell me what you can see', a request which elicited no refusals.

E. *ASSESSMENTS OF POSSIBILITY AND PROBABILITY*

TABLE 5.7 *Elicited modals of possibility*

	MC	*WC*	χ^2	*p*
Picture story	13	0	12·06	0·001

The children rarely used modal adjuncts (e.g. perhaps, probably) to make assessments of possibility and probability. The total number of children using them is only seven, even if we include those using them in role-play speech. It is suggestive, though, that six of these seven children were middle class.

Verbal auxiliaries (e.g. might, could) were much more frequently used. We divided them into two groups: elicited and non-elicited. The elicited were those that occurred in the child's answers to the additional role-play speech questions: e.g. Interviewer: 'What do you think he *might* be saying?'—Child: He might be saying . . . The middle-class children were the only ones to take over 'might' from the interviewer's speech ($\chi^2 = 12{\cdot}06$, $p < 0{\cdot}001$). This result, of course, has to be considered in relation to the 'refusals' results; in particular, to the fact that 30 middle-class children were given these additional questions whereas only 8 working-class children were given them. Forty-three per cent of these middle-class children took over 'might' whereas none of the working-class children did.

Concerning the non-elicited modals, at first sight there appears little difference between the social classes: 18 middle-class and 16 working-class children used them. But when we sub-classified the clauses in which these modals occurred, it was possible to discriminate between the social classes. Nine middle-class children used these modals in ascriptive clauses concerned with particular concrete entities (e.g. might be a tunnel actually might; could be a funny aeroplane), as were the ascriptive clauses associated with the ego-centric sequence, whereas no working-class children did so ($\chi^2 = 7{\cdot}69, p < 0{\cdot}01$).

F. *SUPPOSITIONS BASED ON PERCEPTION*

TABLE 5.8 *2 (+) occurrences of 'look as if/as though/like'*

	MC	*WC*	χ^2	*p*
Picture story and Trotin	8	1	4·23	0·05

When we divided the children into users and non-users of this category, little difference between the classes was evident, 18 middle-class children being users and 12 working class. But a class difference emerged when we asked how many children used the category more than once ($\chi^2 = 4{\cdot}23, p < 0{\cdot}05$).

Discussion

This study has demonstrated that the major operating variables of social class and verbal ability have relevance to the individual's use of expressions of uncertainty. Social class is related to the use of the ego-centric sequence, certain types of question, refusals, the assessment of possibility and suppositions based on perception; whereas verbal ability is related to the use of one type of socio-centric sequence and certain types of question. These results support the hypothesis that the orientation towards the use of expressions of uncertainty is more strongly related to social class than to verbal ability. The other variable, sex, gives just one differentiation and that within the working-class sample only.

In every case in which social class has been shown to be related to the use of expressions of uncertainty, it was the middle-class children who used more of them. This is a point of some theoretical significance and in the course of the discussion we shall relate the findings to Bernstein's socialization theories.

Before we focus on the more important results in some detail, it will be useful to make a few comments about the interview situation. There are two instructions in the interview schedule that have to be considered. First, there is the general instruction that if a child asks a question, the interviewer should answer the child's question briefly and wherever possible return the responsibility for answering the question to the child, for example, 'I don't know. What do *you* think . . .?' Second, there are the specific instructions about the role-play speech questions: if a child refused to answer 'What's X saying?', the additional question 'What do you think X *might* be saying?' was to be put. Since we have established that the middle-class children asked more wh- questions and gave more refusals to the role-play speech questions, it is pertinent to inquire what effect the additional questioning incurred is likely to have had on the children's speech. Previously, we made a distinction between elicited speech and non-elicited speech. Here we are not concerned with elicited speech, that is, speech that bears evidence of the direct influence of the interviewer's speech, but with non-elicited speech. The question we are asking is: did the additional interviewer's questions tend to encourage a set towards the expression of uncertainty in the middle-class subjects?

It is not an easy question to answer. If all the categories we have examined are measures of uncertainty—let us say of a 'tentative disposition'—then we should not be surprised if we found that the subjects who gave refusals and asked questions were also the ones who tended to use the ego-centric sequence, to make assessments of possibility and so on. This could be expected even if it were not the case that refusals and questions elicited such utterances as 'What do you think X *might* be saying?' and 'What do *you* think . . . ?' on the part of the interviewer. In other words, if these children did make more tentative statements, etc., it would not necessarily follow that this was largely due to the influence of the interviewer's speech. Nevertheless, we made an attempt to evaluate the effect of the interviewer's speech.

We divided the middle-class children into two groups: those who had received additional questions from the interviewer ('What do you think *X* might be saying?' after refusals to the role-play speech questions on the picture story task and/or 'What do *you* think . . . ?' after wh- questions on the Trotin task) and those who had not. This division split the middle-class sample in half. We then asked which children used the ego-centric sequence: we concentrated on this sequence since both types of additional question used 'think'. Of the 40 children who received these questions (111 instances), 11 used the ego-centric sequence; whereas of the 40 who did not receive these questions, 16 used the ego-centric sequence. There is, then, little evidence to suggest that the additional questions had a marked effect on the children's use of the ego-centric sequence: almost three-quarters of the children who received these questions did not use the ego-centric sequence; and, further, the number of children in this group who did use the ego-centric sequence is lower than the number of comparable children in the other group, 11 as compared with 16. Of course, we do not rule out the possibility that the additional questions exerted some influence on the children; we are just saying that the influence does not appear to have been great.

We shall now consider the more important findings in some detail.

EGO-CENTRIC SEQUENCE

Several investigators have reported findings on the use of the ego-centric sequence. Bernstein (1962) and Lawton (1964a) got groups of teenage boys, either middle class or working class, to discuss capital punishment and analysed their speech. Lawton (1964b) also interviewed his subjects individually and tested their control over descriptive and abstract language. Cook (1968) examined the speech of adults, that of mothers describing how they control their children. All these investigators agree in finding that middle-class speakers used the ego-centric sequence more than working-class speakers did. Lawton (1964b) showed too that there is a differential usage of the sequence according to context, it being associated with abstract language rather than descriptive language.

On the question of interpretation, Bernstein (1962) provides the fullest account. Bernstein associates the sequence with the expression of uncertainty but stresses the social function of the sequence. In Bernstein's words, the ego-centric sequence 'invites a further "I think" on the part of the listener'; it is 'an invitation to the listener to develop the communication on his own terms'. The discussion groups that Bernstein organized, in which individuals were free to express their opinions on capital punishment and to take issue with their peers, offered ideal conditions for participants to adopt individualized roles if they so wished. The middle-class subjects appear to have taken this opportunity and to have used '*I* think'.

Loban's (1966) concern in his 'tentative statements' category was with 'I *think*', which could be grouped with 'I'm not exactly sure', etc.; he gives the example 'That, I *think*, is in Africa'. If Bernstein focuses on a social function of the 'I think' sequence, Loban focuses on a psychological function. He associates it with flexibility in thinking, with a capacity for seeing more than one alternative.

Hymes (1968), taking up a point raised by Cazden (1966), asks whether Bernstein's subjects said '*I* think' (ego-centric) and Loban's said 'I *think*' (cognitive flexibility) and comments on the value of examining intonational and expressive signals. We might add that if there were such a difference, as seems likely, this seems largely explainable in terms of the differences existing between the two types of experimental situation. The differences between (*a*) the discussion group and the individual interview and (*b*) the tasks involved seem crucial.

Certainly, we would interpret the difference between Bernstein's results (as we have interpreted them) and the results obtained in the present experiment in terms of differences in the experimental situations. It is thought that the rare use of '*I* think' (3 users only) and the relatively frequent use of 'I *think*' (35 users in all) reflect the structure of the interview. In order to effect a standardized interview situation, opportunities were not created for a free give-and-take, a truly two-sided conversation, between the interviewee and interviewer. The interviewer was instructed to keep to the fixed schedule and, otherwise, to say as little as possible. Such an interview is much less conducive than a discussion group to speech that signals difference and invites the hearer to adopt an individualized role.

How should we interpret these 'I *think*' sequences? Lawton's (1964b) finding that the ego-centric sequence went with abstract language rather than descriptive language is suggestive. We cannot, however, press this distinction in the case of our data: the five-year-old children were asked few, if any, questions of the type Lawton used to elicit abstract language; for example, they were asked to tell the story about some boys playing football (descriptive)—they were *not* asked to say what they thought the point of the story was (abstract). Loban's (1966) association of 'I *think*' and 'I'm not exactly sure' etc., with cognitive flexibility is also suggestive. We must be beware of circularity, however, of taking as evidence of cognitive flexibility only what is given in the language. Further evidence is needed and here Bernstein's work on types of familial socialization is important.

Bernstein's work, both theoretical and empirical, suggests that the forms of socialization typically employed in middle-class families are likely to give the children reared in these families greater scope for self-regulation, for operating within a wide range of alternatives. These socialization procedures, it is thought, are likely to give these children a greater awareness of uncertainty in certain areas of experience and are likely to encourage the children to be flexible in their thinking. We shall now consider two areas of experience in some detail: inter-personal relationships and the acquisition of basic skills.

Concerning inter-personal relationships, Bernstein (1964 and 1972) has argued that middle-class children are likely to be given more share in the decision-making process in the family than their working-class contemporaries. Middle-class parents tend not to assign the child's role to him (so many options and no others) but rather they give him opportunity to *make* his own role. More precisely, the middle-class child, relative to the working-class child, may *achieve* his role: he may win it by reasoning, by explaining his intentions and justifying his judgments. There is a kind of built-in uncertainty in this type of socialization: the decision-making is not clear cut, cut and dried; discussion is involved and this is likely to involve the use of questions and tentative statements. On the person-oriented family system (the type in which this kind of socialization is found in its purest form) Bernstein (1972) has written: 'Children socialized within such a role and communication system learn to cope with ambiguity and ambivalence, although clearly there may well be pathological consequences if sufficient sense of boundary is not provided.'

Concerning the acquisition of basic skills, Bernstein and Henderson (1969) have argued that the form of socialization used by middle-class parents is one which emphasizes the autonomy of the child: he is encouraged to take an active role in learning and to explore experience in his own terms. The implicit theory of learning in the skill area is 'self-regulating'. By contrast, working-class parents assign their child a passive role in learning: their implicit theory of learning is 'didactic'. It is thought that the self-regulating type of learning will involve the child, in the early stages of the learning process, in more states of uncertainty than the didactic type of learning. Furthermore, a child socialized in this way may find that he has more need (and indeed more opportunity) to express his uncertainty. There is another aspect to this type of learning: if a child is put in an active role in the learning process, if he is encouraged to find his own solutions, he is likely to make mistakes—but mistakes are not likely to be rewarded. This, it is thought, will tend to generate anxiety in the child: he will tend to become more concerned about getting things right or wrong than a child who is assigned a passive role in the learning process. This concern is likely to foster tentativeness in the child.

To summarize, the socialization procedures typically employed in middle-class families are likely to encourage the middle-class child to perceive reality in terms of more than one alternative, in terms of a range of possible interpretations. Further, these procedures may tend to create anxiety in the child, for not only is he made aware of a range of interpretations, he is also expected, to a certain extent, to make an individual choice from the range, and, further, to choose correctly. These socialization procedures are, in our opinion, the main sociological antecedents of an orientation towards the use of expressions of uncertainty. They are thought to underlie the middle-class children's use of the ego-centric sequence and also their use of other expressions of uncertainty.

SOCIO-CENTRIC SEQUENCES

There are three points to be discussed concerning the socio-centric sequence results: (*a*) the extreme rarity of the 'you know' type; (*b*) the absence of a social class difference in the use of the reversed polarity type; and (*c*) the verbal ability difference in the use of this latter type.

Bernstein (1962) and Lawton (1964a and 1964b) reported finding that working-class subjects used proportionally more socio-centric sequences. They did not distinguish between the 'you know' type and the 'isn't it?' type, however. Robinson and Rackstraw (1967) did distinguish them: they found no significant difference in the mothers' use of the 'isn't it?' type, but a significant difference in the girls' mothers' use of the 'you know' type. Of interest to us is the fact that approximately three times as many mothers used the 'you know' type as used the 'isn't it?' type. In our data, the picture is quite dissimilar: the 'you know' type was rarely used at all, whilst the 'isn't it?' type was frequently used. Both sets of results are alike, though, in that in both cases the 'isn't it?' type is not associated with a social class difference. One wonders whether it is mainly the 'you know' type that is used by older working-class speakers. Some support for this interpretation is provided by Cook's (1968) preliminary findings: she found that there were more occurrences of the 'you know' type than the 'isn't it?' type in the mothers' speech.

If the 'you know' type was used so frequently by working-class mothers, why was it so rare in the children's data? There are at least two possible factors: (*a*) the age of the subjects (Do the 'you know/see' sequences come relatively late in the child's monitoring of his social relationship?); and (*b*) the structure of the interview and the task (What would have happened if a discussion situation had been used, for example, a discussion about who the child chose as his friends?). Probably, both factors are relevant but it is thought that (*b*), the structure of the interview and the tasks, may have been decisive. Further experimentation is needed in this area.

Concerning the verbal ability difference, the most likely explanation is that the medium-ability children felt more insecure, less certain of their ability to perform the tasks, and needed to seek more confirmation that they were on the right lines. This interpretation is in accord with that of Bernstein (1962) and also that of Sinclair (1965). Bernstein writes: 'It is as if the speaker is saying "Check—are we together on this?" On the whole the speaker expects affirmation.' Sinclair writes of the reversed polarity tag: 'The contextual meaning of a sentence with such a tag clause is of a question which predicts a confirmatory answer.' It is also true that more medium-ability children asked (direct) wh- questions, that is, those usually glossed 'information-seeking' rather than 'confirmation-seeking'. Is there likely to be any connection between these two results? We should avoid a too superficial interpretation of the wh- questions. The fact that a person asked a wh- question does not necessarily mean that that person does not possess the information sought in the question. He may have an interpretation, a possible answer, which he wishes to check against someone else's answer. This is pertinent to our present study. The fact that a considerable number of children were able to offer an answer to their wh- questions, either spontaneously or when prompted by the interviewer, suggests that they were perhaps using the wh-questions to try and check their interpretations against the interviewer's. In other words, for some children the use of the reversed polarity tags and the use of direct wh- questions may have had somewhat similar motivations.

QUESTIONS

There are a number of reasons why middle-class children might ask more wh- questions than the working-class. (1) The two groups of children are likely to have experienced different modes of social control (Bernstein, 1964 and 1972; Cook, 1972). Bernstein (1972) has distinguished two main modes of control: the imperative mode and the mode based on appeals. Middle-class children are less likely to be controlled in terms of the imperative mode. The imperative mode does not tolerate challenges—if the child questions the mother's request, the mother quickly moves towards physical coercion; whereas the mode based upon appeals, in varying degrees, does allow questioning—in its purest form, if the child challenges his mother, he is given reasons for the request and further questioning and discussion is encouraged. (2) There is evidence that questioning (not just in social control situations) is likely to be a rewarding activity for middle-class children. Bernstein and Brandis

(1970) found that middle-class mothers were less likely than working-class mothers to avoid or evade answering difficult questions put to them by their children. Further, Robinson and Rackstraw (1967) reported that 'middle-class mothers differed from working-class mothers in that they evaded fewer questions, gave more accurate answers, gave more information in their answers, used fewer "noisy" items, used fewer social psychological checks of agreement and preferred certain modes of answering "why" questions'. (3) If middle-class parents tend to encourage their children to take an active role in the (skill) learning process, as Bernstein and Henderson (1969) suggest, then it is thought that this mode of socialization will at least give these children more opportunity for asking questions.

Some of the factors we have mentioned are measured along with certain other factors in a 'maternal index of communication and control' (Bernstein and Brandis, 1970). Briefly, this index measures the extent to which the mother is likely (*a*) to use coercive methods of control, (*b*) to explain to the child why she wants a change in his behaviour, (*c*) to take up the child's attempts to talk to her, (*d*) to avoid or evade answering difficult questions put to her by her child, and (*e*) to value the general explorative/cognitive function of toys. Index scores were available for the mothers of 79 middle-class children in our sample and of 59 working-class children. In order to give a rough estimate of the different socialization experiences of these groups of children, we may give the group means and standard deviations: MC, $\bar{x} =$ 123·04, s.d. 18·43; WC, $\bar{x} =$ 102·78, s.d. 23·57. These figures suggest that there may well be considerable differences in the socialization experiences of the children—in experiences that are particularly relevant to their use of language.

Questions were a relatively rare phenomenon in Loban's speech data. Their average incidence totalled for four years (Grades three to six) was 14 for the high-proficiency group and 16 for the low-proficiency group, the comparable figures for tentative statements being 159 for the high group and 27 for the low group. Loban explains the result in terms of the structure of the interview which was such that questions would not ordinarily be elicited. It is not possible, then, to compare our findings with Loban's.

REFUSALS AND THE ASSESSMENT OF POSSIBILITY

Why did middle-class children relative to working-class children, refuse to answer role-play questions of the form 'What's X saying?'? Were they bored and unco-operative or just uncertain what to answer? The fact that most of the children *did* answer probes of the form 'What do you think X might be saying?' suggests that they were just uncertain. This interpretation is reinforced by the fact that 43 per cent of the children who answered these additional probes took over 'might' from the interviewer's speech and said 'X might be saying . . .'

Why were these children uncertain about answering the role-play speech questions? There seem to be three main types of explanation possible. (1) The *wording* of the role-play speech questions troubled them. (2) The content of the picture stories troubled them. (3) Role-play speech as such troubled them.

Support is given to the first type of explanation by the facts we mentioned above, namely that most of the children did answer the more tentative probes and 43 per cent of them gave tentative answers. In other words, these children did not find the wording of the original role-play speech questions specific enough: they responded better to the contextually-specific questions; they needed to have the hypothesis made explicit. This perhaps suggests that the middle-class subjects are more *reality-bound* than the working-class subjects: they find it less easy to fantasize. It may be that MC children require a *specific directive* to go beyond what is given. This may arise out of their concern to give a 'right answer'. The above explanation may also partly account for the greater number of MC children who refused to answer the question 'What's happening?' or who gave little response to 'What's going on in this picture?' On the question of specificity to context, some support for this interpretation comes from Henderson's (1971) work on the maternal interviews. Henderson has noted a greater sensitivity to context in middle-class mothers.

Concerning the second type of explanation, the most direct evidence comes from Turner (1972). Turner examined the responses on the first picture story from the point of view of social control. It was found that middle-class and working-class subjects did tend to interpret the story differently, the differences being in line with predictions based on Bernstein's socialization theories. There was no evidence, however, to suggest that the middle-class children found the content more troublesome (more ambiguous, etc.) than the working-class children did.

Finally, are middle-class children less familiar with a model which encourages role-play speech than working-class children? To answer 'yes' to this question sounds improbable. But we have found that working-class children not only refuse to answer the role-play speech questions *less* than middle-class children, but they also spontaneously offer role-play speech *more* than middle-class children on the Trotin task, a task in which none was demanded. Significantly more working-class children, particularly girls, used a communication verb associated with direct speech on this task. One wonders whether the working-class mother provides a model for this type of speech. It is thought that working-class mothers tend, in their conversations, to give or to purport to give verbatim accounts of their conversations with others. Middle-class mothers probably tend to go beyond the actual words spoken, to make inferences, to summarize and so forth.

Of the three types of explanation the first one, namely that the children required a specific request to hypothesize, perhaps seems to fit the facts best. Once the contextual constraints had been made clear, the children generally did not hesitate to give role-play speech.

We have discussed the more important findings at some length. There is not space to consider the other results in detail. We shall end the discussion with a general comment. Except in the case of a small number of categories, notably the refusal and wh- question categories, the incidence of the categories was low. This was unfortunate, since ideally one would have liked to have constructed a correlation matrix (ϕ co-efficients) for the categories to show the degree of association between them. This could not be done. Older children may provide more suitable data. We hope it may be possible to extend the investigation to speech samples obtained from the same children at age seven years.

Conclusion

The results of this study support the hypothesis that the orientation towards the use of expressions of uncertainty is more strongly related to social class than to verbal ability. Moreover, this orientation has been shown to be mainly a middle-class phenomenon. This would suggest that the orientation to use such expressions is related to the child's socialization experiences. Bernstein's work on socialization emphasizes that the forms of socialization a middle-class child is likely to experience make available to the child a wide range of alternatives. Such socialization procedures are likely to encourage the child to be flexible in his thinking but also may tend to generate anxiety in the child. In either case, they are likely to encourage the use of expressions of uncertainty.

The results direct attention to the need for further research into the speech of *mothers* as well as their children in critical contexts in order to establish links between the forms of speech.[7]

Postscript

Since the completion of this report further information concerning the mothers' use of tentative expressions has become available. In the report we made reference to the preliminary findings of Cook (1968): this analysis has now been completed and the results are presented in Cook (1972). Briefly, Cook took a sample of 236 mothers, 127 of whom were mothers of children in our sample. She examined the speech the mothers gave in response to questions about their methods of controlling their children. Nine hypothetical control situations were described to the mothers and they were then asked what they would say or do. The most relevant findings are presented below. To save space we give the proportions for the users only.

TABLE 5.9 *Maternal speech*

	WC (n = 75) %	*Mixed C (n = 81) %*	*MC (n = 80) %*	χ^2	*p*
Ego-centric sequence	55	65	85	16·99	< 0·001
Socio-centric sequences	68	65	40	15·34	< 0·001
Conditional statements with *if*	75	90	85	6·61	< 0·05
I might/I'd probably/ I'd possibly/it depends	29	53	65	19·35	< 0·001

Of particular interest to us are the last two results. The result on conditional statements introduced by *if* clearly suggests that middle-class mothers, relative to working-class mothers, possess an awareness of alternative modes of interpretation. The χ^2 test, in the case of these statements, gives only a weak indication of the extent of the difference between the social classes. The middle-class mothers who used these statements tended to use them more frequently than mothers from the other social classes, as may be judged from the totals for the number of occurrences: 153 (WC), 255 (Mixed C) and 351 (MC).[8] The result on the last category, which is broadly similar to the 'assessments of possibility and probability' category we used, indicates a tendency for middle-class mothers, as compared with the other two groups of mothers, to express what they would say or do in hypothetical or probabilistic terms. Briefly, Cook's findings suggest two things: (*a*) middle-class mothers tend to view their children's behaviour (transgressional behaviour) in terms of more than one interpretation; and (*b*) middle-class mothers tend to see their own behaviour in relation to their children in terms of more than one alternative. They are not dogmatic about how they would act: they tend to make tentative assessments about what they would say or do. Cook's findings provide valuable supportive evidence for the interpretations we made concerning the socialization experiences of middle-class children in the area of inter-personal relations.

Notes

1 Our concern in this paper is with linguistic form, with the ways in which the grammar and lexis may be organized to express uncertainty. A complete account of the expression of uncertainty would include an examination of hesitation phenomena (articulation rates, filled and unfilled pauses, false starts, and so on).

2 Throughout the paper the following initials are used: MC = middle class; WC = working class; MIQ = medium verbal ability; HIQ = high verbal ability; B = boy; G = girl.

3 A computer program to handle this test was written by R. E. Pickvance. A copy of the program is available at the Computing Centre, University of London Institute of Education.

4 Grateful acknowledgment is made to M. Goldberg, Research Assistant in the Sociological Research Unit, for his help with the statistical calculations.

5 For reasons of space, only the numbers for 'users' are given in these tables.

6 The numbers for the picture story and Trotin combined need not be the sums of the numbers for the two tasks considered individually, since there may be subjects who scored in both tasks.

7 It is important to stress that we are not saying that working-class mothers do not have a range of expressions of uncertainty *available* to them, but rather that they may tend to use these expressions less in certain types of context.

8 The totals for the other three categories are as follows:

	WC	*Mixed C*	*MC*
Ego-centric sequence	100	205	244
Socio-centric sequences	192	231	69
I might/I'd probably/ I'd possibly/it depends	39	83	123

References

BERNSTEIN, B. (1962), 'Social class, linguistic codes and grammatical elements', *Language and Speech*, 5, pp. 31–46.

BERNSTEIN, B. (1964), 'Family role systems, socialization and communication', paper given at the Conference on Cross-Cultural Research into Childhood and Adolescence, University of Chicago.

BERNSTEIN, B. (1965), 'A socio-linguistic approach to social learning', in J. Gould (ed.), *Social Science Survey*. London: Penguin.

BERNSTEIN, B. (1972), 'A socio-linguistic approach to socialization: with some reference to educability', in J. Gumperz and D. Hymes (eds), *Directions in Sociolinguistics*. New York: Holt, Rinehart & Winston.

BERNSTEIN, B. and BRANDIS, W. (1970), 'Social class differences in communication and control', in W. Brandis and D. Henderson, *Social Class, Language and Communication*. London: Routledge & Kegan Paul.

BERNSTEIN, B. and HENDERSON, D. (1969), 'Social class differences in the relevance of language to socialization', *Sociology*, 3, and in this volume.

BRANDIS, W. (1970), 'Appendix I: An index of social class', in W. Brandis and D. Henderson, *Social Class, Language and Communication*. London: Routledge & Kegan Paul.

CAZDEN, C. B. (1966), 'Subcultural differences in child language: an inter-disciplinary review', *Merrill-Palmer Quarterly of Behavior and Development*, 12, pp. 185–219.

COOK, J. (1968), 'The mother's speech in answering the child control questions', unpublished document, Sociological Research Unit, University of London Institute of Education.

COOK, J. (1972), *Social Control and Socialization*. London: Routledge & Kegan Paul.

HALLIDAY, M. A. K. (1963), 'Intonation systems in English', in A. McIntosh and M. A. K. Halliday, *Patterns of Language: Papers in General, Descriptive and Applied Linguistics*. London: Longmans, 1966.

HALLIDAY, M. A. K. (1967a), 'Notes on transitivity and theme in English: Pt. I', *Journal of Linguistics*, 3, pp. 37–81.

HALLIDAY, M. A. K. (1967b). 'Notes on transitivity and theme in English: Pt. II', *Journal of Linguistics*, 3, pp. 199–244.

HALLIDAY, M. A. K. (1968), 'Notes on transitivity and theme in English: Pt. III', *Journal of Linguistics*, 4, pp. 179–215.

HALLIDAY, M. A. K. (1969), 'On finiteness and modality in the English verb', prepared for Center for Applied Linguistics Tenth Anniversary Conference on the English Verb (April 1969); an interim version of a paper entitled 'On finiteness, tense and modality in the English verb'.

HASAN, R. (1968), 'Grammatical cohesion in spoken and written English', Part II. London: Nuffield Programme in Linguistics and English Teaching.

HAWKINS, P. R. (1969), *Social Class, the Nominal Group and Reference* (provisional title of forthcoming monograph). London: Routledge & Kegan Paul.

HENDERSON, D. (1970), 'Social class differences in form-class usage among five-year-old children', in W. Brandis and D. Henderson, *Social Class, Language and Communication*. London: Routledge & Kegan Paul.

HENDERSON, D. (1971), 'Contextual-specificity, discretion and cognitive socialization', *Sociology*, 4, and in this volume.

HUDDLESTON, R. D. *et al.* (1968), 'Sentence and Clause in Scientific English', University College London, Communication Research Centre: Report of the OSTI Programme in the Linguistic Properties of Scientific English.

HYMES, D. H. (1968), 'On communicative competence'. This paper is revised from the one presented at the Research Planning Conference on Language Development among Disadvantaged Children, held under the sponsorship of the Department of Educational Psychology and Guidance, Ferkauf Graduate School, Yeshiva University, 1966.

LAWTON, D. (1964a), 'Social class language differences in group discussions', *Language and Speech*, 7, pp. 182–204.

LAWTON, D. (1964b), 'Social class language differences in individual interviews', unpublished document.

LOBAN, W. D. (1966), *Language Ability: Grades Seven, Eight and Nine*. Washington: U.S. Government Printing Office. Co-operative Research Monograph, no. 18, U.S. Dept. of Health, Education and Welfare, Office of Education.

RACKSTRAW, S. J. and ROBINSON, W. P. (1967), 'Social and psychological factors related to variability of answering behaviour in five-year-old children', *Language and Speech*, 10, pp. 88–106.

ROBINSON, W. P. and RACKSTRAW, S. J. (1967), 'Variations in mothers' answers to children's questions, as a function of social class, verbal intelligence test scores and sex', *Sociology*, 1, pp. 259–76.

SINCLAIR, J. MCH. (1965), *A Course in Spoken English* Part 3: *Grammar*. Oxford University Press.

TURNER, G. J. (1972), 'Social class and children's language of control at age five and age seven', in the present volume.

Chapter 6 Perceptual and verbal discriminations of 'elaborated' and 'restricted' code users

W. P. Robinson and C. D. Creed

Introduction

Several investigations (Bernstein, 1962a, 1962b; Lawton, 1963, 1964; Robinson, 1965a, 1965b) have testified to the fruitfulness of Bernstein's distinction between 'elaborated' and 'restricted' codes in that they have revealed a number of grammatical, lexical, semantic, and para-linguistic differences in the language used by working- and middle-class subjects. While these studies have each controlled for intelligence test scores of their experimental subjects, allocation to different code groups has always been based upon social class.

As Bernstein (1961b) has argued, the association between membership of the working class and confinement to a restricted code is contingent rather than necessary, so that it is important to examine the possibility of using more direct measures of the elaboratedness of the code, either by the utilization of appropriate social psychological controls within social class or by a direct examination of appropriate language samples taken from children, again within class.

A second feature common to the previous studies referred to is their use of language samples obtained in the relatively unstructured situations of group discussions, essays, and letter-writing. The language produced was only constrained by the general topic offered, the mode of linguistic communication and the social psychology of the situation; there were no right or wrong brief answers for example. It has not yet been shown that confinement to a restricted code is associated with a reduced probability of efficient functioning in a task requiring a constrained precision of language.

It became possible and desirable to investigate both possibilities in the work undertaken by the Sociological Research Unit. Subsamples of infant-school children could be selected from those being studied in at least two ways, each opposing elaborated and restricted code users; one basis of selection was dependent upon experimental manipulation and the other upon naturally occurring individual differences.

In some schools a language programme[1] had been mounted, whose function was to encourage children towards the use of an elaborated code. The effectiveness of this programme required assessment and this provided the first dichotomy of subjects into 'elaborated' and 'restricted' code users. The second variable was a direct control on the language of the children. At the commencement of the project, over a year earlier, samples of speech had been taken from each child, and it was possible to use linguistic criteria to divide these children in terms of code elaboration.

If the experimental situation selected showed no significant differences between the experimentally defined elaborated and restricted code users, the failure might be attributed to the unreliability or invalidity of the scores in the particular task used, so an additional subject variable was incorporated into the design, which would be almost certainly associated with the dependent variables. If this variable gave significant differences in performances, a failure to find differences between code users would then have to be assigned to faulty allocation of subjects to their respective groups or a faulty theoretical basis rather than to the performance scores obtained. Verbal intelligence test scores were selected as such a validating criterion (English Picture Vocabulary Test, Brimer and Dunn, 1962).

Three areas of interest were selected for study: (1) curiosity and attentiveness, (2) perceptual discrimination, and (3) verbal discrimination. Bernstein's (1961a, p. 164; 1961b, pp. 296–302) exposition of the consequences of a confinement to a restricted code enable the following predictions to be made. The elaborated code user should be higher than the restricted code user on the following three sets of variables:

(1) his greater facility for cognitive experience will lead him to spend more time studying and analysing a new situation,
(2) as a further consequence he will see more relationships between objects in a new situation; he will notice more attributes, and similarly,
(3) these discriminations are more likely to have effective verbal correlates which can be used to communicate the discriminations to a second person.

The task chosen for an examination of the validity of these predictions required a child to look at a painting for as long as he wished and then report what was in the picture. He was then shown a second painting identical to the first except for a limited number of deliberately introduced differences and had to point to the differences. When this had been done, he had to say what the differences were.

It was predicted that children with either high intelligence test scores or elaborated codes would:

(1) study the first picture for a long time without seeking further instruction,
(2) point to more differences, and
(3) describe these differences more efficiently.

Method

Criteria for the allocation of subjects to 'restricted' and 'elaborated' code groups

LANGUAGE PROGRAMME

The language programme was initiated in three schools (E1), a second group of schools (C1) was given some intervention, while a third group of schools was used only for before and after measurements (C2). The extra control group C1 was used to control for such possibilities as the heightened motivation of teachers which may have affected E1 schools over and above the language programme. The teachers in E1 schools met fortnightly with the Unit psychologists who were organizing the language programme to discuss the techniques and materials to be used. The teachers implemented the programme for at least twenty minutes a day and the Unit psychologists observed the teachers once a week to check that agreed procedures were being used. The teachers in C1 schools met fortnightly to discuss general problems arising in infant-school teaching and conducted a number of investigations to obtain information about possible improvements: language and speech did not arise as a substantive issue in these discussions.

The language programme was designed with three general aims in mind: first, to make speech and language more salient, second, to improve and expand the range and type of grammatical, lexical, and semantic facility available to a child, and third, arising out of the previous two, to give the child an increased awareness of new ways of describing and categorizing the perceptual world, both material and social. To achieve these aims the children performed a series of different tasks during the twenty-minute period each day. Two or three of these tasks were performed in one session and variations in tasks were repeated with different materials. A few examples are given:

Variations of the O'Grady game were used ('O'Grady says all

children to raise their left hands.' Those who fail drop out of the game, etc.). This task was intended to enhance the ability to discriminate qualitative and quantitative physical and social differences and act upon them. To succeed, children had to analyse their own attributes and those of relatives and friends. In variations of 'I-Spy' game, specified new vocabulary was introduced. For 'The Surprise Box' the children had to describe and communicate to another child the nature of unseen objects. 'The Five Minute Story' (listened to on tape recorders) offered new vocabulary, exposed the child to increasingly complex syntax and had a 'Spot the mistake' in it. Telephones were used for children to describe familiar objects to each other without mentioning the usual name. 'Question Time' and 'News Time' were made use of to develop the vocabulary and syntax by questioning and reporting. 'Picture stories' were frequently used. Children were given sets of pictures and had to discuss all possible features of the social and physical situation. Pictures were omitted and the order of presentation was reversed, so that the children could develop an inferential and hypothetical approach to the stories.

A general intention of the language programme may be summarized by stating that the hope was that children participating in it would move towards the use of an elaborated code in appropriate circumstances, while their control counterparts would not. E1 children could be used as a sample for 'elaborated' code users, while either C1 or C2 children could be used for the 'restricted' code sample, but since the E1/C1 comparison is the tighter contrast, C1 girls were selected.

The programme was introduced into E1 schools during the children's first term at school and had been running for some four terms (fifty weeks) at the time of this experiment.

DIRECT MEASURE OF ELABORATION/RESTRICTION

When the children first entered infant school, a language sample was taken from each one. The child was interviewed in a permissive atmosphere and performed six tasks designed to provide a range of types of speech. First, the child arranged a model room and answered questions about the activities and speech of the family. This was followed by three sets of pictures forming the basis of narrative stories. The child then talked about what was going on in postcard reproductions of three detailed paintings by Trotin. For the fourth task the child said what he might do in a completely free day. Fifth, the child was asked how to play the game Hide and Seek, Musical Chairs, or Ring-a-ring o' roses, and finally he was required to describe and explain the actions of a mechanical elephant which made a number of movements when an attached rubber bulb was squeezed. This speech is being subjected to a grammatical analysis based upon Halliday's scale and category grammar (Haliday *et al.*, 1964). (For a subsidiary analysis, see Rackstraw and Robinson, 1967.) Certain grammatical variables were selected as being likely to separate elaborated from restricted code users and, while a stronger justification of this selection must await later analyses, it seemed worth while to attempt a separation for experimental purposes. The criteria used for division were among those previously found to differentiate between social class groups. The precise selection followed discussions with linguists. The scores used were: (1) number of subordinate clauses, (2) number of rank-shifted clauses, (3) number of adverbial groups, and (4) number of verb tenses. These criteria were generally consistent in their ordering, ($W = 0{\cdot}75$, $p < 0{\cdot}001$) and summed unweighted rank-orders were used for the final allocation.

SUBJECTS

Boys had been used in other experiments to evaluate the language programme and to reduce the extent to which particular individuals were exploited for such comparisons, girls were chosen for this experiment. The experimental variables of language programme participation, elaboration of code and intelligence test scores have already been described. Subjects were also matched as closely as possible on a ten-point social class scale. This scale compounded the occupation and education of both parents. Occupations were classified on the Hall-Jones scale (Hall and Jones, 1950), while the educational contrast was between basic secondary education and some extension of this. That the subjects were predominantly lower working class is shown by two examples: only 5 of the 48 parents left school after the age of 15 and 15 of the 24 fathers' occupations could be allocated unambiguously to the unskilled or semi-skilled categories of the Hall-Jones scale.

At the time of experiment the mean age of the girls was 6 years and 8 months (standard deviation 1·5 months). Twenty-four girls were selected, 12 from the language programme schools (E1) and 12 from the stricter control group (C1). In each group 4 were high IQ and 8 low. Of the 8 low IQ, 4 were labelled 'elaborated code' users, 4, 'restricted code' users. As far as possible a matched-pairs design was used. E1 and C1 were matched pairs on EPVT verbal intelligence test scores (mean discrepancy 1·42 points) (see Table 6.1) and on the ten-point social class (mean discrepancy 1·36, difference

TABLE 6.1 *Basic data: intelligence test, perceptual discrimination and verbalization scores*

	LANGUAGE PROGRAMME GROUP (E1)			CONTROL GROUP (C1)		
	EPVT IQ	*Perceptual discrimin-ation*	*Verbal-ization*	*EPVT IQ*	*Perceptual discrimin-ation*	*Verbal-ization*
High IQ	125	28	21	127	28	16
	119	27	24	118	22	9
	118	22	19	118	24	14
	106	26	16	109	27	20
Mean scores	117·0	25·75	20·0	118·0	25·25	14·75
Low IQ						
	85	18	10	86	8	0
Elaborated	86	23	16	87	9	2
code	91	19	8	91	15	9
	94	25	13	92	18	14
Mean scores	89·0	21·25	11·75	89·0	12·5	6·25
	86	20	1	86	26	14
Restricted	86	16	0	88	9	0
code	91	18	9	86	16	0
	91	24	15	91	21	0
Mean scores	88·5	19·5	6·25	87·8	18·0	3·5

between group means 0·4). Elaborated and restricted code users were similiarly matched (mean EPVT discrepancy 1·38 points) and social class (mean discrepancy 1·1, difference between group means 0·7), but the variances were so low in these groups that analyses of variance could be used. The subjects were predominantly lower working class.

MATERIALS

Five pairs of pictures were painted of which four pairs were used for this analysis: dock scene, school playground, motor-car/bus, living room and child feeding pet. Twenty-seven differences were intended, but 32 were subsequently categorized: 8 were omitted objects, 7 were differences of colour, 7 involved shape or position, 8 were differences in the faces or clothes of boys and girls with one spelling and one number difference.

Two stop-watches were used to measure relevant time intervals, all conversation was tape recorded, and a check was available for noting differences pointed to.

PROCEDURE

Twelve randomly selected orders of presentation of the pictures were used, the order being the same for each E1/C1 pair. The order in which each member of a pair was offered was systematically varied. The experimenter was a quietly spoken young man of below average height. The atmosphere was friendly and relaxed.

The subject sat opposite the experimenter and the following instructions were given: Each girl was shown the first member of the first pair of pictures as the experimenter said:

'Here is a picture, I'd like you to look at it—for as long as you like.'

The amount of time that the child spent looking was recorded from this moment until she had looked away from the picture for fifteen seconds at one time. A cumulative stop-watch was switched on every time the child looked back at the picture. When a fifteen-second gap had been registered or after three minutes, the experimenter said,

'Now tell me what is in the picture.'

(This instruction ensured that the child studied the picture with some care.) Each time the child stopped, she was asked, 'What else is there?', and this was continued until she said, 'Nothing'. One extra probe was given, 'Are you sure?' The child was then given the second picture of the pair and was told, 'There are some differences between this picture and the one you've been looking at. I want you to point to all the differences you can see. I want you to point to them, but not to say anything.' If the child only pointed to one of the pictures the experimenter said, 'Now show me on the other picture.' The 'What else is there?' procedure was carried out as before. The experimenter then said, 'Now you've pointed to the differences, can you *tell* me what they are?', and the 'What else is there?' procedure was repeated. For two picture-pairs the child was also asked, 'In what ways are these pictures alike?', 'Can you tell me if there is anything the same?', but these data are not reported.

Finally the child was probed on those items where she had reported a difference, but had not made its essence explicit. 'Now we're just going to look at this picture pair again. When we looked at these before, you said the X [name of objects] were different. Can you tell me how they are different?'

Treatment of results

The motor-car/bus pair of pictures was dropped from the analysis and no comments about similarities were included. Two scoring methods were used. For pointing there was no problem, but for the verbal description four gradations were common: (1) simple statement of difference, (2) recognition of relevant variable (shape, colour, etc.), (3) recognition of variable plus a statement of the value of the variable in one picture (it's round there), (4) recognition of both values of variable (that is red and that is green). For one scoring system 0, 1, 2 and 3 were given for the four types of answer, if these were given without probing. If a probe was used, statements at levels (3) and (4) were both given a score of 1. A second scoring system coded (3) and (4) as 1 and all others as 0. The more complex system involved dubious assumptions about the weighting of the parts of answers, and since it gave substantially similar results to the simple scoring, the results of only the latter are reported.

Times were measured in seconds.

Two main techniques of analysis were employed, analyses of variance and co-variance, the latter for E1/C1 and sometimes elaborated/restricted code comparisons, but because of the unequal numbers, high versus low IQ comparisons were confined to analyses of variance. For E1/C1 comparisons all twenty-four subjects were used, but elaborated/restricted code differences could only be tested in the low IQ sub-sample ($n = 16$).

Results

Attentiveness and curiosity

Three sets of scores were tabulated: (1) a D score: the amount of time in seconds for which the subject looked at the first of each pair of pictures, (2) a C score: the amount of time spent looking away and (3) a G score: the number of glances away from the pictures. All measures were only for the period prior to the beginning of the pointing instructions.

Two indices were obtained: D and the ratio G/C. Both were reliable estimates and rankings across the four pictures gave coefficients of concordance (W) of 0·88 for D ($p < 0{\cdot}001$) and 0·69 for G/C ($p < 0{\cdot}001$). The values of the middle two scores of each subject were summed for subsequent analyses, but neither measure gave significant differences between any comparison groups and no trends were indicated.

Errors

Some differences pointed to and described by subjects were not intended by the experimenters, but were in fact reasonable judgments, others were simply not there. Where there was no doubt that a mistake had been made, an error score was noted.

Pointing errors were not associated with IQ or language programme in the analysis utilizing all subjects, but differences were suggested in the low IQ sub-sample. An analysis for main effects showed the language programme ($F = 4{\cdot}21$, $df = 1, 12$, $p < 0{\cdot}10$) to have a weak relevance and the subsequent analysis for simple effects showed two significant differences: E1 made fewer errors than C1 within the restricted code group ($F = 6{\cdot}52$, $df = 1, 12$, $p < 0{\cdot}05$) and elaborated code users made fewer errors than restricted code users in the C1 group ($F = 8{\cdot}65$, $df = 1, 12$, $p < 0{\cdot}025$). Verbal errors reflected a similar pattern at the same levels of significance.

Perceptual discrimination scores

Bartlett's test for homogeneity of variance gave an insignificant χ^2 and uncorrected scores were used (see Table 6.1). High-IQ girls pointed to more differences than Low-IQ girls ($p < 0{\cdot}001$), and the analysis of simple effects (for the Low-IQ sub-sample) showed that E1 girls pointed to more differences than C1 girls within the elaborated group ($p < 0{\cdot}05$) (see Table 6.2).

TABLE 6.2 *Perceptual discrimination: variation of scores as a function of IQ, participation in the language programme and elaboratedness of code.*

Total sample (n = 24)				
Source of variation	*df*	*Mean square*	*F ratio*	*p*
IQ	1	315·22	15·57	< 0·001
E1/C1	1	42·11	2·08	< 0·2
Interaction	1	28·41	1·40	—
Within cells	20	20·24		

Low IQ sample (n = 16)				
Source of variation	*df*	*Mean square*	*F ratio*	*p*
Elab./restrict.	1	14·06	—	—
E1/C1	1	105·06	4·27	< 0·1
Interaction	1	52·57	2·14	< 0·2
Within cells	12	24·56		

Verbalization scores

For the simple scoring technique Bartlett's test of homogeneity of variance permitted the use of untransformed scores and once more IQ was of considerable significance (see Table 6.3). When analyses of co-variance were used to eliminate the relevance of differing perceptual discrimination scores, IQ and the language programme were both significant, while in the low-IQ sub-sample the elaborated code users performed significantly more effectively (see Table 6.4).

TABLE 6.3 *Verbal discrimination: variation of scores as a function of IQ, participation in the language programme and elaboratedness of code*

Total sample (n = 24)				
Source of variation	*df*	*Mean square*	*F ratio*	*p*
IQ	1	580·97	18·39	< 0·001
E1/E2	1	117·26	3·71	< 0·1
Interaction	1	1·65	—	—
Within cells	20	31·58		

Low IQ sample (n = 16)				
Source of variation	*df*	*Mean square*	*F ratio*	*p*
Elab./restrict.	1	68·06	1·77	—
E1/E2	1	68·06	1·77	—
Interaction	1	7·57	—	—
Within cells	12	38·27		

TABLE 6.4 *Verbal discrimination: variation of scores as a function of IQ, participation in the language programme and elaboratedness of code, partialling out perceptual discrimination scores*

Total sample (n = 24)				
Source of variation	*df*	*Mean square*	*F ratio*	*p*
IQ	1	567·85	19·40	< 0·001
E1/E2	1	163·38	5·08	< 0·05
Interaction	1	0·95	—	—
Within cells	19	29·26		

Low IQ sample (n = 16)				
Source of variation	*df*	*Mean square*	*F ratio*	*p*
Elab./restrict.	1	134·67	8·08	< 0·05
E1/E2	1	2·04	—	—
Interaction	1	11·95	—	—
Within cells	11	16·65		

Discussion

The results generally confirmed expectations. For perceptual and verbal discriminations no differences were contrary to expectation and all differences were in the predicted directions, even though they were smaller and less stable than originally hoped, especially in the E1/C1 and elaborated/restricted comparisons.

Intelligence test scores gave clear and strong differentials, attesting to the reliability and validity of the materials used. These results have relevance also to the problem of how far the EPVT is a verbal rather than a non-verbal test. Efficiency of unverbalized perceptual discrimination is strongly associated with EPVT scores, but when pointing scores have been partialled out, the extra efficiency of verbalization remains significantly associated.

This strong association between the intelligence test scores and both perceptual and verbal discrimination was possibly responsible for the attenuation of E1/CI differences when analyses of variance were used: the variance of discrimination scores within groups was probably increased by the small variation in the intelligence test scores.

No measure of attentiveness or curiosity bore a relationship to the dependent variables examined, although the measures of internal consistency suggested that the time periods recorded had satisfactory degrees of reliability. Either these measures are invalid or the original theoretical framework requires modification. Bernstein's comments about curiosity are general rather than specific. The implication of his viewpoint is that curiosity mediated through verbal communication will be lower in restricted code groups. The restricted code child will be discouraged from continuing to ask questions, because the answers he initially receives from his restricted code parents will have been unsatisfactory. This has now been supported empirically: asking questions of his mother, he is less likely to receive an answer, and any answer received is likely to contain less information of a less accurate nature and to be embedded in more 'noisy' sentences (Robinson and Rackstraw, 1967). Similarly with attentiveness, it is the attentiveness to speech which may be lower in the restricted code child, so that the lack of differentiation with the measures of attentiveness and curiosity made here suggests that their proposed relevance should be restricted to situations involving verbal components.

The results with the errors and pointing scores both support the prediction that elaborated code children perform more efficiently than those confined to a restricted code. Both the language programme and the direct measure of elaboration give significant differences on errors, but pointing differences are only significant between E1 and C1 for the elaborated code low IQ group. Both measures of elaboration relate to verbalization, but only when perceptual discrimination scores are partialled out.

An examination of the verbalization scores (see Table 6.1) reveals one reason why the significance of E1/C1 and elaborated restricted differences are attenuated. One child in the restricted code C1 group made the third highest verbalization score of the sixteen low IQ girls. Furthermore, for the analyses of co-variance in the E1/C1 comparison she was paired with the second to weakest E1 child. The elimination of this subject from the analyses left all predictions supported at high levels of significance. Are there good reasons for thinking that this C1 restricted code child was wrongly allocated? A check of her scores in the speech sample confirmed her assignment to the restricted code group. Her WISC verbal score, taken six months before the experiment, was 97; this was 11 points higher than the earlier EPVT estimate, while the mean difference for the low IQ C1 group was only 4. A further feature of possible relevance is social class. This subject was the highest in the low IQ C1 group. Although her father had only basic secondary education and was a dock labourer, her mother had not left grammar school until she was 17 and had subsequently worked as a laboratory technician. Her matched pair in E1 achieved her higher social class by virtue of the father's self-employment. There are some special features differentiating this child from others in her group, but insufficient for dropping the child from the analysis. The case is mentioned in some detail because it illustrates the importance of a close examination of the bases of allocation when using small groups of subjects, and it seems that the use of the compound social class index may have been mistaken. In fields of inquiry such as this, the mother's education may be a more important index than father's occupation, and the true relevance of the variables examined may have been underestimated by this oversight. Nevertheless, significant differences were found and these were not just between extended samples of language in free situations.

The experimental situation constrained subjects severely. There were right and wrong answers, to be achieved by pointing and subsequent explicit verbal labelling of the different values of the relevant variable. For the verbalization, an elaborated grammar was unnecessary: only a contextually appropriate range of adjectives or nouns was required for perfect answering. Whereas the characteristics of the working-class language samples found in earlier studies could be attributed to a preference for certain modes of expression rather than an inability to use other grammatical structures or lexical elements, the results here support the view that group differences are more than matters of selective preferences. Further, this has been demonstrated with elaborated and restricted codes controlled more directly than heretofore.

Both indices proved satisfactory in spite of controls for verbal IQ and social class. The confirmation of the effectiveness of the language programme is the more important result educationally, but the other has greater surprise value. The speech sample from which only four variables were used to classify the children was taken eighteen months before the experiment was conducted. This is a substantial proportion of the speaking life of the children tested and implies a high reliability of the original estimate, as well as its validity as an empirical basis for making predictions about behaviour in other situations. As far as can be ascertained, this is the first demonstration that general differences in language samples, with IQ and social class controlled, are associated with perceptual and verbal discriminations. Since these results are consistent with Bernstein's distinction between elaborated and restricted codes, it would be of considerable theoretical and practical interest to examine the full range of behavioural differences in psychological and social psychological test situations between children whose major difference appears to be in speech code only.

Notes

1 This programme was devised and administered by D. M. and G. Gahagan and published in a book by the above authors entitled *Talk Reform: an exploratory language programme for infant school children*, Routledge & Kegan Paul, 1970.

References

BERNSTEIN, B. (1961a), 'Social structure, language, and learning', *Educational Res.*, 3, 163.

BERNSTEIN, B. (1961b), 'Social class and linguistic development: a theory of social learning', in A. H. Halsey, J. Floud, and C. A. Anderson (eds), *Education, Economy and Society*. New York: Free Press.

BERNSTEIN, B. (1962a), 'Linguistic codes, hesitation phenomena and intelligence', *Language and Speech*, 5, 41.

BERNSTEIN, B. (1962b), 'Social class, linguistic codes and grammatical elements', *Language and Speech*, 5, 221.

BRIMER, M. A. and DUNN, L. M. (1962), *The English Picture Vocabulary Tests*. London: National Foundation for Educational Research.

HALL, J. and JONES, D. C. (1950), 'Social grading of occupations', *Brit. J. Sociol.*, 1, 31.

HALLIDAY, M. A. K., MCINTOSH, A. and STREVENS, P. (1964), *The Linguistic Sciences and Language Teaching* (London).

LAWTON, D. (1963), 'Social class differences in language development: a study of some samples of written work', *Language and Speech*, 6, 120.

LAWTON, D. (1964), 'Social class differences in group discussion', *Language and Speech*, 7, 102.

RACKSTRAW, S. J. and ROBINSON, W. P. (1967), 'Social and psychological factors related to variability of answering behaviour in five-year-old children', *Language and Speech*, 10, 88.

ROBINSON, W. P. (1965a), 'Cloze procedure as a technique for the investigation of social class differences in language usage', *Language and Speech*, 8, 42.

ROBINSON, W. P. (1965b), 'The elaborated code in working-class language,' *Language and Speech*, 8, 243.

ROBINSON, W. P. and RACKSTRAW, S. J. (1967), 'Variations in mothers' answers to children's questions as a function of social class, verbal intelligence test scores, and sex', *Sociology*, 1, 259.

Part III Aspects of the speech of seven-year-old children

Chapter 7 Social class and children's language of control at age five and age seven

G. J. Turner

Introduction

General background

There is a long history of research into parental discipline, particularly maternal discipline. Generally, the research has had two foci of attention: (*a*) the techniques used by the parents; and (*b*) the consequences of the disciplinary techniques. If one compares work carried out mainly in the 1940s and 1950s with some of the more recent work, there are apparent, as Hess has pointed out, two important differences in emphasis and orientation (Hess *et al.*, 1968).

(1) In the earlier period researchers tended to focus on the *affect* of the parents and on the *degree* of the control exerted, whereas more recently they have focused on the *type* of control. Schaefer (1959, 1961) has shown, by means of factor analytic studies, that most of the concepts developed in the earlier period can be reduced to a combination of two main dimensional concepts, namely love *v*. hostility and control *v*. autonomy. Becker (1964) has offered an alternative (but similar) model in which Schaefer's control *v*. autonomy dimension is sub-divided into two dimensions, the three dimensions in Becker's model being warmth *v*. hostility, restrictiveness *v*. permissiveness and anxious emotional involvement *v*. calm detachment. A number of researchers in this earlier period investigated social class differences in the disciplinary techniques used (Bronfenbrenner, 1958; Sears, Maccoby and Levin, 1957; Miller and Swanson, 1960). Becker (1964) has summarized the social differences:

> Generally, the research has shown that middle-class parents provide more warmth and are more likely to use reasoning, isolation, show of disappointment, or guilt-arousing appeals in disciplining the child. They are also likely to be more permissive about demands for attention from the child, sex behaviour, aggression to parent, table manners, neatness and orderliness,

> noise, bedtime rules, and general obedience. Working-class parents are more likely to use ridicule, shouting, or physical punishment in disciplining the child, and to be generally more restrictive.

In the more recent research, a greater emphasis has been placed on the type of control exercised, on the nature of the values transmitted, particularly by means of linguistic appeals (Kohn, 1959a, b, 1963; Bernstein, 1958, 1962a, 1970a; Hess and Shipman, 1968; J. and E. Newson, 1968). Aspects of this later work are considered in detail in this paper.

(2) In the earlier period researchers tended to focus on the orectic development of the child—they examined how parental control influenced the development of the emotional, social and ethical aspects of the child's personality; more recently researchers have focused on the linguistic and cognitive consequences of parental control. In order to illustrate how the earlier research has illuminated the orectic development of the child, we may refer to Becker's (1964) summary of the effects of power-assertive techniques (which include physical punishment, yelling, shouting, forceful commands and verbal threats) and of love-oriented techniques (praise, reasoning, isolation, show of disappointment and withdrawal of love):

> Power-assertive techniques of discipline tend to be used by hostile parents and in this context tend to promote aggression in young children, resistance to authority, power assertion to other children, and externalized reactions to transgression (fear of punishment, projected hostility) . . . Love-oriented techniques of discipline tend to be used by warm parents and in this context tend to provide acceptance of self-responsibility, guilt and related internalized reactions to transgression.

By contrast, some of the more recent research has been designed to show how the control a child is subject to may exert a strong influence on the way he communicates with others and on the development of his powers of reasoning. For this later work, Bernstein (e.g. 1961, 1965) has provided the theoretical bridge relating social structure, linguistic codes and cognitive orientation. Bernstein's theory provides the sociological framework for the present study.

Specific background

Since January 1964 Professor Bernstein has been conducting a large programme of theory-based research, concerned with five main topics:

(1) Social class differences in the way mothers prepare their children for the experience of the infant school.
(2) Maternal communication and control.
(3) The speech of children at age five and age seven and the social factors affecting it.
(4) The development of a language programme for working-class infant school children.
(5) An evaluation of the effects of the language programme.

The present study falls under topic 3, but information concerned with topic 2 is also very relevant. We may briefly describe the two data sources relevant to our study, the maternal interviews and the child interviews. Reports were obtained from mothers (twice within a three-year period) concerning matters pertinent to Bernstein's theories, for example, the extent to which the mother is likely to take up her child's attempts to talk to her, to avoid or evade answering difficult questions put to her by her child, to use coercive methods of control, to explain to the child why she wants a change in his behaviour and so on. Their children were also interviewed twice (at age five and at age seven); they were required to perform several tasks, designed to elicit different kinds of speech, important kinds being regulatory, narrative, descriptive and explanatory speech.

In this paper we are concerned with the responses of the children at age five and at age seven to a picture story cards task. The children were shown picture story cards depicting a transgressional situation and were asked to tell the story and to say what certain people in the story were saying. The task was primarily designed to elicit narrative and role-play speech, but as a subsidiary analysis we examined the children's responses from the point of view of social control. We sought to answer four main types of question:

(1) Do children at these ages reveal social class differences in their choice of social control?
(2) If the children do show such differences in their choice of control, are these differences likely to be a direct reflection of their parents' usage or rather an indirect reflection, influenced in part by the age of the children, their stage of moral development?
(3) Are the class differences greater at age five than at age seven? Does exposure to school for two years tend to make working-class children more like middle-class children in their choice of control?
(4) To what extent are class differences in the choice of control relatable to code differences?

It was thought that the information gained might usefully augment the information obtained in the maternal interviews and elsewhere in the child interviews (Cook, 1972).

To help us answer these questions we have drawn on two sociolinguistic theories: Bernstein's and Halliday's. We shall consider briefly the aspects of these theories that are the most relevant to our problem. We shall begin with Bernstein's work.

In broad terms, Bernstein has suggested that familial inter-action within social strata is governed by different characteristic role structures. Different familial role structures give rise to different linguistic codes. The linguistic code is transmitted to the child in four critical contexts, one of which is the regulative ('social control') context. In this paper as we are more concerned with the mechanics of social control than with family role structure, we shall concentrate on the modes of control recognized by Bernstein and on the linguistic codes with which they have been associated.

Bernstein (1970a, see also 1962b) has distinguished two modes of control: the imperative mode and the mode based upon appeals. The imperative mode is quite similar to the power-assertive mode recognized by previous researchers; the mode based upon appeals is a much more novel conception. Underlying Bernstein's distinctions in modes of control is the role discretion (the range of alternatives) accorded to the person regulated. The imperative mode 'reduces the role discretion accorded to the regulated [child]' (Bernstein, 1970a); the child may only rebel, withdraw or accept. With the mode based upon appeals 'the regulated [child] is accorded varying degrees of discretion in the sense that a range of alternatives, essentially linguistic, are available to him'. Two broad types of appeal are recognized, positional appeals and personal appeals, and each type has several sub-classes (the social control coding manual differentiates seven sub-classes of positional appeal and seventeen sub-classes of personal appeal—see Cook, 1972). Briefly, positional appeals are *communalized*—they refer the child's behaviour to the norms which inhere in a particular or universal status, e.g. 'Little boys don't play with dolls'; by contrast, personal appeals are *individualized*—they take into account the child's intention and his disposition, e.g. 'I know you meant well but . . .' and 'How would you like it if someone took something which belonged to you?' In the case of positional control, rules are *assigned*, whereas in the case of personal control, they are *achieved* by the child in contexts which uniquely fit him. Also, positional control—with its emphasis on external proscription—is likely to lead to the development of *shame*, whilst personal control—with its emphasis on the inner state of the child—is likely to lead to the formation of *guilt*.

Bernstein has associated these modes of control with linguistic codes in the following way. The imperative mode has been associated with a restricted code (or with physical coercion), whilst the mode based upon appeals has been associated with both restricted and elaborated codes, irrespective of whether the appeals be positional or personal.

Clearly, it is necessary to indicate how the codes are distinguished. Below we outline Bernstein's basic theoretical definition and then consider two further definitions which are related to the basic definition but are oriented towards empirical research.

As we have seen, it is Bernstein's contention that the codes, elaborated and restricted, are generated by a particular form of social relation—that they are likely to be a realization of different social structures. The codes may be distinguished in four main ways, which represent aspects of the same basic distinction. (1) 'A restricted code will arise where the form of social relation is based on closely shared identifications, upon an extensive range of shared expectations, upon a range of common assumptions. Thus a restricted code emerges where the culture or sub-culture raises the "we" above the "I" ' (Bernstein, 1970a). By contrast, 'An elaborated code will arise wherever the culture or sub-culture emphasizes the "I" over the "we". It will arise wherever the intent of the other person cannot be taken for granted. Inasmuch as the intent of the other person cannot be taken for granted, then speakers are forced to elaborate their meanings, and make them both explicit and specific.' (2) 'The use of a restricted code creates social solidarity at the cost of the verbal elaboration of individual experience. The type of social solidarity realized through a restricted code points to mechanical solidarity, whereas the type of solidarity realized through elaborated codes points to organic solidarity' (Bernstein, 1970a). (3) 'An elaborated code, in principle, presupposes a sharp boundary or gap between self and others which is crossed through the creation of speech which specifically fits a differentiated "other". In this sense, an elaborated code is oriented towards a person rather than a social category or status' (Bernstein, 1970a). By contrast, a restricted code 'presupposes a generalized other rather than a differentiated other'. (4) In the case of an elaborated code the principles and operations underlying behaviour are made relatively explicit whereas in the case of a restricted code they remain largely implicit: 'Where codes are elaborated, the socialized has more access to the grounds of his socialization, and so can enter into a reflexive relationship with the social order he has taken over. Where codes are restricted, the socialized has less access to the grounds of his socialization, and thus reflexiveness may be limited in range' (Bernstein, 1970c).

In the course of the development of the theory there have been two major definitions of the codes in operational terms: (1) in terms of syntax; and (2) in terms of meaning.

For a syntactic definition of the codes we may refer to Bernstein (1970a): 'These codes will be defined in terms of the relative ease or difficulty of predicting the syntactic alternatives which speakers take up to organize meanings.' In the case of an elaborated code the speaker selects from a wide range of syntactic alternatives, whereas in the case of a restricted code the speaker draws from a narrow range: an elaborated code is marked by flexibility in syntactic organization, whereas a restricted code is marked by rigidity. It is important to note that Bernstein makes reference to meaning even in the syntactic definition of the codes; he refers to 'the syntactic alternatives which speakers take up to organize meanings'. It is clear from Bernstein's writings that he is not interested in syntax *per se*, but rather in the syntactic devices which enable the speaker to elaborate meanings, to make them 'both explicit and specific' (Bernstein, 1970a). Not surprisingly, certain contexts of situation offer more scope for verbal elaboration than others; a number of situational variables (e.g. the topic, the locale, the time available, the number of people present) could have a constraining effect, either singly or in combination; hence Bernstein's (1970a) comment: 'It is clear that context is a major control upon syntactic and lexical selections; consequently it is not easy to give general linguistic criteria for the isolation of the two codes. Derivations from the theory would be required in order to describe syntactic and lexical usage by any one speaker in a specific context.' As it stands, the syntactic definition of the codes presents two difficulties, both of which have been commented on by Bernstein (1970d, 1971). One source of difficulty is the notion of predictability which 'can be given little statistical meaning' (Bernstein, 1970d). Another source of difficulty is the relation that exists in language between syntax and meaning. There is no one-to-one correspondence between syntax and meaning. On the one hand, a syntactic option may be used to realize more than one semantic option; thus, a 'conditional' clause may be associated with a 'threat', e.g. 'If you do that once more, I'll punch you', or with a 'child-oriented cognitive appeal', e.g. 'If you don't go to school, you won't learn to read'; on the other hand, a semantic option may be realized in more than one way; thus, a 'command' may be realized by an 'imperative' clause, e.g. 'Don't do that!', or a 'declarative' clause (with 'modulation'), e.g. 'You mustn't do that'. Of these two difficulties, the former, concerning the notion of predictability, is the critical one. The latter difficulty, when examined, resolves itself into a question of economy. Clearly, the syntactic alternatives which speakers take up to organize meanings and the meanings expressed have to be related at some point; the question is whether it is more economical for the socio-linguistic researcher to take the syntactic alternatives used as his starting point or the meanings expressed. In our opinion, Bernstein's work, especially his work on social control (Bernstein, 1962b, 1970a, d; Bernstein and Cook, 1965), has shown that it is in general more economical to take semantic categories as one's starting point when investigating code differences; it is, of course, the case that Bernstein has always associated conditional threats with a restricted code and child-oriented cognitive appeals with an elaborated code.

In his more recent work, Bernstein (1970 b, c, d, 1971) has distinguished the codes in terms of the meanings they transmit. He draws a distinction between particularistic meanings and universalistic meanings. In broad terms, particularistic meanings are severely context-bound whereas universalistic meanings are less bound to a given context. More specifically, there are two distinct but related senses in which particularistic meanings are context-dependent and universalistic meanings context-independent. In the wide sense, speech is closely tied to the context in which it is uttered if the speaker takes for granted a knowledge of the context and relies on his listener's awareness of relevant features of the situation to achieve comprehension, whereas speech is freed of the context in which it is uttered if the speaker takes little for granted and uses the potentialities of language to make his meanings both explicit and specific. In the former case the meanings are only fully available to those with a knowledge of the context, whereas in the latter case the meanings are in principle available to all; hence the terms, particularistic meanings and universalistic meanings. In a less wide sense, speech may be categorized as context-independent or context-dependent according to the extent to which the speaker makes principles and operations verbally explicit and elaborates them: 'Universalistic meanings are those in which principles and operations are made linguistically explicit whereas particularistic orders of meaning are meanings in which principles and operations are relatively linguistically implicit. If orders of meaning are universalistic, then the meanings are less tied to a given context' (Bernstein, 1970d). Bernstein states that particularistic meanings point to a restricted code, whilst universalistic meanings point to an elaborated code. He says that, in general, the linguistic realizations of particularistic orders of meaning are very different from the linguistic realizations of universalistic orders of meaning, that the linguistic realizations of a restricted code are very different from those of an elaborated code, but he does allow for some overlap. In Bernstein's view (1970c), it is critically important to distinguish between speech variants and linguistic codes.

> A speech variant is a pattern of linguistic choices which is specific to a particular context—for example, when talking to children, a policeman giving evidence in a court . . . Because a code is restricted it does not mean that a speaker will not in some contexts, and under specific conditions, use a range of modifiers or subordinations, or whatever. But it does mean that where such choices are made they will be highly '*context-specific*'.

The concept code refers to 'the transmission of the deep-meaning structure of a culture or subculture—the "core" meaning structure'. The code is transmitted—initially in the family—within four types of context: the regulative, the instructional, the imaginative or innovating and the inter-personal.

> If these four contexts are realized through the predominant use of restricted speech variants with particularistic—i.e. relatively context-tied—meanings, then the deep structure of the communication is controlled by a restricted code. If these four contexts are realized predominantly through elaborated speech variants, with relatively context-independent—i.e. universalistic-meanings, then the deep structure of communication is controlled by an elaborated code (Bernstein, 1970c).

Bernstein (1970d) gives additional criteria for distinguishing the codes in terms of meaning. These criteria are based upon a concept of degrees of contextual specificity and are clearly relatable to Bernstein's earlier theoretical definition of the codes in which, as we have seen, he associated the elaborated code with meanings that are 'both explicit and specific' (Bernstein, 1970a). He introduces the notion of contextual specificity in a discussion of code realizations in the regulative context:

> It is likely that where the code is restricted, the speech in the regulative context may well be limited to command and simple rule-announcing statements. The latter statements are not context-dependent in the sense previously given for they announce general rules. We need to supplement the context-independent (universalistic) and context-dependent (particularistic) criteria with criteria which refer to the extent to which the speech in the

regulative context varies in terms of its *contextual specificity* . . . the general rule may be transmitted with degrees of *contextual specificity*.

Where the code is restricted we should expect simple rule-announcing statements but where it is elaborated we should expect:

1. Some developed grounds for the rule;
2. Some qualification of it in the light of the particular issue;
3. Considerable *specificity* in terms of the socialized, the context and the issue.

These criteria represent an important elaboration of the definition of code realizations in the regulative context and, as Bernstein (1970d) indicates, can be given a more general application: 'It may be necessary to utilize the two sets of criteria for *all* socializing contexts.'

There is one further point to mention concerning the definition of the codes in terms of meaning. Just as in the case of context-dependent and context-independent meanings, when we distinguished a wide sense in which the terms may be used and a less wide sense associated with principles and operations, so in the case of the concept of contextual specificity we can distinguish a comparable wide sense and a less wide sense associated with principles and operations. Clearly, there will be contexts where it is appropriate to interpret the terms in their wider sense and *not* in their narrower sense and there will be other contexts where the terms must be interpreted in their narrower sense. It is important to bear this in mind when dealing with the speech of young children. Young children are unlikely to dwell on principles and operations to any great extent, largely as a result of their stage of development. For this reason, Bernstein emphasizes that it is important to interpret the terms mainly in their wider sense when investigating code differences in the speech of young children.

What is necessary, then, for the identification of the codes is a fairly detailed analysis of the meanings that are expressed in particular types of situation—a by no means easy task. And it is here that we shall draw on Halliday's socio-linguistic work, paying particular attention to his concept of a 'meaning potential'.

Halliday (1970c) argues that the innumerable social uses of language are, to a certain extent, relatable to generalized *situation types*, the social contexts and behavioural settings in which language is used. The classification of situation types is naturally subject to variation in detail; examples of situation types (with more detailed situation types given in brackets) are as follows: shop transactions, consultations (e.g. going to the doctor), personal services (e.g. having one's hair cut) and, of course, a mother controlling her child's behaviour. In situation types such as these the social uses of language are determinate and may be specified fairly closely. For any one such situation type, Halliday argues, it is possible to identify a 'meaning potential', that is, the range of semantic options available to the speaker in the context of the particular situation type. The semantic options available are represented in the form of a network, the network being a device for showing how the options are systematically related to each other. A salient characteristic of the semantic network is that it is open-ended; it permits one to represent finer and finer distinctions in meaning. The point at which it is no longer necessary to make further differentiations in meaning is determined by the type of problem that is being investigated. For illustrations of semantic networks, including some based on Bernstein's social control work, see Halliday (1970c, 1971).

A semantic network, Halliday (1970c) states, is a hypothesis about patterns of meaning; for it to be valid it must satisfy three requirements. These requirements are based on a stratificational model of language. (1) The semantic network has to account for the range of alternatives at the semantic stratum. (2) It has to relate these 'upwards' to what we might call the behavioural stratum. Meaning potential is strictly one realization of behaviour potential, but the behaviour potential may be realized by other means. (3) The semantic network has to relate 'downwards' to the categories of linguistic form at the stratum of grammar.

The concept of the semantic network as the realization of behaviour patterns is one that is of great relevance to our research. Halliday (1970c) makes a distinction between behaviour patterns that are socially significant, for example, a mother controlling her child's behaviour, and those that are not socially significant, for example, playing a card game. Halliday argues that we need sociological theory to identify the contexts and the meanings that are socially significant; he instances Bernstein's theories of socialization and social learning. As we have seen, Bernstein has identified four social contexts that are of critical importance in the socialization of the child, and for these, in varying degrees of detail, he has specified the meanings that are of social significance. Halliday argues that, to be valid, the meaning potential must rest on and be the expression of socially significant categories such as these.

In essence, the Sociological Research Unit's 'Social control coding manual' (Bernstein and Cook, 1965) gives us the basis for a meaning potential for the regulative context. There is, however, one point to be borne in mind, namely that the coding frame was compiled in 1965. Since that time there has been considerable exploration of the theory, particularly, as we have seen, in the area of the definition of the codes in terms of their contextual realizations. The coding manual contains highly generalized categories—they refer to the regulative context conceived of as a general type of context: they are not specific to particular types of social control situations. If we are to take account of the greater emphasis on explicitness and contextual specificity in Bernstein's recent work, then it seems likely that certain categories in the original coding frame will require further specification, taking into account the parameters of the particular type of situation under examination. It is not difficult to add such further specification of meanings whilst preserving the basic structure of the coding system.

As it stands, the Sociological Research Unit's work on social control eminently meets the first two requirements mentioned by Halliday; however, it only partially meets the third requirement, namely that the semantic options should be related downwards to categories of linguistic form, the grammar and lexis. At the time of the compilation of the coding manual, the functional approach to language, despite the work of Firth (1935, 1950), Hymes (1962, 1964) and others, was still largely unexplored in socio-linguistic research. To our knowledge, there was no model of description available which enabled one to relate systematically the social uses of the English language and its structure. It is only in recent years, since Halliday's work in this area, that it has become feasible to attempt this kind of description. We may briefly consider Halliday's approach to linguistic structure.

For Halliday (e.g. 1970b) there is a sense in which language is as it is because of the uses to which it is put; in order to explain the structure of language we need to consider its use. One has to make a distinction between use and function (generalized use) in the case of the language of the adult (but not, Halliday suggests, in the case of the language of the very young child). The innumerable social uses of language are not represented *directly* in the language system, one use equalling one component in the organization of the language system, but rather they are represented *indirectly* through a small set of functional components, or 'macro-functions'. These functional components are the highly abstract linguistic reflexes of the multiplicity of social uses of language.

Three main functional components have been distinguished: the ideational, the inter-personal and the textual, the ideational being further divided into two sub-components, the experiential and the logical. Briefly, the experiential sub-component is concerned with 'the linguistic expression of the speaker's experience of the external world, including the inner world of his own consciousness—his emotions, perceptions and so on' (Halliday, 1968); the logical sub-component provides for 'the linguistic expression of such universal relations as those of "and", "or", negation and implication' (Halliday, 1968); the inter-personal component is concerned with the linguistic expression of the inter-relations between speaker and hearer in a communication situation; it covers the traditional speech functions (e.g. statement, question, command) and also the speaker's attitude (e.g. confirmation, reservation, contradiction) and his comment on the message (e.g. concerning its probability, relevancy, etc.); and finally, the textual component is concerned with the creation of texts, a text being 'a connected and contextualized piece of discourse, as opposed to a random collection of unrelated sentences' (Halliday, 1969). The textual component is somewhat different from the other two functions, the difference lying in the nature of its relationship with non-linguistic phenomena. Whereas the ideational component and the inter-personal component are directly related to non-linguistic phenomena, the textual component is only indirectly related to such phenomena; it is an enabling function whereby language itself is enabled to perform the other two functions just specified.

The functional components represent sub-groupings of the total system of grammatical (including lexical) options, sub-systems of the total language system. Table 1 in the Appendix (reproduced from Halliday, 1970b) shows how the main grammatical systems of English may be grouped according to function. It is important to stress that Halliday argues that most sentences express a combination of functions. Moreover, the functions are expressed simultaneously. The grammatical options associated with the different functions are realized in *integrated* structures, the structures being formed by the mapping on to one another of configurations of elements derived from each of the relevant functional components. For an illustration of this kind of organization, see Halliday's (1970b) discussion of the sentence *Smith died*.

The concept of a meaning potential seems to offer a fruitful way of relating Bernstein's work on social control and his most recent work on code realization. And it is this possibility that is explored in the present paper. Needless to say, all empirical studies have their limitations. The present study has a number of severe limitations which are best stated at the outset.

One can distinguish three major kinds of restriction on the limits of the present inquiry. There are restrictions concerned with (*a*) the nature of the interview situation; (*b*) the content of the picture story cards task; and (*c*) the age of the subjects.

The interview situation was a highly structured one; the interviewer was given a fixed schedule and was directed to keep to it as rigorously as possible. As we have mentioned earlier, the picture story cards task was primarily designed to elicit narrative and role-play speech. We are limited to the social control speech offered in this context. In the event the picture story cards task proved an effective stimulus to social control speech, but clearly, as there were no questions in *this* task specifically designed to examine social control, there are definite limits to the depth of our inquiry into the children's social control concepts.

There is a further point to be borne in mind about the interview. The social control situation was very much a situation within a situation. It was not the case, for example, that the child was given the role of controller and was told to direct someone else present in the interview situation. Our data are much less immediate than this, and this can complicate the analysis a good deal, particularly the analysis of context-dependent and context-independent meanings. It should be remembered that Hawkins' (1969) study of reference in the picture story cards task—which showed impressive class differences in the use of context-dependent meanings, with the working-class children using more—was largely concerned with the interview situation, with the relationship between the interviewee and the interviewer, and not with the social control situation as such.

The second restriction on our inquiry is imposed by the content of the picture story cards task. The story, in its most obvious interpretation, is about the social institution of property. It is concerned with the rights of the property-owner, his right to take steps to protect his property and his right to demand redress if his property is damaged. Although personal control is possible (for example, if the intention of the transgressor is taken into account), it seems clear that positional control and imperative control are more likely to occur.

The third restriction is imposed by the age of the subjects. Earlier we described the influence of parental control on the orectic and cognitive development of the child. At that time we looked at the matter in one way only. It is important to bear in mind that there may be effects in the other direction. The orectic and cognitive development of the child may influence how he comprehends the control employed by others and which types of control he uses himself. The work of Piaget (1948), Kohlberg (1964) and others has indicated that there are *stages* in the development of moral judgment in the child. (To say this, of course, is not to say that environment is not important—see Cook's (1972) discussion). Thus, Piaget has noted 'intentionality in judgment' in young children. According to Piaget, young children tend to judge an act as bad mainly in terms of its physical consequences, rather than in terms of the intent to do harm. If this is the case, then it seems unlikely that the children in the present experiment will opt for that kind of personal control that takes into account the intention of the transgressor.

Method

Subjects

The Sociological Research Unit obtained speech samples from 439 children at age five and similar speech samples from 298 of these children at age seven; for a complete account of sampling procedures and the number of drop outs, the reader is referred to Cook (1972). The present inquiry was originally limited to the children's responses at age five; it was later extended to include their responses at age seven. The population of 439 children at age five was sub-sampled according to a factorial design, one with a two-way division on social class, sex and verbal intelligence test scores. This factorial sample, which we shall call Sample A, comprised 160 subjects, with 20 subjects per cell, shown diagrammatically as follows:

	MC[1]		WC	
	HIQ	MIQ	HIQ	MIQ
B	20	20	20	20
G	20	20	20	20

When the inquiry was extended to take account of the responses of the children at age seven, the same factorial design and the same subjects were used but there was a sample loss of 33 subjects. So the sample of children at age seven, which we shall call Sample B, comprised 127 subjects. The distribution of the subjects in the cells is shown below:

	MC		WC	
	HIQ	MIQ	HIQ	MIQ
B	17	14	16	16
G	16	15	16	17

The age comparisons reported in this chapter are confined to the 127 subjects for whom speech interviews were available at age five and at age seven. At age five these subjects are referred to as Sample A(i) to distinguish them from the full sample of 160 subjects.

At this point it is important to mention the language programme that was run in a group of schools in the working-class area (see Gahagan and Gahagan, 1970). This programme started in the children's second term at school (the spring term) and lasted for five terms. Seventeen children in our sample of seven-year-olds (Sample B) took part in this programme: 14 working-class (i.e. 22 per cent) and 3 middle-class (i.e. 5 per cent). The inclusion of these children in Sample B introduces some bias. Cook *et al.* (1970) compared the control styles of children who had taken part in the programme with those of a control group and found that the control styles of the programme children involved 'less coercive and more linguistically elaborated, more flexible approaches to the control of others'. The suggestion is that working-class children who had taken part in the programme moved towards a kind of control more typical of the middle class. We are justified in including the programme children on the grounds that the bias introduced would tend to work against our hypothesis, not for it.

Indices

Social class was measured in terms of the occupation and education of each parent, according to a procedure worked out by Brandis (1970). Briefly, occupational status was defined in terms of the Hall-Jones scale (with a range of 1–7 points) and educational status was measured in terms of a two-point scale (non-minimal education scoring 1 and minimal education scoring 2). The educational items were given three times the weight of occupational status and the summed scores were compressed into a ten-point scale, 0–9, such that 0–2 is 'totally MC', 3 is 'predominantly MC', . . .7 is 'predominantly WC' and 8–9 is 'totally WC'. The mean social class position of the middle-class group is 2·31 and that of the working-class group is 7·15.

The intelligence test score categories defined high as being at the 90th percentile or higher on the Crichton vocabulary scale and medium as 50th to 75th (the mean for the high group was 90·83 and the mean for the medium group 63·84). Sixteen children in the sample (10 per cent) deviated from this criterion but made appropriate scores on a second test: the English picture vocabulary test. The tests were administered to the children three weeks after they had started school.

Materials

The children were interviewed individually on two occasions: (*a*) early in their first term at school; and (*b*) late in their sixth term at school. On these occasions the children were asked to perform a number of different tasks and their responses were tape-recorded. The materials with which we are concerned formed part of the second task administered to the children, the picture story cards task.

The picture story cards task had three parts; in each part the interviewer laid down a set of four picture cards (in correct sequence), which together told a story. We are concerned with the first set of picture cards. The other two sets were less suitable for the kind of social control analysis we envisaged. Only one of these sets was used on both occasions, and this set depicted a story in which an animal (a fish) played a central role.

The instructions (used at age five) for administering the first set of picture story cards are given below. The actual cards are reproduced in chapter 4.

'Now we are going to play another game. I've got some pictures that tell a story. I'm going to show them to you and I want you to tell me the story: This one, and this one . . . and this one tell a story' (laying cards down fairly slowly, but not so slowly that the child interrupts).

'This is a story about some boys playing football. The boy breaks a window (point to card 2). The story starts here (point to card 1).' If the child stops after the first card, say: 'What happens next?' pointing to card 2. Repeat this for all cards if necessary. When the child has told his story:

Point to picture 3: 'What's the man saying?'
Point to picture 4: 'What about the lady?'
Probe: (if the child says 'I don't know')
'What do you think he *might* be saying?'

The instructions for administering the task to the children at age seven were slightly briefer; the introductory sentences 'This is a story about . . . window' were omitted.

Coding frame

The coding frame is essentially based on the Sociological Research Unit's 'Social control coding manual' (Bernstein and Cook, 1965), which is reproduced, with commentary, in Cook (1972). It differs from the earlier coding frame, however, in that a number of finer differentiations are made within categories such as 'threats' and 'commands'. It differs, too, in that, wherever possible, the categories pertaining to verbal behaviour are defined in formal linguistic terms, using a mode of description based on 'systemic grammar' (see, e.g. Halliday, 1967a, 1967b and 1968). Besides the grammatical definitions, it has been occasionally found useful to make reference to sections in Roget's *Thesaurus* to indicate the lexical items used.

We make a distinction between role-play speech and non-role-play speech. Role-play speech occurs when the child purports to quote or report the speech of the people in the story (e.g. The man said: '*You're very naughty*'; The man said *that they were very naughty*). Non-role-play speech occurs when the child is not giving the speech of the participants but is referring to them—perhaps mentioning their roles (e.g. The policeman comes along; Their father's come out), perhaps characterizing their affective state (e.g. A man was angry; Their mother was cross) or describing their actions, either verbal (e.g. A man told them off) or non-verbal (e.g. That man smacked him).

The coding frame has two main sections, A and B. The former is concerned with non-role-play speech; the latter with role-play speech: it gives a meaning potential for the verbal strategies of control used in this context. Theoretically, we could have constructed a behaviour potential to cover non-verbal as well as verbal strategies. However, an inspection of the data revealed that very few children made reference to non-verbal strategies, such as 'physical punishment', e.g. That man smacked him, and 'loss of privilege', e.g. They had to stay out of doors. We decided, therefore, to treat the non-verbal strategies briefly, and to concentrate on the verbal ones, attempting to construct a meaning potential for them.

Although we are not constructing a behaviour potential, it will, none the less, be useful to indicate how the main non-role-play speech categories may be related to socially significant behaviour patterns. We shall briefly consider three categories: reference to the affective state of the participants; reference to their non-verbal action; and reference to their verbal action. Concerning the first, Bernstein would relate statements about the affective state of the adult participant(s) such as 'Their mother was cross' to positional control, more specifically to the affective component of positional control (cf. I'm very cross with you; You've made me very angry). For Bernstein, punitive acts such as smacking the child or depriving him of some privilege are realizations of imperative control, for they allow the child very little discretion. Finally, references to punishment by verbal means such as 'A man told them off' suggest coercion and point to imperative control; the relationship here, however, would seem to be one of frequency; there are some children in the present experiment who categorize the speech event as 'telling off' and who then give positional strategies of control, rather than imperative strategies, in their role-play speech.

The coding frame now follows. For reasons of space, we have had to keep the information concerning the coding of the categories down to a minimum.

A. *NON-ROLE-PLAY SPEECH*

A1. *Authority figures*

Under this category were scored the authority roles that were ascribed to the adult participants in the story. Two types were recognized: (1) parental (e.g. Daddy/Their mummy was cross); (2) other (e.g. The policeman comes along). Parental authority figures were sub-divided into two further types: (*a*) father; (*b*) mother.

A2. *Affective state of the participants*

The ascription of affective states to the participants was associated with clauses selecting 'relational: attributive' in the transitivity system network (see Halliday, 1968). A distinction was made between (1) states ascribed to the adult participants and (2) those ascribed to the children. For the adults two types of involvement were distinguished: (*a*) anger (e.g. Mummy's cross with them; A man was angry); (*b*) any other (e.g. A people were sad; He was disappointed). For the children in the story only one type of involvement was necessary: fear (e.g. He's scared; They're frightened of the man).

A3. *The speech event*

'One good ethnographic technique for getting at speech events, as at other categories', writes Hymes (1962), 'is through words which name them.' The expression, *tell off* and *tick off*, used by subjects in the present experiment, suggest that the speech event was seen as one of 'punishment'.

A4. *The non-verbal action*

Two types of non-verbal actions were distinguished: (1) physical punishment (e.g. That man smacked him); (2) loss of privilege (e.g. They had to stay out of doors; The mother sent them all to bed).

B. *ROLE-PLAY SPEECH*

For typographical convenience, the meaning potential for the verbal strategies of control is presented in several sections. The first broad differentiations of meaning are given below; the finer differentiations are dealt with in sections B1–5. The notational conventions used are those of Halliday (1970a). A summary of them is given in the appendix.

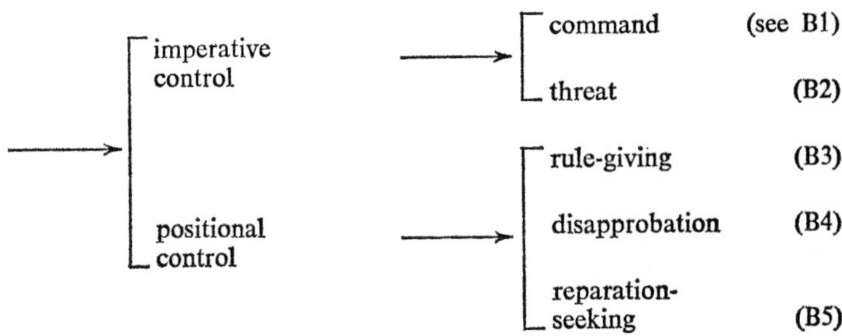

B1. *Command*

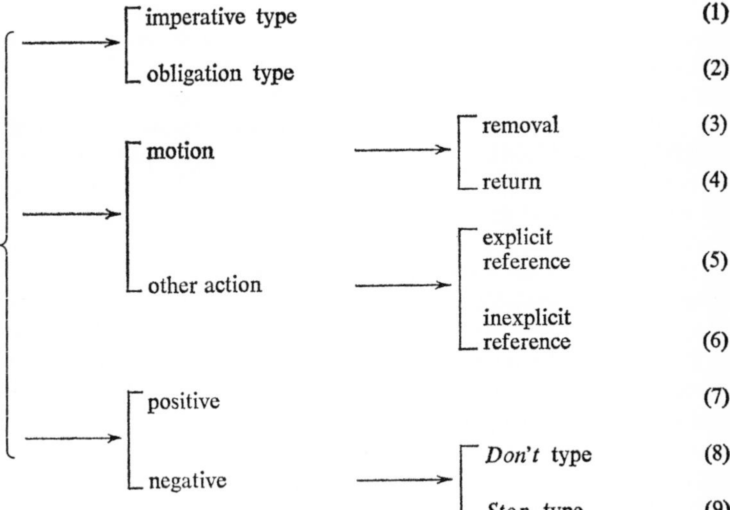

Examples

Go away. You go away. Get off. Get out of it. Get away from this house. (1,3,7)

You must go away. You'd better go away. (1,3,7)
Come here. You come here. Come back. (1,4,7)
Don't come back ever again. (1,4,8)
You're not to come back. (2,4,8)
Don't you knock my window again. (1,5,8)
Don't do it again. Don't do that again. (1,6,8)
You mustn't do it again. You must not do that. (2,6,8)
Stop bashing my window. (1,5,9)
Stop it. (1,6,9)

The figures following the examples indicate, by reference to the network, the options expressed.

Commentary

I. A distinction was made between (1) the imperative type, i.e. those realized by clauses selecting 'imperative: jussive: exclusive' in the mood system (e.g. Go away; Don't do it again) and (2) the obligation type, i.e. those realized by clauses selecting 'indicative: declarative' in the mood system and 'modulated: passive/neutral: necessity: compulsion' in the modulation system (e.g. You must go away; You must not do that). For mood and modulation, see Huddleston *et al.* (1968) and Halliday (1970b) respectively.

II. Commands were sub-divided into (1) those concerned with motion (e.g. Come here; Go away) and (2) those concerned with any other action (e.g. Don't knock my window again). Both types are associated with 'actional' clauses, the former being 'middle', i.e. one-participant clauses, and the latter tending to be 'non-middle', i.e. two-participant clauses (see Halliday, 1968). Type (1) commands were sub-divided into two further types: (*a*) those specifying removal from the controller or scene of transgression (e.g. Go away; Go, get out of my sight); (*b*) those specifying return to the controller or scene of transgression (e.g. You come here; Come back to me). Sub-types (*a*) have a verb from Roget §287 (Recession) or §293 (Departure) and usually an adverb or preposition of direction: 'from a place', *away, off, away from, out of*; whilst sub-types (*b*) have a verb from Roget §286 (Approach) or §292 (Arrival) and usually an adverb or preposition of direction: 'in the opposite direction, so as to return to starting point', *back, back to*, or an adverb of place: 'near to speaker', *here*. Type (2) commands were also sub-divided into two further types: (*a*) explicit (e.g. Don't you knock my window again); (*b*) inexplicit (Don't do it again). The inexplicit ones have the verb *do* and a pronoun, *it* or *that*, the reference of the pronoun being usually, in the most likely interpretation, exophoric, i.e. to the context of the situation.

III. Finally, commands were sub-divided into (1) positive and (2) negative. Two sub-types of negative were recognized: (*a*) the *don't* type; (*b*) the *stop* type. In the former type negation is realized grammatically—in the verbal group (e.g. Don't crash my window in; You mustn't do it again) and/or in the adverbial group (e.g. Don't do that no more; Never do it again); in the latter type it is realized lexically by means of *stop* (e.g. Stop bashing my window).

B2. *Threat*

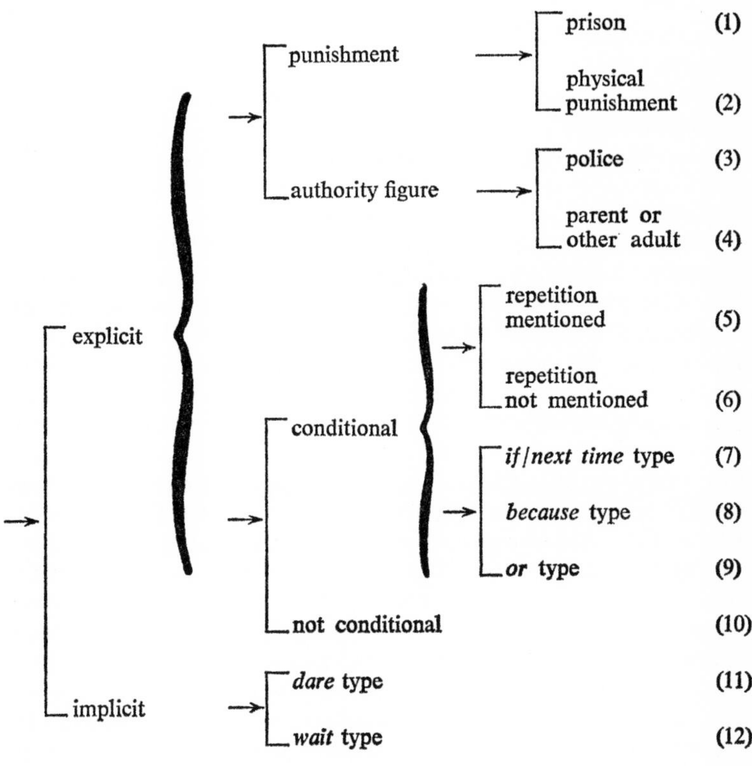

Examples

I'll get you in prison. (1,10)
I'm going to give you a smack. (2,10)
I'll tell the police. (3,10)
I'm going to tell your mum. I'll tell the lady. (4,10)
If you do that once more, I'll punch you. Next time you come round here, I'm going to spank you. (2,5,7)

If you do that once more, I'm going to tell the police. (3,5,7)
If you do that again, I'll go and tell your mum. (4,5,7)
If you don't go, I'll call the police. (3,6,7)
Don't do it again 'cos you'll go in prison. (1,5,8)
Don't come back because I'd give you a spank. (2,5,8)
Never do that again or you'll get smacked. (2,5,9)
Go on, go on or I'll get a stick and whack you. (2,6,9)
You come back or I'll tell a policeman. (3,6,9)
You pay for this, boys, or I take you to the police. (3,6,9)
You mustn't do that or else he'll go and tell their mother. (4,6,9)
You dare play football here again. You dare do this again. (11)
Don't you dare break that window again. Don't you dare do that again. (11)
You wait. Just wait. Wait until you come back. (12)

Commentary

I. That which is threatened may be (1) explicit (e.g. I'll get you in prison; I'm going to give you a smack) or (2) inexplicit (e.g. You dare play football here again; You wait). The explicit threats are realized by clauses selecting 'indicative: declarative' in the mood system and the inexplicit ones by clauses selecting 'imperative: jussive: exclusive'. A characteristic of the explicit threats is that they are almost always associated with the selection of future tense, either simple 'future' (e.g. I'll call the police) or 'future in present' (e.g. I'm going to spank you). For an example without future tense, note 'You pay for this, boys, or I take you to the police.'

I.1.1. Two types of explicit threat were recognized: (1) those referring to punishment (e.g. I'll punch you; You'll go in prison); (2) those involving an authority figure (e.g. I'm going to tell the police; I'll go and tell your mum). Threats of abandonment, loss of privilege and withdrawal of love were not mentioned by the children. To a large extent, the punishment threats and the authority figure threats may be distinguished in terms of their transitivity selections, the former being associated with 'actional' clauses and the latter with 'mental process: verbalization' clauses (see Halliday, 1968). However, not all authority figure threats are associated with 'mental process' clauses; clauses such as 'I'll call the police', 'I'm going to report you to the police', for example, are probably best regarded as 'actional' clauses concerned with 'verbal action'. As a rough guide, we may add that type (1) threats have a verb from Roget §972 (Punishment), or the inter-section of §972 and §276 (Impulse) (e.g. I'll punch you), or §784 (Giving) (e.g. I'd give you a spank); whereas type (2) threats usually have a verb from §527 (Information). Two sub-types of punishment threat were distinguished. (*a*) those mentioning prison (e.g. I'll get you in prison; you'll go in prison); (*b*) those involving physical punishment (e.g. I'm going to spank you; I'll get a stick and whack you). Somewhat similarly, two sub-types of authority figure threat were recognized: (*a*) those mentioning the police (e.g. I'll tell the police); (*b*) those mentioning a parent or other adult (e.g. I'm going to tell your mum; I'll tell the lady).

I.1.2. Threats that are explicit may be (1) accompanied by a condition (e.g. If you do that again, I'll go and tell your mum; Never do that again or you'll get smacked), or (2) not accompanied by a condition (e.g. I'm going to tell your mum). The conditions may (*a*) make reference to repetition (e.g. If you do that once more . . .) or (*b*) not make such reference (e.g. Go on, go on . . . ; You pay for this . . .). The reference to repetition is usually made by an aspectual adverb (*again, never . . . again, once more, no more*) but the binder *next time* may be used (e.g. Next time you come round here . . .). We also decided to regard *don't come back* (because I'd give you a spank) as making reference to repetition.

Threats that are accompanied by a condition are associated with clause complexes of both the hypotactic and paratactic types. The *if/next time* type and the *because* type, recognized in the semantic network, are associated with hypotaxis (subordination) whereas the *or* type is associated with parataxis (co-ordination). For definitions of the terms 'hypotaxis' and 'parataxis', see Halliday (1965). There is an important difference between the *if/next time* type and the *because* type. In the case of the *if/next time* type the condition is given in the dependent (hypotactic) clause (e.g. If you do that again . . . ; Next time you come round here . . .), whereas in the case of the *because* type it is given in the independent clause (e.g. Don't do it again 'cos you'll go in prison). In this respect the *because* type is similar to the *or* type (cf. Never do that again or you'll get smacked). In the present context the independent clauses that the *because* clauses and *or* clauses are related to may realize either a command (e.g. Don't come back . . . ; You mustn't do that . . .) or a demand for reparation (e.g. You pay for this . . .). The choice available could be represented as below:

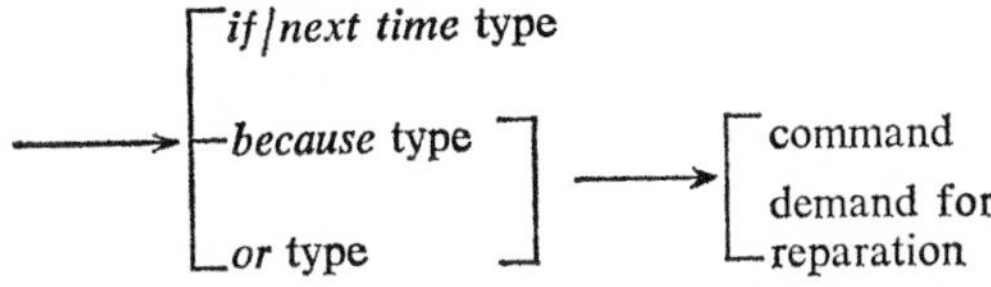

The question arises: in our counts of clauses such as 'Don't do it again', should we make a distinction between those clauses that occurred by themselves and those that occurred accompanied by a threat? In other words, is the social meaning of such a clause the same, irrespective of whether it is accompanied by a threat or not? It is Bernstein's view that there is a difference in meaning—that an accompanying threat does colour one's interpretation of the command or demand for reparation—and that therefore separate counts should be made. This viewpoint is adopted here.

The above question about how we treat commands or demands for reparation that are accompanied by a threat is, of course, an aspect of a wider question that might be raised: how do we allow for the possibility that the speaker might select the same option more than once, e.g. Go away (command) and don't come back again (command), or select several different options, e.g. Don't come back again (command). If you come back, I'll smack you (threat), in the course of giving the role-play speech? These possibilities are in principle handled by the fact that one can go through the network more than once. This capability could be formally represented in the network by introducing an option with the terms 'stop'/'go'. Had more children offered extended stretches of role-play speech, we would have included this option in the network.

I.2. Two types of inexplicit threats may be distinguished: (1) the *dare* type (e.g. You dare do this again; Don't you dare do that again); (2) the *wait* type (e.g. You wait; Wait until you come back). Both types are associated with clauses selecting 'imperative: jussive: exclusive', the former with *dare*, the latter with *wait*.

B3. *Rule-giving*

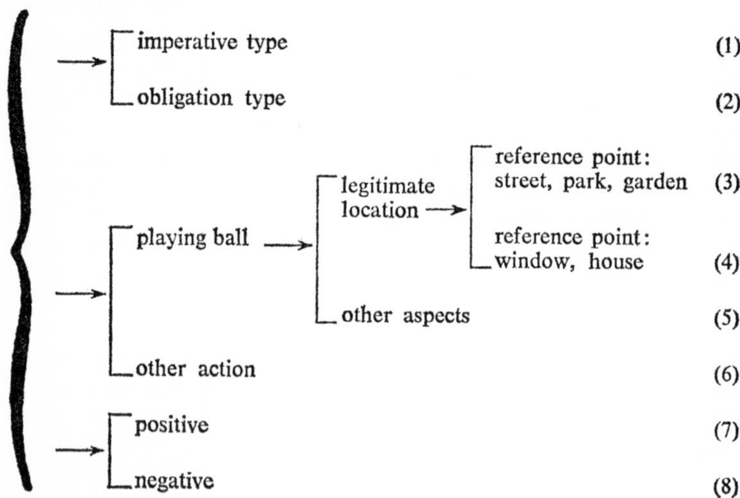

Examples

Always go in the park to play football (in case you do some more damage).	(1,3,7)
Play football in your own garden.	(1,3,7)
You should go over the park to play football.	(2,3,7)
He should keep it on the ground (not in the air).	(2,5,7)
Don't play football out in the street.	(1,3,8)
You shouldn't have played football in the street.	(2,3,8)
Now you've not to kick balls out in the road; (it's dangerous; you'll get run over by someone else).	(2,3,8)
Don't play football near our house again.	(1,4,8)
You shouldn't play right in front of the window.	(2,4,8)
You mustn't play ball outside our window.	(2,4,8)
You mustn't smash windows.	(2,6,8)

Commentary

I. As in the case of commands, a distinction was made between (1) the imperative type (e.g. Always go in the park to play football) and (2) the obligation type (e.g. You shouldn't have played football in the street; You mustn't play ball outside our window). It is noticeable that *should* is quite frequently used with rules, but not with commands.

II. A distinction was made between (1) rules pertaining to playing ball (e.g. You should go over the park to play football) and (2) those referring to other actions (e.g. You mustn't smash windows). Type (1) rules were sub-divided into (*a*) those referring to the legitimacy of the location (e.g. Play football in your own garden; Don't play football near our house again) and (*b*) those concerned with other aspects (e.g. He should keep it on the ground, not in the air; Somebody told him not to put the ball up on the wall). Finally, sub-type (*a*) were further sub-divided according to the reference point mentioned: (i) street, park, garden; (ii) house, window. The basic distinction is between rules that forbid (either directly or by implication) playing football in the street (sub-type (i)) and those that do not forbid playing football in the street as such (sub-type (ii)). Examples of sub-type (i) are: You shouldn't have played football in the street; Always go to the park to play football; examples of sub-type (ii) are: You shouldn't play right in front of the window; Don't play football near our house again. The various sub-types of type (1) rules seem best distinguished in terms of the prepositional groups used; for example, sub-type (i) is associated with a prepositional group of place: 'within the limits of' (in the street, in your own garden, in the park) whereas sub-type (ii) is associated with a prepositional group of place: 'in a position close to' (near our house, in front of the window, outside our window).

III. Rules were sub-divided into (1) positive, i.e. those stating what one is obliged or required to do (e.g. Always go in the park to play football) and (2) negative, i.e. those stating what one is prohibited from doing (e.g. Don't play football out in the street). It is perhaps worth stressing that this difference is not just a matter of inserting a *not* or *n't*. Positive and negative rules concerned with, say, the legitimate location for playing football, do not fall into pairs representing exact opposites. It is not a matter of saying 'You have to x' *v.* 'You haven't to do x', but rather a matter of saying 'You have to do x' *v.* 'You have to not do y'. Thus, in the case of rules concerned with the legitimate location for playing football, the location mentioned will vary according to whether the rule is positive or negative. If a negative rule is given, it is arguable that a positive rule is also needed to make explicit what is required (e.g. You shouldn't be playing football in the street. You should go over the park to play football).

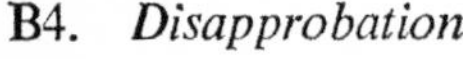

B4. *Disapprobation*

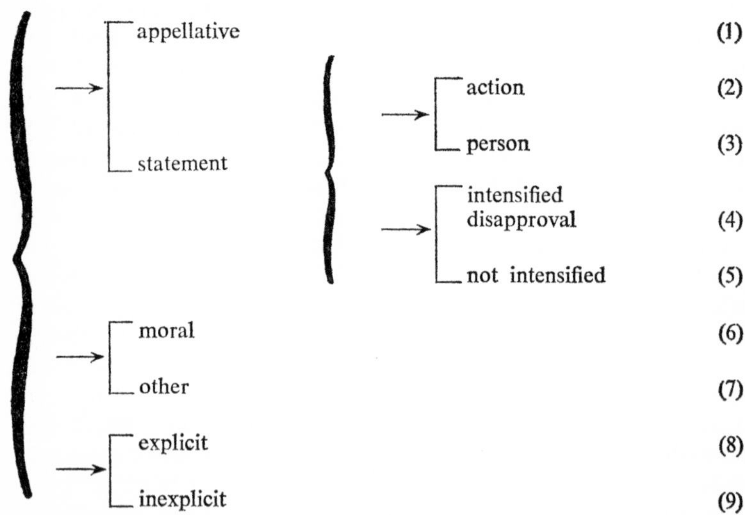

Examples

Naughty boys. You naughty boys. You bad boy.	(1,6,9)
You silly idiots. You horrible things.	(1,7,9)
You bad boys for smashing the window.	(1,6,8)
It was naughty.	(2,5,6,9)
It's very naughty smashing my window.	(2,4,6,8)
You're naughty boys.	(3,5,6,9)
You're a very, very, very naughty boy.	(3,4,6,9)
You're very naughty to play football in the street.	(3,4,6,8)
You're very, very naughty children to break that window.	(3,4,6,8)

Commentary

I. Expressions of disapprobation were sub-divided into two types: (1) appellative (e.g. Naughty boys; You silly idiots); (2) statement (e.g. You're naughty boys). The appellative is usually realized by a 'moodless' clause with a vocative element, whereas the statement type is realized by an 'indicative: declarative' clause. Both types are associated with attribution but there is a difference. Type (1) is associated with attribution at group rank, whereas type (2) is associated with attribution at clause rank, 'relational: attributive' being selected in the transitivity system. The statement type has two sets of choices open to it which are not available to appellative type. The controller may disapprove of (*a*) the action (e.g. It was naughty) or (*b*) the person (e.g. You're naughty boys). In the case of disapproval of the action the attribuend is usually *it* or *that* whereas in the case of the person the attribuend is *you* in direct speech, *he* or *they* in indirect speech. Further, the controller may express (*a*) intensified disapproval (e.g. You're a very, very, very naughty boy) or (*b*) disapproval that is not intensified (e.g. You're naughty boys). Intensification, as defined here, is associated with the use of the sub-modifier *very*.

II. Two types of disapprobation were distinguished: (1) moral (e.g. Naughty boys; You bad boy); (2) other (e.g. You silly idiots; You horrible things). The first type has an adjective from Roget §945 (Vice), whilst the second type has one from §499 (Imbecility, Folly) or §830 (Painfulness).

III. Finally, expressions of disapprobation were differentiated according to whether they (1) contained an explicit reference to the transgression (e.g. You bad boys for smashing the window; It's very naughty smashing my window; You're very naughty to play football in the street) or (2) did not contain such a reference (e.g. You bad boy; It was naughty; You're naughty boys). As the examples illustrate, there are several ways in which the speaker may make explicit reference to the transgression.

B5. *Reparation-seeking*

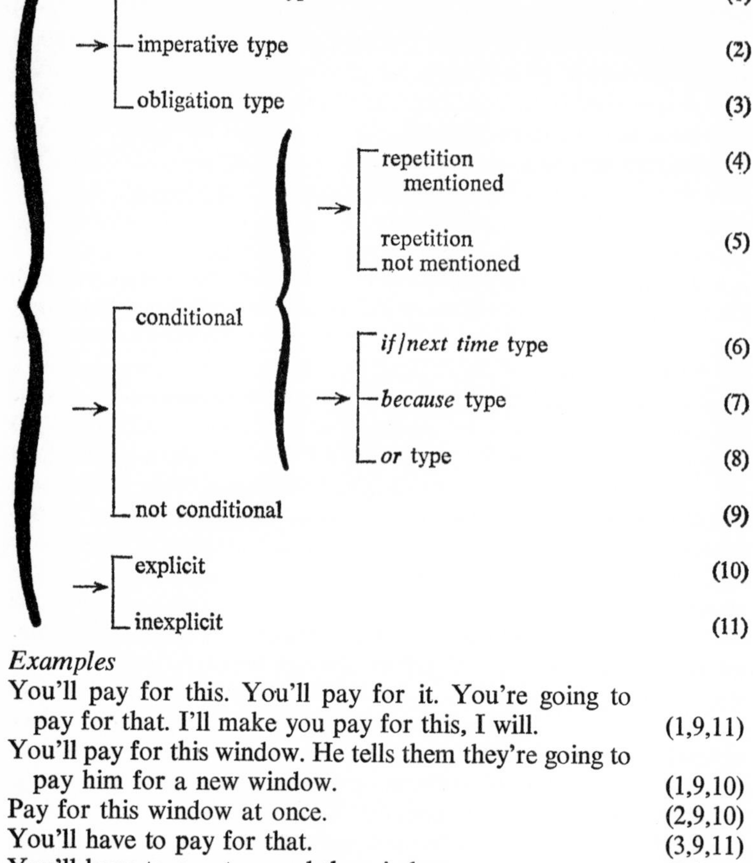

Examples

You'll pay for this. You'll pay for it. You're going to pay for that. I'll make you pay for this, I will.	(1,9,11)
You'll pay for this window. He tells them they're going to pay him for a new window.	(1,9,10)
Pay for this window at once.	(2,9,10)
You'll have to pay for that.	(3,9,11)
You'll have to pay to mend the window.	(3,9,10)
You've got to pay for this window mended.	(3,9,10)
You can buy another pane of glass.	(3,9,10)
If you do that again, you can pay for my window.	(3,4,6,10)
Don't come back 'cos you have to pay for it.	(3,4,7,11)

Commentary

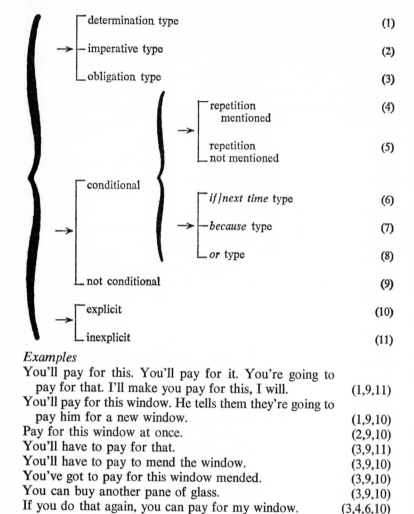

I. Three types of reparation-seeking were recognized: (1) the determination type (e.g. You'll pay for this window; You're going to pay for that); (2) the imperative type (e.g. Pay for this window at once); and (3) the obligation type (e.g. You've got to pay for this window mended). As the names suggest, the distinction between type (2) and type (3) is comparable to the distinction recognized in the case of commands and rules. Notice, however, that the type (3) forms are *you'll have to . . .* , *you've got to . . .* , *you'd better . . .* , *you can . . .* , not *you must . . .* , *you should . . .* From a grammatical point of view type (1) demands for reparation are similar to certain type (1) threats (cf. You'll pay for this window; You'll get smacked; You'll go in prison). To a large extent, the two types may be distinguished in terms of their lexis, the demands for reparation being concerned with payment, the threats being concerned with punishment. A number of utterances, such as 'You'll pay for it', 'You'll pay for this', are ambiguous. It is thought that these utterances in their more likely interpretation are demands for reparation; nevertheless, we have taken the precaution of presenting two sets of figures, one in which they are treated as threats and one in which they are regarded as demands for reparation.

II. Like the threats, the demands for reparation may be (1) conditional (e.g. If you do that again, you can pay for my window; You're going to pay for this next time I see you; Don't come back 'cos you have to pay for it) or (2) not conditional (e.g. You'll pay for this window). Several sub-types of conditional demands for reparation were distinguished, using the same classificatory scheme as was used in the case of the conditional threats. We need not duplicate the details here.

III. Finally, a distinction was made between (1) demands for reparation that are explicit, i.e. those that make reference to the window (e.g. He tells them they're going to pay him for a new window; You'll have to mend the window) and (2) those that are inexplicit (e.g. You'll pay for it; You're going to pay for that). The inexplicit ones have a pronoun, *it*, *this* or *that*, the reference of which is, in the most likely interpretation, exophoric.

B6. *Explanation*

Commands, threats and rules may be (1) accompanied by an explanation (e.g. Get out, mate, because you broke my window; I'll get you 'cos you've broken our glass; Now you're not to kick balls out in the road—it's dangerous—you'll get run over by someone else; . . . he's not to play with the ball on the street so that he doesn't kick the window), or (2) not accompanied by an explanation. In most cases the explanation is given either in a dependent clause of 'reason' or in an independent clause standing in a similar semantic relationship to a previous clause. To the extent that the explanation often takes the form of an explicit reference to the transgression (e.g. I'll get you 'cos you've broken our glass), this category has a good deal in common with the explicit reference category recognized in the analysis of expressions of disapprobation (e.g. You're very, very naughty to break that window). The explanation category, however, has a broader scope, as may be shown by the following examples: Always go in the park to play football in case you do some more damage; Don't get near the windows again 'cos you will smash them; Get away from here—you might break my window; You get out from my room because this is my own house; Go away—I don't want you round here. An important form of explanation, illustrated by the first three examples above, is one which points to the future and warns of the possible consequences of future behaviour. Note that the children may offer explanatory speech other than in the course of giving role-play speech. Examples are: He's all cross 'cos it's his house; She's shouting at them because they've broken her glass and she doesn't want it broken; A man shakes his fist 'cos he's very angry; The boys run away because they're frightened of the man. Such instances were counted separately.

B7. *Questions*

A small number of children gave questions which seemed predominantly regulative in function (e.g. Why don't you go round your own places?; Why don't you play with your ball in the park?; Why don't you pay for it?). We could have included an extra category in the sub-classification of commands, rule-giving and reparation-seeking in the network to cover such utterances. However, as these utterances occurred extremely rarely, we decided not to complicate the network further on their account. The other questions that occurred may be sub-classified on a number of dimensions.

I. A distinction was made between (1) questions that imply some knowledge of the transgression (e.g. Who broke my window?; What have you done to my window?) and (2) questions that do not imply any direct knowledge of transgression—such questions being usually ascribed to the female onlooker in the story (e.g. Where have those boys been?; What are you running for?; What's wrong with you boys?). The first of the two types is clearly the more relevant from the point of view of our inquiry.

II. A broad distinction was made between (1) questions concerned with identification (e.g. Who's bust this window?; Which one of you had done this?) and (2) questions concerned with explanation, mainly the *why, what . . . for* questions (e.g. Why did you kick that ball through my window?; What did you do that for?). It is possible to sub-classify the identification questions in two ways: according to the type of specification; and according to the type of orientation. A variety of types of specification may be recognized: (*a*) person (e.g. Who done it?; Did you do that?); (*b*) action (e.g. What have you done to my window?; What are you doing to my house?); (*c*) object (e.g. What have you broken the window with?); and so on. Concerning the orientation, questions may be (*a*) information-oriented (e.g. Who broke my window?) or (*b*) confirmation-oriented (e.g. Did you do that?), the former questions being associated with Wh- clauses, the latter with polar or Yes/No clauses (see Huddleston *et al.*, 1968).

Hypotheses

The following predictions were made. They are based on Bernstein's theoretical work and on the empirical work of Cook (1972) and others.

Concerning the non-role-play speech, it was predicted that the middle-class children would tend to focus on the affective state of the controller, ascribing feelings of anger to him, whereas the working-class children would focus on the event, categorizing it in terms of verbal punishment. This prediction is based on Bernstein's association of expressions such as 'Their mother is cross' with positional control, more specifically with the affective component of positional control, and on his association of expressions such as 'A man told them off' with imperative control.

Concerning the role-play speech, in view of the severe situational constraints, it was expected that the children, irrespective of their social class, would tend to make selections from both the imperative mode and the positional mode of control. In broad terms, it was predicted that more working-class children would use the imperative options, commands and threats, and also reparation-seeking, whereas more middle-class children would mention disapprobation and rule-giving. However, because of the situational constraints it was thought that certain sub-divisions within these general categories would prove to be important. Two types of more specific prediction were made. One, it was predicted that the working-class children would tend to choose the forceful options (imperative type rather than obligation type in the case of commands and reparation-seeking, appellative rather than statement in the case of disapprobation), whereas the middle-class children would choose the less forceful, potentially more reflective options. Two, it was predicted that the working-class children would tend to be less explicit than the middle-class children in their reference to the transgression, choosing the options we have labelled inexplicit rather than the explicit ones.

Treatment of results

For the children's responses at age five and at age seven a three-way comparison was made wherever possible, contrasting social class, verbal intelligence test scores and sex. The basic strategy was to compare with χ^2 tests the relative proportions of children in the opposed groups who used a particular option.

For the age comparisons McNemar's test for the significance of changes was used.

For a small number of summed scores it was possible to do a correlational analysis.

To reduce the number of individual results reported, comparisons yielding no significant differences are either ignored or only mentioned briefly.

Results

A1. *Authority figures*

TABLE 7.1 *Authority figures*

	B	%	*G*	%	χ^2	*p*
Parental (Sample A)	15	(19)	27	(34)	3·91	$< 0{\cdot}05$
Parental (Sample B)	16	(25)	16	(25)		
Parental: mother only (A)	10	(13)	23	(29)	5·47	$< 0{\cdot}02$
Parental: mother only (B)	14	(22)	14	(22)		
Non-parental (Ai & B)						

		At age seven −	At age seven +	χ^2	*p*
At age five	+	16	1		
	−	108	2	9·39	$< 0{\cdot}01$

At age five 26 per cent of the children ascribed a parental role to at least one adult participant in the story, and similarly at age seven 25 per cent of the children did so. At the earlier age there is a sex difference: significantly more girls (34 per cent) than boys (19 per cent) ascribed this role, $\chi^2 = 3{\cdot}91$, $p < 0{\cdot}05$. A sharper sex difference is apparent if the parental role is differentiated into 'father' and 'mother': 29 per cent of the girls ascribed the role 'mother' to the female participant whereas 13 per cent of the boys did so, $\chi^2 = 5{\cdot}47$, $p < 0{\cdot}02$. At the later age there is no sex difference, the ascription of parental roles being made by boys and girls in equal proportion.

Authority figures other than parental were mentioned with reference to the male participant only. For most children who made such reference he was 'a/the policeman' or 'the police'; for just two children he was 'the headmaster' and 'the soldier' respectively. More children referred to these figures at age five than at age seven. This change in the children is significant, $\chi^2 = 9{\cdot}39$, $p < 0{\cdot}01$ (McNemar).

A2. *The affective state of the participants*

TABLE 7.2 *Anger*

	MC	%	*WC*	%	χ^2	*p*
Adult: anger (A)	16	(20)	2	(3)	10·58	< 0·01
Adult: anger (B)	17	(27)	3	(5)	10·78	< 0·01
Adult: intensified anger (A)	6	(8)	0	(0)	4·33	< 0·05
Adult: intensified anger (B)	10	(16)	2	(3)	4·88	< 0·05

At age five 14 per cent of the children made some reference to the feelings of the participants in the story: 12 per cent referred to the adults; just 2 per cent referred to the children, e.g. They're frightened of the man. Similarly, at age seven 17 per cent of the children made reference to the affective states of the participants, and again just 2 per cent referred to the feelings of the children.

At five years the affective state ascribed to the adult participants was—with two exceptions only—one of 'anger'. Significantly more middle-class children (20 per cent) than working-class children (3 per cent) made this ascription, $\chi^2 = 10{\cdot}58$, $p < 0{\cdot}01$. Two middle-class children who did not mention 'anger' gave the following: He was disappointed; A people were sad. Again, at seven years the state ascribed was one of 'anger'—this time without exception. The social class difference at this age is very similar to the one at the earlier age: 27 per cent of the middle-class children and 5 per cent of the working class made the ascription, $\chi^2 = 10{\cdot}78$, $p < 0{\cdot}01$.

At both ages 'anger' was associated almost exclusively with expressions with *cross*, with just a few instances of *angry* and *annoyed*.

At both ages significantly more middle-class children intensified the anger, e.g. The father's very, very, very cross; A man shakes his fist 'cos he's very angry. 8 per cent of the middle-class children *v.* 0 per cent of the working class at age five, $\chi^2 = 4{\cdot}33$, $p < 0{\cdot}05$; and 16 per cent of the middle class *v.* 3 per cent of the working class at age seven, $\chi^2 = 4{\cdot}88$, $p < 0{\cdot}05$.

A3. *The speech event*

TABLE 7.3 *Verbal punishment*

	MC	%	*WC*	%	χ^2	*p*
Verbal punishment (A)	10	(13)	22	(28)	4·73	< 0·05
Verbal punishment (B)	15	(24)	27	(42)	3·57	< 0·1
Verbal punishment (Ai & B)						

		At age seven −	At age seven +	χ^2	*p*
At age five	+	13	13	6·88	< 0·01
	−	55	29		

Significantly more working-class children (28 per cent) than middle-class children (13 per cent), at five years, categorized the speech of one or both of the adult participants in terms of verbal punishment, $\chi^2 = 4{\cdot}73$, $p < 0{\cdot}05$. There is also a trend difference in the same direction at age seven, $\chi^2 = 3{\cdot}57$, $p < 0{\cdot}1$.

Irrespective of social class, more children mentioned verbal punishment at age seven than at age five, the change being significant, $\chi^2 = 6{\cdot}88$, $p < 0{\cdot}01$ (McNemar).

A4. *The non-verbal action*

Very few children at either age made reference to physical punishment or loss of privilege. The former was mentioned by 1 WC and 5 MC children at age five and 2 WC and 2 MC at age seven, whilst the latter was referred to by 3 WC and 3 MC at age five and 5 WC and 2 MC at age seven.

B1. *Commands*

Commands were mentioned by 53 per cent of the children at age five and by 41 per cent of them at age seven. There are no social class differences apparent in the use of commands at either age when the commands are undifferentiated. There are, however, verbal ability differences. At both ages significantly more medium-ability children than high-ability children used commands: 63 per cent *v.* 43 per cent at age five, $\chi^2 = 5{\cdot}64$, $p < 0{\cdot}02$; 53 per cent *v.* 28 per cent at age seven, $\chi^2 = 7{\cdot}58$, $p < 0{\cdot}01$.

It is of interest to note that the verbal ability difference at age five is much stronger in the middle-class group than in the working-class group—relatively few middle-class children of high verbal ability used commands. Thus, in the middle-class group 30 per cent of the high-ability children mentioned commands, whilst 63 per cent of the medium-ability children did so, $\chi^2 = 7{\cdot}24$, $p < 0{\cdot}01$; the comparable figures for the working-class group are: 55 per cent of the high-ability children *v.* 63 per cent of the medium-ability children. By contrast, at age seven the two social groups are closely alike in the patterning of the verbal ability differences.

When the commands are differentiated into two main types, the imperative and the obligation types, the relevance of social class (as well as verbal ability) becomes more apparent. Verbal ability is related to the use of the imperative type of command

TABLE 7.4 *Commands*

		HIQ	%	*MIQ*	%	χ^2	*p*
Commands	(A)	34	(43)	50	(63)	5·64	< 0·02
Commands	(B)	18	(28)	33	(53)	7·58	< 0·01
Imperative type	(A)	31	(39)	48	(60)	6·40	< 0·02
Imperative type	(B)	14	(22)	30	(48)	8·95	< 0·01
		MC	%	*WC*	%	χ^2	*p*
Imperative type	(A)	32	(40)	47	(59)	4·90	< 0·05
Imperative type	(B)	20	(32)	24	(37)		
Obligation type	(A)	5	(6)	1	(1)		
Obligation type	(B)	9	(15)	2	(3)	3·90	< 0·05
Imperative type: removal	(A)	15	(19)	32	(40)	7·71	< 0·01
Imperative type: removal	(B)	12	(19)	10	(15)		

Imperative type: removal (Ai & B—WC only)

		At age seven −	At age seven +	χ^2	*p*
At age five	+	23	3	7·50	< 0·01
At age five	−	32	7		

(the much more frequently used type): at both ages significantly more medium-ability children used this type of command: 60 per cent *v.* 39 per cent at age five, $\chi^2 = 6{\cdot}40$, $p < 0{\cdot}02$; 48 per cent *v.* 22 per cent at age seven, $\chi^2 = 8{\cdot}95$, $p < 0{\cdot}01$. Verbal ability, however, is not related to the use of the obligation type of command. By contrast, social class is related to the use of both types. At age five significantly more working-class children (59 per cent) than middle-class children (40 per cent) used commands of the imperative type, $\chi^2 = 4{\cdot}90$, $p < 0{\cdot}05$. And at age seven significantly more middle-class children (15 per cent) than working-class children (3 per cent) used commands of the obligation type, $\chi^2 = 3{\cdot}90$, $p < 0{\cdot}05$. As these results clearly reveal, it is not just the social class of the child that is important here, but also the age of the child. It is possible for us to look at an aspect of this relationship between social class and age in more detail, if we further subclassify the commands.

At the earlier age many of the imperative commands mentioned were positive and concerned with motion, with telling the children to go away (very common) or come back (considerably less common). Significantly more five-year-old working-class children (40 per cent) than middle-class children (19 per cent) gave imperative commands concerned with removal, $\chi^2 = 7{\cdot}71$, $p < 0{\cdot}01$. (It is interesting to note that there is no significant verbal ability difference on this measure, the relevant figures being: 35 per cent of the medium-ability children *v.* 24 per cent of the high-ability children.) At age seven, however, there is a clear reduction in the proportion of working-class children using commands specifying removal; at this later age the proportion of working-class children using such commands is roughly similar to the proportion of middle-class children using them: 15 per cent and 19 per cent respectively. The change in the working-class children is significant, $\chi^2 = 7{\cdot}50$, $p < 0{\cdot}01$ (McNemar).

B2. *Threats*

TABLE 7.5 *Threats*

		MC	%	*WC*	%	χ^2	p
Threats	(A)	10	(13)	17	(21)		
Threats	(B)	8	(13)	22	(34)	6·60	< 0·02
Threats: conditional	(A)	0	(0)	8	(10)	6·45	< 0·02
Threats: conditional:	(B)	3	(5)	9	(14)		

At age five no group differences emerged for the use of threats when the threats were undifferentiated, but at age seven there is a social class difference: 34 per cent of the working-class children gave threats as opposed to 13 per cent of the middle-class children, $\chi^2 = 6{\cdot}60$, $p < 0{\cdot}02$. At age five a significant difference emerged from the sub-classification of threats: 10 per cent of the working-class children used conditional threats, whereas no middle-class children gave such threats, $\chi^2 = 6{\cdot}45$, $p < 0{\cdot}02$. At the later age 14 per cent of the working-class children used conditional threats as compared with 5 per cent of the middle class; this difference is not significant, but clearly the direction of the difference is the same as that at age five.

The figures given above do not include the children who gave ambiguous utterances such as 'You'll pay for it'. It is thought that, in the present context, these utterances are more likely to be demands for reparation than threats (cf. You'll pay for this window). Nevertheless, it behoves us to present two sets of figures. If we treat these utterances as threats, the figures for the seven-year-old children are as follows: 10 middle-class children (16 per cent) *v.* 27 working-class children (42 per cent), $\chi^2 = 8{\cdot}73$, $p < 0{\cdot}01$. It seems desirable that future work should make use of intonational clues in order to resolve this type of ambiguity.

B3. *Rule-giving*

Relatively few children mentioned rules. Almost all the rules mentioned were concerned with playing football, either referring to *where* it may be played or specifying *how* it may be played appropriately in the given situation. At age five 3 per cent of the sample gave such rules (1 MC *v.* 3 WC), and at age seven 13 per cent of the sample did so (11 MC *v.* 5 WC). If we focus on the rules concerned with the legitimacy of the location, it is possible to discriminate between the social groups at age seven: no working-class children gave rules forbidding playing football in the street whereas eight middle-class children (13 per cent) did, $\chi^2 = 6{\cdot}90$, $p < 0{\cdot}01$. We may add that three further middle-class children gave questions which seemed to imply the above rule: 'Why are you playing football out in the road?', 'Why don't you play with your ball in the park?', and 'Isn't he being a bit naughty by doing it in the street?' If we include these three children, the social class difference is sharpened: 18 per cent of the middle-class children *v.* no working-class children, $\chi^2 = 10{\cdot}48$, $p < 0{\cdot}01$.

B4. *Disapprobation*

TABLE 7.6 *Disapprobation*

		MC	%	*WC*	%	χ^2	p
Disapprobation	(A)	31	(39)	9	(11)	14·70	< 0·001
Disapprobation	(B)	30	(48)	23	(35)		
Disapp.: appellative	(A)	17	(21)	4	(5)	7·89	< 0·01
Disapp.: appellative	(B)	16	(26)	20	(31)		
Disapp.: statement	(A)	17	(21)	6	(8)	5·08	< 0·05
Dissap.: statement	(B)	16	(26)	4	(6)	7·82	< 0·01
Intensified disapp.	(A)	7	(9)	0	(0)	5·38	< 0·05
Intensified disapp.	(B)	10	(16)	2	(3)	4·88	< 0·05

Disapprobation (Ai & B—WC only)

		At age seven −	At age seven +	χ^2	p
At age five	+	2	4	15·43	< 0·001
	−	40	19		

At age five 25 per cent of the subjects used expressions of disapprobation, characterizing the children (or much more rarely their behaviour) mainly in terms of moral disapproval. At age seven 42 per cent of the subjects used such expressions. There is a highly significant social class difference at age five: 39 per cent of the middle-class children used expressions of disapprobation as compared with 11 per cent of the working-class children, $\chi^2 = 14{\cdot}70$, $p < 0{\cdot}001$. There is also a verbal ability difference: 33 per cent of the high-ability children *v.* 18 per cent of the medium-ability children, $\chi^2 = 4{\cdot}03$, $p < 0{\cdot}05$. By contrast, there is no social class (or verbal ability) difference at age seven when these expressions are undifferentiated: 48 per cent of the middle-class children used them as compared with 35 per cent of the working-class children. There is, then, a large increase in the proportion of working-class children using these expressions at the later age: this change in the working-class children is significant, $\chi^2 = 15{\cdot}43$, $p < 0{\cdot}001$ (McNemar).

If we sub-divide the expressions of disapprobation into two types, the appellative and the statement types, it is possible to do two things: (1) to discriminate between the social class groups at both ages; and (2) to show which expressions are favoured by the working-class seven-year-olds. At both ages significantly more middle-class children used the statement type: 21 per cent *v.* 8 per cent at age five, $\chi^2 = 5{\cdot}08$, $p < 0{\cdot}05$, and 26 per cent *v.* 6 per cent at age seven, $\chi^2 = 7{\cdot}82$, $p < 0{\cdot}01$. At age five the middle-class children also made more use of the appellative type, 21 per cent *v.* 5 per cent, $\chi^2 = 7{\cdot}89$, $p < 0{\cdot}01$, but not at age seven, the comparable figures being 26 per cent *v.* 31 per cent. It is, therefore, the appellative type that is favoured by the working-class children at the later age.

One important difference between the appellative type and the statement type is that the latter permits the speaker to use intensification. At both ages significantly more middle-class children expressed intensified disapproval: 9 per cent *v.* 0 per cent at five. $\chi^2 = 5{\cdot}38$, $p < 0{\cdot}05$, and 16 per cent *v.* 3 per cent at seven, $\chi^2 = 4{\cdot}88$, $p < 0{\cdot}05$. It seems legitimate to relate this finding to a finding reported earlier under B2, namely that more middle-class children attributed intensified anger to the adult participants. At five years 13 per cent of the middle-class children referred to intensified anger and/or intensified disapproval, whereas none of the working-class children did, $\chi^2 = 8{\cdot}64$, $p < 0{\cdot}01$. At seven years 27 per cent of the middle-class children made such reference as compared with 6 per cent of the working-class, $\chi^2 = 8{\cdot}91$, $p < 0{\cdot}01$.

It was found that most children did not make explicit reference to what was disapproved of. At age five just three middle-class children made such reference, and at age seven five middle-class and two working-class children.

B5. *Reparation-seeking*

At age five the children rarely mentioned demands for reparation but at age seven nearly a third of them mentioned such demands. The change in the children between five years and seven years is highly significant, $\chi^2 = 24{\cdot}32$, $p < 0{\cdot}001$ (McNemar).

TABLE 7.7 *Reparation-seeking*

		MC	%	*WC*	%	χ^2	p
Reparation	(A)	2	(3)	3	(4)		
Reparation	(B)	14	(23)	20	(31)		
Reparation (Ai & B)							

		At age seven −	At age seven +		
At age five	+	4	1	24·32	< 0·001
	−	89	33		

The figures given above do not include the subjects who gave ambiguous utterances such as 'You'll pay for it'. If these utterances are counted as demands for reparation, the totals for the seven-year-olds are as follows: 25 working-class children (38 per cent) *v.* 16 middle-class children (26 per cent). On these figures, considerably more working-class children than middle-class children mentioned demands for reparation, but the difference is not great enough to be significant.

The sub-classification of demands for reparation did not reveal any significant differences. It did, however, reveal a tendency for working-class children to make references that were inexplicit; this result is presented in more detail in the section on reference below. It also revealed a slight tendency for more working-class children to use conditional demands for reparation: 9 per cent *v.* 2 per cent at age seven.

B6. *Explanation*

The commands, threats and rules given by the children were very rarely accompanied by an explanation. At the earlier age just five children offered explanations (3 MC and 2 WC), and at the later age nine children (6 MC and 3 WC).[2]

The explanation category is somewhat similar to the explicit reference category recognized in the analysis of expressions of disapprobation, which also had a very low incidence of occurrence. If we combine the two categories, the following results are obtained: 6 MC and 2 WC at age five, 11 MC and 5 WC at age seven.

B7. *Questions*

At age five there is a sex difference in the use of questions, when the questions are not differentiated. Significantly more girls than boys ascribed questions to the adult participants: 23 girls (29 per cent) *v.* 11 boys (14 per cent), $\chi^2 = 4{\cdot}52$, $p < 0{\cdot}05$. At age seven, however, there is no sex difference, the figures being: 19 girls (30 per cent) *v.* 19 boys (30 per cent).

The sub-classification of questions did not reveal any further differences.

Forceful options

A number of the results already reported have seemed to suggest a pattern, namely that working-class children tend to select the forceful options available, whereas middle-class children tend to select the less forceful options. In the present section we shall attempt to summarize the selections made by the children in terms of the forceful/less forceful distinction, in order to investigate further this apparent pattern in the data. We shall concentrate on the children at seven years since at this age the children used a wider range of alternatives and there is, thus, greater scope for variation.

Our approach is to take each strategy and to recognize for each a forceful option (or a set of forceful options) and a less forceful option (or set of less forceful options). Besides taking the five main role-play speech strategies—commands, threats, rule-giving, disapprobation and reparation-seeking—we also tried to fill in the picture by including some information concerning the children's non-role-play speech; we asked whether the child focused on the speech of the controller, categorizing it in terms of verbal punishment, or whether he focused on the controller's feelings. Following Bernstein, we regarded the latter as the less forceful option.

Below we present the options grouped according to the forceful/less forceful distinctions:

	Strategy	*Forceful options*	*Less forceful options*
1.	Commands	imperative type	obligation type
2.	Threats	all threats except those listed under 'less forceful options'	conditional threats associated with commands or demands for reparation of obligation type
3.	Rule-giving	imperative type	obligation type
4.	Disapprobation	appellative	statement
5.	Reparation-seeking	imperative type determination type	obligation type
6.	Non-role-play speech	focus on verbal action of controller, seen as punishment	focus on affective state of controller

We scored the children according to the number of *different* strategies they used, not according to the total number used (so two commands and one threat would count as two instances, not three). It was, thus, theoretically possible for the children to have up to six instances of strategies of the forceful type and up to six instances of those of the less forceful type.

It was found that no children used more than four strategies of either type and that, in fact, relatively few children used three or more. In Tables 7.8 and 7.9 (given below) the children are grouped according to social class and according to the number of strategies used, measured on a scale, 0–3(+).

Most children used at least one forceful option (see Table 7.8). The major class difference emerges when we oppose those children with 0 or 1 instance and those with 2 or 3 (+) instances. It is not the case, however, that most of the children used at least one of the less forceful options (Table 7.9). Many working-class children used none of these options; here the major class difference emerges when we oppose those children with no instances and those with 1, 2 or 3(+) instances. χ^2 tests were run on these two sets of opposed groups (see Tables 7.10 and 7.11 below).

TABLE 7.8 *Forceful options*

No. of instances	*MC*	*%*	*WC*	*%*
0	11	(18)	6	(9)
1	39	(63)	19	(29)
2	12	(19)	28	(43)
3(+)	0	(0)	12	(18)

TABLE 7.9 *Less forceful options*

No. of instances	*MC*	*%*	*WC*	*%*
0	20	(32)	46	(71)
1	28	(45)	17	(26)
2	10	(16)	2	(3)
3(+)	4	(6)	0	(0)

TABLE 7.10 *Forceful options*

	Users of 0,1	*Users of 2,3(+)*	χ^2	*p*
MC	50 (81%)	12 (19%)		
WC	25 (38%)	40 (62%)		
			21·64	< 0·001

TABLE 7.11 *Less forceful options*

	Users of 0	*Users of 1,2,3(+)*	χ^2	*p*
MC	20 (32%)	42 (68%)		
WC	46 (71%)	19 (29%)		
			17·34	< 0·001

The class differences are highly significant: 62 per cent of the working-class children used two or more forceful options as compared with 19 per cent of the middle-class children, $\chi^2 = 21{\cdot}64$,

$p < 0{\cdot}001$; by contrast, 68 per cent of the middle-class children used one or more of the less forceful options as compared with 29 per cent of the working-class children, $\chi^2 = 17{\cdot}34$, $p < 0{\cdot}001$.

The existence of these summed scores for the children's use of the forceful options and the less forceful options created for us the possibility of doing a correlational analysis and of including in the matrix not only the variables we have mentioned—sex, class and verbal ability—but also the 'maternal index of communication and control' constructed by Brandis (1970). Briefly, this index measures the extent to which the mother is likely (*a*) to use coercive methods of control, (*b*) to explain to the child why she wants a change in his behaviour, (*c*) to take up the child's attempts to talk to her, (*d*) to avoid or evade answering difficult questions put to her by her child, and (*e*) to value the general explorative/cognitive function of toys. This information was obtained from the mothers when their children were five years old, but there is reason to suppose that the mothers' attitudes towards communication and control remain fairly stable and that the index is still relevant when the children are age seven.

Communication and control index scores were available for the mothers of 60 middle-class children in Sample B and of 44 working-class children. So a correlational analysis was performed, using these 104 children. Six variables were used. These are listed below:

(1) Sex
(2) Social class
(3) Communication and control index (CCI)
(4) Crichton vocabulary scale
(5) Forceful options (summed score)
(6) Less forceful options (summed score)

The correlation matrix calculated is given in full (see Table 7.12).

The pattern of the correlations is quite clear. Sex is not important; there are no significant correlations between sex and any other variables. Verbal ability is not important. (It should be remembered, by the way, that we are dealing with a factorial sample; otherwise, there would have been a significant correlation between verbal ability and social class). What is important is social class. Mother's orientation towards communication and control (CCI) and social class emerge as closely related, but the communication and control index does not emerge as a more effective discriminator than social class with respect to the forceful options and less forceful options variables. Social class has a highly significant positive correlation with the forceful options (i.e. working-class children using more), $r = 0{\cdot}454$, $p < 0{\cdot}001$, and a highly significant negative

TABLE 7.12 *Product—Moment correlation (r) : MC and WC children (n = 104)*

Variables	*1*	*2*	*3*	*4*	*5*	*6*
1. Sex	x					
2. Social class	−0·012	x				
3. CCI	−0·073	−0·571	x			
4. Crichton	−0·058	−0·040	0·106	x		
5. Forceful options	0·014	0·454	−0·266	−0·031	x	
6. Less forceful options	−0·104	−0·382	0·156	0·021	−0·327	x

$p < 0{\cdot}05$ for r = 0·193
$p < 0{\cdot}01$ for r = 0·249
$p < 0{\cdot}001$ for r = 0·322

correlation with less forceful options (i.e. middle-class children using more), r = −0·382, $p < 0{\cdot}001$. The communication and control index has a significant negative correlation with the forceful options (roughly, the lower the score for forceful options the higher the score for the mother's orientation towards communication and control, which is what we would expect), r = −0·266, $p < 0{\cdot}01$, but the correlation between CCI and the less forceful options does not reach significance. Further, it is clear from the matrix that the correlation between CCI and the forceful options is largely a reflection of the relationship between CCI and social class, the correlation between these two variables being −0·571,[3] $p < 0{\cdot}001$—the highest correlation in the matrix. There remains one further relationship to mention, namely that between the forceful options and the less forceful options; these two variables emerge, as we would expect, as significantly negatively correlated, r = −0·327, $p < 0{\cdot}01$.

Two further correlation matrices were calculated, one for the working-class children (n = 44) and one for the middle class (n = 60), since previous work had suggested that the communication and control index discriminates more powerfully between working-class strata than between middle-class strata (Brandis, 1970). These two analyses did not reveal any significant correlations between CCI and the forceful options and less forceful options variables, nor was there any clear suggestion that the index discriminated more powerfully in the working-class sample.

A note on the distinction between forceful and less forceful options

In order to clear up possible misconceptions, it should be stressed that the grouping of the options used by the children into two groups, the forceful and the less forceful groups, was done on the basis of the researcher's intuitions as an adult speaker of the language; in these intuitions, the obligation type seemed less forceful than the imperative type, the statement type less forceful than the appellative and so on. The assignment of options to the groups followed a consistent pattern—thus, for example, the obligation type (associated with four strategies) was always assigned to the less forceful group, and never to the forceful group—and the resultant groupings revealed very large social class differences. There is no claim, however, that the seven-year-old children would perceive the options in exactly the same way as the researcher. Nor is there any claim that the working-class children would perceive the options in just the same way as the middle-class children; it is quite possible, for example, that an option that middle-class children would tend to perceive as a forceful option would be viewed as a less forceful one by working-class children. To the extent that the terms 'forceful options' and 'less forceful options' seem to imply claims such as these, their use is inappropriate. Clearly, there are great difficulties in investigating how children of differing social classes interpret and respond to the control strategies used by their parents and others, and a variety of types of data would certainly be needed in order to throw light on these matters.

It has to be said that, in the terms of reference adopted by the researcher, the grouping of the options is not free from difficulty and has an obvious limitation. One source of difficulty is intensified disapprobation. Assuming that the categorization of appellative disapprobation as forceful and of statement disapprobation as less forceful is correct, to what extent is this distinction neutralized when the statement type is associated with intensification? An obvious limitation is that the analysis did not take into account intonational signals, and tone is an important way of manifesting attitude, for example, reserved, mild, insistent. But, of course, had we included an analysis of such signals, we still could not have said that young children of differing social classes would interpret them in exactly the same way.

The division of the options into two groups—perhaps, at the present state of knowledge we should call them simply Group A and Group B, rather than forceful options and less forceful options —is best regarded as a hypothesis about the clustering of these variables. Briefly, the expectation is that, in a correlational analysis, these variables would tend to cluster together in the way suggested, even after the influence of social class has been controlled for. The researcher is now working on more extensive data and it is hoped that it may be possible to test this hypothesis.

Inexplicit reference

The distinction we drew between inexplicit reference and explicit reference relates to a number of contrasts. One, it may relate to the pronominal/nominal contrast—and this is perhaps the most important contrast (cf. You'll have to pay for that; You're going to pay for that window). Two, the verb may also be involved; *do* plus pronoun may be used to refer to the action (cf. Don't do it again; Don't you knock my window again). Three, a clause may be involved—in one construction, a clause may be related to a pronoun (cf. It was naughty; It's very naughty smashing my window); in other constructions, there is no pronoun involved (cf. You're very naughty; You're very naughty to play football in the street).

In the case of the first two contrasts mentioned above, the question of degrees of inexplicitness arises. We may put our basic view briefly. Drawing on Hasan (1972), we would argue that a pronoun functioning exophorically (i.e. one making reference to something in the non-linguistic context) is less explicit in its reference than one functioning anaphorically (i.e. one making reference to something previously mentioned in the language of the message). For precise definitions of types of reference and a detailed discussion of this point, the reader should consult Hasan's work. The basic distinction between a pronoun functioning exophorically and one functioning anaphorically is in itself quite straightforward; its application in the present analysis, however, is not so straightforward. As we pointed out in the introduction, the analysis of our data is complicated by the fact that we are, to a large extent, focusing on a situation within a situation. Our chief point of focus is the role-play speech—the speech that the children assign to the adults in the story, giving them the role of controller and the children that of controlled. If we could justifiably focus on this speech alone and ignore the other speech given by the children, there would be no problem. Thus, if a child said 'You'll have to pay for it', we could ask whether the pronoun *it* referred back to something mentioned earlier by the child whilst giving role-play speech. If it did refer back to something in the role-play speech (for example, *this window* in 'Who's bust this window?'), we could say that the pronoun was functioning anaphorically; if it did not make such reference, we could say it was functioning exophorically. But can we focus on the role-play speech solely and disregard the other speech? The crux of the matter is this: most of the children are likely to have referred to the participants (persons and objects) and the actions concerned with the transgression *before* they give the speech of the adults in the story—the role-play speech we are interested in. (How the children made this initial reference is the concern of Hawkins's paper in this volume, and is not our central concern here.) So, if a child said 'You'll have to pay for it', one is likely to be able to find something in the preceding speech of the child (even if it is not in the role-play speech) to which *it* can be said to refer (for example, *the window* in the following: The ball breaks the window). If this is the case, should we regard *it* in 'You'll have to pay for it' as functioning anaphorically, rather than exophorically? In our view, the more likely interpretation is that *it* is functioning exophorically—not so much in the sense that the child is making reference to something present in the picture in front of him (i.e. something in the interview situation) but rather in the sense that the child, in enacting the role of a man or woman controlling some children, makes reference to something present in the control situation. Nevertheless, we can see some truth in the view that if a child has already referred to an object once, his subsequent references to this object are likely to be influenced by this fact, even if these later references occur in role-play speech; the initial reference may be explicit or inexplicit (probably explicit in the case of the middle-class child and inexplicit in the case of the working-class child (Hawkins)), but whatever the initial reference, subsequent references will tend to be inexplicit. Because of these interpretative difficulties, we felt unable to measure degrees of inexplicitness in terms of the anaphoric/exophoric reference distinction. Instead we operated with a rather less informative but easier to apply distinction; we distinguished between inexplicit reference associated with anaphoric reference to preceding role-play speech and any other inexplicit pronominal reference, regarding the former as less inexplicit than the latter.

It was found that most of the children who gave inexplicit references did not give references of the type we have labelled 'less inexplicit'; just one middle-class child at age five and just three middle-class and two working-class children at age seven gave references involving anaphoric pronominal reference to preceding role-play speech. To a large extent, this result reflects the children's length of output; most children did not offer long stretches of role-play speech.

Table 7.13 below is concerned with the children who made inexplicit pronominal references other than those involving anaphoric reference to preceding role-play speech. In the table the children are grouped according to the type of linguistic context in which they made the reference. Five main types are recognized; two of them, threats and reparation-seeking, are also sub-divided according to whether the inexplicit reference was made in the threat or demand (e.g. You dare do this again; You'll have to pay for that) or whether it was made in an accompanying condition (e.g. If you do that once more, I'm going to tell the police; If you do that again, you can pay for my window).

TABLE 7.13(*a*) *Number of children making inexplicit references, grouped according to type of linguistic context*

		At age five		*At age seven*	
		MC	*WC*	*MC*	*WC*
Commands		13	8	6	4
Threats	in threat	2	0	0	2
	in condition	0	5	1	6
Disapprobation		0	1	0	0
Reparation seeking	in demand*	1	1	3	10
	in condition	0	0	0	2
Questions		4	4	3	3

* Children giving ambiguous utterances such as 'You'll pay for it' were included here.

TABLE 7.13(*b*) *Number of children making one (or more) inexplicit reference(s)*

	MC	%	*WC*	%	χ^2	*p*
At age five (*a*)	19	(24)	18	(23)		
At age seven (*b*)	13	(21)	26	(40)	4·54	$< 0{\cdot}05$

The grouping of the children according to the types of context in which they made inexplicit references revealed no significant differences (see Section (*a*) above). It is noticeable that the number of children grouped under any particular type was generally quite low. Nevertheless, the figures seem such as to suggest that it could be important to control for type of linguistic context when investigating social class differences in the use of reference. We shall consider this point further in our discussion of the results reported in Section (*b*).

At age five there is virtually no difference between the social class groups in their use of inexplicit reference when this use is not differentiated according to type of linguistic context, the proportions of users being: 24 per cent MC *v.* 23 per cent WC. But at age seven there is a significant social class difference, the proportions of users being: 21 per cent MC *v.* 40 per cent WC, $\chi^2 = 4{\cdot}54$, $p < 0{\cdot}05$. It is clear that the figures for the middle-class children are similar at the two ages (24 per cent and 21 per cent) whereas those for the working-class children are quite different (23 per cent and 40 per cent). There is, then, a considerable increase in the proportion of working-class children making inexplicit references, between age five and age seven. Section (*a*) of Table 7.13 reveals that this increase in the making of inexplicit references is associated with the linguistic contexts of threats and reparation-seeking. We know from Tables 7.5 and 7.7 that more working-class children mentioned threats and reparation-seeking at age seven than at age five. We also know that considerably more working-class than middle-class children mentioned these two strategies: in all, at age seven, 43 working-class children (66 per cent) mentioned threats and/or reparation-seeking as compared with 21 middle-class children (34 per cent). These facts prompt the question: is the result on inexplicit reference at age seven largely a reflection of the working-class children's greater use of threats and demands for reparation, rather than a reflection of a tendency for them to make inexplicit references as such? To suggest an answer to this question we have to consider not only the children who made inexplicit pronominal references but also those who made explicit nominal references *in comparable linguistic contexts*; in other words, we have to present the children using inexplicit pronouns (in the sense defined above) as a percentage of the total number of children using constructions of a like kind in which an inexplicit pronoun could have been used. It was found that 16 middle-class children and 28 working-class children offered threats and demands for reparation in which such a pronoun could have been used: 4 of the middle-class children (i.e. 25 per cent) actually used a pronoun as compared with 20 of the working-class children (i.e. 71 per cent). In our opinion, these figures do not lend support to the view that the result on inexplicit reference at age seven is largely a reflection of the working-class children's greater use of threats and demands for reparation. Of course, we would not deny the importance of controlling for type of linguistic context; in fact, we would emphasize this. But what we would argue is that, when one does tightly control for type of linguistic context, the indications are that the middle-class and working-class children tended to make different types of reference, with the working-class children using the inexplicit type.

Discussion

In the introduction we stated that the study sought to answer four main types of question. We sought to discover (*a*) whether children at these ages exhibit social class differences in their choice of control; (*b*) whether the children's choice of control *directly* reflects their home experience or whether it appears to be influenced in part by their stage of development; (*c*) whether class differences are greater at age five than age seven; and (*d*) whether such differences are relatable to code differences. We shall now try to answer these questions in the light of the results obtained. Our basic strategy is to take each question in turn, but clearly it is not always practicable to adhere to this procedure—in the detailed discussion of some of the results several of the questions are considered together.

(*a*) **Social class differences**

The study provides clear evidence of the relevance of social class to the child's definition of the control situation and his choice of control at both ages. By comparison, the verbal ability and sex of the child appear to have only limited relevance; there is only one variable that verbal ability significantly relates to at both ages ('commands') and there is no variable that sex relates to at both ages. It is striking that the social class results obtained at the two ages reveal a largely consistent pattern—there are some changes but there are no reversals. To a large extent the results are in line with expectations and in the sections on particular results which follow we shall relate them to Bernstein's and Cook's work.

'TELLING OFF' AND 'BEING CROSS'

Before we discuss the social class differences in the use of these expressions, it is necessary to give our reasons for distinguishing them, regarding a clause such as 'A man told them off' as focusing on the verbal action and one such as 'The man is very cross' as focusing on the affective state of the person. This is necessary since it may be held that both types of expression refer to the speech event, the difference between them being largely one of social dialect. There are two main considerations which dissuade us from making this interpretation. One, 'telling off' necessarily involves speaking whereas 'being cross' does not. One middle-class child, when asked 'What's the man saying?', actually replied: 'He wasn't saying anything. He's just very cross.' Two, significantly more children used 'telling off' at seven years than at five years (irrespective of social class) but there is no comparable increase in the number of children using 'being cross'; in our view, this strongly suggests that there is a meaning difference between the two types of expression and that they are not just different ways of saying the same thing, one being used by working-class speakers and the other by middle-class speakers. In the absence of any evidence to the contrary we took the grammatical selections at face value, 'telling off' being associated with 'actional' clauses and 'being cross' with 'relational: attributive' clauses.

Concerning the social class distribution of speech events labelled 'telling off', it is valuable to consult Cook (1972). Cook grouped 'tell off' with 'tick off', 'scold', 'have a nag', 'give a good talking to', 'shout at', 'holler out' and so on as instances of verbal punishment. Cook found that more working-class mothers (of five-year-olds) mentioned verbal punishment; interestingly, though, the social class difference was not just one of frequency. There was some suggestion that the social class groups differed in terms of the conditions under which they would resort to verbal punishment. From the maternal reports it appears that working-class mothers, in certain situations, tend to use verbal punishment as a first control strategy and resort to physical chastisement if the first strategy fails, whereas middle-class mothers tend not to use verbal punishment in the first instance, but resort to it rather than physical punishment later. This indication in Cook's data that both working-class and middle-class mothers tend to use verbal punishment *under certain conditions* suggests perhaps an explanation for our finding that significantly more children (irrespective of their social class) mentioned verbal punishment at age seven than at age five. It may well be that mothers of both social classes find that they have to use verbal punishment more as their children grow older and it is this greater use of scolding that is reflected in the children's responses at age seven. Of course, it is possible, too, that the children's responses at age seven reflect in part the practice of their teachers.

Turning to the 'being cross' expressions, our finding that more middle-class children at both ages made reference to the affective state of the adult participants in the story, attributing feelings of anger to them, has points of contact with another finding of Cook (1972) on the maternal data. Cook found that in the responses to one particular question (namely, 'What would you say or do if [your child] wasn't watching what he was doing and spilt tea over the table-cloth?') significantly more middle-class mothers mentioned to the interviewer that this type of incident made her feel angry, e.g. 'She's always doing things like that and I get very cross'; 'this tends to make me a little bit cross.'

The similarities between the children's data and the mothers' data suggest that middle-class mothers tend to put their feelings into words and to express them to their children, presumably saying such things as 'I'm very cross with you' and 'It makes me angry to see that.' If this is the case, then it illustrates a sense in which Bernstein's (1958) formulation is true: 'Within middle-class and associative levels direct expressions of feeling, in particular feelings of hostility, are discouraged. The word mediates between the expression of feeling and its approved social recognition, that is, a value is placed upon the verbalization of feeling.' We would emphasize that, in our view, putting feelings into words in this way is not the same thing as telling somebody off. A mother may state her feelings to her child, to let him know what effects his actions have on her, without necessarily attacking or abusing the child.

COMMANDS, RULES AND EXPLANATIONS

Most mothers are concerned to impart to their child certain broad principles governing behaviour, e.g. respect for other people's property, well before the child's fifth birthday. The importance of the role of language in imparting these principles needs no emphasizing. Much of Bernstein's work has been focused on this area and, as we have discussed in the introduction, the main criterion for distinguishing elaborated and restricted codes in the regulative context is the extent to which the principles governing behaviour are made explicit and specific and are explained. In general, it may be expected that explicit verbal communication, particularly when the mother shapes it to take into account her child's particular needs, aids the child's comprehension of the principles and enables him to carry them in his mind. It may be expected, too, that such communication will influence and develop two things in the child simultaneously, his use of language and his power of reasoning. To avoid possible misunderstanding we should stress that when we talk about explicit verbal communication we are concerned with the meanings; we are certainly not concerned with correct English ('good' grammar) or even grammatical complexity. There may well be a correlation between explicit communication and grammatical complexity (complex sentence structure, complex nominal group structure and so forth) but grammatical complexity is certainly not a necessary condition for explicit verbal communication; in fact, it seems clear that such complexity could be a stumbling-block to a child's comprehension.

Several empirical studies, besides those undertaken by the Sociological Research Unit, have suggested that, in general, middle-class mothers are more likely to use explicit verbal communication than working-class mothers. Strodbeck's study (referred to by Bereiter and Engelmann, 1966) indicated that working-class mothers made more use of simple imperatives and less of explanations and statements than middle-class mothers. Hess *et al.* (1968) examined how Negro mothers prepared their child for his first day at school and found that working-class mothers made more use of 'imperative communication', i.e. unqualified commands, whilst middle-class mothers made more use of 'instructive communication', i.e that which provides some rationale for the behaviour expected of the child. Finally, the Newsons (1968), on the basis of their investigations, came to the conclusion that the middle-class mother 'will try to give the child an explanation rather than a bald command, and will be (theoretically at least) prepared to countenance argument and to meet it with calmness and further explanation.' By contrast, 'working-class mothers . . . are less likely to embark upon a course which looks like involving them in lengthy verbal explanations of the whys and wherefores of their actions; on the whole, they show a preference for short-cut methods which get results quickly for the minimum of outlay in time and thought.'

Our finding that significantly more five-year-old working-class children gave abrupt commands specifying removal, e.g. Go away; Get out of it, would seem to be in line with the findings of previous investigators but there is a complication. In the situation depicted such a response seems a little inappropriate: a person who has had his window broken is probably more likely to demand reparation than simply to send the offenders away. It is thought that, whilst the use of these removal commands by working-class children clearly reflects a difference in their control experiences, it also reflects their moral development. Very few children of either social class mentioned reparation-seeking at age five, whereas approaching a third of the children mentioned it at age seven. At five years, 40 per cent of the working-class children gave removal commands, whereas only 4 per cent of them mentioned demands for reparation; by contrast, at seven years, 15 per cent of the working class gave removal commands, whereas 31 per cent of them mentioned demands for reparation. It seems unlikely that the reduction at age seven in the proportion of working-class children using removal commands and the increase at this age in the proportion of those using demands for reparation are unrelated. This finding indicates the value of controlling for the age factor when examining social class differences in children's regulatory language.

Rules and explanations—especially explanations—were rarely mentioned by the children, and in this particular data there is little suggestion that middle-class children made more use of these strategies. More middle-class children at age seven, however, mentioned rules of a particular type, those forbidding the playing of football in the street—a finding that seems directly relatable to their cultural values and environmental conditions. The relative rarity of rules and explanations in the present data suggests that the age of the children, their stage of development, was very important. It seems likely, too, that the interview situation (the control situation depicted and the questions asked) had a constraining influence with respect to the use of rules and explanations; though it is of interest to note that the results obtained for these categories are similar to those obtained by Cook (1972), using a larger sample of seven-year-old subjects and employing a different interview technique—doll-play—and a variety of situations. The suggestion is, then, that in the present experiment the children's stage of development and the situational constraints had the effect of overriding the influence of social class with respect to the use of speech giving principles and explanation.

THREATS

Our prediction that more working-class children would mention control by means of threats—this being one of the main ways of realizing imperative control—was largely supported by the results obtained.

The finding that more working-class children mentioned conditional threats at age five and, to a certain extent, at age seven is of considerable interest, even though the number of children using them is not large. These threats are of interest because of their association with grammatical complexity; they are realized by compound linguistic structures, either hypotactic structures (i.e. those involving subordination), e.g. If you do that once more, I'll punch you; Don't do that no more, because I'm going to come after you, or paratactic (co-ordinate) structures, e.g. You come back or I'll tell a policeman. Now there have been several studies of the use of subordination linking it (*a*) with linguistic development and (*b*) with social class—with middle-class children using more (e.g. Templin, 1957; Bernstein, 1962a; Lawton, 1964; Loban, 1966). The suggestion in our data that there is a linguistic context in which working-class children use more subordination than middle-class children indicates the importance of tightly controlling for linguistic context when investigating social class differences in the use of grammatical categories (see Bernstein, 1970a, b, d).[4] As we stated in the introduction, the same grammatical option may be selected to realize quite different semantic options; thus, a subordinate clause may be associated with a conditional threat, e.g. If you do it again, I'll call the cops, or with a child-oriented cognitive appeal, e.g. If you don't go to school, you won't learn to read, a control strategy which has been shown to be favoured by middle-class mothers (Cook, 1972). To a large extent it is not possible to make sense of social class differences in the use of grammatical categories, unless one looks at the contexts which control the meanings.

Conditional threats and certain child-oriented cognitive appeals have a good deal in common grammatically; it is instructive to consider how they differ semantically and in their behavioural effects. Let us compare a threat such as 'If you do that once more, I'll punch you' and appeals such as 'If you don't go to school, you won't learn to read' and 'If you eat cookies now, you won't want your dinner' (called a cognitive-rational appeal by Hess and Shipman, 1968). The threat is concerned with reprisal, with stating the counter-action to be taken if the child continues to offend, whereas the appeals are concerned with explanation, with giving a logical (no matter how simple) cause-effect account of the child's action. Both the threat and the appeals mention ill-effects but there is a difference: in the case of the threat the ill-effects are brought about by an external agent, whereas in the case of the appeals they are caused by the child himself. In Ginott's (1970) opinion, threats are a self-defeating control strategy; they are invitations to misbehaviour. They fail because they are perceived by the child as challenges to his autonomy; he must transgress again or lose some self-respect. If Ginott is right, it is probably the mentioning of counter-action by another that serves as a challenge to the child. Ginott also says that threats should be avoided on affective grounds; they create hate and resentment. Without denying this possibility, we would argue that, if threats are to be avoided, there are also cognitive grounds. Whereas child-oriented cognitive appeals encourage the child to reason for himself and to reflect on the logical consequences of his actions, threats encourage the child to think mainly of possible punishment. The appeals teach the child to avoid the act itself; threats teach him to avoid punishment, and in situations in which there seems little likelihood of the child being found out, he may well feel free to commit the wrong-doing. The distinction we are making here has points of contact with the distinction that Bernstein (1970a) makes between guilt and shame; see also Fantini and Weinstein's (1968) discussion of personal and positional control.

DISAPPROBATION

There is a sense in which the strategy of disapprobation contrasts with all the other control strategies used in this situation: the commands, threats, rules and demands for reparation are all action-oriented—they all refer to action of one type or another; whereas the expressions of disapprobation are not primarily action-oriented; instead they attribute a state to the child. This attribution has both a cognitive and an affective component; briefly, the cognitive component may be characterized in terms of the opposition 'good'/ 'bad' (in most cases) and the affective component in terms of the opposition 'liked'/'disliked'. Now when an adult uses or hears these expressions the affective component may or may not be dominant, but when a child uses or hears these expressions the affective component is extremely likely to be dominant, because of the state of his cognitive and moral development. It is important to bear this in mind. We regarded expressions such as 'You're naughty boys' as exemplifying positional rather than personal control, on the grounds that the attribute assigned to the controlled is of the generalized type, not the particularized. There seems no reason to doubt the validity of this interpretation. Nevertheless, because of the strength of the affective component in these appeals, it seems reasonable to suggest that there is a sense in which they are more personal than the other control strategies. To put the matter simply, a young child is probably more likely to burst into tears if his mother says he is naughty or silly than he is if she tells him not to do something again and threatens him with punishment if he does. It may well be that expressions such as 'I'm very cross with you' and 'It makes me angry to see that' work in a similar way; though one doubts whether they carry the same emotional charge. Anyway, it seems to us that of all the control strategies we have considered in this study, disapprobation—because of its strong emotional component—is the one that is most likely to lead to internalized reactions to wrong-doing and foster feelings of guilt.

Our prediction that more middle-class children would mention disapprobation was confirmed at age five and was fairly well supported at age seven. At the earlier age significantly more middle-class children mentioned the appellative type and the statement type; at the later age significantly more mentioned the statement type, there being no class difference in the use of the appellative type.

The finding that almost two-fifths of the middle-class five-year-olds mentioned disapprobation as compared with approximately one-tenth of their working-class contemporaries suggests most strongly a real difference in the home experience of these children.

To say this, however, is not to say that the children's use of disapprobation necessarily mirrored their parents' practice. Indeed, there seems good reason to doubt that it did.

In general, the children (at either age) did not seem to distinguish between disapproval of an action and disapproval of a person. Nor did they seem to distinguish between an action done on purpose and one done accidentally. Few children mentioned the actor's intention (in any context), just two at age five and three at age seven. In general, their reasoning seems to have been: the children broke a window; therefore, they were naughty. This type of reasoning would seem to be a clear instance of an aspect of development in moral judgment noted by Piaget (1948)—namely 'intentionality in judgment'. Briefly, young children tend to judge an act as bad chiefly in terms of its physical consequences, not in terms of the intent to do harm.

There is reason to think that middle-class parents tend to focus on the child's intent rather than on the physical consequences of his actions; see, for example, Kohn's (1959a) study. Kohn investigated the conditions under which parents punish their pre-adolescent children physically. His work suggested that middle-class parents are more likely to respond in terms of their interpretation of the child's intent, working-class parents in terms of the immediate consequences of the child's actions. Kohn contends, we may add, that the reactions of parents of both social classes are appropriate to their cultural values. Working-class parents value for their children qualities that assure *respectability*; desirable behaviour consists essentially of not violating proscriptions. Middle-class parents value the child's development of internalized standards of conduct; desirable behaviour consists essentially of acting according to the dictates of one's own principles.

The main social class differences have been discussed at some length. There is not sufficient space to allow us to consider the other results in similar detail. We shall conclude this section with a brief consideration of the inexplicit reference and forceful options results. Our expectation that more working-class children would make inexplicit references was fulfilled at age seven. The origins of this association of inexplicit reference with the working class and the consequences of it have been considered in detail by Hawkins (1969), Bernstein (1970b, c, d; 1971) and Hasan (1972); the reader is referred to these works for the discussion. As we mentioned earlier, our own treatment of inexplicit reference drew most heavily on Hasan (1972). Our expectation that more working-class children would choose the forceful options was also fulfilled (at age seven). Since the summed scores for the forceful options and the less forceful options to a large extent summarize the results that we have already discussed in detail above, we need not add more here. There is, however, one matter that requires comment, namely the finding that the communication and control index was not related to the forceful options and less forceful options variables, except through its relationship with social class. The distinctions we made, for example, imperative type *v.* obligation type in the choice of command, and appellative *v.* statement in the choice of disapprobation, were too fine to be picked up by the communication and control index, though not too fine to be picked up by social class. It should be remembered that the index, although it takes into account a considerable range of phenomena, does not take into account all aspects of the communication and control that exists between a mother and her child. The index is necessarily selective. Thus, in the area of social control, it takes account of two sets of choices that are *sharply distinct* from each other; to illustrate this, we may mention 'physical punishment' (taken from the punishment sub-index) and 'recognition of the child's intent' (taken from the child-oriented reasoning sub-index). Had the children made such sharply distinct choices the index may have proved relevant.

(*b*) Home experience and stage of development

By and large, the social class differences observed in the children's use of control seem to reflect *directly* the children's home experiences, if we take into account the findings of Cook and others on maternal data. There are just two main areas where there is a suggestion that, although the children's choice of control *did* reflect their home experience, it did not do so *directly*, there being reason for thinking that the children's choice was influenced in part by their stage of development. We have already had cause to refer to these areas, commands and disapprobation, so we need not consider these results in detail. There seems an important comment that can be made about these results. In these areas the effect of the development of the child was such as to reinforce and strengthen class differences rather than to weaken or obliterate them. By contrast, in the area of explanation, if the development of the child had an influence here (and we are not saying that it was the *only* possible influence here), it appears to have had the effect of overriding the influence of social class.

(*c*) Exposure to school

Although there is a sense in which the social class differences are greater at age five than at age seven (cf. the results for imperative commands and disapprobation), it would be unwarranted to suggest that two years' exposure to school has brought the children very close together in their choice of control. For although there are significant changes between five and seven in the working-class children's use of commands and disapprobation, their use of these strategies at the later age is sharply distinct from that of the middle-class children: significantly more middle-class seven-year-olds mentioned commands of the obligation type and significantly more middle-class seven-year-olds mentioned disapprobation of the statement type. It is, of course, likely that the children's experience of control in the infant school had some influence on their choice of control, but the overall consistency in the patterning of the social class results at the two ages suggests that the influence of the school as an instrument of change is not great. In fact, it is possible that the control that the children experience in the infant school might serve to *maintain* initial social class differences. This view is supported by evidence from the work of Bernstein, Brandis and McGovern (forthcoming) which indicates that teachers in the working-class area, relative to teachers in the middle-class area, are much more likely to use physical punishment, when controlling the children.

(*d*) **Code differences**

Any attempt to relate data of the type we are dealing with—in which the mean number of utterances offered by the subjects was extremely low—to Bernstein's codes must be viewed as highly tentative. The assignment of speech to codes is much more feasible when extended discourse is offered. Speech samples of the size of those we are concerned with offer no scope for the kind of discourse analysis that Bernstein's work really demands.

Our approach to the question of relating the social class differences to code differences is to take first the choices that are associated with imperative control. Bernstein has associated imperative control far more with a restricted code than with an elaborated code, so it is a useful starting point. At age five, more working-class children mentioned 'telling off', imperative commands, especially abrupt ones specifying removal, and conditional threats; similarly, at age seven, more working-class children mentioned 'telling off' ($p < 0{\cdot}1$) and threats. At the later age more middle-class children mentioned commands of the obligation type. There are two other results to be mentioned; these are concerned with both imperative and positional choices. At age seven, more working-class children made inexplicit references, associated with threats and demands for reparation, and more of them gained 'high' scores for the use of 'forceful options'. What emerges from the above is a broad association of the working-class children with imperative control and a restricted code. We should add that the working-class children's use of conditional threats would appear to be a clear instance of what Bernstein (1970b, c, d,) has called an elaborated speech variant associated with a restricted code. Bernstein hypothesizes that the working-class children's use of conditionals is highly context-specific; the view taken is that the working-class children would use them in the regulative context, but they would use them much more rarely in the instructional context. Current work being performed in the Sociological Research Unit is designed to test this hypothesis.

We shall now consider the choices associated with positional control. At age five, more middle-class children mentioned the affective state of the controller ('being cross') and disapprobation; at age seven, more middle-class children mentioned the affective state of the controller, disapprobation of the statement type and rules of a particular kind, those forbidding the playing of football in the street. There remains one further result to mention, which is related to the above: more middle-class seven-year-olds gained 'high' scores for the use of 'less forceful options'. What emerges from the above is a broad association of the middle-class children with positional control, especially that kind of positional control which focuses on states and feelings. There is a strong suggestion. then, in the patterning of the statistically significant results, that the working-class and middle-class children are different in their orientations towards control: the working-class children are oriented towards imperative control which is primarily action-oriented, whereas the middle-class children are oriented towards positional control, particularly that type which is not primarily action-oriented but which focuses on states and feelings. Are these differences in orientation associated with code differences? Did the middle-class children express meanings that were more explicit and more specific than those that the working-class children expressed? There are a number of suggestions, especially at age seven, which we shall now list.

1. *Explicitness*
   (*a*) Middle-class children were more likely to make explicit obligation (e.g. You mustn't . . . , You should . . .).
   (*b*) Middle-class children were more likely to assign attributes, making explicit (i) the controller's evaluation of the offenders or the offence (e.g. You're naughty

boys) and (ii) the effect of the offence on the controller (e.g. The man's cross).

2. *Specificity*
Middle-class children made greater use of intensification (e.g. You're very naughty; Mummy's very cross with them) to distinguish and emphasize relative severity.

3. *Implicitness*
(*a*) Middle-class children were *less* likely to use abrupt imperative commands specifying removal (e.g. Go away; Get out of it).
(*b*) Middle-class children offered *fewer* examples of implicitness than working-class children, as measured by the use of inexplicit pronominal reference.

It is the case that very few children indeed offered any examples of principles and their explanation. The emphasis of the children was more upon control as such than upon principles and explanation. We would suggest that the absence of the latter is directly related to the developmental stage of the children and also to the limitations placed upon the children by the context. As we have stated earlier, our inquiry was limited to a relatively narrow range of choices within the imperative and positional modes of control. It is the case that within this range of choices the middle-class children's linguistic usage indicates *greater* explicitness, specificity and *less* implicitness than the working-class children's usage. Within the constraints of the children's developmental age and the limitations of the context, we would suggest that the linguistic usage of the middle-class children, relative to the working-class children, indicates an orientation towards an elaborated code.

Conclusion

We believe that one of the major points of interest in this analysis is the use of Professor M. A. K. Halliday's concept of meaning potential. This concept should enable researchers to integrate sociological concepts and linguistic concepts. The sociological theory identifies the socially significant meanings. Once these are specified, their grammatical and lexical realizations are also capable of specification. We believe that this concept will lead to a greater clarity and precision in the operationalization of sociolinguistic theories, in particular those constructed by Bernstein. At a number of points in this paper we have indicated that only two sub-systems of the Bernstein-Cook model of control have been explored in the present study, namely the imperative and positional modes of control. There are, in fact, six sub-systems. The author is currently engaged in constructing meaning potentials for other sub-systems in the model.

We should emphasize our agreement with Halliday's (1971) suggestion that the same sentence may have different meanings for speakers from different social groups; see, for example, Bernstein's (1961) discussion of commands. Halliday gives the imaginary example, *they don't want children in here*, and discusses how it may have more than one meaning, even in the regulative context, 'given two distinct social groups one of which typically exploited one area of meaning potential (say "elaborated code") and the other another ("restricted code")'. We may quote Halliday's final comments on the example in full:

> Within a 'code' in which the typical appeal was positional and non-discretionary this example would be interpreted as an imperative, whereas in one tending towards more personal and more challengeable appeals it could be taken as a partially explicit rule. The meaning of selecting any one particular feature would be potentially different in the two 'codes', since it would be selected from within a different range of probable alternatives.

At the present time we are still collecting information concerning the frequency with which different social groups select a particular option and the frequency with which the option co-occurs with other options; it is hoped that it will be possible eventually to use this information to make statements of the type that Halliday suggests.

To end, we shall summarize the main findings. (1) It is a matter of some interest that the verbal ability of the children, relative to their social status, was only weakly related to their control choices. This finding confirms that of Cook (1972), who used a larger sample of seven-year-old children and a larger sample of regulative contexts. (2) We have shown that social class differences are maintained to a large degree when we examine the same children's speech at age five and at age seven. (3) On the whole working-class children were more likely to take up options within the imperative mode and middle-class children were more likely to take up options in the positional mode of control. Finally, some evidence has been offered which indicates that the middle-class children's linguistic usage within the above two modes is more explicit and specific and the working-class children's linguistic usage is more implicit.

Appendix

TABLE 1 *The main grammatical systems of English grouped according to function* (reproduced from Halliday, 1970b)

rank \ function	IDEATIONAL Experiential		Logical		INTERPERSONAL	TEXTUAL	
CLAUSE	TRANSITIVITY types of process participants & circumstances (identity clauses) (things, facts & reports)	HYPOTACTIC COMPLEXES OF CLAUSE, GROUP & WORD	condition addition report POLARITY	PARATACTIC COMPLEXES (all ranks) co-ordination apposition	MOOD types of speech function modality (the *WH*-function)	THEME types of message (identity as text relation) (identification, predication, reference, substitution)	COHESION ('above the sentence': non-structural relations) reference; substitution & ellipsis; conjunction; lexical cohesion
Verbal GROUP	TENSE (verb classes)		catenation secondary tense		PERSON ('marked' options)	VOICE ('contrastive' options)	
Nominal GROUP	MODIFICATION epithet function enumeration (noun classes) (adjective classes)		classification sub-modification		ATTITUDE attitudinal modifiers intensifiers	DEIXIS determiners 'phoric' elements (qualifiers) (definite article)	
Adverbial (incl. prepositional) GROUP	'MINOR PROCESSES' prepositional relations (classes of circumstantial adjunct)		narrowing sub-modification		COMMENT (classes of comment adjunct)	CONJUNCTION (classes of discourse adjunct)	
WORD (incl. lexical item)	LEXICAL 'CONTENT' (taxonomic organization of vocabulary)		compounding derivation		LEXICAL 'REGISTER' (expressive words) (stylistic organization of vocabulary)	COLLOCATION (collocational organization of vocabulary)	
INFORMATION UNIT					TONE intonation systems	INFORMATION distribution & focus	

Summary of notational conventions* (reproduced from Halliday, 1970a)

$a \longrightarrow \left[\begin{array}{l} x \\ y \end{array}\right.$ there is a system x/y with entry condition a (if a, then either x or y)

$a \left\{\begin{array}{l} \rightarrow \left[\begin{array}{l} x \\ y \end{array}\right. \\ \rightarrow \left[\begin{array}{l} m \\ n \end{array}\right. \end{array}\right.$ there are two simultaneous systems x/y and m/n, both having entry condition a (if a, then both either x or y and, independently, either m or n)

$a \rightarrow \left[\begin{array}{l} x \rightarrow \left[\begin{array}{l} x \\ n \end{array}\right. \\ y \end{array}\right.$ there are two systems x/y and m/n, ordered in dependence so that m/n has entry condition x and x/y has entry condition a (if a, then either x or y, and if x, then either m or n)

$\left.\begin{array}{l} a \\ b \end{array}\right\} \rightarrow \left[\begin{array}{l} x \\ y \end{array}\right.$ there is a system x/y with compound entry condition, conjunction of a and b (if both a and b, then either x or y)

$\left.\begin{array}{l} a \\ c \end{array}\right] \rightarrow \left[\begin{array}{l} m \\ n \end{array}\right.$ there is a system m/n with two possible entry conditions, union of a and c (if either a or c, or both, then either m or n)

* An expanded version appears in the Appendix to this volume.

Notes

1 Throughout the paper the following initials are used: MC = middle class; WC = working class; MIQ = medium verbal ability; HIQ = high verbal ability; B = boy; G = girl.
2 Similar figures were obtained when we asked how many children offered explanations in the course of giving non-role-play speech.
3 This correlation is exactly the same as that obtained by Brandis (1970) for the overall sample of mothers (n = 351).
4 Bernstein's comments on the working-class use of conditionals are discussed in section (*d*), p. 194.

References

BECKER, W. C. (1964), 'Consequences of different kinds of parental discipline', in M. L. Hoffman and L. W. Hoffman (eds), *Review of Child Development Research*, I, New York: Russell Sage Foundation, 169–208.

BEREITER, C. and ENGELMANN, S. (1966), *Teaching Disadvantaged Children in the Preschool*. New York: Prentice-Hall.

BERNSTEIN, B. (1958), 'Some sociological determinants of perception: an enquiry into sub-cultural differences', *British Journal of Sociology*, 9, 159–74.

BERNSTEIN, B. (1961), 'Social class and linguistic development: a theory of social learning', in A. H. Halsey, J. Floud and C. A. Anderson (eds), *Education, Economy and Society*. New York: Free Press, 288–314.

BERNSTEIN, B. (1962a), 'Social class, linguistic codes and grammatical elements', *Language and Speech*, 5, 221–40.

BERNSTEIN, B. (1962b), 'Family role systems, socialization and communication', manuscript, Sociological Research Unit, University of London Institute of Education; included in 'A socio-linguistic approach to socialization', *Directions in Sociolinguistics*, 1972, J. Gumperz and D. Hymes (eds). New York: Holt, Rinehart & Winston.

BERNSTEIN, B. (1964), 'Family role systems, socialization and communication', paper given at the Conference on Cross-Cultural Research into Childhood and Adolescence, University of Chicago.

BERNSTEIN, B. (1965), 'A socio-linguistic approach to social learning', in J. Gould (ed), *Social Science Survey*. London: Penguin.

BERNSTEIN, B. (1970a), 'A socio-linguistic approach to socialization: with some reference to educability', *The Human Context*, II, 1–9, 233–47. Also in J. Gumperz and D. Hymes (eds), *Directions in Sociolinguistics*, 1972. New York: Holt, Rinehart & Winston.

BERNSTEIN, B. (1970b), 'A critique of the concept "compensatory education" ', in D. Rubinstein and C. Stoneman (eds), *Education for Democracy*. London: Penguin.

BERNSTEIN. B. (1970c), 'Education cannot compensate for society', *New Society*, 26 February, 344–7.

BERNSTEIN, B. (1970d), 'Social class, language and socialization', to appear in A. S. Abramson, *et al.* (eds), *Current Trends in Linguistics*, vol. 12. The Hague: Mouton.

BERNSTEIN, B. (1971), 'Introduction', *Class, Codes and Control: Theoretical Studies towards Sociology of Language*. London: Routledge & Kegan Paul.

BERNSTEIN, B. and COOK, J. (1965), 'Social control coding manual, unpublished document, Sociological Research Unit. To appear in J. Cook (1972).

BERNSTEIN, B., BRANDIS, W. and MCGOVERN, E. (forthcoming), *Social Class and Teachers' Evaluations of Infant Schoolchildren*. London: Routledge & Kegan Paul.

BRANDIS, W. (1970), Appendix I 'Social class index'; Appendix II 'Communication and control index', in W. Brandis and D. Henderson, *Social Class, Language and Communication*. London: Routledge & Kegan Paul.

BRONFENBRENNER, U. (1958), 'Socialization and social class through time and space', in E. E. Maccoby, T. M. Newcomb and E. L. Hartley (eds), *Readings in Social Psychology*. New York: Holt, 400–25.

COOK, J. (1972), *Social Control and Socialization*. London: Routledge & Kegan Paul.

COOK, J. *et al.* (1970), Appendix 3 'Differences in the control of others', in Gahagan and Gahagan (1970).

FANTINI, M. D. and WEINSTEIN, G. (1968), *The Disadvantaged: Challenge to Education*. New York: Harper & Row.

FIRTH, J. R. (1935), 'The technique of semantics', *Transactions of the Philological Society*. Also in J. R. Firth, *Papers in Linguistics 1934–1951*. London: Oxford University Press, 1957, 7–33.

FIRTH, J. R. (1950), 'Personality and language in society', *Sociological Review*, 13, 2. Also in J. R. Firth, *Papers in Linguistics 1934–1951*. London: Oxford University Press, 1957, 177–89.

GAHAGAN, D. M. and GAHAGAN, G. A. (1970), *Talk Reform*. London: Routledge & Kegan Paul.

GINOTT, H. G. (1970), *Between Parent and Child*. London: Pan Books,

HALLIDAY, M. A. K. (1965), 'Types of structure', Nuffield Programme in Linguistics and English Teaching Work Paper, 1.

HALLIDAY, M. A. K. (1967a, b), 'Notes on transitivity and theme in English', parts I & II, *Journal of Linguistics*, 3, 37–81, 199–244.

HALLIDAY, M. A. K. (1968), 'Notes on transitivity and theme in English', part III, *Journal of Linguistics*, 4, 179–215.

HALLIDAY, M. A. K. (1969), 'The components of a grammar', prepared for Programme in Linguistics and English Teaching, University College, London.

HALLIDAY, M. A. K. (1970a), 'On functional grammars', in paper read to seminar, 'The Construction of Complex Grammars', Boston, Mass. (mimeographed).

HALLIDAY, M. A. K. (1970b), 'Functional diversity in language', *Foundations of Language*, 6, 322–61.

HALLIDAY, M. A. K. (1970c), Sections 1–7 of chapter 11, 'Sociological applications', *Introduction to System-Structure Theory of Language*. New York: Holt, Rinehart & Winston (forthcoming).

HALLIDAY, M. A. K. (1971), 'Language in a social perspective', *Educational Review*, 23, 165–88.

HASAN, R. (1972), 'Code, register and social dialect', in the present volume.

HAWKINS, P. R. (1969), 'Social class, the nominal group and reference', *Language and Speech*, 12, 125–35, and in the present volume.

HESS, R. D. and SHIPMAN, V. C. (1968), 'Maternal influences upon early learning: the cognitive environments of urban pre-school children', in R. D. Hess and R. M. Bear (eds), *Early Education: Current Theory, Research and Action*. Chicago: Aldine.

HESS, R. D. *et al.* (1968), 'The Cognitive Environments of Urban Preschool Children', the Graduate School of Education, The University of Chicago.

HUDDLESTON, R. D. *et al.* (1968), 'Sentence and Clause in Scientific English', report of the O.S.T.I. Programme in the Linguistic Properties of Scientific English. Communication Research Centre, University College, London.

HYMES, D. (1962), 'The ethnography of speaking', in T. Gladwin and W. C. Sturtevant (eds), *Anthropology and Human Behaviour*. Washington, D.C.: Anthropological Society of Washington.

HYMES, D. (1964), 'Introduction: toward ethnographies of communication', in J. Gumperz and D. Hymes (eds), *The Ethnography of Communication*. Washington, D.C.: Anthropological Society of Washington.

LAWTON, D. (1964), 'Social class language differences in group discussions', *Language and Speech*, 7, 182–204.

LOBAN, W. D. (1966), *Language Ability: Grades Seven, Eight and Nine*. Co-operative Research Monograph, no. 18, U.S. Dept. of Health, Education and Welfare, Office of Education. Washington: U.S. Government Printing Office.

KOHN, M. L. (1959a), 'Social class and the exercise of parental authority', *American Sociological Review*, 24, 352–66.

KOHN, M. L. (1959b), 'Social class and parental values', *American Journal of Sociology*, 64, 337–51.

KOHN, M. L. (1963), 'Social class and parent-child relationship: an interpretation', *American Journal of Sociology*, 68, 471–80.

KOHLBERG, L. (1964), 'Development of moral character and moral ideology', in M. L. Hoffman and L. W. Hoffman (eds), *Review of Child Development Research*, I. New York: Russell Sage Foundation, 383–431.

MILLER, D. R. and SWANSON, G. E. (1960), *Inner Conflict and Defense*. New York: Holt.

NEWSON, J. and NEWSON, E. (1968), *Four Years Old in an Urban Community*. London: Allen & Unwin.

PIAGET, J. (1948), *The Moral Judgement of the Child*. Chicago: Free Press.

SEARS, R. R., MACCOBY, E. E. and LEVIN, H. (1957), *Patterns of Child Rearing*. Evanstan, Ill.: Row, Peterson.

SCHAEFER, E. S. (1959), 'A circumplex model for maternal behaviour', *Journal of Abnormal Social Psychology*. 59, 226–35.

SCHAEFER, E. S. (1961), 'Converging conceptual models for maternal behaviour and for child behaviour', in J. C. Glidewell (ed.), *Parental Attitudes and Child Behaviour*. Springfield, Ill.: Charles C. Thomas.

TEMPLIN, M. C. (1957), *Certain Language Skills in Children: Their Development and Interrelationships*. Minneapolis: University of Minnesota Press.

Acknowledgments

I should like to express my gratitude to Professor Bernstein and Professor M. A. K. Halliday who gave valuable advice and criticism on an earlier draft of this paper. I should also like to thank my colleagues Dr Ruqaiya Hasan and John Lawrence, for many helpful discussions.

Chapter 8 Where do children's answers come from?

W. P. Robinson

Introduction

The last ten years have seen changes in the clarity and detail of Bernstein's ideas about language and society. The early development has been traced by Lawton (1968), who illustrates how questions about his theory can be set at various different levels of analysis, be these sociological, social psychological, psychological, linguistic or inter-actions of these. In this study, we focus upon what mothers make available for their children to learn within the particular area of answering children's questions. The first half of the paper presents a somewhat extended reanalysis of the problem posed at Bernstein's original level of a sociological contrast between middle and lower working-class socialization practices. The second half attempts to shift the level to social psychological variations among individual mothers within each social class category. In both halves, the variations among mothers' answers are analysed in relation to differences in the ways in which their children answer questions.

In the development of his ideas about child-rearing and social class, Bernstein has argued for the usefulness of a more basic contrast between what he calls positional and personal systems of control (Bernstein, 1966). In the positional system, the emphasis is upon the induction of role appropriate behaviour, roles themselves being defined in relation to general status categories such as age, sex, and status differentials. Norms and rules governing what is and is not appropriate are conveyed, either overtly in such forms as 'Little boys of five do not . . .', or implicitly by direct punishing or unexplained commands like 'Stop that!'. Whether or not the child can manage to extract what is 'implicit' we do not know. Whether there are regularities to be extracted can also be doubted. In this system, the use of language is primarily directed towards the immediate control of behaviour.

In the personal system, language is used not only to the end of immediate and mediated control, but also for the transmission of more general information. A personal system of control uses verbally based explanations which direct attention to the consequences of behaviour for individuals: how specified people will feel or would feel and what they will or would have to do, given that certain events occur. In this system, children are given reasons for behaviour which transcend the limitations of the ascribed roles of the positional system, and language can function indirectly as a means of control in that it is used to convey information relevant to conduct.

In Bernstein's thesis, the lower-working-class[1] families will tend to use positional systems of control, the middle-class personal systems. This does not mean that members of the middle class invariably rely solely on the personal system, but that in general when other pressures on parents are not too great they will begin with the personal system. It does not mean that LWC families always issue abrupt commands or move into non-verbal action. That these systems of control are differentially associated with social class has been checked empirically in a number of investigations. Social class differences have been found in mothers' attitudes to control problems (Bernstein and Henderson, 1970; Jones, 1966), in the reported control behaviour of mothers (Cook, 1972; Bernstein and Brandis, 1970; Newson and Newson, 1970) and their observed behaviour (Hess and Shipman, 1965).

But investigations have also begun to move on from studies of social class differences to an examination of relationships between the behaviour of individual pairs of mothers and children, showing direct associations between individual differences in mothers and children within class. Bernstein and Young (1967)* and Bernstein and Brandis (1970) have shown that certain mediating social psychological variables can be used to predict a child's performance over and above social class. The present study is an attempt to extend such work within the area of answers to 'wh' questions (who, where, when, what, why and how).

In a previous article, Robinson and Rackstraw (1967) tested several predictions derived from Bernstein's theoretical framework. Mothers had been asked how they would reply to a number of 'wh' questions supposedly posed by their five-year-old children. For two 'where from' and four 'why' questions, it was predicted and found that, relative to LWC mothers, MC mothers evaded fewer questions, gave more accurate information in their answers, gave a greater amount of information, used fewer common 'filler' words irrelevant to the facts, inserted fewer socio-centric sequences and

* See this volume, chapter 1.

gave different types of answer to 'why' questions: they were more likely to use appeals to higher order categories, analogies, cause and consequence, but less likely to repeat the question as its own answer or make appeals to the simple regularity of events. The answers of the LWC mothers could be construed as having the function of controlling rather than informing. A subsequent study (Robinson and Rackstraw, 1972, chapters 7 and 8) extended the work to seven-year-old children and to a wider variety of possible differences in answering behaviour, with similar and additional results.

Since the social class differences found in answers to 'wh' questions were very similar in both mothers and children, it is reasonable to assume some causal link between the two. However, it is preferable to demonstrate direct associations, and this is what has been attempted here. To specify relationships between individual mothers and children is a goal at a far remove from the purposes of the original investigation, and there are consequent methodological weaknesses in the adaptation and enlargement of the original design. For example, the children answered their twenty-nine 'wh' questions two years after their mothers had reported how they would answer questions. In the intervening period the children had been at school and had therefore been exposed to sources of influence that should have generally acted to reduce the probability of finding direct links between mothers and children, in so far as experiences in schools differed from those at home. There were also losses of sample members. In all, data were available on a sample of fifty-five mother/daughter pairs, of which twenty-three were LWC and twenty-two MC, the remainder being intermediate.

The analysis was conducted in stages. The first two of these were concerned with replication and an assessment of the relevance of the control and communication index to answering:

Stage 1. For a selected sample of both maternal and child variables, a check was made on the previous results. Correlations were run between social class and various indices of question answering to confirm that previously found social class differences were upheld within this sample of subjects.

Stage 2. Correlations were run within the MC and LWC samples separately to see whether the Control and Communication Index (CCI) used in other work of the Sociological Research Unit (Brandis, 1970) accounted for within-class variance.

The third stage involved the construction of indices of answering in both mothers and children for application to the fourth stage, in which associations between mothers and children were examined within the two social class groups.

Stage 3. In the construction of a usable social psychological indices, joint consideration was paid to empirical co-variation and theoretical interest as guides for the reduction of the rather large number of maternal and child variables in the study. This was a prelude to the examination of direct mother–child links.
Stage 4. Finally, analyses were conducted to examine the links between the mother and child answering indices within each social class.

Expectations were that similar results to those obtained before would be found for relationships between social class and language used. It was hoped that the CCI would reveal a similar pattern within social class groupings. It was also predicted that the maternal answering variables would be directly associated with their children's scores on corresponding variables within social class in a similar fashion.

Method

Subjects

There were too few boys available from the original studies for a within-class analysis to be feasible, but 55 mother/daughter pairs were selected, of whom 22 were clear middle class, 23 unambiguously working class, and 10 were intermediate. Brandis (1970) had produced a ten-point social class index which gave equal weight to mother's and father's education and occupation. A score of 9 indicated that neither parent had experienced more than basic secondary education nor held more than an unskilled job (Hall-Jones category 7), while a score of 0 showed that both parents had enjoyed more than secondary education and had held jobs which were clearly middle class (Hall-Jones categories 1, 2 and 3). In this sample the mean score for the middle class was 2·50 (max. 1, min. 4: s.d. 1·01) and for the working class 7·57 (max. 6, min. 9: s.d. 1·15). Hence, the middle class were solid middle class and the working class mainly lower working class.

Although in the earlier studies a control had been maintained on verbal intelligence test scores (EPVT, Brimer and Dunn, 1962), this was not feasible here and the MC girls ($\bar{x}$ = 103·5, s.d. 8·5) made somewhat higher scores than their LWC peers ($\bar{x}$ = 95·4, s.d. 6·6). Since these scores were only of minor significance in both previous studies, this difference was not adjudged serious.

Materials

The materials used have been described in detail previously (Robinson and Rackstraw, 1972). Mothers reported how they would answer one 'who', two 'where from' and four 'why' questions supposedly asked by their five-year-old children: Q1 Why does Daddy shave every morning? Q2 Where does the water in the tap come from? Q3 Why do leaves fall off the trees? Q4 Why did Mrs Jones cry when Johnny went into hospital? Q5 Where did I come from? Q6 Who is the man who brings the milk? Q7 Why do I have to go to school in September?

The children answered 29 'wh' questions: 2 'where from', 'what for', 'how well', 'who', and 'what', 3 'when', 'where' and 'how' and 10 'why' questions—4 'why' questions dealt with the physical world, 4 with morals and two with social matters (see Appendix I).

The Index of Control and Communication was taken from Brandis (1970). It was based on five aspects of mother–child inter-action: willingness to answer difficult questions, willingness to chatter in a variety of situations, an attitude to toys which noted their use for development, the absence of punishment (use of physical punishment, verbal reproof and imperative command), and the presence of reasoning (appeals oriented to consequences for the child and taking the child's intention into account). A higher score means more communication.

Procedure

Questions to the mothers were given as part of a protracted interview schedule in their own homes. The daughters answered their questions at school in an informal and friendly individual interview conducted by a familiar female research worker. Precise specifications of the scoring procedure of individual categories can be found elsewhere (Robinson and Rackstraw, 1972). Here, descriptions are confined to short comments and the provision of typical examples.

Scoring procedure

MATERNAL DATA

While much of this second analysis was similar to the first, further categories were added, categories that subsequent research and thinking had suggested might be fruitful. The total set of categories could be grouped under four headings:

(i) *Strategies of answering*

1. *Truth has to be told.* For some questions mothers would say explicitly that they felt that their children should never be given untrue or inaccurate answers.

2. *Appeals to differences,* and 3. *Appeals to similarities.* Particularly for the question 'Who brings the milk?', mothers were likely to mention similarities to and differences from father's job. Such tactics should provide the child with opportunities to organize and co-ordinate knowledge about the world. Analogies with a metaphorical flavour were excluded and left under the appeal to analogy mode.

4. *Question-answer mismatch.* Where answers were semantically unrelated to the question, a note was made of an 'irrelevant' answer.

5. *Ignorance of what to say.* This category included statements of not knowing an answer, not knowing what to say, and unqualified claims that questions would be answered later.

6. *Untrue answers.* Answers which cited clearly inaccurate facts were scored. Marginal cases were ignored, and religious answers, especially to the 'baby' question were not included. (This reverses the procedure adopted in the earlier article.)

7. *Questions like this not asked.* Mothers occasionally made explicit statements to the effect that questions like these were never posed. While this may have been true, it might also be taken as an indication that such mothers would be very uncertain how to handle such questions, i.e. they had no prior policy to call upon.

(ii) *Style of answering*

Mothers could *add* a variety of words and phrases to the kernel structure of their answers that carried no extra information, and they could *substitute* relatively uninformative general-purpose nouns. adjectives, verbs and adverbs. The categories of Simplifiers (e.g. just), Additional words and phrases (e.g. really), Redundant finishers (e.g. and that), Indefinite modifiers, qualifiers, heads and adjuncts (e.g. something, sort of) and Indefinite adjuncts attached to verb (e.g. he like pushed me), and Socio-centric tags (you know) were viewed as likely LWC preferences for addition and substitution. Minimizers (of unpleasantness of hospitals), and Adjuncts and verbs of hypothesis (possibly, I wonder) were included as possible indicators of MC style. The probable relevance of the latter is supported by the finding of Turner and Pickvance (1972) that such verbs of hypothesis and uncertainty were more commonly used by MC children.

(iii) *Amount of information*

The previously scored units of information were counted for both 'where from' questions. For 'Where does the water in the tap come from?', four processes of collection, purification, storage and distribution could each receive a point as could a mention of each installation or sources involved. For the baby question similar units were extracted.

It was noticed that the answers to the 'leaf falling' and 'hospital' 'why' questions were frequently supplemented by the provision of additional facts. Hence these two were included in the information count and given a maximum score of 2 for each question.

(iv) *Types of information*

The nine previously used modes were used with no amendments. The seven actually occurring were:

(1) Repetition of questions as statement (20)*, e.g. Because they do.
(2) Unqualified appeals to regularity of events (21), e.g. They fall every year.
(3) Appeals to wants and wishes (25) (36, Q4), e.g. Because I want to.
(4) Appeals to analogy (26), e.g. The tree falls asleep and . . .
(5) Categorization of event or object (24) (35, Q1), e.g. Leaves are alive and all living things die.
(6) Appeals to cause (27, Q3) (28, Q4), e.g. The strong winds of autumn blow them off.
(7) Appeals to consequence (29, Q1 beard removal) (30, Q1 other reason) (31, Q3) (32, Q7 to learn on its own) (33, Q7 number of specific skills) (34, Q7 long term reasons), e.g. So that new leaves can come in the spring.

In the previous study, it was noticed that appeals could differ considerably in their complexity, and sub-divisions were introduced to take this into account. For instance, in answer to 'Why does daddy shave every morning?', the simplest appeal to consequence was 'To remove his beard', and this was separated from more complex answers. Similarly, 'To learn' as a reason for going to school could be separated from more detailed specifications. Other details will be mentioned in the text and tables. Modes 1 and 2

* Numbers in brackets refer to code numbers in the tables of results.

above (20 and 21) were summated to give a single score 'Focus as proposition' (22). Rackstraw had argued earlier (Robinson and Rackstraw, 1972) that such answers had a degree of similarity in that they require no special empirical knowledge relevant to the content of the question in hand.

Mothers sometimes used a single mode in their answers (37), but they could mention more than one, and it seemed useful to include a count of those answers which utilized more than one mode of explanation (28).

CHILD DATA

In the earlier analysis the emphasis was on types of information and this is reflected here also. Only a few categories dealt with anything else: most of these were concerned with aspects of grammar, lexis, and context, each of these being examined for instances of inappropriateness or incompleteness. Inappropriateness involved a sin of commission, where some feature present was unacceptable in terms of the rules of adult grammar or lexis or did not correspond to the world as it is (context). Incompleteness was similar except that it involved a sin of omission, where the insertion of an extra element or elements would yield an acceptable sentence. Contextual completeness was the number of units of information. 'No answer', 'Don't know' and answer irrelevant to the question were also scored.

The other items were concerned with the various modes of answers to 'why' questions, but modes for 'when', 'where' and 'who' questions were incorporated in addition to those for 'why'. Objective modes of answering 'where' and 'when' questions were distinguished from relative modes. 'Objective' answers were those that used the least relative system of location, e.g. addresses or days and years, while 'relative' answers were couched in terms of distance from present place or time etc. Allowance in the scoring was made for the possibility that in some contexts for some 'when' and 'where' questions it would be odd not to give a 'relative' answer. Children's answers to 'where' questions sometimes mentioned places that the experimenter was most unlikely to know by the names the children used, and this was noted as an index of 'not taking the other into account'—inappropriate contextual presupposition. The use of the teacher's or doctor's name was included as being more likely to be informative to an inquirer than a report of the role label.

Stages 1 and 2: Social class and Control and Communication Index in relation to answers of mothers and children

Treatment of results

The analysis of the results proceeded in two stages:

(1) A large number of individual and a few combined items from both mother and child were included in a correlation matrix along with social class and control and communication index (CCI).
This analysis was conducted for several reasons. First, it was important to check whether or not this sample exhibited the same relationships between mother and child answering and social class as those found earlier. Second, it gave information relevant to the subsequent reduction of the number of scores for both mother and child.

(2) Separate correlation matrices were calculated for the MC and LWC samples. This provided some data about possible differences in association between variables within classes, but the main intention was to investigate the role of the communication and control index as a significant source of variance, with social class controlled.

Results

Stage 1: Social class in relation to answers of mothers and children

MOTHERS' ANSWERS

Table 8.1 shows both the correlations between social class and the total set of individual items and the significance of the differences in the mean scores of MC and LWC mothers. Of the 37 items, 11 gave significant correlations with social class, while the same number gave correlations with CCI—five were common to both. Thirteen items showed up differences in mean incidence of usage by the two social classes. Taken together, 18 items gave at least one significant relationship with social class.

Within the set dealing with strategy of mothers' answers, ignorance of what to say, answers being to other questions, wrong facts in reply to questions, and an absence of differences being pointed out, occurred more frequently in the lower working class.

For amount of information, MC mothers gave more units of information in reply to both the 'babies' and the 'hospital' questions. The indices of style gave only one significant correlation—the lower working class using more simplifiers. However, the directions of the other seven correlations were consistent with previous results.

For modes, the most impressive result was the tendency of the MC mothers to give multiple category answers. Among individual modes for individual questions, they showed preferences for appeals to wants, categorization and consequence on the 'shaving' question, and wants and cause on the 'hospital' question. Of the individual modes summed over questions, only appeals to wants and categorization gave significant degrees of association, although directions for other items were again in line with expectations.

CHILDREN'S ANSWERS

Table 8.2 shows the relationships between social class, CCI and aspects of children's answers. Social class had ten significant correlations, while nine items discriminated between the middle and lower working class on the tests. CCI gave only two significant relationships.

Grammatical incompleteness and the provision of irrelevant answers were more common among LWC girls. Few of the modes gave significant associations. For those which did, the lower working class were more likely to make appeals to regularity alone, to unspecified authority and to the avoidance of punishment to self as a reason for not doing things, while the middle class were more likely to use combined appeals to wants and consequence, to use the teacher's or doctor's name, and to use objective modes for answering 'when' questions. Again, many other correlations were in appropriate directions.

Stage 2: Control and Communication Index within class

Within each main social class, the correlations between class and CCI were reduced respectively to $-0{\cdot}16$ in the middle class and $-0{\cdot}05$ in the lower working class. With social class removed as a source of variance, a number of correlations remained significant (see Table 8.1). MC mothers high on CCI were likely to give more units of information in reply to the 'babies' question (in spite of a general reluctance to say how 'babies' got there), were less likely

TABLE 8.1 *Mothers' answers in relation to social class and the control and communication index*

	Total sample		Middle class	Working class	Middle class		Working class		
	SC	*CCI*	*CCI*	*CCI*	*Mean*	*S.D.*[2]	*Mean*	*S.D.*[2]	*t*
(i) *Strategy of answering*									
1. Truth to be told	—09	14	20	—03	0·27	0·21	0·17	0·15	0·77
2. Differences pointed out	—38*	05	—18	—	0·32	0·23	0	0	3·13*
3. Similarities pointed out	—22	16	24	—03	0·50	0·26	0·30	0·22	1·34
4. Irrelevant answers	38*	—15	—	0	0	0	0·35	0·24	3·28*
5. Ignorance of what to say	35*	—33†	—09	—34	0·85	0·05	0·35	0·42	2·02†
6. Inaccurate facts in answer	32†	—27‡	—17	—21	0·05	0·05	0·26	0·20	1·93‡
7. Questions like this not asked	08	—08	04	10	0·09	0·09	0·26	0·20	1·46
(ii) *Style*									
8. Simplifiers	33†	—05	11	08	0·23	0·18	1·78	5·09	3·10*
9. Indefinite in nominal group	—07	0	39‡	—14	0·23	0·28	0·26	0·47	0·16
10. Indefinite verb adjuncts	11	—15	—01	—31	0·05	0·05	0·52	1·81	1·58
11. Redundant finishers	13	—18	16	—05	0·09	0·09	0·83	3·15	1·89‡
12. Additional words and phrases	19	—15	11	04	0·55	0·83	1·35	3·87	1·69‡
13. Socio-centric tags	08	—05	25	0	0·55	1·02	1·39	4·89	1·59
14. Markers of hypothetical	—04	15	20	09	1·32	3·75	1·22	3·18	0·18
15. Minimizers	—09	37*	27‡	37‡	0·68	0·61	0·35	0·78	1·29
(iii) *Amount of information*									
16. Units: tap water (Q2)	—07	16	19	0	2·09	1·71	1·48	1·99	1·47
17. Units: baby (Q5)	—54*	43*	48†	22	1·41	0·63	0·48	0·35	4·37*
18. Units: leaf fall (Q3)	—24‡	—04	11	0	0·95	0·52	0·52	0·44	2·03†
19. Units: hospital stay (Q4)	—32†	22	29	—09	0·27	0·21	0·04	0·04	2·15†
(iv) *Modes*									
20. Repetition as statement	08	—17	—	—03	0	0	0·17	0·24	1·59
21. Simple appeal to regularity	—01	—36*	—45†	—35‡	0·36	0·43	0·43	0·36	0·36
22. Focus on proposition	13	—37*	—45†	—23	0·36	0·43	0·74	0·38	1·96‡
23. Number of multiple category answers	—34†	29†	—11	31	1·45	0·55	0·61	0·52	3·76*
24. Categorization	—34†	17	—22	26	0·95	0·33	0·35	0·33	3·42*
25. Wants and wishes	[illegible]	[illegible]	[illegible]	[illegible]	[illegible]	[illegible]	[illegible]	[illegible]	[illegible]

26.	Analogies	[illegible]	[illegible]	[illegible]	[illegible]	[illegible]	[illegible]	[illegible]	[illegible]	[illegible]
27.	Cause (Q3)	−11	03	51†	28	0·27	0·21	0·48	0·26	1·42
28.	Cause (Q4)	06	14	−09	37‡	0·45	0·26	0·52	0·26	0·45
29.	Consequence (beard removal, Q1)	−08	33†	26	50†	0·68	0·23	0·65	0·24	0·20
30.	Consequence (other reason, Q1)	0	0	0	−05	0·23	0·18	0·13	0·12	0·85
31.	Consequence (Q3)	−24‡	−04	−20	−10	0·23	0·18	0·04	0·04	1·90‡
32.	Consequence (to learn, Q7)	11	08	13	20	0·32	0·23	0·39	0·25	0·47
33.	Consequence (number skills, Q7)	−19	04	−15	−04	0·91	1·04	0·48	0·81	1·47
34.	Consequence (long-term reasons Q7)	−09	30†	18	34	0·68	0·70	0·30	0·22	1·85‡
35.	Categorization (Q1)	−25‡	32†	0	62*	0·45	0·26	0·13	0·12	2·42†
36.	Wants and wishes (Q4)	−38*	34†	13	22	0·91	0·09	0·52	0·26	3·05†
37.	Single category answers	14	−13	11	−01	2·55	0·55	3·04	0·50	2·23†
n		55	55	22	23	22	—	23	—	

* means $p < 0{\cdot}01$, † $p < 0{\cdot}05$, ‡ $p < 0{\cdot}1$

TABLE 8.2 *Children's answers in relation to social class and the control and communication index*

	Total sample SC	Total sample CCI	Middle class CCI	Working class CCI	Middle class Mean	Middle class S.D.²	Working class Mean	Working class S.D.²	t
(i) *Strategy of answering*									
40. No answers	12	02	20	04	1·23	5·42	2·61	12·07	1·52
41. Don't knows	−16	22	31	06	4·73	10·02	3·74	11·29	0·99
42. Irrelevant answers	50*	−14	−05	11	0·41	0·35	1·83	2·97	3·58*
43. Contextual inappropriateness	21	−09	−21	−12	0·50	0·26	0·87	0·94	1·55
(iii) *Amount of information*									
44. Contextual completeness	−29†	−19	04	25	5·18	5·97	3·61	4·70	2·23†
(iv) *Modes*									
45. Restatement	−08	02	−02	08	2·45	3·69	2·00	3·45	0·78
46. Regularity alone	28†	−12	12	−07	0·14	0·12	0·39	0·25	1·89‡
47. Focus on proposition	20	−24‡	−27	−19	7·18	12·06	8·26	22·75	0·84
48. Unspecified authority	30†	−10	−21	06	0·14	0·22	0·74	1·47	2·12†
49. Regularity qualified	−21	12	28	−23	0·18	0·16	0·04	0·04	1·68‡
50. Categorization (m)	−21	04	−23	16	1·18	0·63	0·83	0·88	
51. Cause (p)	−19	−01	−03	−16	4·32	4·99	2·87	4·21	2·22†
52. Wants and wishes	07	04	−61*	51†	0·18	0·25	0·30	0·40	0·69
53. Combined wants and consequences (m)	−28†	18	−54*	58*	2·59	4·35	1·22	3·54	2·26†
54. Consequence (p)	18	−12	−05	−07	0·86	1·17	1·70	3·22	1·85‡
55. Consequence (s)	−03	−04	−17	01	1·64	0·91	1·48	0·81	0·56
56. Consequence (m)	10	−08	−43*	19	4·18	6·25	4·30	6·86	0·15
57. Consequence (m) negative actor-punishment	47*	−21	−28	01	1·14	1·65	2·48	3·44	2·74†
58. Consequence (m) action, other or actor effects (not punishment)	−25‡	09	−35‡	34‡	3·14	5·93	1·87	3·39	1·93‡
59. Objective modes (when)	−48*	37*	25	29	2·14	0·50	1·04	1·04	4·09*
60. Objectives modes (where)	−20	21	20	10	2·27	0·49	1·91	0·72	1·51
61. Answers not using colloquial place names	−32†	31†	−18	02	0·86	0·69	1·52	0·62	2·67†
62. Naming (who)	−30†	14	30	−08	0·64	0·24	0·39	0·43	1·41
Formal									
63. Grammatical inappropriateness	11	06	46†	−02	0·95	0·71	1·30	0·68	1·37
64. Grammatical incompleteness	43*	−18	−10	−28	1·73	2·02	3·39	2·98	3·43*
65. Lexical inappropriateness	−25‡	−25‡	−16	−34‡	0·73	1·16	1·13	1·39	1·16
66. Lexical incompleteness	04	04	08	−11	1·23	2·28	1·04	1·04	0·48
n	55	55	22	23	22	—	23	—	

* means $p < 0·01$, † $p < 0·05$, ‡ $p < 0·1$

to use unqualified appeals to regularity and more likely to use causal explanations. In the lower working class, high CCI mothers were more likely to use categorization, one of the appeals to consequence answer, as well as multiple category answers on the 'shaving' question. Eight other correlations were above 0·30.

For the child data, high CCI MC girls were less likely to use appeal to wants and the combined appeal to wants and consequences, while the exact reverse was true in the lower working class. High CCI MC girls were also less likely to appeal to consequences in moral questions. Such results do suggest a measure of relevance of CCI to answering behaviour with social class controlled, particularly for modes of answering by mothers.

Discussion

The previously found differences between MC and LWC answers to 'wh' questions were replicated for both mothers (Robinson and Rackstraw, 1967) and children (Robinson and Rackstraw, 1972). This is not surprising, since the subject samples on the two occasions had a common nucleus. Some further results were obtained with a number of new coding categories. The previous result that MC mothers were likely to give more information than LWC mothers in their answers to 'where from' questions was supplemented by the demonstration that this was also true for two 'why' questions. Under the general heading of 'strategy of answering', two new categories are of interest: differences and similarities being pointed out. Of these, the tendency to mention differences gave significant relationships with social class. Both categories were assumed to be important, because they are relevant to the *ordering* of knowledge acquired. It is a long time since Aristotle mentioned that two desirable aspects of the definition of any term or concept are its differences from and similarities to related terms and concepts, and the result obtained here provides some support for the idea that MC mothers are more likely than LWC to attempt to organize the knowledge of their children in this way.

For modes, the 'focus on proposition' category gave a significant difference, with the LWC mothers being more likely to use it. Rackstraw's idea (Robinson and Rackstraw, 1972) that a small number of sentence frames can be used to answer any 'why' question without the answerer needing any knowledge other than that provided in the question has a theoretical and aesthetic appeal, but did not receive substantial empirical support in the earlier study. Here it fared better. Although the correlations with social class were significant for both mothers and daughters, the difference in means between the MC and LWC mothers was nearer acceptable levels of significance, and it did give significant correlations with the Control and Communication Index. In the MC sample, the mothers' use of weak modes was associated with the use of 'focus on the proposition' modes in the children, and in the LWC sample, the mothers' use of weak modes was related to two constituents of the 'focus on proposition' modes in their daughters (see pp. 227 and 229).

No attempt was made to bring together 'strong' modes of explanation for the analysis of social class differences, and when it was used for the within-class predictive analysis, some apparently odd results were obtained. This issue is taken up again later.

From the theoretical standpoint, the social class differences lend support to Bernstein's thesis. We originally derived the following predictions: that, relative to LWC mothers, MC mothers should:

(1) Evade fewer questions (5)
(2) Give more accurate answers (6)
(3) Give more information in their answers (16, 17, 18, 19)
(4) Show less structural disorganization in their answers (not tested)
(5) Use fewer 'noisy' additional items (8, 11, 12)
(6) Use fewer socio-centric tags (13).

Those examined were supported by the results. There was also a seventh multiple prediction concerning modes, to the effect that the MC mothers should use relatively more appeals to categorization (24), arguments from analogy (26), appeals to cause (27,28) and consequences (29–34), but fewer denials of oddity (no instances), repetitions of the question as a statement (20), appeals to authority (not tested in isolation), essence (not tested in isolation) and simple regularity (21) (see Table 8.1).

The latter types of explanation were relatively rare, some not occurring at all. (Those not tested in isolation were simply too uncommon for significant differences to be possible.) However, when combined as 'focus an proposition' explanations, the expected differences appeared.

Of the others, categorization, appeals to consequence for the 'leaf' question, and long-term consequences of going to school were associated with social class. Appeals to cause and relatively simple immediate consequences did not differentiate between the classes. This introduces the problem of *level* and *extensiveness* of explanation as well as mode.

An argument could be advanced which would assert that very simple, short, concrete, and particular causal or consequential explanations are available to many mothers for many questions. If this is so, the empirical problem of describing the social class differences in detail will require some more thorough detective work than is possible with our data. If it is true that the appeals to cause and consequences by the LWC mothers are simpler and less developed than those used by the MC, it would also be interesting to know what happens, when these are followed by a second 'why' question—whether, for example, there is a speedy switch to a 'focus on proposition' mode, an admission of ignorance, or a provision of further empirical information.

Differences between MC and LWC girls were similar to those found between their mothers. For strategy of answering, the provision of irrelevant answers (42) clearly differentiated between the classes and inaccurate answers (43—contextual inappropriateness) nearly so; the amount of information likewise (44—contextual completeness).

For the 'focus on proposition' modes, both appeals to simple regularity (46) and unspecified authority (48) yielded differences, but the summary score, which included what were termed *simple* categorizations, did not achieve significance. Modes of answering among the girls were generally weak in their association with social class. Cause and appeals to wants and wishes gave differences. Appeals to consequence were confounded by two initially worrying problems, similar to those mentioned in the section on mothers' answers. We have to consider level and complexity of explanation as well as type. For example, with questions about the physical world, some appeals to consequence invoked human-centred rather than other reasons for natural events (e.g. the sea has waves so we can swim in it). This type of thinking has been mentioned by Piaget (1927) as characteristic of the young child's ego-centric approach to problems of causality, but on our scoring it is incorporated into total appeals to consequence. Similarly, the category 'consequence-negative' actor punishment (e.g. 'Because I'd get smacked') is a consequence, but, in developmental terms it is alleged to characterize only the first stage of successively more difficult reasons for not doing certain things (Kohlberg, 1963). From earlier work, we would expect children of seven to include such reasons in their explanations, but to be moving on to other reasons as well. It is noteworthy that both sorts of reasons are more common in LWC than in MC answers. However, that LWC children are giving appeals to consequence, means that our theoretical framework must be developed to cope with complexity and level of explanation as well as type.

We may also note that for the 'when' questions (and to a lesser extent for 'where') strong social class differences were obtained. MC girls were more likely to give names than roles in answer to 'who' questions and less likely to mention places by colloquial names outside their listener's knowledge.

The results with the Control and Communication Index may be less satisfactory than an optimist might have hoped for, but they are better than a pessimist would have predicted. For mothers' answers, CCI was as powerful a discriminator as social class. While the success might have accrued from the common variance with social class ($r = 0{\cdot}33$), this correlation represents only 10 per cent of the total variance and thus renders such an interpretation unlikely. Certainly, the pattern of results is sufficiently consistent to suggest both that the move to social psychological variables will prove useful and that the verbal output of mother to child is the most sensible domain to explore.[2] To extricate the particularly relevant variables and to specify the nature of their relationships with children's behaviour may prove difficult, but one obvious strategy is to explore this within sub-culturally homogenous groups. What follows in the second half of this paper is one example of how this can be pursued within the context of question-answer exchanges.

Two aspects of the relationships between CCI and the children's answers are worth noting. The first is that there are hints that the CCI index relates to children's answers differently in the two social class groups. The use of regularity qualified and categorization, appeals to wants or wishes and moral consequence, all gave correlations different in sign in the two groups. Other items may be similar. At this point in time nothing constructive can be added, but this contingency should be borne in mind.

It may also be observed that social class of mothers is more relevant to children's answers than is CCI, although this was not so for their own answers. If we argue that social class predisposes mothers towards the adoption of certain attitudes to child rearing, which predispose them to adopt some patterns of behaviour rather than others and that these patterns are *one* source of the child's learning opportunities, which in turn will be *one* set of factors influencing the child's answers to our interviewer's questions, then it can be seen that CCI and maternal answers to children's questions are more closely linked in this 'causal' chain than are CCI and children's answers. One complication arising from the actual design of the investigation is the two-year gap between the collection of data from the children and their mothers. For prediction to be successful across this gap it is necessary to assume some continuity of maternal behaviour. While there may well be consistency of attitudes, the realization of these may well change as children develop. In fact, one would expect that socialization procedures that accommodate to the child's development will change; the particular behavioural tactics optimally efficient for encouraging development in five year olds will be different from those efficient for seven-year-olds. Of course, in so far as mothers producing best tactics at one point in time do so at others, such variables as CCI could be predictive of children's behaviour.

However, it would still not be surprising to find that social psychological variables other than CCI are more closely associated with children's answers and the maternal answering behaviours themselves are the most obvious starting points for investigation.

This is examined next.

Stages 3 and 4: Relationships between mothers' and children's answers

Treatment of results

The decision to analyse within social class was taken because social class covers a complex set of variables, many of which might be linked to children's answers. By looking at the two social class groups separately, this source of contamination is at best eliminated or at least reduced.

The next difficulty lay in the existence of 37 maternal and 27 child variables. If these were to be reduced to manageable proportions, how could this be achieved and what form should any compression take? Since the objective was to predict from mothers' behaviour to children's, it was considered more important to construct summary indices of maternal than child behaviour. Further, we might expect mothers' behaviour to be more stable and consistent than that of developing seven year olds, so that there is also a greater probability of achieving success with them. The construction of summary indices was based on the dual principles of theoretical interest and empirical co-variance.

Where a summary heading could be applied to a set of scores such as 'amount of information' or 'focus on proposition' modes, scores might be combined on these criteria, especially if the scores co-vary empirically. On the other hand, if a number of scores correlate positively with each other, this clustering may suggest a common heading which would justify summation. To anticipate, if four scores, each labelled 'units of information', all have positive correlations with each other, a summary score can be justified on both counts.

The construction of indices proceeded in this manner.

Stage 3: Construction of summary indices

MOTHERS' DATA

(i) *Strategy of answering*

Table 8.3 gives details of the correlations of the items which might be combined to give a single index. Although the matrix suggests a weak general positive factor among the items, it was decided that item 7 (question such as this never asked) should not be included, on the grounds that it was only an incidental observation of mothers. The others each have some readily inferred possibility of relevance to the child's competence to answer questions in a semantically satisfactory way. A voluntary announcement of an insistence that answers should be true (1) and the actual offering of instances of differences (2) and similarities (3) should not only give the child a basis for correlating verbal and non-verbal experience, but should also help him to order and systematize both. On the other hand, ignorance of what to say (5), the provision of answers irrelevant to the question posed (4) and inaccurate facts (6) are different ways of failing to build up an understanding of the rules governing question-answer exchanges.

(ii) *Style of answering*

The indices of style were intended to include items associated with the usage of each social class group. However, the use of verbs and adverbs indicative of a tentative attitude by mothers (14) and the use of units that might attenuate the unpleasantness of stays in hospitals (15) were unrelated to each other, and the first quite unrelated to social class. Minimizers showed weak negative relationships with the other variables, while the signs of tentativeness gave mainly positive associations. These possible signs of middle classness had therefore little support for their inclusion. Of the possible indicators of working-class speech, the use of simplifiers (8) had correlated strongly with social class ($r = +0{\cdot}33$), but it did not have strong positive associations with items 9 to 13. These last five did form a positive cluster and they were therefore combined to form a general index of vagueness, indefiniteness and 'noise'.

TABLE 8.3 *Association among strategies of answering ($n = 55$)—mothers*

	1	2	3	4	5	6	7
1. Truth has to be told	x						
2. Differences pointed out	33†	x					
3. Similarities pointed out	27†	26	x				
4. Irrelevant answers	−04	10	11	x			
5. Ignorance of what to say	21	17	30†	39*	x		
6. Inaccurate facts in answer	21	17	08	05	08	x	
7. Questions like this not asked	17	22	21	20	29†	08	x

* $p < 0{\cdot}01$, † $p < 0{\cdot}05$

TABLE 8.4 *Association among indices of style ($n = 55$)—mothers*

	8	9	10	11	12	13	14	15
8. Simplifiers	x							
9. Nominal and adverbial group indefinites	−03	x						
10. Verbal group indefinites	06	11	x					
11. Redundant finishers	14	46*	16	x				
12. Additional words and phrases	15	47*	06	43*	x			
13. Socio-centric tags	16	50*	55*	35*	38*	x		
14. Markers of hypothetical	14	15	15	31†	11	14	x	
15. Minimizers	20	−10	−14	−20	−16	−04	08	x

* $p < 0{\cdot}01$, † $p < 0{\cdot}05$

TABLE 8.5 *Association among units of information ($n = 55$)—mothers*

	16	17	18	19
16. Units information: tap water	x			
17. Units information: babies	38*	x		
18. Additional information: leaf fall	43*	26	x	
19. Additional information: hospital	29†	51*	06	x

* $p < 0{\cdot}01$, † $p < 0{\cdot}05$

(iii) *Amount of information*

Information was counted for four questions. The two 'where from' questions were scored for units of information given in the answer, while the 'leaves' and 'hospital' question answers were often supplemented with additional information, facts not strictly requested were voluntarily added. Table 8.5 shows that there is a sufficient degree of association among the four variables to make a single summed score sensible.

(iv) *Modes of answering*

There were several difficulties anticipated in the problem of summating modes:

(1) Although a simple-minded initial division into 'strong' and 'weak' modes might be made, with 'strong' being those which could help the questioner to extend and order his knowledge about the apparent focus of his question, this may well be inadequate, because considerations of appropriateness, level and amount of information within mode may also be relevant. 'Because it's wrong' in answer to a question about a moral matter could be coded under 'categorization' along with a much more complex and abstract answer involving appeals to moral principles; similarly with cause and consequence. The possible inappropriateness of the mode used did not in fact arise, although it is easy to conceive of explanations which would use 'strong' modes in a 'bad' way, for example, appeals to little men working away inside refrigerators or televisions or human-centred appeals for natural events, e.g., 'The sun shines to make us happy'. Some account was taken of this in the coding frame. The simple purposes 'To remove his beard' for Q1 and 'To learn' for Q7 were separated out from more complex answers. Nevertheless, in the current situation it is impossible to pass judgment about optimal answers. If mothers use relatively simple explanations, this may be a function of the limitations of their own understanding or it may represent their judgment of what is optimal for the present capacity of their five-year-old child.

(2) The questions raised under (1) could be partially answered empirically, if there were certain items that could be inarguably defined as 'strong' modes. However, there are no such criterial items available, although there are tactics for lifting oneself by one's bootstraps. Through an examination

TABLE 8.6 *Association among modes of answer ($n = 55$)—mothers*

	20	21	22	36	27	28	29	30	31	32	33	34	37	26	24	25	23
20. Repetition as a statement	x																
21. Simple appeal to regularity	−03	x															
22. Focus on proposition	33†	82*	x														
36. Wants and wishes (Q4)	−36*	−04	−28†	x													
27. Cause (Q3)	15	−28†	−18	−19	x												
28. Cause (Q4)	−09	01	07	07	05	x											
29. Consequence (beard removal) (Q1)	01	−30†	−22	04	23	−13	x										
30. Consequence (other reason Q1)	−02	−36*	−29†	15	−15	15	−02	x									
31. Consequence (Q3)	06	−25	−21	10	−30	−23	13	12	x								
32. Consequence (to learn Q7)	−02	−07	−04	07	05	24	07	00	−02	x							
33. Consequence (number skills, Q7)	−12	20	16	−02	05	−18	03	00	−02	−36*	x						
34. Consequence (long-term reasons Q7)	−22	−21	−30	36*	−16	24	−05	20	−01	−08	00	x					
37. Single category answers	37*	04	16	−34†	05	−45*	31†	−11	08	−30†	12	−37*	x				
26. Analogies	−12	−30†	−35*	26	25	11	−03	05	19	12	20	27†	−10	x			
24. Categorization	−29†	−08	−16	18	−07	13	−19	01	−06	09	07	24	−44*	08	x		
25. Wants and wishes	−25	−15	−32†	69*	02	00	01	04	08	18	−01	23	−45*	27†	18	x	
23. Number of multiple categories	−30†	−14	−19	39*	05	50*	−10	14	−01	27†	−01	38*	−89*	10	54*	52*	x

* $p < 0{\cdot}01$, † $p < 0{\cdot}05$

of what goes with what and a tentative construction of clusters, it is possible to develop a picture with a pattern in it.

(3) The items in the matrix are not independent of each other. With such a small sample of answers and the mothers' preferences for giving only one or two modes in any answer, items are likely to show negative inter-correlations, not so much, for example, because mothers who frequently offer causal explanations do not also appeal to consequences, but because in this limited study, they tended to make a disjunctive choice. Hence, to examine successfully which modes co-vary in answers, a much larger sample of question answers would be required.

Two processes of analysis were exploited to provide summary scores of modes.

(i) It was judged that certain modes (20,21) were weak and that certain others were stronger (23,24) and correlations between these and other items were inspected.

(ii) Relationships with social class were inspected with the expectation that these modes preferred by the middle class were more likely to be the 'stronger' ones.

Adopting these tactics led to certain conclusions.

Multiple category answers (23), appeals to wants and wishes (25), the use of analogies (26), and categorization (24) formed a loose cluster. These items correlated positively with each other and social class and negatively with items 20 and 21. Items 30 (appeal to consequence, additional reason Q1), 28 (cause, Q4) and 34 (appeal to long-term consequences, Q7) might have been included.

Items 20 (restatement) and 21 (regularity) generally showed negative associations with the items in the other cluster and social class and these were summed to give a 'focus on proposition' mode. Items 29 (consequence, simple removal of beard, Q1) and 32 (consequence, to learn, Q7) might also have been included. Their tenuous association with the 'weaker' modes serves as a reminder of the point made above that level and complexity as well as type of explanation are relevant (see Table 8.6).

CHILD DATA

A similar procedure was adopted with the children's data, with a weaker constraint that, although it was deemed desirable to attempt to match up child and mother summed scores, there was a willingness to leave more scores uncombined on the grounds that the final analysis was intended to predict from mother to child and not in the reverse direction.

(i) *Strategy of answering*

Items 40 (no answer), 41 ('don't know'), 42 (irrelevant answers) and 43 (contextual inappropriateness) were possible candidates for summation, but were left separate because they showed no empirical evidence of co-variation. (r40/41 = −0·02, r40/42 = 0·07, r41/43 = −0·24, r40/43 = 0·02, r41/42 = 0·04, r42/43 = 0·08).

(ii) *Style of answering*

There were no such scores for children.

(iii) *Amount of information*

Contextual completeness (44) was the name given to amount of information in the children's data and was the sum of items of information given in response to the two 'how' questions.

(iv) *Modes of answer*

Summary scores were extracted for three sets of items. The use of objective modes of answering 'when', 'where', and 'who' questions were added (r Q1/Q2 = 0·23, r when/who = 0·05, r where/who = 0·25).

A strong modes set was formed by adding regularity qualified (29), wishes (52), categorization (moral) (50) and cause (physical) (51). A weak mode set (47) was constructed from restatement (45), unqualified appeals to regularity (46), appeals to unspecified authority (48) and appeals to simple categorization, e.g. because it's naughty.

Results

Stage 4: Relationships between mother and child within social class

Mothers were divided into 'high' and 'low' groups on the basis of the five summary scores, the precise dividing point differing for the various indices. Either Mann Whitney U or χ^2 tests were run to examine the extent of differences in the children's scores, U tests being used when scores were sufficiently distributed to render this feasible and sensible. Where possible, divisions of 'high' and 'low' were made to give maximal and equal contrast, but maintain numbers. The ideal was of one third 'high', one third 'low' and the remainder omitted, but the distributions of the scores did not permit this very often. Results are reported for the lower working class first.

LOWER WORKING CLASS

Strategy of answering

Mothers who made high scores (e.g. relevant, etc.) were more likely than mothers who made low scores to have children whose answers were: relevant ($p < 0{\cdot}01$), grammatically complete ($p < 0{\cdot}01$), contextually complete ($p < 0{\cdot}05$) and which mentioned the teacher's name ($p < 0{\cdot}05$). There was no suggestion of any relationship with the children's modes of answering.

Hence, that maternal strategy which includes the use of relevant answers is associated with relevant answers from the children. The 'no answer' category did not differentiate between the groups in the analysis, but of 13 children saying that they did not know the answer to more than 3 questions, 10 were from the 'low' mother group ($p <= 0{\cdot}046$).

Style of answering

Although there were no corresponding stylistic variables scored in the children's speech, mothers who were high on this index were more likely than mothers who were low to have daughters whose answers: were grammatically inappropriate ($p < 0{\cdot}025$), contained appeals to regularity alone ($p < 0{\cdot}05$) and consequence (physical, human-centred) ($p < 0{\cdot}025$) and made mention of the teacher's name ($p = 0{\cdot}05$).

Amount of information

Mothers who were high were more likely than mothers who were low to have daughters whose answers: were contextually complete ($p < 0{\cdot}025$), appealed to consequence (physical, human-centred, $p = 0{\cdot}05$) and offered appeals to categorization. The provision of more knowledge by mothers was therefore associated with a correlatively higher amount of information in their daughters' answers.

Use of strong modes

LWC mothers high on 'strong' modes had daughters who differed from those of mothers classified as low in both expected and unexpected ways. Their daughters were less likely not to give answers ($p < 0{\cdot}025$) and more likely to give more contextually complete answers ($p < 0{\cdot}01$). While the fact that their daughters were not likely to appeal to consequence for moral questions ($p < 0{\cdot}05$) and gave 'objective' modes to 'where' ($p < 0{\cdot}05$) is not inconsistent with expectation, three other results were. Their daughters were more likely to appeal to unspecified authority ($p < 0{\cdot}05$), to use simple categorization ($p < 0{\cdot}05$) and to use the modes labelled 'focus on proposition' ($p < 0{\cdot}05$)—which is equivalent to 'weak' modes in the mothers' usage. Their girls were also more likely to mention punishment to self as a reason for not doing things.

Use of weak modes

LWC mothers high on 'weak' modes have daughters who differed from those of mothers who made low scores in that they were less likely to give contextually more complete answers ($p < 0{\cdot}05$), more likely to give grammatically incomplete ($p < 0{\cdot}05$) and contextually inappropriate ($p < 0{\cdot}025$) answers. They were more likely to appeal to unspecified authority ($p < 0{\cdot}05$) and simple categorization ($p < 0{\cdot}05$). These are two of the 'weak' mode categories in the children's answers.

Summary

Although the data are weak in several respects and the use of 'strong' modes of explanation has some apparently anomalous relationships to the children's answering behaviour, two conclusions seem warranted. The four indices of maternal answering behaviour do correlate weakly with each other and have predictive value for the daughters' answering behaviour on scores *not* immediately likely to have direct relationships, e.g. maternal strategy predicts daughter's grammatical incompleteness. This implies a weak general factor, such that a semantically rich strategy, an absence of linguistic 'noise', high information content, the presence of 'strong' modes and the absence of 'weak' modes of explanation do co-vary and have general predictive significance for the quality of the children's answers.

However, there also appears to be a measure of specificity such that maternal use of irrelevance is associated with daughters' use of irrelevant answers, but not with daughters' use of one mode rather than another. Similarly, the amount of information given by mothers can be used to predict the amount of information in their children's answers, their use of 'weak' modes predicts children's use of 'weak' modes and their use of 'strong' modes predicts children's use of 'strong' modes as well as 'weak' ones. Direct links are discernible.

MIDDLE CLASS

Strategy of answering

MC mothers making high scores were more likely than those who had low scores to have daughters whose answers: did not use particular proper names ($p < 0{\cdot}05$), did not restate the questions as an answer ($p < 0{\cdot}025$) and did not use 'focus on propositions' modes of answering ($p < 0{\cdot}025$).

Expectation might have been that irrelevant answers and contextual inappropriateness would have been related to maternal strategy, but in both cases these were such *rare* occurrences that there was virtually no differential use to explain. Only nine MC girls gave any irrelevant answers, and only eight any contextually inappropriate ones.

Style of answering

Many additions and substitutions in the mothers' answers were weakly associated with a higher number of 'no answers' from their daughters ($p < 0{\cdot}05$).

Amount of information

In this case MC mothers scoring high on information were more likely to have daughters who: gave more 'no answers' ($p < 0{\cdot}1$), used appeals to regularity alone ($p < 0{\cdot}1$) and were less likely to use combined emotion/consequence appeals ($p < 0{\cdot}05$). Each of these is the reverse direction to any difference that might have been anticipated, although for the total sample there are no relationships between maternal amounts of information and these three. However, the result raises possibilities of a different pattern of co-variation in middle- and working-class samples.

Use of strong modes

The use of strong modes predicted only an absence of grammatical inappropriateness in the children's answers.

Use of weak modes

By contrast with the other maternal indices in the middle class, when this variable was high, it showed a strong positive association not only with the use of 'focus on proposition' modes in the children ($p < 0{\cdot}01$) but was also negatively associated with objective modes for 'where' ($p < 0{\cdot}05$), and positively with answers containing particular unknown proper names ($p < 0{\cdot}1$), lexical inappropriateness ($p < 0{\cdot}05$) and lexical incompleteness ($p < 0{\cdot}01$).

Summary

The degree of specificity between the maternal tactics of answering and daughters' answers found in the working-class break down within the middle-class sample. Only the mothers' use of weak modes directly predicts the correlative behaviour in their daughters, with the subsidiary result that it also predicts the use of non-objective modes answering 'where' questions as well as lexical inappropriateness and incompleteness. It might be tempting to speculate that mothers who make extensive use of 'focus on proposition' modes will not be providing their children with a varied lexis used appropriately, and that this may be relevant to the lexical weaknesses of their children.

Although the generally high level of proficiency in the relevance and contextual appropriateness of the daughters' answers can be invoked to explain why maternal strategy of answering did not relate to these two categories, and MC mothers were low on their usage of stylistic features which might interfere with the reception of their answers, the weakness of the other two maternal indices, viz. amount of information and strong modes, cannot be explained in a similar fashion.

Discussion

In the examination of possibilities of predicting daughters' behaviour from that of their mothers within social class, it is necessary to decide first of all whether the relationships found within the two classes are such as to merit retaining the differences. Other work in Bernstein's Sociological Research Unit has suggested rather different associations of variables within class.

Both strategy of answering and style gave more significant and meaningful associations in the lower working class than in the middle class. Irrelevant answers in both mothers and children co-varied in the former, but not the latter, but this result was inevitable because the MC girls gave so few irrelevant answers ($\bar{x} = 0{\cdot}48$) or contextually inappropriate ones ($\bar{x} = 0{\cdot}50$), that it is sensible to suggest that MC girls of this age appear to have grasped the semantic requirements that answers need to bear to questions (at least for the questions posed here). The same was true for their mothers, who gave no irrelevant ($\bar{x} = 0$) and very few inaccurate answers ($\bar{x} = 0{\cdot}05$). With so little variance among either mothers or children to capture, the results are not surprising. Similarly, MC mothers used few of the additional and substitutional markers of 'noisy' style ($\bar{x} = 1{\cdot}45$, s.d.$^2 = 3{\cdot}21$) compared with the working class ($\bar{x} = 3{\cdot}21$, s.d.$^2 = 18{\cdot}27$). As can be readily inferred from the variances, some LWC mothers made very high scores on this index, and it is perhaps not all that surprising that their daughters are relatively high on grammatical inappropriateness in their answers, while the general incidence of such features in the MC mothers' speech may have been so low as to be insignificant.

Amount of information might have been expected to show no complications. In the working class there were none: mothers high on information had children whose answers were high on information. But in the middle class this was not so. The daughters of mothers who made high scores were somewhat less likely to answer questions and more likely to use appeals to simple regularity (a weak mode) and less likely to use the combined emotion/consequence appeal (a strong mode). At present, no immediately testable reasons for these results can be given. It could be that some mothers consistently overload their children with the answers they give, resulting in a reduced absorption; giving answers extending beyond the cognitive capacities of their children leading to a failure to assimilate anything.

For mothers who use a relatively high incidence of 'weak' modes, the pattern was similar in both social classes—their daughters were more likely to use 'weak' modes. Prediction was possible.

The use of 'strong' modes by mothers could not be used to predict similar behaviour by their daughters. As far as the middle class is concerned, it looks as though it is necessary to think again and develop a more complicated theoretical analysis to predict what the consequences of the use of strong modes might be. For the lower working class, the mothers' use of 'strong' modes had some predictive significance in consistent directions, but further results were superficially odd: use of 'strong' modes by mothers predicted use of appeals to unspecified authority, simple categorization, avoidance of punishment to self, and more generally 'focus on proposition' modes by their daughters. One interpretation that might be offered would rely upon a consideration of the relative proportion of 'weak' to 'strong' modes employed by mothers in the two social classes. In the middle class, 'strong' modes made up 91 per cent of the total (3·41 to 3·77), while in the lower working class they constituted 72 per cent (1·91 to 2·65). It could be the case that this higher proportion of 'weak' modes in the lower working class is what is significant. The incidence of the use of 'strong' and 'weak' modes is still sufficiently similar for the child to be unable to make a clear distinction between the two, and with her lesser understanding, she may opt for the easier mode rather than not answering at all. This is a weak argument, but it could be examined by appropriate questioning of and experimentation with mothers and children. At present, we know very little about how mothers answer their children's questions and nothing about the way these answers change as the children develop.

With modes as well as with strategy and style, there is a suggestion again that the gross differences between the MC and LWC mothers may lead to rather different consequences for the children. Those few MC mothers who used 'weak' modes were likely to have children who used 'weak' modes. The variation among the many who used mainly 'strong' mode answers has not been discriminated in terms of consequences for the children in this study. The higher proportion of LWC mothers using many 'weak' modes had daughters who used more 'weak' modes. The relatively few who used 'strong' modes frequently were also using a high incidence of 'weak' modes, and their children had not yet at least achieved a strong discrimination between them and hence used both more than other children. However, they were not producing no answers or irrelevant ones!

As with the relationships between social class, CCI and the children's answers, so with maternal answering behaviours and children's answers, the two-year gap in data collection may be important as a source of weakness of the associations found. The differences in the relationships found in the two social class groups raise an additional possibility. Perhaps the simple and more pronounced associations found in the working class stem from a greater *stability* of maternal answering behaviours. It could be that LWC mothers do not adapt their answers to their children's present competence, but give similar answers to seven- and five-year-olds. If this is so, and maternal answering behaviour is the major source of learning for the children, then the two-year gap should have less significance for them. In the middle class, any differential development among children during the gap may have been matched by accommodative behaviour of mothers, so that their answering tactics at five will be correspondingly less informative of children's answers at seven.

It would be premature to come to firm conclusions on the mechanisms of transmission or what exactly is transmitted on the basis of this study. Whether or not the mothers' answers function only as a source for modelling, or whether mothers who adopt certain answering strategies and tactics also employ incentives and correctives which are of relevance, we cannot say. The data here are not inconsistent with the simplest view that the modelling role alone may be sufficient. We might expect the child to repeat what he can assimilate from the mother and to learn these maternal answers within the limitations imposed jointly by the message complexity and his own cognitive constraints.

This view is supported by the existence of specific as well as general relationships between the answers of mothers and children. Overall, mothers whose answers used language more powerfully and efficiently had children whose mastery of language was greater: maternal strategy, style, information and modes could be used to predict aspects of grammatical, lexical and contextual expertise in children. But it was also true that where sufficient variance existed to make tests feasible, specificity of prediction could be achieved. Maternal strategy predicted child strategy. Amount of information predicted amount of information. 'Weak' modes predicted 'weak' modes. To answer how specific such specificity is, requires data not available here.

Acknowledgments

I would like to express my appreciation to the Joseph Rowntree Memorial Trust for the financial support to develop this work. A similar acknowledgment must be made to the Department of

Education and Science and the Ford Foundation for their support of the original investigations.

Appendix The questions asked of seven-year-old children

In so far as words in questions are stressed, those in italic should carry it.

1. *When* do you go home from school?
2. *Where* is your home?
3. *What* is a *home* for?
4. *Where* does your best friend live?
5. *What* is a *friend*?
6. *Where* is your favourite sweet-shop?
7. *How* do you buy sweets?
8. *How well* can you read?
9. *Who* gives you lessons at school?
10. *What* is a *school*?
11. *When* did you start at *Infant* school?
12. *Who* is the man who sees you when you are ill?
13. *Why* are people sometimes ill? (2 probes)
14. *Why* shouldn't you hit children smaller than yourself? (2 probes)
15. Can you tell me *how* to ride a bicycle?
16. *Why* does wood float? (2 probes)
17. *Where* does milk come from? (If child answers 'cow', ask Why?)
18. *When* was your birthday?
19. *What* are birthdays *for*?
20. *Why* shouldn't anyone tell lies? (2 probes)
21. *Why* does Daddy shave every morning? (2 probes)
22. *How tall* would you like to be when you are grown up?
23. *Why* do the leaves fall off the trees? (2 probes)
24. *How* do the leaves fall off the trees?
25. *Why* does a ball come down when you throw it up in the air? (2 probes)
26. *Why* shouldn't anyone steal? (2 probes)
27. *Why* does the sea have waves? (2 probes)
28. *Where* does the water in the tap come from?
29. *Why* should children do what their parents tell them to? (2 probes)
30. Tell me all the different things you can do with a piece of string.

A probe was a further question which sought an elaboration of the child's initial answer.

Notes

1 Subsequently lower working class as a modifier is abbreviated to LWC, middle class to MC.

2 Bernstein has made the valid observation that CCI is an index of effected policies rather than detail and that it relates most strongly to modes of mothers' answers (Table 8.1), themselves indicative of policy.

References

BERNSTEIN, B. (1966), 'Elaborated and restricted codes: their social origins and some consequences', in J. J. Gumperz and D. H. Hymes (eds), *The Ethnography of Communication, American Anthropologist* special publication, 66, no. 6, pt. 2.

BERNSTEIN, B. (1972), 'A socio-linguistic approach to socialization with some reference to educability', in *Directions in Sociolinguistics*, J. Gumperz and D. Hymes (eds). New York: Holt, Rinehart & Winston.

BERNSTEIN, B. and BRANDIS, W. (1970), 'Social class differences in communication and control', in W. Brandis and D. Henderson, *Social Class, Language and Communication*. London: Routledge & Kegan Paul.

BERNSTEIN, B. and HENDERSON, D. (1970), 'Social class differences in conceptions of the uses of toys', in W. Brandis and D. Henderson, *Social Class, Language and Communication*. London: Routledge & Kegan Paul.

BERNSTEIN, B. and YOUNG, D. (1967), 'Social class differences in conceptions of the uses of toys', *Sociology*, 1, 2.

BRANDIS, W. (1970), 'Measure of the mother's orientation towards communication and control', in W. Brandis and D. Henderson, *Social Class, Language and Communication*. London: Routledge & Kegan Paul.

BRIMER, M. A. and DUNN, L. M. (1962), *The English Picture Vocabulary Tests*. London: National Foundation for Educational Research.

COOK, J. (1972), *Social Control and Socialization*. London: Routledge & Kegan Paul.

HESS, R. D. and SHIPMAN, V. C. (1965), 'Early experience and the socialization of cognitive modes in children', *Child Development*, 36.

JONES, J. (1966), 'Social class and the under-fives', *New Society*, 221.

LAWTON, D. (1968), *Social Class, Language and Education*. London: Routledge & Kegan Paul.

KOHLBERG, L. (1963), 'Moral development and identification', in H. Stevenson (ed.), *Child Psychology*. University of Chicago Press.

NEWSON, E. and NEWSON, J. (1970), *Four Years Old in an Urban Community*. London: Penguin.

PIAGET, J. (1927), *The Child's Conception of Physical Causality*. New York: Harcourt.

ROBINSON, W. P. and RACKSTRAW, S. J. (1967), 'Variations in mothers' answers to children's questions', *Sociology*, 1.

ROBINSON, W. P. and RACKSTRAW, S. J. (1972), *A Question of Answers*. London: Routledge & Kegan Paul.

TURNER, G. J. and PICKVANCE, R. E. (1972), 'Social class differences in the expression of uncertainty in five-year-old children', *Language and Speech*, 1971, 14, and reprinted in this volume.

Chapter 9 The influence of sex, social class and pause-location in the hesitation phenomena of seven-year-old children

P. R. Hawkins

Introduction

The research reported in this paper was stimulated by the work on hesitation phenomena carried out by F. Goldman-Eisler, and by Bernstein's theoretical and practical work in connection with the differences in language which correspond to different social class groups. Goldman-Eisler has demonstrated, in a series of studies, the relationship between hesitation in speech, verbal planning, and information content (Goldman-Eisler, 1958 a and b, 1961 a–d). Bernstein, in an experiment performed in 1962, applied these findings to samples of speech (group discussions) taken from adolescent boys, and compared the hesitations of a group of middle-class boys with those of a group of working-class boys. He predicted that the users of a 'restricted code', i.e. the working class, would pause less frequently and spend less time pausing, than the middle-class 'elaborated code' speakers. An elaborated code is associated with 'higher levels of structural organization and lexical selection' and with 'the preparation and delivery of relatively *explicit* meaning', and will therefore entail more verbal planning, and hence longer and more frequent pauses (Bernstein, 1962). Bernstein's experiment gave findings in the predicted direction, but was based on a small sample, with great variation in the output of individual speakers.

More recently, Bernstein (1972) has suggested, in connection with a discussion on positional- and person-oriented families, possible differences in language use within the working class, between boys and girls. Some working-class girls, he suggests, have more complex roles within the family, controlling and 'mothering' their younger brothers and sisters, and mediating between them and their parents. These roles demand 'forms of control based upon linguistically elaborated meanings, [rather] than upon physical coercion. [The girls] are placed in a situation involving a variety of role and code switching', which is 'likely to develop their orientation towards a more differentiated, more individualized use of language'.

The present study investigates further the relationships between social class, sex, and hesitation pausing. It is based on a comparatively large sample (186) of seven-year-olds in a speech situation involving creative narrative.

The sample

Two hundred and ninety-eight children, aged between six and a half and seven, were given individual interviews (at school), which were tape-recorded. Of these children, 174 were drawn from schools in a predominantly working-class district of east London, while 124 came from schools in a largely middle-class suburb of south-east London. Some of the children from the working-class population had been given a special programme of 'language enrichment' during the preceding year and a half, and this group, known as the E1 group, must be considered separately. Apart from this, the sample is divided into boys and girls, and children of high, medium and low IQ. The social class of the families to which the children belonged was determined by interviewing the mothers, the scale being based on the occupation and education of both parents (Brandis and Henderson, 1970). (For further details of this research project, see Bernstein, 1971.)

During the individual interviews, the children were given a series of tasks to perform, each designed to elicit speech of various kinds. For the final task, which is the one we shall be concerned with, the child was asked to make up a bedtime story for a teddy-bear. The interviewer presented first the bear, then the four dolls who were to be the 'characters' of the story, and the instruction was as follows: 'This bear is going to sleep. Can you make up a bedtime story for him? Tell him a story about a little boy, a little girl, a sailor, and a dog.' If the child made no response, one further probe was allowed: 'There's no hurry. See if you can think up a story.'

In fact, not many children needed this second probe. The response was good, and most of the children were not at a loss for words. The quality of the recordings, however, varied considerably. The recordings were later transcribed, in traditional orthography but without any 'editing', i.e. the transcription included all *ums*, *ers*, false starts and repeated words.

From the original sample of 298, a number of children had to be excluded. Goldman-Eisler had shown (1968, p. 22) that utterances of less than 100 syllables give an unreliable measure of speech-rate, so that all stories of shorter length than this were excluded. In addition, 17 children (12 working class, 5 middle class) refused a story or admitted they could not think of one, and 10 children (7 working class, 3 middle class) produced very long, mainly incoherent stories which were considered unsuitable for analysis. The resulting sample of 186 stories was distributed as follows (Table 9.1):

TABLE 9.1 *Characteristics of the sample*

	E1 group	*Working class*	*Middle class*	*Total*
Boys	14	34	37	85
Girls	16	49	36	101
Total	30	83	73	186

The first measure to be taken was the speech-rate, i.e. the number of syllables uttered per minute. The mean speech-rates were calculated and an analysis of variance was performed to compare the groups with each other. The results of this are presented in Table 9.3.

After this a sub-sample of 48 children was devised, 12 from each group—(excluding E1), i.e. middle- and working-class, boys and girls. These children were selected so as to be representative, in fluency, of the sample as a whole. A division was made into fluent, medium, and slow speakers, the cut-off points being 140 and 90 syllables per minute, i.e. one standard deviation on either side of the overall average of 115. The tapes of these children's stories were played into an oscillograph to obtain a visual record of the speech (speech being recorded as an oscillating line and silence as a continuous one). This enabled the location of each pause, and its length, to be determined precisely. The data were then used to determine: (*a*) whether the distribution of pause-length and pause-frequency is affected by social class or sex differences (see Results, iv); (*b*) whether pause length and frequency is related to grammatical structure. The results of a fairly extensive study of pausing in relation to grammar are reported in another paper (Hawkins, forthcoming), but in so far as they are relevant to sex and social class differences, they will be mentioned below (Results, v). Basically, pauses were classified according to their occurrence at clause-boundaries, or at positions within the clause, or at positions within the group (or phrase).

Results

(i) The speech-rate (number of syllables per minute)

Table 9.2 presents the mean and standard deviations of the speech-rate for each group of children.

TABLE 9.2 *Speech-rate*

		E1 group	*Working class*	*Middle class*
Boys:	Mean	107·1	108·0	109·8
	S.D.	21·2	33·4	25·7
Girls:	Mean	123·7	128·3	111·7
	S.D.	31·2	26·7	26·7

An analysis of variance of the speech-rate of the middle- and working-class children (excluding the E1 group) was then carried out. The method of unweighted means, for unequal cells, was used, following Myers (1966, pp. 106–8). The results are given in Table 9.3.

TABLE 9.3 *Analysis of variance: speech-rate*

	d.f.	*Variance*	*F-ratio*	*p*
Sex	1	123·51	8·72	0·01
Social class	1	55·43	3·91	0·05
Inter-action	1	85·30	6·02	0·02
'Error'	152	14·17		

(ii) Distribution of pause-length

The pauses measured on the oscillograph, for the sub-sample of 48 children, were distributed according to length. Goldman-Eisler's studies indicated that pauses of less than one-quarter of a second could not be regarded as true 'hesitation' pauses but may be due to factors of articulation (Goldman-Eisler, 1968, p. 12). In the present study, then, 0·3 sec. was taken as the minimum length for a hesitation pause. There was no theoretical maximum, but in fact the longest pause recorded lasted 67·1 secs. The distribution of pause-length, which may be inferred from Table 9.5, was roughly uni-modal with a long 'tail', the shortest pauses (0·3–0·5 secs) being the most frequent, the longest pauses the least frequent.

(iii) **Influence of pause-length and pause-frequency on speech-rate**

Pause-length (in seconds per pause), and pause-frequency (in syllables per pause) were each correlated (by the ranking method) with speech-rate, to discover whether the latter is determined rather by the number of pauses, or their length. Since length correlated 0·755 with speech-rate, and frequency 0·254, we may conclude that for this speech sample, the rate is determined more by length than by frequency. Slow speakers *are* slow, therefore, because they make long, rather than frequent, pauses.

This result may be seen as a function of the speech situation. The child was under no pressure to keep up a high level of fluency as he might be in, for example, a group discussion where prolonged silence would mean losing the conversational 'ball' to someone else. The task itself also demands considerable powers of invention and the speech is likely to be less fluent than if, for example, the child were narrating one of his own experiences. The overall average speech-rate of 115 is thus considerably lower than the rates found by Goldman-Eisler in adult group discussions, which ranged from about 180 to 250 syllables per minute (1968, p. 20); and long pauses of more than ten seconds, of which there are seventeen in our data, would be unusual in many other situations. These long pauses will obviously have a considerable effect on the overall speech-rate.

(iv) **Influence of social class and sex on pause-length and frequency**

A distribution of pauses according to length, for each group of children separately (middle- and working-class boys and girls) shows tendencies for class differences in the pauses of intermediate length, that is between 2 and 5 seconds. The distribution is given in Table 9.4.

Overall, the total number of pauses is about the same for each group—though middle-class boys appear to pause rather more frequently than working-class boys. But the middle-class children have more pauses of 2–5 seconds duration. The difference, for boys only, in the 2–3 second category was statistically significant ($t = 2{\cdot}32$, $p < 0{\cdot}05$), and for boys and girls combined, the difference was more significant ($t = 2{\cdot}96$, $p < 0{\cdot}01$). Taking the 2–5 second category as a whole, the class difference was again significant ($t = 2{\cdot}64$, $p < 0{\cdot}02$). A comparison of the girls' pauses shows that working-class girls tend to have more short pauses, up to 1 second ($t = 1{\cdot}91$, $p < 0{\cdot}10$), while the middle-class girls have more inter-

TABLE 9.4 *Pauses distributed according to length*

Pause-length (secs)	*WC boys*	*MC boys*	*WC girls*	*MC girls*
0·3–0·5	109	100	143	117
0·6–1·0	88	128	116	82
1–2	75	64	61	81
2–3	14	31	19	34
3–5	13	23	8	14
5–10	10	1	4	8
10+	8	1	2	6
Total pauses	317	348	353	342

mediate pauses, from 1 second onwards (for the 2–5 second category, t = 1·87, $p < 0{\cdot}10$).

Working-class boys appear to have more long pauses of 5 seconds or more. The class difference was assessed by a χ^2 test but gave a tentative result only ($\chi^2 = 2{\cdot}85$, $p < 0{\cdot}10$). Of the twelve children in each group, seven working-class boys had pauses in this range, compared with only two middle class (see Discussion (3)).

(v) **Grammatical incidence of pausing**

From the grammatical analysis of pause occurrences, four categories of pause-position were devised; these were:

(*a*) At the beginning of the clause, before or after any conjunction but definitely preceding the first information item of the clause (usually the subject)—these are clause-initial, or clause-boundary pauses.

(*b*) Before the main verb or predicator of the clause, but after the subject (or other initial item of information).

(*c*) At other places within the clause, but excluding (*d*).

(*d*) Within the group or phrase, e.g. the . . . sailor, on . . . the ship.

It was then possible to observe how many pauses occurred in each of these positions, and how much time was spent pausing there. The results are given for boys and girls separately, in Tables 9.5 and 9.6, in order to observe class differences.

It will be observed, first, that most pauses, and most of the pausing time, occur at the boundaries of clauses. Second, clause-boundary pauses can be seen to be relatively longer pauses than the

TABLE 9.5 *Frequency and duration of pauses for each grammatical category (boys only)*

Category	No. of pauses		Duration (secs)	
	WC boys	*MC boys*	*WC boys*	*MC boys*
(*a*) Clause-initial	213	222	459·1	295·6
(*b*) P after S	33	41	41·4	37·0
(*c*) Within-clause	43	46	39·5	47·7
(*d*) Within-group	23	36	15·0	35·6
Total	312	345	555·0	415·9

TABLE 9.6 *Frequency and duration of pauses for each grammatical category (girls only)*

Category	No. of pauses		Duration (secs)	
	WC girls	*MC girls*	*WC girls*	*MC girls*
(*a*) Clause-initial	238	216	298·4	363·5
(*b*) P after S	30	33	22·8	25·7
(*c*) Within-clause	44	52	36·3	85·9
(*d*) Within-group	38	39	23·6	29·9
Total	350	340	381·1	505·0

N.B. The total number of pauses for each group does not quite correspond with the totals given in Table 9.4. This is because a few pauses did not fit into any of the four categories satisfactorily.

others, if we divide the duration by the number of pauses (this is discussed more fully in another paper—Hawkins, forthcoming). Third, middle-class boys (Table 9.5) appear to have more within-group pauses (category *d*) and certainly to spend more time on within-group pauses. The former difference was not significant ($t = 1{\cdot}53$, $p =$ n.s.) but the latter was significant (by a Mann-Whitney U test, $U = 32$, $p < {\cdot}025$). The biggest apparent difference, however, and perhaps the most interesting, is in the amount of pause-time taken up by clause-boundary pauses. Working-class boys totalled 459·1 seconds, compared with the middle-class 295·6 seconds, although the pause-*frequency* is almost the same (213 and 222). The difference is due to some very long pauses by a few slow speakers. It is not statistically significant ($U = 58$, $p =$ n.s.), because not all speakers were involved, but these long pauses affected the overall speech-rate, and their significance is considered in sections (2) and (3) of the Discussion.

Discussion

(1) The speech-rate is a general measure of the children's fluency in telling the stories. It will be observed that the analysis of variance did not include a division of the sample according to the IQ of the children, though IQ could be an important factor in determining pause-behaviour. The division was not made originally, because it would have been impossible to match the cells across sex and social class as well. But IQ was included as a variable in a set of correlations carried out with this and other data, and it was clear from these results that IQ had no effect on hesitation. Similar conclusions have been reached by Goldman-Eisler, and the exclusion of IQ was therefore justified.

(2) A glance at the average speech-rates for each group (Table 9.2) shows us that the only group to differ appreciably from the others is the working-class girls, who are clearly more fluent than any of the other groups. The analysis of variance (Table 9.3) gives a significant F-ratio (measure of difference) for both sex and social class, sex being greater because middle-class girls are also slightly more fluent than middle-class boys; but there is also a significant inter-action factor, which shows that the main variables are not operating independently of each other—in fact, it reflects the imbalance created by the higher fluency of one cell only, working-class girls. Testing the individual groups against each other, we find working-class girls significantly more fluent than working-class boys ($t = 3{\cdot}05$, $p < 0{\cdot}005$) and more fluent than middle-class girls, again significantly ($t = 2{\cdot}83$, $p < 0{\cdot}01$).

How is this finding to be interpreted? There seems to be an inherent paradox in the assumptions we make about hesitation pauses. In the first place, hesitations, irrespective of social class or language codes, are linked with verbal planning, and fluent speech is interpreted to mean 'poorer quality', because less time is devoted to planning. Following from this, speakers using a 'restricted' code, which is relatively unplanned, may be expected to be more fluent than those using an 'elaborated' code. If the use of these codes is a function of social class, we should find working-class children more fluent than middle class; and since working-class girls use a more 'elaborated' code than working-class boys, by virtue of their more comprehensive family role, working-class boys should be the most fluent speakers of all. Our results, however, show working-class boys to be the least fluent, working-class girls the most fluent, group.

Perhaps we need to question, then, our original assumption that greater fluency inevitably means less planning and hence inferior quality. It seems at least equally plausible to say that fluency indicates more experience, and/or greater confidence in language use on the part of the speaker and hence perhaps even *better* quality. Certainly, fluent speakers are often regarded as having greater control over their linguistic resources. Is it possible, then, that in the present case working-class girls are displaying greater, rather than less, linguistic expertise?

The question can best be resolved by examining the quality of the utterances produced. If working-class girls invent rambling, incoherent stories, while the more hesitant middle-class girls give well-constructed, thoughtful ones, we could conclude that the former are doing less verbal planning—that their fluency is 'mere garrulousness'. But if there is no loss of quality despite the greater fluency, we should perhaps conclude that the working-class girls are showing greater confidence in using their linguistic resources. In this case, what functions are the pauses serving? Are they not indicative of verbal planning, after all?

I believe we have to isolate two different kinds of pauses with different functions. We must note that Goldman-Eisler's experiments, which originally established the relationship between hesitation and speech-planning, were based on *within-sentence* hesitations. But we must also take account of pauses at the boundaries of, i.e. *between*, sentences since the speech-rates (our measure of fluency) are based on total pausing time, including sentence-boundary pausing.[1] I shall argue that some of these latter pauses function rather differently from the others; that they do not contribute to subsequently better-planned speech; and that their presence may indicate a less effective, rather than a more effective, story.

In interpreting the findings we shall therefore need to take account of two factors: (*a*) the quality of the stories the children offered, and (*b*) the grammatical location, and relative length of the pauses. Investigation of these involves the sub-sample of forty-eight children.

(*a*) The assessment of the quality of a story in a scientific, non-impressionistic way is a long and complex task, and work on this is still being carried out at the Sociological Research Unit. The sub-sample of forty-eight stories was however submitted to an experienced infant-teacher for a preliminary assessment of content on an impressionistic basis. She was asked to grade the stories on a five-point scale, from 'much better than average' to 'much worse than average'. The results suggested that the quality of the working-class girls' stories was in no way inferior to that of the middle-class girls: if anything, it was slightly better. Seven out of twelve working-class girls told 'better than average' stories, compared with four out of twelve middle class. In a points system applied to the grading, working-class girls scored 42, middle-class girls 39. My own impressions of the quality, based on the larger sample, were similar; in spite of greater fluency, there was no loss of quality. It seems in this case, then, that fluency is the result of greater confidence and better control of linguistic resources[2] by the working-class girls. This may be connected either with the more demanding role they play within the family or, in relation to this particular task, these girls may be less constrained, relative to the middle-class girls, over considerations of the narrative's formal structure. These points will be developed later in the discussion.

(*b*) In view of this conclusion, it is necessary to ask how greater fluency is compatible with equal quality. To answer this, we must take into consideration the grammatical location, and relative length, of the hesitation pauses. The argument is as follows:

If a child is uncertain or inexperienced in story-telling, the narrative is likely to be interrupted, perhaps only once or twice, by long pauses. These pauses are occasioned by the search for an appropriate overall direction to the story, as the speaker tries to decide how the story will go on. Since they involve 'overall content' decisions, such pauses will occur at clause-boundaries rather than within a clause. Furthermore, they have a considerable effect on the total speech-rate; we have already seen that the latter correlates more strongly with length than with frequency of pauses, and we shall see (below) that the slow speech-rates of a number of working-class boys can be directly attributed to a few very long pauses. But if these pauses affect the speech-rate so much, it is clear that they are not serving to plan the speech ahead in detail, in the way 'classical' hesitation pauses have been shown (by Goldman-Eisler, for example), to do, since if they did, the subsequent utterance would be faster and more fluent, and there would be little or no effect on the overall speech-rate. This is not to say that the long pauses are totally devoid of verbal planning, but only to point out that they are not giving 'value' for the amount of time they consume: in other words, they are not as productive, as far as planning is concerned, as the shorter pauses.

Pauses occasioned by the search for, and selection of, a particular lexical item, on the other hand, are more likely to occur *within* the clause, i.e. preceding the lexical item, and to be shorter in duration. These are the 'genuine' hesitations which are giving full value for time, which serve to improve the 'quality' of the utterance by permitting selections from a wide range of possibilities, and which make the difference between considered, thoughtful speech and 'mere garrulousness'.

The data from our present study supports this postulated division of pauses according to length and grammatical location. If we take the pauses of 5 seconds or more as our 'long' pauses, and examine their occurrence (in the sub-sample), we find that 36 of the 40, i.e. 90 per cent, occur at clause-boundaries. They are also distributed among 18 children, 15 of whom have only one or two of these long pauses, which shows they occur only once or twice in each story (where they occur at all, that is). Thus these long pauses, it is suggested, are occasioned by difficulties in deciding how the story is to go on; and since they affect the speech-rate strongly, they are not giving value in planning for the time devoted to them.

Returning to the discussion of the greater fluency of working-class girls, we can now see, from Table 9.4, that middle-class girls produce more of these long pauses, even in a sub-sample that was matched for overall fluency. Thus, working-class girls produce 6 (of which 1 can be discounted because it occurred within a clause), middle-class girls, 14 (of which 2 can be discounted for the same reason); 3 working-class girls were involved, compared with 6 middle-class girls. We also observe, from Table 9.6, that although middle-class girls had fewer category (a) (clause-boundary) pauses, the total time devoted to them is 22 per cent greater than the corresponding time for working-class girls. These differences illustrate the tendency for working-class girls to have fewer long pauses, hence higher speech-rates. In view of what we said about the function of these pauses (deciding how the story shall go on), we may conclude that working-class girls are more confident in telling stories; relative to middle-class girls, they have no need for the occasional long pause to determine the further direction the story is to take.

This greater confidence may be due, in part, to the more complex role these girls play within the family. Alternatively, it may be due to the fact that they are less constrained, relative to the middle-class children, by the demands of this particular task. Bernstein (1971) suggests that middle-class children are in general more concerned with 'getting their answers right', and that in this case, being more aware of the *form* a narrative should take, they may be attempting to meet the requirements of the form, as well as organizing the content. Middle-class children are more aware of narrative form because they hear or read more stories than working-class children do—Jones (1966) found, for example, that the former have stories read to them more often. This concern with correct 'form' does not necessarily make for a better story; it may indeed produce a worse one, since the restraints put a greater burden on the child's imagination; but it will most probably result in the story being less fluent. Working-class girls, on the other hand, being less familiar with narrative structure, will feel less constrained by its demands, and hence tell their stories more freely and fluently.

(3) Let us next consider the differences between working- and middle-class boys. We see (from Table 9.2) that the average speech-rates of these groups differ very little, but the working-class group has a higher standard deviation. A distribution scatter of the speech-rates shows that the working-class group is not homogeneous; it contains, in fact, among the 34 boys, a small group of very slow speakers, with speech-rates between 50 and 60 sylls/min., and an exceptional one with 33 (the whole group's average is 108). As with the middle-class girls, the stories from this group contain a number of very long pauses, occurring at clause-boundaries, and indicative, it is suggested, of a lack of confidence and ability in devising an integrated, continuous narrative. The dis-fluency here, however, is much more serious than with the middle-class girls, who were hesitant only by comparison with working-class girls (only 2 middle-class girls out of 36 had rates below 70, these being 69 and 65). This group of boys encountered real difficulty in devising a story, and there is no doubt that hesitation in this case did *not* contribute to quality: of the four non-fluent stories which were assessed, one was rated 'average', two 'worse than average', and one 'much worse than average'.

The results from the sub-sample suggest that these long pauses are quite frequent among working-class boys generally—they were encountered in seven of the twelve stories, compared with two for the middle class ($p < 0{\cdot}10$—see Results, iv, and v). A glance at Table 9.5 also reveals how the working-class boys spend a vastly greater amount of time on clause-boundary (category a) pauses than the middle class, in spite of the pause-frequency here being roughly equal for the two groups (213 as against 222 pauses). This extra time spent is not reflected in better quality, the working-class boys' stories being rated on the whole worse than the middle class, in fact worse than any other group.

There is little doubt that these boys found story-invention a difficult, perhaps even distasteful, task. This is to be expected if, as Bernstein (1972) suggests, working-class boys are tied more strongly to 'activity-oriented, peer-group dominated social structure', than girls are. Thus, these boys might prove to be fluent and very competent in the sort of language which accompanies and co-ordinates activity, whereas a task such as the present one would be outside their competence. Within the middle class, on the other hand, the differences between the roles of boys and girls may be smaller, and hence we find a much smaller difference in performance between middle-class boys and girls—indeed, the middle class as a whole forms a homogeneous group, both boys and girls telling stories with comparable speech-rates and comparable in type and quality. This is not true of the working class, where there is a wide divergence between the sexes, both in fluency (the girls being significantly more fluent, $p < 0{\cdot}005$), and in quality: a test to compare boys and girls telling better-than-average stories was significant in favour of the girls ($p < 0{\cdot}05$, from Mainland and Murray, fourfold contingency Tables).

(4) A further finding of some significance is that the middle class (both boys and girls) have more pauses of an intermediate length, i.e., between two and five seconds. These pauses, we have suggested, may be regarded as the longest 'genuine' hesitation pauses, i.e. those likely to contribute to better-planned speech. In the 2–3 second category, the class difference was highly significant ($p < 0{\cdot}01$), and for the 2–5 second category, a significant result was also obtained ($p < 0{\cdot}02$). The differences applied across both sexes, but more especially among the boys. Many of these pauses occurred at clause-boundaries, but it is interesting to note that a considerable percentage of them were located *within* the clause. The percentage differs according to social class, being 29 per cent for the middle class, but only 18 per cent for the working class. The latter produce 13 such pauses, the former 37, a difference which is significant both by χ^2 test ($\chi^2 = 4{\cdot}12$, $p < 0{\cdot}05$) and by t–test ($t = 3{\cdot}03$, $p < 0{\cdot}01$).

Middle-class children, then, not only have more 'intermediate' pauses, but also devote more of them to within-clause lexical planning. If our assumptions are correct, these children spend more time on lexical decisions than the working-class children. And time spent in planning speech in this way is generally time well spent; it results in subsequent utterances of higher quality, more carefully chosen and better organized. This result thus fits in quite well with the concept of an 'elaborated' code, which entails more precise choices from a wider selection of items, and hence longer pauses to resolve the choices.

(5) Finally, we must make a brief mention of the experimental E1 group of children who received the 'language-enrichment' programme. Since no study of their pauses was made in depth, it is not possible to draw similar conclusions about their performance. We can however note that the overall average speech-rate of the E1 boys is similar to that of the working-class boys, while the E1 girls approach the working-class girls, but are slightly less fluent

(see Table 9.2). As the programme had run only briefly when the stories were collected, and as it had not included specifically the invention of stories, no great differences in performance for this group are to be expected. The lower standard deviation of the E1 boys' group, however, indicates that there was no sub-group there with very slow speech-rates, such as was found among the working-class boys; nor were there any very slow speakers among the girls. The enrichment programme may therefore have served to improve the all-round confidence and control of language resources among both boys and girls.

Conclusion and summary

(1) The working-class girls were found to be the most fluent group. Examination of pause-location showed that this was because they hesitated less in determining the general direction of the story, as shown by less time devoted to clause-boundary pauses. They thus appear to be more self-assured and confident in story-telling than their middle-class counterparts, perhaps because they were less aware of any restrictions imposed by the demands of the task itself. Their greater fluency however did not result in the output being of inferior quality.
(2) The working-class boys were the least fluent. One group among them was particularly slow; they used long pauses while they searched for ideas to continue the story. This resulted, not in a subsequently better-planned speech output, but as far as could be assessed, in a considerable worsening of quality. The inability of these boys to invent fluently may result from the type of social structure they participate in and their orientation towards physical activity; neither of which would favour the telling of bedtime stories or provide them with experience in it. The sex-difference within the working-class children was marked by comparison with the middle-class children, where the sex roles are perhaps less discrete.
(3) Middle-class children as a whole were found to have more 'genuine' hesitation pauses at within-clause locations which suggested an inclination to pause for the selection of individual lexical items.

Finally, let us note the importance, for the present study, of classifying the pauses according to their length and grammatical location. This study suggests pauses may have two different functions. The first function relates to the selection of lexical items; the second function may indicate a failure to meet the specific demands of the task: in this case a failure to invent and sustain a story. We would not have been able to infer these functions if we had *limited* our analysis to a consideration of the total speech-rate.

Notes

1 I.e. what we have called above (Results, v) clause-boundary, or clause-initial, pausing. The distinction between sentence and clause is not important here.

2 This is not quite the same thing as 'more differentiated' language. I would suggest that these girls possess better control over existing linguistic resources, rather than necessarily a wider range of vocabulary and structures (which 'more differentiated' implies); thus Henderson (Brandis and Henderson, 1970) found significant differences between WC boys and girls in the frequency of adjectives (both types and tokens) but not for nouns, verbs or adverbs.

References

BERNSTEIN, B. (1962), 'Linguistic codes, hesitation phenomena and intelligence', *Language and Speech*, 5, 31–46.

BERNSTEIN, B. (1971), 'Social class, language and socialization', *Current Trends in Linguistics*, vol. 12, A. S. Abramson *et al.* (eds). The Hague: Mouton.

BERNSTEIN, B. (1972), 'A socio-linguistic approach to socialization: with some reference to educability', *Directions in Sociolinguistics*, J. J. Gumperz and D. Hymes (eds). New York: Holt, Rinehart & Winston.

BRANDIS, W. and HENDERSON, D. (1970), *Social Class, Language and Communication*. London: Routledge & Kegan Paul.

GOLDMAN-EISLER, F. (1958a), 'Speech production and the predictability of words in context', *Q.J. Exp. Psychol.*, 10, 96–106.

GOLDMAN-EISLER, F. (1958b), 'The predictability of words in context and the length of pauses in speech', *Language and Speech*, 1, part 3, 226–31.

GOLDMAN-EISLER, F. (1961a), 'The continuity of speech utterance: its determinants and its significance', *Language and Speech*, 4, 220–31.

GOLDMAN-EISLER, F. (1961b), 'The distribution of pause durations in speech', *Language and Speech*, 4, 232–7.

GOLDMAN-EISLER, F. (1961c), 'Hesitation and information in speech', *Information Theory*, Colin Cherry (ed). London: Butterworth.

GOLDMAN-EISLER, F. (1961d), 'A comparative study of two hesitation phenomena', *Language and Speech*, 4, 18–26.

GOLDMAN-EISLER, F. (1968), *Psycholinguistics: Experiments in Spontaneous Speech*. London and New York: Academic Press.

HAWKINS, P. R. (forthcoming), 'The syntactic location of hesitation pauses', *Language and Speech*.

JONES, J. (1966), 'Social class and the under-fives', *New Society*, 22 December.

MACLAY, H. and OSGOOD, C. E. (1959), 'Hesitation phenomena in spontaneous English speech', *Word*, 15, 19.

MYERS, J. L. (1966), *Fundamentals of Experimental Design*. Boston: Allyn & Bacon.

Part IV Two theoretical issues

Chapter 10 Code, register and social dialect

R. Hasan

Introductory remarks

The main aim of this paper[1] is to examine the notions 'code', 'register' and 'social dialect'. Each of these categories is without doubt relevant to the field of socio-linguistics; at the same time, their recognition adds valuable dimensions to theories regarding the nature of language. The examination of these concepts, therefore, raises issues which appear to be of fundamental importance both to socio-linguistics and general linguistics.

I start with the assumption that there exist specifiable correlations between language and elements of social structure. The nature of the correlations may vary in given cases but what is basic to the assumption remains true and may be formulated as follows. Language is primarily a social phenomenon; despite the fact that some of man's biological attributes play a decisive part in the acquisition and subsequent use of language, it remains the property of social man rather than that of animal man. This gives rise to the possible hypothesis that aspects of social structure would be reflected in language. Such an assumption forms the very basis of socio-linguistics. Although accounts of coherent theories and methodologies for this field are conspicuous almost by their absence, the literature does vindicate the above hypothesis.

I sympathize with Fishman's view that socio-linguistics is probably a misnomer for what goes on in the field (Fishman, 1970). The label may suggest that socio-linguistics is a matter of applying linguistic techniques to the study of language placed in some socially significant context. No doubt it is true that more and more socio-linguists are at present employing the techniques for the description of language evolved by linguistics; none the less this does not appear to be the significant characterizing factor. What seems to be central to socio-linguistic studies is not that linguistic techniques are employed; it is rather that the structure of language is related at various levels of abstraction to social structure. It is, perhaps, not often recognized that such study, where it is explanatory, is of theoretical significance to general linguistics, extending its scope in a manner which has potentially far-reaching consequences, not only for the description of some of the essential properties of human language, but also for a study of the patterns of language acquisition by members of given communities and sub-communities. The relationship of socio-linguistics and general linguistics is such that one may find it difficult indeed to draw a definite boundary line between the two. Does the work of the functionalist linguists of the Prague School represent one or the other? One would like to be able to answer that it represents both in that it relates the structure of language to social elements and at the same time provides a model for the description of language in general and of language in particular.

Perhaps it needs to be pointed out that although the bulk of literature in linguistics is currently concerned with some aspect of the writing and construction of grammars, general linguistics itself cannot be equated with grammar even where the word is used to cover other aspects of the internal patternings in language than just syntax. Instead of going into a detailed discussion of the scope of general linguistics, I would here refer to Firth's 'A synopsis of linguistic theory 1930–55' (1957) as presenting one of the most catholic and systematic brief accounts of the concerns of general linguistics. On this particular issue Firth's views are generally shared by other linguists. Within the same general tradition, may be mentioned names such as Sapir (1921), Whorf (1956), Pike (1954) and Firth's own colleagues and students.

Firth maintains that 'linguistics accepts speech and language texts as related to the living of, and therefore to the "meaning" of life, and applies its theory and practice as far as it is able, to the statement of such "meaning" in strictly linguistic terms'. It is Firth's view that the 'meaning of language can be stated in linguistic terms if the problem is dispersed by analysis at a series of congruent levels'. Firth's use of the word 'meaning' has been criticized by linguists (Lyons, 1966; Langendoen, 1968). I am not concerned in this paper with an evaluation of the Firthian concept of 'meaning'; but as the discussion of the three concepts code, register and social dialect continues, it will be seen that the question of meaning in language, as opposed to meaning in individual items constituting the entries in the lexicon, indeed, cannot be handled adequately except by dispersion at a series of congruent levels of analysis; moreover, some of the levels of analysis may not be identified entirely by reference to the formally recognized components of syntax, lexicon and phonology. It would appear that underlying Firth's view of meaning is the assumption that a given linguistic utterance is capable of conveying a composite of different types of meanings rather than just one type. There seems to be no *a priori* reason for suggesting that, say, the content-meaning of an utterance is *ipso facto* more important or more deserving of attention in a verbal inter-action than its affective meaning. As users of language, we would seem to take into account all the components of the meaning of an utterance and our response appears to be conditioned by the totality of the meaning rather than by any one particular component.

This concern with the meaning of a linguistic event, in the wide sense of the word 'meaning', provides the Firthian schema with one of the justifications for a binary distinction in the study of language in general. Language can be studied formally; and it can be studied institutionally. The formal study of language is concerned with the network of relationships obtaining amongst the 'bits' of a given language, whereas the institutional study of language places it in relation to some circumstance of the speech community. It should be added that the segmentation between the two types of studies is not as discrete as the above statement might suggest; indeed were that the case, it might be taken as argument for regarding either the one or the other but not both as the 'proper concern' of general linguistics.

Social dialect

Aspects of the formal study of language are of peripheral interest to this paper. I turn my attention then to institutional linguistics, which studies language in relation to some circumstance of the speech community. At the risk of over-simplification, I shall restrict myself here to the brief examination of only three of the generally accepted categories of institutional linguistics. These are:

(1) *État de langue.*
(2) *Geographical dialect.*
(3) *Social dialect.*

The assumption in each case is that a language L has (or 'is a sum of') some varieties a, b, c . . . ; that a, b, c . . . all share certain formal features which justifies their being regarded as instances of L; that the variety La has certain formal features (or a pattern of formal features) belonging to it exclusively; by virtue of these La is differentiated from Lb, from Lc . . . Thus, in order to be accorded the status of varieties of L, each of the categories a, b, c . . . *must* simultaneously be alike and different from others in respect to some specifiable formal properties. The differences between a, b, c . . . can be correlated with some extra-linguistic factors, to which reference has been made earlier under the general label 'some circumstance of the speech community'. In the case of *état de langue*, a term much in use since F. de Saussure, the difference is correlated with time; in the case of geographical dialect, with space, and in the case of social dialect, with some social attribute of the speech group in question. Of these, the last is of special interest to the discussion; the first two are referred to in determining the nature of the category of social dialect.

Halliday *et al.* (1964) define dialect thus: 'Each speaker has learnt . . . a particular variety of the language of his language community, and this variety may differ at any or all levels from other varieties of the same language learnt by other speakers . . . Such a variety, identified along this dimension is called a dialect.' Geographical dialect is a variety of language determined by 'who you are', and 'in general, "who you are" for this purpose means "where you come from" '. If geographical dialect may be defined thus, by analogy social dialect may be defined as a variety differing at any or all levels from other varieties of the same language according to 'who you are', where 'who you are' would mean 'what social class you belong to'.

There are problems in the measurement of nominal social class membership. These problems arise out of the question of the range and the weighting of attributes which are considered as demarcation criteria. However, a parallel may be found in the case of geographical dialects, where a variability in the demarcation may result from a variation in the delicacy of focus. We may, for instance, recognize both a Scottish dialect and a Glaswegian one, where the latter is subsumed in the former. Similarly, we may recognize a social dialect A, spoken by members of a social group defined by reference to its members' income level. If, with reference to, say, the education of its members, the same social group can be sub-divided into sub-groups 1, 2 and 3, and if, corresponding to these sub-groups, further distinctions within dialect A can be established, then we would have at least three social dialects pertaining to sub-groups 1–3. The relationship of the latter to A would be the same as that of Glaswegian to Scottish. Just as Glaswegian is a more specific instance of the broader category 'geographical dialect: Scottish', so social dialects pertaining to subgroups 1–3 would be more specific instances of the broader category 'social dialect: A'. Social parameters such as those of income, education and occupation etc. may be used individually or in combination to define the boundaries of given social groups; the larger the number of attributes combined to define a social group, the more specific the social dialect pertaining to the group will be.

Geographical and social dialects may thus be seen as roughly parallel descriptive categories of institutional linguistics. In both cases, the linguist's approach is essentially the same: the identity of the dialect is defined by those of its formal properties which distinguish it from other dialects of the same general category. The search for language-external factors correlating with the distinctions in formal properties is based upon the assumption that consistent patterns of formal variation do not occur randomly; that if there exist different varieties of the same language, then some extra-linguistic factor(s) will indicate in general terms the boundaries of their operation.

It is to be noted in this context, that normally in the study of dialectology, the manifest in language is related to the manifest in non-language. If one asks: why does a particular person speak a particular social dialect, the answer in all likelihood would be that he has an affinity with a particular social group. The question is seldom answered or even asked: why does a particular social dialect differ from another just in these specific respects? This, it appears, happens because the extra-linguistic factor(s) correlating with the distinctions are regarded as only incidental to, but not constituting an explanation of, the specific peculiarities. There being no true causal connection between the dialect boundaries and their respective extra-linguistic correlates, at least in theory the possibility is to be granted that one may, for instance, be a native of Glasgow without possessing a Glaswegian dialect; similarly, one may belong to a particular social group with a particular income level and education, without possessing the social dialect said to pertain to the group in general. This is related to the observation that the identity of a dialect is crucially defined by reference to its distinctive formal properties, not by the extra-linguistic factors as such. Consequently the geographical and social provenance of a speaker does not, in itself, constitute an argument for his membership in a given dialect community. In the mouth of a born Londoner, Glaswegian still remains Glaswegian; it does not become Cockney.

Thus the internal formal patterns of a dialect, be it temporal, geographical or social, are studied purely descriptively; they are not related in any specific manner to 'the living of life' by the speech community in question. This characterization of dialect is not presented as a criticism of dialectology in general. The aim is simply to throw some light on the nature of the category 'dialect'. Indeed, the patterns of the formal levels by reference to which the identity of some dialect is established do not appear to be directly relatable to the 'living of life', except in some restricted areas of the structure of its lexicon, and more doubtfully, in some aspects of its syntax. Dialects, whether they correlate with time, space or social attributes of the speech community, remain a descriptive category, relating the manifest to the manifest. While the boundaries of the dialect will always correlate with some extra-linguistic factor(s), the latter cannot be used to predict the absence or presence of the formal patterns defining the identity of the dialect. The relationship between the two is not of logical dependence or concomitance but of simple co-occurrence.

Code

Having characterized dialect thus, we may inquire if Bernstein's category of code could be regarded as parallel in its nature to that of social dialect. Two outstanding differences between the two immediately draw attention to themselves: while the extra-linguistic factor(s) correlating with social dialect are incidental, those correlating with code are said to be causal; if the relationship between the two in the former case is simply that of co-occurrence, the relationship between the two in the case of code is that of logical dependence, which presupposes co-occurrence. Second, while social dialect is defined by reference to its distinctive formal properties, the code is defined by reference to its semantic properties,[2] thus involving the consideration of the formal levels only indirectly. That is to say, it can be argued that the semantic properties of the codes can be predicted from the elements of social structure which, in fact, give rise to them. This raises the concept code to a more general level than that of language variety; indeed, there are advantages in regarding the restricted and the elaborated codes as codes of behaviour, where the word behaviour covers both verbal and non-verbal behaviour. In the present paper, however, the notion code is discussed mainly in its capacity of controlling verbal behaviour.

Bernstein maintains that 'these two codes, elaborated and restricted, are generated by a particular form of social relation. Indeed, they are likely to be a realization of different social structures' (1969). It would appear that the aspects of social structure most relevant to the definition of codes are those which relate to the principle of social organization.

> The concepts mechanical and organic solidarity can be used to indicate the emphasis within a society of one form of social

> integration rather than another. Organic solidarity is emphasized wherever individuals relate to each other through a complex inter-dependence of specialized social functions. Therefore organic solidarity presupposes a society whose social integration arises out of *differences* between individuals . . . Mechanical solidarity is emphasized wherever individuals share a common system of beliefs and sentiments which produces a detailed regulation of conduct. If social roles are achieved in organic solidarity, they are assigned or 'ascribed' in mechanical solidarity (Bernstein, 1967).

To simplify, the identity of the members of societies characterized by mechanical solidarity can be stated adequately in answer to the question 'what is *x*?', whereas in those characterized by organic solidarity, the question must take the form 'who is *x*?' In the former case the identity is stated in terms of some recognized ascribed social role; for example, *x* may be father, boss or neighbour. In the latter case the identity is completely stated only when some individual characteristic of the member in question is stated in addition to his recognized social role, thus rendering him unique.

For obvious reasons, the form of social integration plays an important part in how a child is socialized. Bernstein approaches the question of socialization through four contexts which he considers to be critical, in that at the level of primary abstraction they exhaust the areas in which socialization takes place. These have been discussed in various writings by Bernstein and may be listed as follows (1970a):

(1) The regulative context—these are authority relationships where the child is made aware of the rules of the moral order and their various backings.
(2) The instructional context where the child learns about the objective nature of the objects and persons and acquires skills of various kinds.
(3) The imaginative context (or innovating) where the child is encouraged to experiment and re-create his world on his own terms and in his own way.
(4) The interpersonal context where the child is made aware of affective states—his own and others.

According to Bernstein, the difference between the forms of social integration will be naturally manifested in the verbal and non-verbal behaviour of the participants—the socializer and the socialized—in all these four contexts. Although more work has been done on the first two contexts (Cook, 1972; Bernstein and

Henderson, 1969; Brandis and Henderson, 1970; Robinson and Rackstraw, 1972; Turner, and Turner and Pickvance, as well as Robinson, in the present volume), implicit in these studies are certain predictions regarding the last two.

In social structures integrated by mechanical solidarity, the institutional and the communal is predominant, the unique meaning of the individual being less relevant. This is a way of saying that any possible set of situations is, as it were, largely pre-categorized by reference to communal beliefs and reactions. Consequently an alternative interpretation of a situation by reference to some specific attribute of a participant or some specific characteristic of the total event will normally neither be sought nor offered. The general propensity to view situations and the participants of the situations simply in terms of the communal pre-categorization, presupposes the propensity not to analyse—much less to question—the principles underlying a category. The emphasis is not on this aspect; rather it is on the process whereby a certain category is manifested. This attitude extends itself not only over the characterization of the moral order but also over the world of personal relations and concrete objects. Some of the consequences of these propensities for the four critical socializing contexts can be predicted in general terms.

In the regulative context, a situation may be characterized morally in absolute terms: 'that's wrong/that's naughty', without conceding the possibility that the individual's intent might not have been 'wrong' or 'naughty'. The emphasis is on punishment, verbal or non-verbal. If any appeals occur, they are likely to be made by reference to the positional status of the participants: 'your dad told you not to do that/boys don't play with dolls'. In the instructional context, an object or phenomenon is characterized by reference to what it does and/or how it does it. To be sure, this does not mean that the underlying principles may not be internalized; simply that characteristically, an explicit formulation of the controlling principles will not be forthcoming. In the interpersonal context, the positional orientation of members functions as a restraint, both upon the exploration of the bases of inter-personal inter-action, and the explicit verbal formulation of the affective states. Since there is a general lack of awareness regarding the controlling principles and the abstract properties of form, in the imaginative context this may lead to a greater freedom for fantasy which is likely to be less constrained by the logic of organized objective facts or by the explicit conventions of artistic form. Innovation in the world of objects—as distinct from artistic creativity—is likely to be tied down to the level of 'doing' and is not expected to arrive at the level of 'explaining the doing' in terms of the underlying principles.

The above is only a highly simplified and brief account of how membership in a certain type of social structure may affect the living of life in the crucial socializing contexts. Persons, objects, situations and their inter-action—phenomena round which the living of life revolves and which in other types of social structures might be the object of scrutiny and analysis—are here less likely to be questioned; they are filtered mainly through the communally recognized beliefs and attitudes. In this manner of living, a lot is taken for granted. The beliefs and attitudes of the members of the community are seen generally as unambiguous, forming part of a largely known paradigm. This is the kind of society in which the general is raised above the particular, the common above the specific and the 'we' above the 'I'. Bernstein has pointed out that the restricted code 'emerges where the culture or sub-culture raises the "we" above the "I" ' (Bernstein, 1969). It is assumed that the language which constitutes the verbal realization of the restricted code of behaviour will display certain semantically characterizable features which are expected to be reflected at the formal levels of syntax, lexis and most probably phonology. The justification of these assumptions can be provided in the following terms: meanings are social and are therefore affected by the characteristics of a social structure. In the description of languages, components of meanings are said to form units of the semantic level; the formal patterns which occur in any verbal inter-action are activated by the semantic components underlying them. Thus, if any crucial characteristic of meaning can be predicted by reference to the nature of codes, then it follows that prediction regarding the possible crucial formal patterns can also be made (Hasan, 1971).

In societies which are integrated by organic solidarity, the differences between individuals are of crucial importance; their recognized social role does not overshadow their personal attributes which are utilized in the achieving of the role. By the same token, special parameters of given situations cannot be ignored. Thus no sets of situations are pre-categorized totally or irrevocably; there is always the possibility that, despite the overall acceptance of communal beliefs and attitudes, some specific attribute of a participant or some specific parameter of a situation will be taken into account, allowing a modified interpretation. The readiness to modify a category presupposes the readiness to separate the elements constitutive of a category. It indicates an attitude which is basically analytic, although the details of the reasoning behind the analysis may be totally or partially wrong when considered from a technical point of view. That is to say, it is not being implied that the members are here 'scientific' or 'knowledgeable' in the technical sense of the word; simply that they have an attitude of scrutiny towards persons, objects and situations.

Again, such an attitude is generally reflected in the crucial socializing contexts, both in the verbal and the non-verbal behaviour of the participants. In the regulative context, the emphasis is upon the inner regulation of the person and this is achieved mainly through the greater use of the verbal elaboration of meanings as they focus upon the inter-personal and intra-personal (for details regarding this point see Bernstein, 1971a). In the instructional context, an object, phenomenon or skill will be characterized not only by reference to what it does and how it does it but also by some explanation regarding the underlying principles (for details see Robinson in this volume). In the inter-personal context, the orientation to differences between individuals and the general concern with the motivation and the personal affects of participants leads to a scrutiny of the bases of inter-personal inter-action, with the implication that the attributes whereby the individuals are rendered unique are likely to be explicit. This constant scrutiny and analysis fosters an awareness of the abstract properties of form with an emphasis on what might be described as the recognized 'objective realities'. In the imaginative context, fantasy is likely to be conditioned by the knowledge of explicit aesthetic frames, while in the innovation of objects the level of explaining the doing can be reached in explicit terms—again without any implication that the explanation would be necessarily correct. It is clear that in this manner of living not much can be taken for granted. The possibility of ambiguity is greater since the status of persons, objects and events is generally not seen in terms of their ascribed functions. The specific, therefore, over-rides the general; the personal, the communal. Elaborated code emerges from this type of society. The language that constitutes the verbal realization of the elaborated code of behaviour can again be characterized semantically, again with the implication that the possible range of crucial formal patterns can be stated by reference to the crucial characteristics at semantic level. As varieties of a language, the verbal manifestations of these two codes—the restricted and the elaborated—will differ from each other in respect to certain mutually exclusive formal patterns. If this assertion could be proved false, then there would be no case for regarding the codes as responsible for leading to varieties in language.

Though the above account is brief, it is hoped that it clarifies the relationship between the social elements and the verbal realizations of the two codes. Members of different types of societies use different codes; ultimately, the codes differ linguistically in some particular respects only because they reflect the two modes of the living of life. It may be best to elaborate upon this comment by discussing one particular example. It has been shown that in the use of language controlled by the restricted code, there is a much higher frequency of exophoric reference (Hasan, 1972; Hawkins, 1969). So far the statement does not appear to be very different in nature from the statement that in Cockney English, the initial 'h' is 'dropped'. This difference emerges only when we concern ourselves with a reasoned explanation of the phenomena referred to in the two seemingly parallel statements. While it is difficult to find any reason why the phenomenon of 'dropping the initial h' should occur in Cockney but not in the suburban dialects of London, the higher frequency of exophoric reference in the variety of language controlled by restricted code can be explained. Although this explanation involves a complex set of arguments, it will be useful to examine it in brief.

The information encoded in an exophoric item is available to an immediate participant of the situation (Hasan, 1968). It is perhaps important to point out that one does not acquire the status of participant in a speech situation by simple physical presence at the moment of verbal inter-action. Rather, the status is allowed to one if one is in possession of the relevant parameters of the situation which motivate the speech. The use of exophoric reference generally implies an assumption on the speaker's part that the hearer knows what the communication is about in general. Characteristically, exophoric references occur frequently where such an assumption can be made; and, characteristically, such an assumption can be made only where the possibility of ambiguity is not very high. It has been pointed out above that in sub-cultures which give rise to the restricted code a lot is taken for granted and ambiguity is generally not anticipated. This is one of the factors which accounts for the predominance of exophoric references in the variety of language controlled by the restricted code.

It is important to realize that the high frequency of the exophoric reference, by itself, is not a crucial characteristic of this variety of language alone. That is to say, there are varieties not necessarily controlled by the restricted code, in which the frequency of such reference may be equally high. However, the formal patterns to be found in the variety controlled by the restricted code will display a 'semantic compatibility' which arises from the deep meaning of the code. For example, consider another prediction related to the observation regarding the preponderance of exophoric references in the language controlled by the restricted code. This prediction maintains that the structure of the nominal phrase will be predominantly simpler in the variety under discussion; in other words, fewer modifying parameters will be selected to set aside the entity modified. Moreover, where the modifying parameters do get selected, they will tend to belong to certain semantically classifiable sets. Now, the formal elements 'modifier' and 'qualifier' are the encoding means of differentiation of any kind as applied to any category of person, object or event; it is through these that the uniqueness of an entity may be made explicit in language. The larger the number of parameters of differentiation, the higher the frequency of the modifiers and the qualifiers would be; the more varied the bases of differentiation in the nature of an entity, the wider the set of items which could perform the function of modification.

It has been noted earlier that in the type of societies which give rise to the restricted code, specific attributes of persons, objects and events are less likely to be emphasized or raised to the level of verbal explicitness; here the positional attributes would be emphasized more characteristically. This allows us indirectly to state the limits imposed upon the parameters of differentiation: if differentiation is to be made in terms of positional attributes for, say, persons, then the sets of items covering the semantic fields of sex, age and social role would be more relevant. The limitation on the parameters of differentiation lowers the possibility of complexity in the nominal phrase, since complexity is here merely a function of the selection of modifier and qualifier elements in permissible structures. To this may be added a fact discussed above—namely, that explicit encoding of meaning is not the primary concern of communicative acts here, since ambiguity is generally not anticipated. These two facts considered in conjunction provide sufficient explanation for the comparative simplicity of the nominal phrase in the variety under discussion. At the same time, the above discussion serves to clarify the meaning of the phrase 'semantic compatibility' as applied to characteristic formal patterns, diagnostic of a variety. Further, the discussion of these examples indicates how meanings may be affected by the characteristics of a social structure and how this may in turn affect the formal patterns of the language used by the members of the society.

In the above discussion the speakers making habitual use of a particular code have been identified by reference to their membership in different types of social structures, characterized by specific types of social integration. However, it would be rare, if not impossible, to find a contemporary society which is totally monolithic in its social integration. This would imply that in most contemporary industrialized societies, the two codes would exist side by side, since the social conditions giving rise to them would do so. Thus there exists the possibility that one and the same person may have access to both codes at once, using them in different contexts. However, given the genesis of the codes, it follows that every person in a society must have access to the restricted code, while social conditions may be created due to the complex inter-relations between industrialization, social class and education, whereby effective access to the elaborated code may become the prerogative of one class through its forms of socialization and access to education (Bernstein, 1971a). That effective access to elaborated code may be restricted, under certain social conditions, only to one class may give rise to the idea that the term 'code' is just another label for what has been known as 'social dialect'. The results of the work carried out in the Sociological Research Unit, under Bernstein's guidance, have indicated a tendency to an orientation to the restricted code on the part of the working-class population, whereas the middle-class population appears to be oriented to the elaborated code (Brandis and Henderson, 1970; Gahagan and Gahagan, 1970; Hawkins, 1969; see also Cook, and Turner and Pickvance in this volume). However, it would be a misinterpretation of this correlation of code orientation with social stratification to argue from it that the terms 'code' and 'social dialect' stand for the same concept. Note that access to the restricted code by all members of a society is not only allowed for in practice but it is essential in theory. It is true that one and the same person may have access to two social dialects; this would however be something determined largely by chance. There is nothing in the nature of the social dialects as such which demands that every member having access to one particular dialect should also have access to another particular one. Where access to codes is concerned the hypothesis that every member of a society would have access to the restricted code, whether or not he also has access to the elaborated code, is ultimately based upon the nature and origin of the two codes; the validity of this hypothesis depends upon the validity of the sociological arguments underlying the very genesis of codes.

The nature of codes differs from that of social dialects in other important respects. In the case of all three types of dialects discussed earlier—the temporal, the geographical and the social—the defining linguistic characteristics of the varieties are said to be located at the encoding levels of syntax, lexis and phonology. In the case of codes, however, the distinctive characteristics can be stated more powerfully and economically by referring to the level of meaning; it is not so much the formal patterns but rather the semantic structure of a message that is under focus when the latter is examined in relation to codes. Moreover, keeping the genesis of the codes in view, one may meaningfully raise the question: if different social strata show a tendency to use different codes in the same social contexts—such as the four crucial socializing ones—what sociological explanation for this may be found in consonance with the theory of codes? This is an interesting question, the answer to which would probably involve a consideration of the structure of power and the control of knowledge in society (Bernstein, 1971b). It will be noted that such questions cannot be asked meaningfully with reference to the social dialects, for there does not appear to be any true causal relation between the defining formal characteristics of a social dialect and the social factor correlating with it.

Being an explanatory socio-linguistic concept, the code is likely to have implications both for the field of sociology and that of linguistics. The concept may be used to throw light on questions important to both these parent fields. Consider, for instance, the question of change and stability, which is crucial to any sociological theory. A sociological theory must provide some hypothesis, not only about how societies change, but also how they continue with their essential characteristics. Bernstein has used the concept of code to put forward a hypothesis regarding stability in society. He postulates a bi-directional relationship between codes of communication and elements of social structure. As the earlier discussion has shown, different forms of social relationships determine what orders of meaning will have relevance for members entering into these different relationships. This in turn determines the kind of communication code to be employed. Stripped to its bare essentials this is the view taken by many linguists, that language reflects, albeit indirectly, the speech community which makes use of it for the living of life. Epigrammatically, society fashions language as it is.

The above is one direction of the relationship between social elements and codes of communication. The other direction points to a factor leading to stability in social structures. Bernstein maintains (1965) that

> the social structure becomes the developing child's psychological reality by the shaping of his act of speech. Underlying the general patterns of his speech are . . . critical sets of choices, preferences for some alternatives rather than others, which develop and are stabilized through time and which eventually come to play an important role in the regulation of intellectual, social and affective orientation.

The origin of these statements can be traced back to the famous Whorfian hypothesis that language creates the orders of perception and the relevance of patterns in terms of which the so-called world of objective reality is segmented by a speech community. Thus, according to this view, reality is relative and the specific shape of its segmentation is determined by the characteristics of the language one speaks. Epigrammatically, language fashions society as it is.

In the context of the present discussion, the relevance of these general comments is as follows: it may be maintained that orientation to a particular code implies a particular kind of experience and attitude on the part of the speaker, making him sensitive to just those aspects of social relationships which underly the use and the origin of the code in question. Thus the code of communication created by a particular form of social relation also perpetuates this same form of social relation by sensitizing the speakers to just these particular social meanings. This naturally raises the question of how the structure of a society admits of any change. Change in social structures can obviously emerge from varied factors, most of which need not concern us here. The factor relevant here is Bernstein's notion of change in the orientation to code. He allows the possibility that orientation to code can change for members. However, this change is not simply a matter of making the member learn certain aspects of the grammar and lexicon of the language; it entails no less than a change in his social identification (Bernstein, 1970b). A prerequisite of change in orientation to code is that the member may be enabled by some agency to perceive forms of relevance and meaning other than those to which he is sensitized by his own code orientation. This in turn entails that he should enter into some forms of social relation other than those which underly the genesis of the code to which he is already oriented. The relevance of this hypothesis to the entire education system is obvious: educational failure may not be as much a result of the pupil's inability to master the concepts, as that of the educational system which fails to establish any relevance between these concepts and the pupil's living of life, especially where the life in school is not a simple extension of life outside.

The relevance of language to social identification has some rather interesting implications for the acquisition of language. No doubt there is some biological attribute in normal humans which enables them to learn language. However, it seems highly improbable that this learning is triggered off simply by the possession of the biological attribute. The motive is furnished by the strongest urge of all—the urge for identification and placement in a social system as a member of a community. An infant remains a simple animal man for a surprisingly short period of his life; and I am suggesting that from very early infancy the learning of communication is simply grasped as a means of learning about one's identity in some social unit. Language being the most efficient medium of communication —and probably the most explicit means of social identification— receives attention in this capacity. A child learns to speak not because otherwise he could not get his mother to give him his bottle, his rusk or his teddy or whatever—these are comparatively low level pragmatic functions of language, although their value for sheer physical survival is great. He learns language because he is a social animal and his relation to society is determined for him most effectively by the mastery of the verbal system of communication.

The claim is then, that if Bernstein's hypothesis is correct, a child exposed physically to human language which is never placed in any social context, so that it does not symbolize forms of social relation, will not learn the language, despite his biological language-acquisition device. An experiment can be suggested —which for humane reasons could not be undertaken: a child exposed to human language only through a tape-recorder would not learn human language, since this stream of noise would in no way be related to his living of life and therefore would have no specific social meaning. He may be able to utter strings of noises which sound like the human language to which he is exposed, but they will not have the essential characteristics of relevance and flexibility. Unlike the learning of walking, running and jumping, the learning of language is a social phenomenon, much like the learning of non-verbal salutation. In all cases the possession of some biological attribute makes the actual operation possible; it is only in the latter two cases that the possession of the biological attribute alone is not enough.

Recently in linguistic theory, the notion of 'competence' has been introduced (Chomsky, 1965) as determining the area of language that a linguistic model must be able to account for. Very simply, competence is an idealization of the speaker's knowledge of language—the description of a language should at least be able to specify explicitly what the speaker knows—perhaps only implicitly— about his own language. It should be clear that the word 'speaker' as used in such statements is an abstraction, resembling in many respects the notion of 'langue' in linguistics and of 'conscience collective' in the field of sociology. In order to bear any relevance to the purpose for which the notion of 'competence' is introduced originally, the speaker in these cases *must be* the 'ideal speaker'. The mythical nature of the 'ideal speaker' is made abundantly clear when considered in the light of Bernstein's views regarding the relationship of codes to social relations. If his hypotheses regarding the origin and function of codes are correct, then it follows that the social relations underlying and determining some of the characteristics of the total meaning system of one code are not the same as those social relations which underly and determine the meaning structure of another one. The implication is that for members with access to only one code, at least some of the meanings of the other codes are filtered through their own code. The 'ideal speaker' even as a theoretical fiction is, therefore, an impossibility in socio-linguistics. His recognition presupposes the existence of a member who can enter into all forms of social relations simultaneously—which is an impossible proposition in sociology. It may be relevant to remark here that the rituals of a social group to which one does not belong appear often meaningless in the absence of technical sophistication.

A logical conclusion of Bernstein's views about the relevance of social elements to codes would be that all meanings are social—what the members can mean is determined by society. Bernstein is not alone in holding this view; ignoring the many sociologists and anthropologists, one could cite names from linguistics such as those of Boas, Bühler, Firth, Halliday, Pike, Sapir and Whorf who have all supported the hypothesis—implicitly or explicitly—that meanings in language cannot be arrived at without reference to society, since they are in the first instance generated by society itself. The various forms of systems of communication only provide the means whereby the totality of social meanings can be encoded and thus made available for transfer to other members. I would suggest that the social origin of meaning would argue strongly for the need to establish a point of contact between elements of social structure and that level of a communication system which is concerned with the meanings that can be encoded through the symbols of the said system of communication. If this premise is granted, it may have interesting implications for the study of language. Here, the level concerned with meaning is generally known as the semantic level. In both the systemic and the stratificational models for the description of language, the semantic level is regarded as the highest language-internal level, bearing a dynamic relation to the encoding levels of syntax, lexis and phonology. In any particular language inter-action, the selection of specific categories from the latter three levels is motivated by the selection of certain semantic components (Hasan, 1971). This view explains the basis of selection from amongst the totality of formal-phonological patterns available to a speaker; it cannot, however, explain what motivates the selection of particular semantic components in any given instance. In view of the social origins of meaning, it is perhaps not far-fetched to suggest that the answer to this question will lie in relating the semantic level to elements of social structure (Halliday, 1971b). Most linguists would agree that the semantic level bridges the gap between language and non-language; there are, however, not very many hypotheses as to how the bridging of the gap takes place. It is being suggested here that perhaps a large part of this bridging would consist in the mapping of the social elements onto the semantic ones.

If the origin of meanings is social, and if there are various forms of systems of communication, at least in theory the possibility has to be granted that the meaning potential of any one form of system of communication may not be identical with that of any other. Moreover, the meaning potential of one particular communication system will always form only a part of the totality of meanings available to the society. Thus, the verbal system of communication may be seen as having communicative control over only a part of the total social meaning potential, and there may be some advantage in remembering that verbal systems of communication do not have the sole monopoly of encoding meanings. In any given situation, various forms of communicative systems may be employed side by side and often it may not be possible to state definitely that the realization of a particular component of meaning was achieved solely through some symbol(s) of one and only one particular communicative system. The meaning of a comment with a smile is the function of the inter-action of the smile with the comment; this meaning can be realized neither by the verbal symbols nor by the smile alone. Where one's primary concern is the study of meanings communicated in a particular instance, it may be necessary to weaken, if not to disregard, boundaries between the verbal and the non-verbal means of communication. These comments may be taken as a plea for considering human behaviour as a unified whole, in which the verbal and the non-verbal merge in the process of what can only be described as the natural living of life. If in the interest of greater clarity, we choose to study some instance of human behaviour in its different aspects, separating each aspect from the others, it is desirable not to lose sight of the fact that the unit itself is greater than its own individual segments and that the meaning of the unit as such cannot be stated if any of its segments are ignored.

It is hoped that the above discussion would justify the claim that code is a 'key concept'; it is productive in that it leads outside itself. With the help of the concept one may raise questions and one may throw light on matters that do not form part of the concept as such.

Register

I have made an attempt earlier to show that code as a concept lies on a level different from that of social dialect and that the two cannot be considered as different labels for the same thing. This is equally true where the pair 'code' and 'register' is concerned; the terms are far from being synonymous.

Register is a variety of language differing at any or all levels of form from other varieties of the same language, 'distinguished according to use' (Halliday *et al.*, 1964). A particular register is said to be characterized by reference to some syntactic, lexical or phonological patterns; that is to say, register varieties differ language-internally by virtue of distinctive formal patterns, such that the totality of distinctive patterns for one particular register is not identical with that of any other register. To this extent they resemble temporal, geographical and social dialects, as well as varieties controlled by the different codes. So far as linguistics is concerned, no category of dialect, code or register can be recognized unless it differs from another category at the same level of abstraction in respect to some formal properties, in a consistent manner. The difference between registers and dialects lies in the fact that, but for a few immaterial exceptions, the distinctive formal patterns characterizing a dialect cannot be shown to be motivated by the circumstance of the speech community correlating with it; by contrast, but for a few immaterial exceptions, the distinctive formal patterns characterizing a particular register can be shown to be motivated by the factors which correlate with register distinction.

These factors can be studied under two main heads: those which form the relevant parameters of the situation giving rise to the use of language and those which arise from the nature of the channel through which language is transmitted. The latter is often referred to as 'medium'. One may question whether it is justifiable to separate the medium from what it is a medium of. Although it is difficult to think of any other medium for human language, I believe I am right in saying that none the less it is an accident that the transmission of human language takes the channels that it does. In essence the symbolic property of the system 'human language' is independent of the medium of its realization. A practical and, perhaps weaker, argument in favour of the separation of the verbal symbolic system from its medium may be found in the observation that individual formal patterns of a language seem to vary according to variation in medium—we do not speak as we write, and often foreigners sound strange, not because their language is ungrammatical, but simply because they have failed to master this distinction. I believe that no contradiction is involved in maintaining that the symbolic system *qua* a symbolic system is independent of the medium while holding the view that different individual bits of the system have a tendency to correlate with different forms of the medium. Somewhere in the acquisition of language, members of a language community, which possesses both basic media, do gather an awareness of the difference between spoken and written language. In most cases they are able to tell from the language, dissociated from its original context, whether it was produced orally or not. Clearly, extreme cases of either such as 'trespassers will be prosecuted' and 'what with one thing and another I wasn't able to make it to the party' will be recognized without any difficulty, though there can arise complications, some of which are discussed below in the discussion of medium.

The total set of factors correlating with the varieties of register can be listed briefly as follows:

(1) Subject-matter of discourse.
(2) Situation-type for discourse.
(3) Participant roles within discourse.
(4) Mode of discourse.
(5) Medium of discourse.

It is assumed that the factors listed above can vary independently, so that any combination of an instance of any is possible. If upon further study it can be shown that some factor listed above independently is in fact a function of some other factor(s), then the former would have to be subsumed in the appropriate category. Thus if it can be shown, for example, that the situation-type fully determines the subject-matter of the discourse, then there would be no need to consider subject-matter as an independent variable, since the specification of the situation-type would in this case be tantamount to the specification of the subject-matter as well. Neither originality nor empirical substantiation on a large scale is claimed for the selection of these factors as relevant to register variation. The factors are largely derivative of the account presented by Halliday *et al.* (1964) (see also Ellis and Ure, 1969), and the only justification for their present arrangement is intuitive; they seem to me to be both independent of each other and important to register variation.

It may be just as well to add in what sense the word 'independent' is being used here. I recognize that the independence of the listed factors is not absolute. That is to say, in actual fact the selection of specific subject-matter may present a fairly reliable basis for the expectation that it would be embedded in specific situation-types. If we take the subject-matter of linguistics, it is highly probable that this particular subject-matter will be embedded in a situation-type which could be labelled generally as 'informative', the exposition of hypothesis/evaluation of hypotheses/comparison of hypotheses etc. being more specific instances of the general situation 'informative'. And it would be rather unlikely to use the subject-matter of linguistics to flatter or to provoke, but neither is totally ruled out and instances of both can be found in linguistic literature. Thus, although specific instances of specific factors may be shown to 'go together' normally, conforming to the pattern of expectations, this co-occurrence is not necessarily pre-determined. It is in this sense that I regard the factors as independent of each other. Certain general statements can be made. For instance, the more technical the subject-matter, the less likely it is that it would be embedded in a situation-type involving the arousal of personal reactions; the more institutionalized the situation-type, the less likely it is that the mode of discourse would vary independently; similarly, the smaller the personal distance in participant roles, the less likely it is that the impersonal mode of discourse would be used. These generalizations have a certain degree of validity as they are based on an intuitive understanding of the social meaning of the categories involved; on the other hand, for the examination of a particular case, these generalizations are not of primary interest, only the actual is significant.

One general point seems worth making here before I embark upon a discussion of the factors listed. It has been too readily assumed that the easiest and most valid form of describing the linguistic characteristics of registers is to state the frequency or likelihood of individual patterns or of their combinations. I would suggest that it might be advantageous to specify the characteristics of given registers by reference to some high-level semantic component. For instance, two semantic components common to all sale situations would be the denigration and the desirability of the object of sale. Admittedly the situations would be somewhat different in societies where bargaining is customary as opposed to those where the fixed price rule obtains, but it seems to be true in both that certain semantic components are functions of the situation-type and the participant roles within the discourse. The characterization of registers by reference to some high-level semantic components would have at least three advantages. In the first place, the description of registers need not be tied down to the specification of individual sets of items or their combination occurring within a particular variety—the presentation of such an inventory seems to me to be almost impossible to achieve. Consider the examples below:

(1) It certainly is lovely but it's expensive.
(2) It *is* expensive but it's unique, made by our own exclusive craftsman.

In most societies—and particularly in those where bargaining is customary—(1) would be a possible statement by a buyer and (2) by a seller. The interesting point to note here is that the two are not different ways of saying nearly the same thing. Despite the use of the item *expensive* in (2), what stands out is the relative cheapness of the item which is an argument for its desirability, while in (1) the item *expensive* has its standard dictionary meaning. One is saying: it is expensive because of some desirable attribute(s) and therefore cheap: the other, that it is expensive despite the attribute(s) and therefore not worth the expense. No item-inventory could handle such features for the simple reason that they are not the property of individual items but of items of often different levels in combination. What distinguishes the two statements is the fact that one denigrates 'it' while the other stresses the desirability.

It is often difficult to know what value to assign to the relative frequencies of items occurring within a text when it is a question of allocating the text to some specific register. If the text is long, there seems to be no explicit criterion for concentrating on certain items rather than on others. I am suggesting that the postulate of a high-level semantic component provides a justification for picking out those items of the encoding levels which are pertinent to the encoding of the said semantic component. I would further suggest that the realization of these high-level semantic components is not 'localized' but that it is likely to be dispersed over the text as a whole (Hasan, 1972). Less technically, the register allocation of a text is impossible without understanding the meaning of the text, and I am suggesting that within the meanings of the text there are constellations of meanings which are crucial to the identity of registers; and these are the very meaning constellations to which I have referred as the high-level semantic components of the text.

Further, the statements of points of similarity and dissimilarity amongst different register varieties may be made easier by this approach. What Davies says (Davies, 1969) regarding the formal patterns of a text on chemistry may be true only of a particular sub-type of chemistry texts. I would doubt that the grammatical structures whose frequency he considers to be crucial to chemistry texts upon Taylor's findings (Taylor, 1968) would be crucial to chemistry texts in pedagogical situations where the participant roles are school-teacher and young pupils; one only needs to look at a school-book of chemistry—or to listen to a teacher in the class—to realize that the density of attributive and locative clauses is not a function of the subject-matter alone. At the same time, the kind of propositional relations cited by him as a property of this register are not specific to it alone—they will be found equally in texts of the same tenor on other physical sciences, if not elsewhere as well. From a consideration of the combinations of specific subject-matter, situation-type, participant roles, mode and medium, may be predicted certain high-level semantic components which will at once display the points of similarity and dissimilarity amongst the various sub-types of a general register such as that of chemistry or politics. This observation is based upon the assumption that the social meanings of the different variable factors correlating with register provide an indication of the total range of what can possibly be meant—they determine what Halliday calls the 'meaning potential' (Halliday, 1971a) of a given variety. Under a specifiable circumstance we can only 'mean' from that set of meanings which the circumstance has set aside as potentially relevant.

To return to the main discussion, the gloss on the subject-matter of discourse may be defined as 'what is the language about?' This is what forms part of the contents of the discourse. The subject-matter controls the range of the lexicon from which selection may be made. This is so obvious that it does not need to be pointed out: in a discussion of the nature of volcanic eruptions, the lexicon referring to, say, the genres of musical composition is, as it were, irrelevant. The correlation between subject-matter and the range of the lexicon functioning as the field of effective choice is the most transparent of all relations—what is being talked about must be referred to, for in everyday life we do not function like the symbolist poet. If specific registers varied from each other only in this respect there would probably be no need to recognize the category of register.

The subject-matter is embedded in the situation-type. Situation-type is a cover term for the nature and purpose of the transaction in which language is being used and only refers to those parameters of the immediate situation (Ellis, 1966) which are encapsulated in the language of a text; that is to say, situation-type is an abstraction from the totality of material situational setting (Hasan, 1972). When two situation-types are very different in nature, it is difficult to realize that the subject-matter in both is the same; this is because subject-matter constitutes only part of the contents of the text, and the nature of the transaction as well as the purpose of the use of language function just as importantly in determining the meanings of the text. Compare two texts regarding a piece of jewellery, one in a situation-type of expert evaluation and the other in sale, perhaps, in Petticoat Lane. The two are likely to run thus:

(3) This chain is 8-carat rolled gold, thirteen inches; the stone is semi-precious. Their total value is approximately £2·10p.

(4) It's a beauty. Lovely stone and the chain is dainty. Want to try it on? It'll go beautifully with your dress—and very cheap for what it is. Lovely workmanship—new design in the market. Came in only yesterday.

In these two examples the difference in the situation-type obscures the fact that the language is in both cases about the same thing—i.e., a piece of jewellery. Such obscurity arises most often in cases where the subject-matter is what is not regarded as belonging to a technical discipline. Conversely, where the subject-matter belongs to a recognized discipline, the situation-type does not obscure the subject-matter—instead it may itself get obscured by this part of the content of the discourse. Criticism of works in recognized fields of discipline on the ground of their not doing what the speaker never set out to do in the first place are based on a misinterpretation of the situation-type. If the subject-matter functions as a control on the general relevant area of the lexicon, the situation-type functions as a modification of this area—excluding some part of what, on the basis of the subject-matter alone, would have been adequate, but what, in the combination of *that* subject-matter in *that* situation type, would not be. At the same time it may argue for the inclusion of some area(s) of lexicon which, on the ground of the subject-matter alone, could not have been predicted. If the situation-type in which the subject-matter of chemistry is embedded is pedagogical as opposed to exposition of hypotheses, this will inevitably modify the area of lexicon relevant to the two. Similarly, if the situation-type in which the subject matter of jewellery is embedded is of ordering a piece of jewellery to be made, then certain areas of the lexicon referring to the weight and design particulars of the object in question would be relevant while they are not relevant *per se* to the situation-type of evaluation or sale. It is expected that the propositional relations holding the particular statements of the text together will vary with a variation in situation-types. Consider the implicit causal relation between the first and second sentences of text (3) above; in (4) the relationship between the sentences is what I have referred to as 'additive' elsewhere (Hasan, 1972).

Participant roles within discourse may be glossed as 'who is using language to communicate with whom?' where *who* and *whom* do not refer to unique individuals but to some communally ascribed role, such as those of older, younger, male, female, mother, father, husband, wife, son, daughter, teacher, neighbour, stranger etc. It will be readily seen that these are all socially defined positional roles. What may not be seen so readily is the fact that in any particular case a speaker may operate in the capacity of some particular role, the others being, as it were, irrelevant. This is why I have considered it necessary to add the qualification 'within discourse', which implies 'only that role which is relevant to the discourse, irrespective of others that the speaker is capable of assuming on other occasions of verbal inter-action involving the self-same persons'. Thus when Mrs Jones, the teacher, inter-acts in the classroom with a student who happens to be also her daughter, the role-relations are likely to be those of teacher–taught, not of mother–daughter which may be assumed on some other occasions. Another attribute of the participants of a discourse which is subsumed in this head is what I have referred to as the 'personal distance'; this is the factor which underlies the distinctions made on the axis of formality–familiarity. It would seem that the roles of the participants are largely determined by the situation-type in which they inter-act with one another. Indeed, the more institutionalized the situation-type, the more likely it is that the role-constellation to be found would be totally predictable from the specific situation-type. In a situation of school pedagogy, the roles are institutionally also determined as those of teacher and taught. However, what cannot be predicted from the situation-type is the personal distance obtaining between the participants, even in institutionalized situations. It is interesting to note here that in some cases the factor of personal distance is built into the meaning of the items of a set; consider *intruder*, *stranger*, *acquaintance*, *friend*, in this light. In any given instance the personal distance factor may override the consequences of the publicly recognized roles. A father and son may in different situation-types inter-act with a different degree of personal distance, often depending upon the subject-matter of the discourse. Thus, the institutional role as such is not a sure indication of the degree of personal distance obtaining within an inter-action, except in cases where the item referring to the ascribed role has this factor built into its meaning.

All things being equal, the participant roles and personal distance together act upon the lexicon and the syntax of a given register. The role and personal distance which allows:

(5) His business has gone phut

is different, however minimally, from that which allows:

(6) His business has come to a sad end

and the following is again different from the above example, in the role relations and the distance obtaining between the roles:

(7) The court have declared him bankrupt.

It may be of interest here to note that the exophorics, whose use has been cited above as one of the characteristics of language controlled by the restricted code, would most probably occur with a greater frequency in those registers where the personal distance is very reduced. The reasons in both cases are the same; the possibility of ambiguity arising is low where the distance between participants is reduced, just as it is low where the paradigm of known and possible behaviour is largely pre-categorized. Thus one and the same feature of language can arise from different sources depending on the context of the discussion; this is not a reason for ignoring these features of language—if anything it argues for an interpretation which takes the relevant factors into account, and therefore probes more deeply into the significance of these features. While it is easier to describe in general terms how the lexicon may vary according to the variation in role and distance, it is comparatively more difficult to make such general statements regarding their effect upon syntax. However, consider the following examples, in which it is assumed that only the personal difference is at variance:

(8) I wondered if I might be allowed to leave earlier today. There are some personal matters I should like to settle this afternoon.

(9) I've got this thing to do at home. Is it all right if I go off earlier today?

It is my tentative suggestion that the greater the stress on the institutionalized aspect of the role and the greater the personal distance, the more likely it is that the high-level semantic components of +/−*tentativeness* and +/−*uncertainty* would be relevant to the text, the plus and the minus signs distributing themselves in a coherent pattern for the dominated and the dominating role. Thus in example (8) the employee's language will have the semantic components +*tentative* and −*certain*, while the employer's is likely to possess −*tentative* and +*certain*. Some of the realization of the component +*tentative*, for example, would be through the modification of whole statements, which may involve at the formal levels the selection of comment adjuncts, modality, modulation (Halliday, 1970) or of some subordinating circumstance. This mode of approach seems to be perhaps more helpful for stating characteristics of registers; it would certainly appear to be somewhat more productive than the counting of subordinate clauses or what-have-you.

Given the same situation-type and the same subject-matter as well as the same participant roles, registers may vary according to variation in the mode of discourse. Often the combination of the specific instances of the former three factors can effectively determine the mode to be employed. For example, in the situation of buying and selling, the mode would normally be 'persuasive'; it would be a-normal to find the 'imperative' mode used here. Non-technically, a salesman wheedles; he does not dictate. Again, in a situation of exposition of hypotheses, the mode is likely to be 'expository'/'explanatory' while it is not likely to be 'supplicatory' in the normal sense of the word. But in theory the mode of discourse *can* vary independently, even in the same given combination of situation-type, subject-matter and participant role. Thus we may have the following different statements from two different mothers:

(10) If you climb up that wall you may hurt yourself.
(11) You climb up that wall and I'll take a stick to you.

One might say that at one level what the mothers are saying is the same, namely *I don't want you to climb up that wall*, but the difference in the mode of discourse certainly changes some aspects of the meaning of the two statements, so much so that it is difficult to realize that they belong to the same situation-type basically, namely that of control. The mode of discourse is most effectively reflected in the mood choices of the clauses in the text. It is possible to make predictions regarding the structural characteristics associated with different types of mode. For instance, the persuasive mode is likely to produce texts in which the various statements are causally linked; the expository mode, those in which in addition to causal relations, relations of elaboration and exemplification will also be found, while in the imperative mode the causal relation between the propositions is likely to be of an arbitrary nature as in (11).

Medium of discourse has already been discussed in some respects earlier. Basically it refers to the channel of communication, which may be either oral (spoken) or graphic (written). Varieties differ according to whether they are spoken or written. It is perhaps important to emphasize that the actual nature of the manifestation is itself not crucial here. The transcript of a recorded conversation is not an instance of the written medium; equally the broadcast of news is not an instance of the spoken medium. Because individual bits of language have a tendency to occur in different media, a somewhat curious situation has emerged. It is possible to produce a text in writing which was never spoken but which is written-as-if-spoken; for example, consider some modern plays. Equally it is possible to speak out a text which was never written but which, as it unfolds itself, bears all the characteristics of written language, save the orthographic manifestation. It is therefore fair to assume that oral and graphic media as factors correlating with register variation, do not refer to the physical manifestations of the text in question, but rather to some properties of the text, which are normally associated with these basic forms.

The medium of discourse is expected to affect the syntactic choices of a text. All things being equal, spoken texts display a greater complexity in syntax than the written ones, a point to which attention was drawn also by Halliday *et al.* (1964). In written discourse, exophoric cohesive devices have an almost negligible frequency, as compared with spoken discourse, where certain types of ellipses occur much more frequently than they do in the former type of discourse. These characteristic features—which do not exhaust all the peculiarities—of the spoken and written varieties stem from the fact that in spoken communication more information regarding the relevant immediate situation is available extra-linguistically to the participants of the discourse. It is therefore not necessary to encapsulate in language all the relevant components of the meaning of the message in an explicit manner. In written communication, on the other hand, extra-linguistically provided information is of a very limited kind and depends much upon the shared contexts between the participants. In order to be decoded appropriately, the relevant components of the meaning of the message must be encapsulated explicitly in language, since whatever is not so encapsulated may not be available to the decoder. The lower occurrences of exophoric cohesive devices and of certain types of ellipses in the written variety of discourse would appear to be governed by these conditions. In the spoken variety an elliptical clause such as *don't*, even when it occurs all by itself, can be interpreted as a request or order to desist from carrying out a particular action—the nature of which would be known to the decoder from extra-linguistic sources; in the written variety, the same elliptical clause cannot be assigned a specific interpretation—

that is to say, the specific process under focus will not be known to the decoder—unless the elliptical clause functions anaphorically presupposing some item cohesively in the text.

Features referred to sometimes as cancellation, repetition and contradiction have been ignored in the above discussion. Although these features are normally associated with the spoken medium, they are not causally related to this factor alone. Rather, in general, they indicate the speaker's familiarity and control over the subject-matter in relation to his listener(s). To the extent that the language of a speaker, on some particular occasion, is more 'well-organized', it points to the fact that what is said and to whom it is said presents little or no problem to the speaker. Thus, these features are not a function of the medium of the discourse as such; they result from an inter-action of the subject-matter, situation-type and participant relations relevant to a discourse (Hasan, 1972).

Throughout the discussion of the category of register, the term 'tenor' of discourse has been avoided. It seems to me to be a particularly suitable term to refer to the 'tonal quality' of texts of various varieties. The tonal quality itself is the product of the inter-action of the five factors listed and discussed above. In other words, the tonal quality of a text is not determined solely by the selection of any one factor, be it that of situation-type, of mode or personal distance or participant role. Instead, it would seem to be a result of the fact that *x* is being talked about, in *y* situation, with participant roles *a* and *b*, with reduced personal distance, in a particular mode and medium. It should be noted that the use of tenor to refer to the tonal quality of texts as a whole is a departure from both Halliday *et al.* (1964) and from Enkvist, Spencer and Gregory (1964). Halliday *et al.* use the term 'style', underlying which are the factors of role-type and personal distance, while Enkvist, Spencer and Gregory use the term 'tenor' for the same purpose, on the ground that the term 'style' is best used exclusively for literary texts.

Hopefully, the above discussion shows that the factors said to correlate with register variation stand in a causal relation to the formal patterns which are characteristic of a particular register. The details of these factors can therefore be used to predict the formal characteristics crucial to a given variety of register. By virtue of this attribute, register can be shown to be distinct from dialect: the correlation of extra-linguistic factors with formal patterns diagnostic of a given dialect variety is based upon what might be described as incidental co-occurrence. On the other hand, this particular type of causal relation is not specific to register alone. It may be recalled that in the discussion of code, some of the crucial formal patterns were shown to be predictable from the social factors underlying a particular variety of code (cf. pp. 264–5). In this particular respect then code and register are alike; however, the terms are not synonymous. They refer to two distinct concepts, involving different levels of abstraction.

The difference between code and register can perhaps be indicated most economically by considering the extra-linguistic factors said to correlate with each category. The factors relevant to register have been discussed in some detail above (cf. pp. 272–81). Where code is concerned the key concept would appear to be that of 'role-system'. The term role has been mentioned as a factor correlating with register variation as well; to be more precise, variation in participant role in discourse is said to result in variation of register. It may be well to state the difference between participant role and role-system as used in the discussion of variation in register and code, respectively. The term role-system as used in the discussion of code variation is more abstract and general than the term participant role, as used in register. Any particular manifestation of participant role would be some instance of that type of role which may be labelled 'institutionalized'; thus the term covers only a fraction of what may be meant by the general term role-system. This is just another way of saying that the term role-system refers to a more general and abstract concept. At this level of abstraction, the role-system lies at the basis of all social relations: it acts upon social inter-action and may itself be seen as a dynamic product of the social relations available to members of a community. The type of social relations underlying the role-system determines whether a particular role would be of the ascribed and communalized type or of the achieved and individuated type; and it is this distinction between the type of role-systems that is pertinent to code variation. The differences between specific ascribed roles in social hierarchies and institutions are, *per se*, not relevant to code variation; the differences between types of roles are. Thus, unlike register, code need not vary according to whether a speaker is operating in the ascribed capacity of father or that of son; it will, however, vary according to whether the role is communalized or individuated.

Role-system acts upon the more specific factors which correlate with code variation; in fact these factors may be seen as a function of role-system. I shall refer to these factors as 'mode of control', 'focus of interest' and 'focus of meaning'. The difference in role-type is expected to affect the nature of control-meaning and interest. In its turn this variation would be relevant to code variation. If we accept as our paradigm, the ideal types of restricted and elaborated code, then the relationship of the various factors discussed above to code variation may be presented as follows:[8]

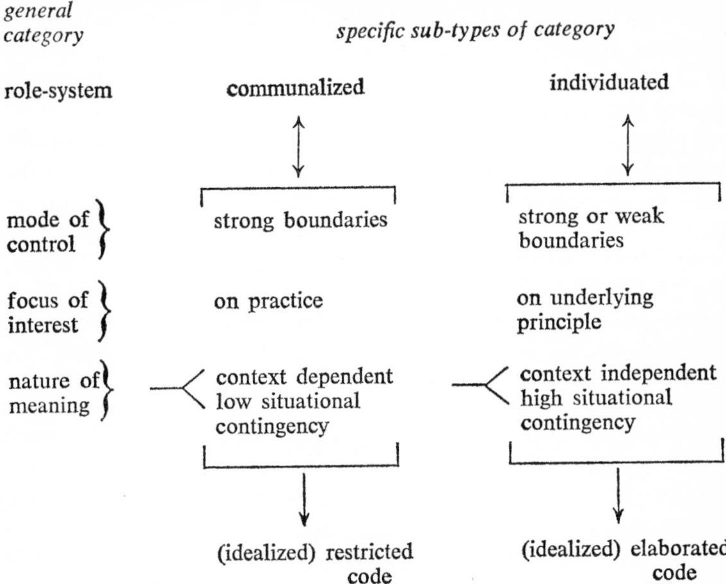

It is important to emphasize that the schematic presentation above is highly simplified; moreover, it presents that combination of factors which underlies the restricted and elaborated codes in their most idealized states, instances of which might not even occur in practice. The first column is labelled 'general category'; it states general factors relevant to code variation. The second and third columns present the more specific sub-types of the latter general category. Thus, looking across the columns, communalized and individuated role-systems are more specific sub-types of the general category role-system. Looking downwards in columns 2 and 3, we find within braces those specific factors which stand in a causal relation to the specific sub-type of role-system: a two-way arrow is used to indicate the bi-directionality of this relationship. Thus, in the above representation, column 2 may be read out as follows: wherever role-systems are of the communalized type, there is a greater likelihood that the mode of control will utilize strong boundary maintenance, that the focus of interest would be on practice and that meanings would be context dependent with low situational contingency; conversely, wherever these particular factors combine, there is a greater expectancy that the role-systems would be of the communalized type. The arrow from the lower brace to the idealized code-type shows that in, say, column 2 the combination would correlate with a maximized restricted code. The labels for most of the factors within braces are self-explanatory, but a word must be added here regarding the sub-types of the factor 'nature of meaning', as this is probably most relevant to code differentiation where the concept is being considered as controlling certain varieties of language.

The term 'context dependent' when applied to language as used in any inter-action may be paraphrased as follows: language that does not encapsulate explicitly all the features of the relevant immediate situation in which the verbal inter-action is embedded. Crucial to this paraphrase is the distinction between 'material immediate situation' and 'relevant immediate situation'; the latter is that sub-set of the former to which reference is made implicitly or explicitly by the language of a message (Hasan, 1972). The implicitness of the context dependent language implies that the correct decoding of the verbal message would be dependent upon an awareness of the relevant immediate situation, which awareness would be derived from sources other than the verbal message under focus. That is to say, in order to have access to the meanings of the verbal message, the decoder has to utilize other sources of information than just the language of the text under focus. As might be expected, 'context independent' has exactly the opposite meaning; context independent language is language that encapsulates explicitly all the relevant features of the immediate situation in which the verbal inter-action is embedded. It follows that here the correct decoding of the message is a simple function of one's understanding of the language, requiring no extra-linguistic sources of knowledge.

The label 'low situational contingency' may be paraphrased as follows: the linguistic means of rendering entities unique are rarely employed. Where there is low situational contingency those details specific to particular persons, objects and situations are not treated linguistically which would set aside the entity under focus as unique. Rather, the attributes by reference to which an entity is characterized are likely to be such general ones as do not lead to an individuation of the entity. Conversely, 'high situational contingency' implies a greater explicit use of verbal means whereby some entity is rendered unique so that it is set aside as a particular case.

It may be of interest here to note that the terms of each pair of contrasting factors cannot be treated as mutually totally exclusive. That is to say, it is not the case, for instance, that in language controlled by the elaborated code, every bit of the message would be explicitly encoded. The question regarding these factors then is not whether they occur or not; rather, it is to be formulated in relative terms. The degrees of, say, context dependence and situational contingency are variable; and there is no absolute point which may be said to be diagnostic of one variety of code or of the other. This is one of the reasons why code variation is better studied in the background of the same social functional contexts, e.g. Bernstein's four socializing contexts. It is also to be noted that the relationship between the type of role-system and the factors (contained within braces) is not absolute; there is no total logical dependence between the two. In theory, at least, the possibility is allowed that social conditions may arise which would allow different re-alignments of the factors. It is therefore possible that we may have an array of the varieties of restricted and elaborated codes rather than just two highly idealized ones.

If we compare the factors which are said to correlate with code variation with those said to correlate with register variation, the difference between the two categories may be formulated. The code-correlating factors are derived directly from a coherent, albeit limited, theory of social structure and cultural transmission. Each factor here is relatable to the central concept of role-system; in its turn, role-system is basic to the theory of social structure and cultural transmission. There is thus a clear chain of causal relation, which traces the origin of the code to its very roots, offering hypotheses as to why certain forms of behaviour are the likely ones under certain specifiable social conditions. Underlying the register-correlating factors, there is no such theoretical coherence. Although largely social in nature, these factors are not relatable to any specific aspect of a social theory; indeed, in some cases the very basis of the distinction between two specific instances of factor is itself non-sociological. For example, the distinction between chemistry and biology as two distinct technical fields is not based upon sociological arguments, although this distinction may be regarded as a sociologically important one. As a concept, code points to something outside itself; register does not. Register does not presuppose a coherent sociological theory; the presupposition of certain observed social facts is sufficient for the discussion. In order for the concept of register to be viable, it is not necessary to establish any relation between the observed social facts which are built into the register-correlating factors.

It is an outcome of these attributes that whereas all code-correlating factors lie at the same level of abstraction, the question whether or not this is true also of register-correlating factors cannot even be raised meaningfully. Presupposing a coherent theory, the code-correlating factors can be placed *vis-à-vis* each other and within the theory. Register-correlating factors on the other hand cannot be so placed.

The code-correlating factors belong to a high level of abstraction. The theory of code is not only the theory of a linguistic variety; it includes a theory of both verbal and non-verbal behaviour in the sense that it offers some hypothesis regarding the effect of certain social phenomena upon the community's living of life. Code is thus a much more global concept than register.

The recognition of the concept of register has some interesting implications for the study of language in general. I have suggested earlier that registers may be better characterized by reference to some high-level semantic components, whose realization would not be a function of individual items of any size or level but rather of a combination of such items throughout the text. It would follow that at least two types of meanings would have to be recognized—those which are localized and those which are text-wide. Thus any text may be seen to contain meanings whose pertinence is limited within some formal unit; at the same time it would contain meanings which are not unit-bound, these latter being realized across formal units and being pertinent to more than any one particular unit—no matter of what size or level—in the text. We may use two different labels for these two distinct types of meaning, referring to the former as 'localized semantic components' and to the latter as 'textual semantic components'. The need for a recognition of these two kinds of semantic components can be justified. Both the localized and the textual semantic components are equally relevant to an adequate decoding of a verbal message. *A priori* there appears to be no reason for suggesting that the study of only one kind—namely the localized semantic components—is the business of linguistics while the other kind of semantic components can be relegated to some vague area, such as that of 'stylistic variation' or 'performance', as if these meanings did not reside in language.

The category of register differentiates texts generally by reference to their textual semantic components. Registers are not set up to account for the semantic differences between the following:

(10) If you climb up that wall you may hurt yourself.
(12) If you climb up that wall you may ruin your nice new shirt.

This is one of the reasons for commenting that if registers varied simply by the variation in subject-matter and consequently showed distinctions only in the selection of lexical items, it would not be necessary to recognize the category of register. The two texts above do differ in meaning but this difference in meaning is not text-wide, as is the case with:

(10) If you climb up that wall you may hurt yourself.
(11) You climb up that wall and I'll take a stick to you.

(10) and (11) belong to two different varieties of register by virtue of variation in the mode factor; this variation is reflected in the text-wide difference in meaning.

Most current theories of semantics are inadequate for dealing with textual semantic components, whether or not they are capable of dealing with the localized ones. Moreover, it would seem that in order to move towards a semantic theory capable of adequately describing text-wide meanings, we may have to revise our linguistic models. A model that can accept and integrate the inter-action of language with non-language as an important part of language study obviously stands a better chance of dealing with text-wide meanings. The autonomy of the verbal symbolic system appears to be restricted to the formal levels alone and it may be that an adequate semantic theory presupposes an adequate theory to account for the nature of contact between the formal linguistic and the extra-linguistic phenomena. The nature of this contact is not exhausted by such isolated notions as those of 'reference', 'representation' or 'naming'. The onomastic function is certainly basic to language; it is perhaps also necessary for other functions that language has. In view of our present state of knowledge, this particular type of relationship between language and non-language is perhaps also the easiest to handle. None the less, there is more to this rather neglected area of language study. Language is used to live, just as social structure is used to live. This introduces a complexity in the description of language and argues for a weakening of boundaries between various systems for communication. The exhaustive description of language is an ideal, which may perhaps never be achieved, but there will certainly be much *less* chance of its being achieved if language is separated from the living of life totally. The semantic structure of language is not absolutely unrelated to the total meaning structure available to a community. Hence, meanings in language cannot be described adequately by remaining enclosed within the formal symbolic system of language.

The adequate use of language must in some sense be a part of our linguistic competence. In actual practice the learning of language cannot be equated with the learning of formal relations obtaining amongst individual 'bits' of verbal symbolic system. Indeed, I have maintained earlier that such learning of language *as language* is impossible—language cannot be learnt in dissociation from how it is used. If 'competence' refers to a speaker's knowledge of his language rather than to just some particular aspect(s) of such knowledge, then it cannot be equated with grammar, unless 'grammar' equals total description—and such a use of the term grammar would be somewhat a-normal. The variation in the tonal quality of two texts is not a superficial matter, resulting from the randomness of performance; it has a meaning as basic to the message as the so-called 'cognitive' meaning. This is not to say that all variation in language is necessarily meaningful. However, when two items occur in a regular pattern, the pattern of their occurrence being generally definable by some such concept as that of code, register or dialect, it seems profitless to insist that they are free variants of each other simply because in some respects the meanings of the two may be similar. In the background of that clustering of register-correlating factors, where a mother may say:

(12) If you climb up that wall you may ruin your nice new shirt.

She could not very well have said:

(12a) If that wall is climbed up by you your nice new shirt might be ruined by you.

This is not because (12) is grammatical while (12a) is not. It is because given the particular clustering of register-correlating factors, (12a) would be highly inappropriate. The meaning components encoded in (12) are not identical with those encoded in (12a) and it is only the former that are appropriate in the register of maternal control with reduced distance; the latter are not. This point is related to the definition of 'deviation' in linguistics. Language is an abstraction, and while it is not only justifiable but also necessary to describe the grammar of language, disregarding those forms which are peculiar only to some specific variety, the limitations of such a grammar should not be forgotten. Consider the following:

(13) She often buys in Switzerland.
(14) They shivered their spears.
(15) He hit many fours during the first Test match.

To say that the above are deviant or ungrammatical tells us little that is worth knowing about these sentences—what it does tell us about is the kind of limitations we have imposed upon the grammar which regards these as deviant—or worse, as ungrammatical.

While the norms of the language, abstracted from its varieties, apply generally, the norms of specific varieties of language cannot be ignored, for in any confrontation with language, we do not encounter the abstraction 'language' itself—only an instance of some variety of it.

Concluding remarks

In the discussion of the three categories—code, register and social dialect—I have attempted to present what seems to me to be the essential difference in their nature. At the same time, I have tried to show the implications of the recognition of these categories to linguistics and to sociology. If socio-linguistics consisted only of the study of social dialects as characterized here, there would be no justification for its recognition as a separate field of study, since it would present little or no extension of either sociology or linguistics. This is not to say that dialect studies have no value; simply, that they can be adequately accommodated within the area of general linguistics known as institutional linguistics. It is a function of cross-disciplinary studies—or so it seems to me—that they pose a set of problems which could not be handled adequately remaining within one of the associated fields, thus providing further new insights important to both in different ways. It is true both of codes and registers that they provide an insight into language which could not be obtained simply by concentrating on the formal relations obtaining between the 'bits' of language.

In the discussion of both codes and registers one may find enough indications to suggest that Firth is correct in his assumption that a language text contains various levels of meaning. These meanings cannot be described simply by having recourse to the lexicon, no matter how complete it is—nor by working out a set of rules which tell us how to interpret sentences in isolation. It may be true that linguistics has not yet reached even this infant stage of describing such meanings explicitly. But this does not seem to be any reason for suggesting that explorations of the statements of meaning at various levels of analysis are either invalid in themselves or shorn of interest. Centuries of linguistic scholarship has allowed us to arrive at a stage where we can, perhaps with some justification, talk about the construction of explicit grammars—but the work of the preceding generations was certainly neither invalid within its own historical context nor a waste of time. The field of language study is wide and so full of legitimate inquiries into its varied aspects that it would be narrow-minded, indeed, to insist that every linguist should approach the study of language in the same manner. In the last resort, the aspects of language one chooses to study and the approach one follows would very much depend upon why one is interested in the study of language at all. The purpose of one's inquiry would seem to push one to emphasize one aspect over some other—as it may also determine the nature of the hypotheses regarding those aspects of language. Some hypotheses may have the substantiation of empirical work, but no hypothesis starts with such substantiation—all are equally suspect when they are first put forward and need recurrent reformulations in the light of better understanding. To this no discipline bears better witness than that of linguistics itself, even within the last decade. It is not too fanciful to suggest that a theory is like an artifact: it justifies itself if its different parts hang together coherently so that the inner logic of the structure is not disturbed and the total bears some viable relation to the 'reality' to which the artifact of theory stands in a symbolic relation. If a linguistic theory can achieve this, it will have made a positive contribution.

Acknowledgments

This paper draws heavily upon the writings of Basil Bernstein and Michael Halliday. Since explicit reference to their work has not been made at every relevant point, I take this opportunity to acknowledge my deep debt to both. My interpretation of Bernstein's concept of code is based not only upon his writings but also on several discussions with him. Although I have made every effort to present an interpretation of the concept code which is faithful to Bernstein's writings and comments in seminars and discussions, the responsibility for the views expressed here is strictly mine, without any implication of agreement on all points on Bernstein's part. To Halliday, I owe the basic framework for the discussion of the concept of register as well as the notion of 'semantic potential' and the relationship of semantics to social structure.

Notes

1 This paper is based upon a talk given at a seminar in the Language and Society series at London School of Economics in June 1969. I am grateful to the Nuffield Programme for the Sociolinguistic Study of Children's Stories for financing the work on this paper.

2 Although in Bernstein's earlier writings mention is often made of the kind of language patterns associated with the two codes at the levels of syntax, lexis and sometimes, phonology, I believe I am right in maintaining that the status of these statements is that of a means to an end—the end, in my view, has always been to characterize the

varieties of code by reference to the differences at the level of meaning.

3 I owe this schematic presentation of the factors correlating with code variation to Basil Bernstein, since its present shape emerged during a discussion with him on the nature of codes.

References

BERNSTEIN, B. (1965), 'A sociolinguistic approach to social learning', *Social Science Survey*, J. Gould (ed.). London: Penguin.

BERNSTEIN, B. (1967), 'Open schools, open societies?', *New Society*, September.

BERNSTEIN, B. (1969), 'A sociolinguistic approach to socialization: with some reference to educability, I', *The Human Context*, vol. I. London: Chaucer Publishing Company.

BERNSTEIN, B. (1970a), 'Education cannot compensate for society', *New Society*, February.

BERNSTEIN, B. (1970b), 'A sociolinguistic approach to socialization: with some reference to educability, II, *The Human Context*, vol. II, no. 2. London: Chaucer Publishing Company.

BERNSTEIN, B. (1971a), 'Social class, language and socialization', to appear in *Current Trends in Linguistics*, vol. 12, A. S. Abramson (ed.). The Hague: Mouton.

BERNSTEIN, B. (1971b), 'On the classification and framing of educational knowledge', *Knowledge and Control*, Michael Young (ed.). London: Collier-Macmillan.

BERNSTEIN, B. and HENDERSON, D. (1969), 'Social class differences in the relevance of language to socialization', *Society*, vol. 3, no. 1.

BRANDIS, W. and HENDERSON, D. (1970), *Social Class, Language and Communication*. London: Routledge & Kegan Paul.

COOK, J. (1972), *Social Control and Socialization*. London: Routledge & Kegan Paul.

CHOMSKY, N. (1965), *Aspects of the Theory of Syntax*. Camb., Mass.: M.I.T. Press.

DAVIES, A. (1969), 'The notion of register', *Educational Review*, vol. 22, no. 1.

ELLIS, J. (1966), 'On contextual meaning', *In Memory of J. R. Firth*, C. E. Bazell, J. C. Catford, M. A. K. Halliday, R. H. Robins (eds). London: Longmans.

ELLIS, J. and URE, J. N. (1969), 'Language varieties: register', *Encyclopaedia of Linguistics, Communication and Control*. London: Pergamon Press.

ENKVIST, N. E., SPENCER, J. and GREGORY, M. (1964), *Linguistics and Style*. London: Oxford University Press.

FIRTH, J. R. (1957), 'A synopsis of linguistic theory 1930–55', *Studies in Linguistic Analysis*. Oxford: Blackwell.

FISHMAN, J. A. (1970), *Sociolinguistics*. Rowley, Mass.

GAHAGAN, D. M. and G. A. (1970), *Talk Reform: Explorations in*

Language for Infant School Children. London: Routledge & Kegan Paul.

HALLIDAY, M. A. K. (1970), 'Functional diversity in language', *Foundations of Language*, 6.

HALLIDAY, M. A. K. (1971a), 'Language in a social perspective', *Educational Review*, vol. 23, no. 3.

HALLIDAY, M. A. K. (1971b), 'Semantics and syntax in a functional grammar: [towards a sociological semantics]', paper to be read at International Symposium on Semantics, Urbino.

HALLIDAY, M. A. K., MCINTOSH, A. and STREVENS, P. (1964), *The Linguistic Sciences and Language Teaching*. London: Longmans.

HASAN, R. (1968), *Grammatical Cohesion in Spoken and Written English*, part I, Nuffield Programme in Linguistics and English Teaching, Paper no. 7, series 1. London: Longmans.

HASAN, R. (1971), 'Syntax and Semantics', *Biological and Social Factors in Psycholinguistics*, John Morton (ed.). London: Logos Press.

HASAN, R. (1972), *Language in the Imaginative Context: A Sociolinguistic Study of Stories Told by Children*, to be published by Routledge & Kegan Paul.

HAWKINS, P. R. (1969), 'Social class, the nominal group and reference', *Language and Speech*, 12, and reprinted in this volume.

LANGENDOEN, D. T. (1968), *The London School of Linguistics: A Study of the Linguistic Theories of B. Malinowski and J. R. Firth*, M.I.T. Research Monograph no. 46. Camb., Mass.: M.I.T. Press.

LYONS, J. (1966), 'Firth's theory of meaning', *In Memory of J. R. Firth*, C. E. Bazell, J. C. Catford, M. A. K. Halliday, R. H. Robins (eds). London: Longmans.

PIKE, K. L. (1954), *Language in Relation to a Unified Theory of the Structure of Human Behaviour*, Part I, (prelim. ed.) Glendale, California: SIL.

ROBINSON, W. P. and RACKSTRAW, S. J. (1972), *A Question of Answers*. London: Routledge & Kegan Paul.

SAPIR, E. (1921), *Language: an Introduction to the Study of Speech*. New York: Harcourt, Brace.

TAYLOR, G. (1968), 'Language and Learning: Deep Structure in a Chemical Text' (unpublished M. Litt. thesis, University of Edinburgh).

WHORF, B. L. (1956), *Language, Thought and Reality*, J. B. Carroll (ed.). Camb., Mass.: M.I.T. Press.

Chapter 11 Language and socialization: a critical review

J. A. Cook

All interpretation of this world is based upon a stock of previous experience of it, our own experiences and those handed down to us by parents and teachers, which in the form of 'knowledge at hand', function as a scheme of references. To this stock of experiences at hand belongs our knowledge that the world we live in is a world of well circumscribed objects with definite qualities, objects among which we move, which resist us and upon which we may act. Philosophical or psychological analysis of the constitution of our experiences may afterwards, retrospectively, describe how elements of this world affect our senses, how we passively perceive them in an indistinct and confused way, how by active apperception our mind singles out certain features from the perceptional field, conceiving them as well delineated things which stand over against a more or less unarticulated background or horizon. The natural attitude does not know these problems. To it, the world is from the outset not the private world of a single individual, but an intersubjective world, common to all of us, in which we have not a theoretical but an eminently practical interest. The world of everyday life is the scene and also the object of our actions and interactions. We have to dominate it and we have to change it in order to realize the purpose which we pursue within it among our fellow men. We work not only within but upon the world. Our bodily movements—kinaesthetic, locomotive, operative—gear, so to speak, into the world modifying or changing its objects and their mutual relationships. On the other hand, these objects offer resistance to our acts which we have either to overcome or to which we have to yield. Thus, it may be correctly said that a pragmatic motive governs our natural attitudes towards the world of daily life. World in this sense is something that we have to modify by our actions or that modifies our actions (*On Multiple Realities*, Alfred Schutz).

Introduction: socialization and the problem of social control

We begin this paper by considering some of the theories that have shaped studies of child socialization.

The problem of socialization enters into all the social sciences in some way. This problem revolves partly around the dual nature of the task. Any study of child socialization concerns both the development of the human individual and the continuance of the culture in a new generation. There is the problem both of the newly-born individual becoming human, a problem of socio-biological development, and becoming a member of a specific society through acquiring that society's culture. Wrong (1961) has described this problem as 'on the one hand socialization means "transmission of culture", the particular culture of the society the individual enters at birth; on the other, the term is used to mean the "process of becoming human", of acquiring human attributes from others. All men are socialized in the latter sense.' Many of the different views of socialization arise from the different emphasis which is placed on either side of this duality. It can be seen as a matter of different levels of abstraction in the theory, whether micro (the individual) or macro (the society, culture) aspects are focused upon. Child and Ziegler (1967) point to different 'models of man' that underlie different theories of socialization, especially the debate over the influence of the environment on the individual, the nature versus nurture controversy, as to whether a child should be considered a 'tabula rasa' or whether he can be considered to have certain innate developmental qualities. This tension between the development of man and society has been the foundation of the problem of social control and is fundamental to the study of socialization.

Wrong's comment clearly places his emphasis in socialization studies on the problem of continuity of order, and of the possibility of change in this order. Wrong considers that 'becoming social' can be assumed; the problem is one of the continuing or changing social order. Social control, when seen in these terms, becomes a means of achieving this continuity through specific social institutions. This view of social control is described by Coser and Rosenberg (1955) quoting E. A. Ross as 'the mechanisms by which the society exercises its dominion over its component individuals and enforces conformity to its norms, i.e. its values'. Such a view is based on the assumed duality of interest between man and the society. The controls of society are seen as *external* to the individual, who by nature will be in conflict with the social order; Wrong describes this as the Hobbesian problem of social control. Yet socialization studies show that if it is to be achieved, social control of the form described by Ross requires the individual to exercise self-regulation that is social in its form. As Wrong has pointed out 'becoming human' is also a socially governed experience. Social control is not only the exercise of controls on individuals, it is also the *practice* of control by individuals. The controls have to be made to work in the daily lives of individuals, who have to be able to recognize and to accept the controls. Durkheim saw this problem and proposed a different view of social control. He suggested that the social order was a moral order, and as such was *constituent*, not merely regulative of the individual.

Society as a moral order

For Durkheim, the conduct of society could only be achieved through its ability to exert an incontrovertible force on the shaping of its component individuals. This was a moral force. Men do not follow the regulations of society out of choice but from the necessity, the moral necessity of being social. He says:

> Moral life begins with membership of a group, however small the group may be. We must understand how it is there are rules called moral rules which we must obey because they command or direct our actions to ends that transcend us, while at the same time appearing desirable . . . Society transcends the individual's consciousness. It surpasses him materially because it is a result of the coalition of all individual forces. Society is something more than a material power, it is a moral power. It surpasses us physically, materially, morally. Civilization is the result of co-operation of men in association through successive generations; it is essentially a social product. Society made it, preserves it and transmits it to individuals (*Sociology and Philosophy*, pp. 53, 56).

From Durkheim's perspective of the moral necessity of the 'transcendental' society, the study of socialization is the study of how the individual comes to be aware of and to acquire the socio-moral rules. He proposed, although not explicitly, a model of the *internalization* of social controls.

> Society is the end of all moral activity. Now (i) while it transcends the individual, it is immanent in him; (ii) it has all the characteristics of a moral authority that imposes respect. (i) Society transcends the individual's consciousness. However small it may be, we do nevertheless always integrate in ourselves a

> part; thus, while society transcends us, it is always immanent in us, and we feel it as such. While it surpasses us, it is within us, *since it can only exist by and through us*. (ii) At the same time, it is a moral authority. The characteristic of a moral authority is that it imposes respect, because of this respect our own will defers to its imperatives. Society, then, has all that is necessary for the transference to certain rules of conduct of that same imperative which is distinctive of moral obligation. (*Sociology and Philosophy*, pp. 54–6).

We have quoted at length from Durkheim because the *internalization* model of cultural norms and social controls that he proposed has been influential in shaping all the studies of socialization. Any summary of his views may overlook certain qualities which we would like to emphasize. Inkeles (1959) and Wrong (1961) have pointed out that Durkheim does not propose the means by which the internalization of the 'moral imperative' of society takes place. His views lack a social psychological perspective on the individual, although as Wrong points out, Freudian theory has provided one. From this tradition come most of the studies of the child's acquisition of social controls. We consider one of the special values of Durkheim's perspective to be its recognition of the *necessity* of 'being social'. Children cannot choose to be socialized, but are born into an already existing social world, in which they have a position described by others. In this sense, it can be said that 'society transcends' the individual; it is there before him and continues after his death. But during the lifetime of each 'component' individual it is this individual's activities that make up the social order which can be seen to exist. Durkheim suggests the imperative nature of social control for the individual but he did not suggest how these controls are translated into effective action by the individuals. The underlined sentence in the quotation above, suggests that he was aware of this problem, that society only exists through the activities of its members. It is interesting to note this because it is usually the Durkheimian view which is said to be responsible for 'reifying' society and social order.

The oversocialized concept of man

Wrong has suggested that the tradition of studies that have resulted from the Durkheim-Freud internalization model have ignored the possibility of conflict between the individual and society. A view is developed that adequate socialization is when the society's requirements become the socialized man's requirements. Wrong suggests that the fit is never that good. Although men are by necessity social, they are not 'socialized'. A distinction needs to be maintained between men's activities as social beings, and the requirements and values of the society or an over-socialized view of man results. Men are continuously *being socialized* throughout the life cycle after the early childhood stage. Wrong suggests that this is 'becoming human'; it is acquisition of basic social skills, especially language. In order to avoid this problem of an over-socialized view, the study of socialization has taken up different perspectives; the psychological, which focuses on the individual's acquisition of social requirements, and the socio-logical, which focuses on the differing values between social groups and how the individual becomes an acceptable member of a group.

The psychological versus the sociological perspectives on socialization

Clausen and Williams (1963) have suggested that the study of socialization refers to 'both a process and to a set of institutional studies and practices'. This difference between psychological and sociological perspectives is often referred to as one of the differences in theoretical level between the macro and micro level of structure. We suggest that it may be a useful heuristic device to study these two aspects of the socialization process separately, but it becomes difficult in the study of child socialization, and in any attempt at a comprehensive socialization theory, to keep these two perspectives apart. Any definition of socialization needs to integrate both the practices of the parents and the acquisition by the child into a single description. Brim's description (1966) of this area of study, which, as Goslin suggests (1969), is probably one of the most acceptable to most sociologists, 'the process by which individuals acquire the knowledge, skills and dispositions that enable them to participate as more or less effective members of groups and of the society', also includes both perspectives. Brim's, simple definition, takes for granted one very important aspect of socialization studies; it assumes that 'everyone knows' what it means to be a 'more or less effective member of the society'. Such a view seems to assume that the requirements for membership exist in a more clearly codified form than is actually the case. The main problem of this area is the need both to describe the conditions of membership at the same time as considering whether these conditions have been adequately acquired by the child. Yet often the requirements of what it is that is necessary to be a 'member' of the society are taken for granted by the researchers who themselves are members of this society. Researchers tend to concentrate on those aspects of socialization which in their own view are seen as more problematic, or the social rules that 'everyone' thinks are important, but which may have a fairly small part in organizing the actual daily conduct of children and their parents. We are suggesting that the study of child socialization is a vantage point from which researchers can consider what is necessary for membership in the society by studying how this membership is practised. Parents, in controlling and inter-acting with their children daily, demonstrate to these less practised members what is necessary for membership of their social group. The recruitment of new members, especially the naïve members who are newly-born children, into the existing social order, can be considered as a 'point of inflexion' for any theorist's view of social organizations. It may require of researchers, as of parents, that some of our taken-for-granted assumptions about how social order is achieved on a day-to-day basis are questioned. For without some attention to the way in which social order is achieved in the daily life of individuals composing the society, any theory of social organization is vulnerable. This was said by Inkeles to be the weakness of Durkheim's theory. From this perspective it becomes more difficult to see separation between psychological and sociological approaches to the study of socialization. Only one contemporary theory, that of Talcott Parsons (1956) proposes to integrate these perspectives and to include a theory of socialization within a theory of social organization.

Society as man's production

If we accept the view which we noted in Durkheim that 'it [the society] can only exist by and through us [its members]', then it appears that not only is the separation between psychology and sociology hard to maintain, but also the separation between man and society. From this perspective it seems that the antagonism, or difference of interest between man and society, that has often been assumed to be fundamental to the problem of social control, may be a false dichotomy (see Spiro, 1959, for a similar discussion about culture/personality). Men *work* co-operatively to produce the social orders that 'constrain' them, and Durkheim's moral imperative extends to the very beginning of life. Men have no choice but to be 'social beings'. For the sociologist, the problem is not man's neglect.

First, we will look at various theories of the child's acquisition of the socio-moral order. We consider four theories which have provided the main theoretical foundation for this area of study.

All four theories are well known so we will only look at them briefly and then at some of the research which has been guided by them. Second, we will look at the influence of the parents on the child's acquisition of social controls. The studies we review in the second section focus specifically on the social influences that the parents experience. The parents are the child's link to the wider social world and present to the child essential knowledge of the social structure. The child learns to understand the world through his parents' eyes. The parents' experience of the social world, described by sociologists as their social class, shapes the child's experience of the world in many ways.

The child's acquisition of the socio-moral order

The four different theories to be discussed are (1) the Freudian theory of development, (2) the social reinforcement learning theory of Sears and others, (3) the cognitive developmental theory developed by Piaget, (4) and social competence (role) theory which has developed from G. H. Mead. These theories all provide explanations of how the child acquires the rules of conduct of society, the socio-moral order of society, which enables the child to act in socially acceptable ways. The first three theories focus on the child's acquisition of an internalized moral order, although as we shall describe, the definition of an 'internalized order' varies between theoretical perspectives. The fourth theory is concerned both with a model of performance and with describing a method of acquisition, although the research emphasis is mostly on the former. The question we will consider is whether, and in what ways, these theories of acquisition of social controls have considered the role of language in socialization.

The Freudian perspective

Freudian theory of personality development is the earliest and one of the most continuous influences on research in child-rearing (Miller, 1969). It initially focused the attention of the anthropologist and social psychologist on the importance of childhood experiences. Freud's proposal for internalized controls provided a solution for the Durkheimian problem of how the moral regulations of society became constituent of the individual. Freud's own concern was with the continuing dilemma of the individual and the society. His position has been described by Philip Rieff (1959): 'human relations are seen in terms of clashing intentions, which society at best can never suppress. Far from being a residual idea left over from his biological training Freud's theory of instinct is the basis for his insight into the powerful source of contradiction in which man and his culture, the individual and society are forever fixed.' It is ironic that Freud's theory of personality became the underpinning for a view of socialization described by Wrong as an 'oversocialized view'.

Although Freud's theory focused on the problem of how the individual achieved a balance between his own desires and the requirements of society, he did not regard the outcome of this process as certain, nor did he think that the individual had any choice but to make the attempt. Men are condemned to be social beings. The individual personality is shaped by the achievement of some balance between the psychic forces of the ego, the super-ego and the id. The super-ego is developed through the emotive process of identification with the parents (or loved adults) and the introjection of their requirements and standards. The child internalizes the parents' standards and through these and the growing awareness of the world of others is able to balance his own desires (instincts) against the pressure of social standards. Freud's tripartite theory of personality has been seen by some writers as an elaborate metaphor to deal with the problem of how the biological existence of man was translated into social forms. Merleau-Ponty (1964) has suggested that Freud's theory represents an important move towards the reintegration of body and mind, through the recognition that social experiences are located in the body. Commenting on Freud's statement 'Psychic facts have a meaning', he says 'this meant that no human behaviour is simply the result of some bodily mechanism, that in behaviour there is not a social centre and a periphery of automatism, and that all our gestures in their fashion participate in that single actuality of making explicit and signifying which is ourselves.' A quality rarely noted is emphasized here that Freud was concerned with the situated nature of men's experience, (men are 'of' the world not merely 'in' it). The focus of the problem between men and society becomes one of communication and understanding. Thus, if this view is taken, the possibility of over-socialization will not arise as the communicative balance will need to be continually achieved, and society becomes as much man's production as man was thought to be society's. Language therefore becomes important as the social expression of bodily experiences; both oral language and the language gestures. At least in Merleau-Ponty's view, language in Freud's theory cannot be considered as the expression of the epiphenomenal.

Yet the research following from Freud's theory did not take this line of development. Maybe the reason is that the complexity of

Freud's theory required the selection of 'researchable' hypotheses and limited statements. The key to the theory of personality became the emotive aspects of the acquisition of morality and social learning. The stress on the emotive led to a neglect of language, especially in the field of child-rearing research.

Two features of Freud's theory have been most influential in socialization research: (1) the concept of identification which, as Bronfenbrenner (1960) points out, in Freud's theory refers to a process of learning; (2) the theory of the critical stages of personality. Early research using the concept of identification (see MacKinnon, 1938) has found that the guilt and concern over rule violation shown by children is not related to the *severity* of parental practices, but to their techniques of emotional control, which MacKinnon called 'psychological' techniques. Later researches, both within a single culture and cross-cultural (Allinsmith, 1957; Murdock, 1957; Whiting and Child 1953; Whiting 1960) have all found evidence of an association between the child's expressions of guilt and the parents' practices of emotional control. In all these studies the expression of guilt was taken to be an indication of the child's successful identification with the parents' standards. Miller and Swanson (1960), using a more complex categorization of parental control, have suggested that different modes of control result in different 'inner defense' strategies or modes of personality expression for the individual child. They have also found a social class difference in the strategies of expression with the lower-class children preferring non-verbal expressive styles. Freud's theory of the critical stages of personality influenced much of the early research on socialization to focus on the child's experiences in his early years of life. The results of this research have been varied and sometimes contradictory (the findings on the social class difference in personality development indicate that the different conceptualizations of parental practices and the different methods of data collection may have had some influence on these findings). In a comprehensive review paper of these studies, Sewell (1961) has pointed out that 'doubts and differences have not led to any widespread rejection of the basic notion of the primary importance of early experiences in shaping later personality'.

Correlational studies have been a particular trap for examining Freudian theory. Since Freud's theory focused on the problem of understanding, it suggests that there would not be a direct relationship between the parents' behaviour and the child's response. Brown (1965) has considered the problem of the acquisition of the superego by quoting Freud as follows: 'Experience has shown however that the child's super-ego in no way corresponds to the severity of treatment it has itself experienced . . . The more righteous a man is, the stricter and more suspicious will his conscience be . . .' One of the greatest contributions of Freudian theory to child-rearing studies which is still to be fully appreciated is this focus upon the non-correlational problem of understanding in child research, (or any social research) .

Social (reinforcement) learning perspective

This theoretical perspective has contributed most towards research in the child's acquisition of morality in the last decade. The concept of identification has been redefined in behaviourist terms (see Bronfenbrenner, 1960; Kagan, 1958; Sanford, 1955). This perspective provides some of the most 'researchable' propositions in the literature of child-rearing. Most of the studies have been concerned, from the behaviourist perspective, with the differing environmental conditions for learning provided by different parental practices. Different explanations have been proposed for the way in which the child acquires 'internalized' standards. One of the most influential approaches in this area is role theory, although at the level of research studies, there is considerable inter-dependence of approach. Social reinforcement theory developed from the work of Hebb (1949), from Miller and Dollard's (1940) frustration-aggression thesis, and from the child-development theory of Sears (1960, 1961). Sears (and see Maier, 1965) has developed certain Freudian concepts of development in behaviourist terms.

Sears (1960) has described three critical stages of development in which the child is influenced by a progressively widening interpersonal environment. He focuses on the child's identification as arising out of both positive and negative experiences. The idea of 'positive conscience' is a development of the concept of identification by social learning theorists. The child identifies with the parents, both out of anxiety for loss of love and fear of punishment, but also out of desire for rewards. Sears suggests that there are two stages to the child's identification-learning, the first is the child's desire for love and affection in which he experiences anxiety over loss of love, the second is the child's desire for mastery and power, in which he learns to control his aggression in order to reach desired goals. Sears stresses that identification-learning from this perspective is more than imitation of the powerful parents.

Research, from this perspective on the child's acquisition of moral standards, focuses attention on the environment created by the parents' practices in which the child sometimes appears to be only a passive 'responder'. Child and Zeigler (1967) have criticized this approach on these grounds. The environment is seen as a system of rewards and punishments, which the child either moves towards or avoids, the child's learning is often described as avoidance and reward patterns. Since the emphasis of this approach is on the contribution of the environment to the child's internalization of standards, the main research problem to be examined is that of the transfer of learning. Evidence of successful (or adequate) identification and internalization will be that the rules (standards) can be used in other contexts than the specific context in which they were learnt. Research examining the relationship between the child's conscience development and control of aggression and the parents' techniques of control has resulted in contradictory findings (see, for example, Burton, Maccoby and Allinsmith, 1961; Grinder, 1962; Sears, Maccoby and Levin, 1957; Sears, 1961.) The parents' use of psychological techniques of control did not always relate to the child's resistance to temptation or other signs of conscience. It is possible as Maccoby (1961b) and Aronfreed (1968) suggest that the contradictory findings may arise from the difficulty of measuring experimentally the child's internalized standards.

Other theories than that of Sears, of the way in which the child acquires internalized standards have been proposed. Hill (1960) suggests that the child experiences vicarious empathy with the parent and is encouraged to imitate and then identify with the parents' affective satisfaction. This theory has been supported experimentally by Bandura and Huston (1961). The two most detailed theories which have developed role-theory perspectives are those of Whiting (1960) and Maccoby (1959). Whiting's theory of *status envy* proposes that the child internalizes his parents' standards through his envy of the parents' greater power and status. This seems an extension of Sears's desire for mastery. The parents control scarce resources that the child would like (toys, food, love). This is the manifestation of their power. The child's desire to be like the parents motivates him to observe, practice and acquire the parents' role and standards.

Bandura with Ross and Ross (1963) has tested these three theories of identification in game situations with young children. They found that children are more likely to identify with the adult who has social power than the adult who receives scarce resources, and they suggested that on this evidence Sears's theory was the more acceptable. Whiting (1960) has suggested that the problem of this work is that children cannot distinguish between control and consumption of resources and that control may not entail the latter. He suggests that the children have cognizance of several roles, but are only motivated to perform some. This raises the problem, critical to all the work in this area, of the neglect in these experiments of the child's understanding. Aronfreed (1968) mentioned this as a problem of motivation, which also brings in the child's experience outside a testing situation. Maccoby (1959) has suggested that the child acquires the parents' roles and so internalized standards by *covert practice*. She says that the mother and child form a complementary role-system in which the child learns to 'run through the mother's views and practices in his head'. This approach is a move towards a cognitive and communicative view of internalization. It suggests the linguistic internalization of the parents' roles. This view would need research which focused in more detail on the child's own understanding of his experiences, which would need verbal evaluation.

Research by Aronfreed (1961–9) and Hoffman (1959–67) has focused on the role of language in the child's process of internalization and in the experimental evaluation of signs of conscience. Aronfreed's work in particular has looked in some detail, in a series of studies, at the child's reparation, self-criticism, and resistance to temptation. He found (1963) that if the mother used verbal techniques of control the child was more likely to be self-critical and to use verbal reparation. Hoffman looked both at parent's power assertion and at the child's consideration of others, in the development of positive conscience. He found that if parents used other-oriented rather than consequence-oriented discipline, the child was more likely to acquire concern for others. Hoffman's research is unusual in that it focused on detailed observation techniques, and the mother's use of explanations with the child. These studies show that the orientation of social learning theory research in child-rearing has moved both towards some evaluation of the child's cognitive processes, and to some recognition of the importance of language. The problem in this work is its approach to language, which is viewed as a complex and detailed *cue system*. This limited view of language is shown in this comment from Becker (1964) in which he also quotes from Aronfreed on the parents' use of reasoning.

> The frequent concurrence of use of reasoning by parents and internalized reactions to transgression by the child suggests two possibilities. First, the parent who talks and reasons with the child about his misbehaviour is more likely to provide the child with a clear understanding of what he did wrong, so that

> the anxiety about misbehaviour is connected to the right cues. Secondly, as Aronfreed has suggested, explanations and reasons provide the child with internal resources for evaluation of his own behaviour; that is, the child gains explicit training in making moral judgements.

This view of language and the value of reasoning seems to take a too simplistic view of the problem of the child's understanding. In the following review of Piaget's work we can see the developmental constraints of this process.

The recent social reinforcement studies have made a greater move away from the consideration only of rewards and warmth against punishment and control, towards the recognition of the child's cognitive perception and evaluation of the control situation. This work has also raised one of the most critical questions for this whole area of research—how generalizable or how specific is the moral response? (see Maccoby, 1968). Can the child experimentally show that he can transfer his rule learning to other contexts? If he can, is this evidence of 'internalization'? In these studies we need to consider what kind of rules the child acquires in childhood. This is a question to which we will return in a later section. The problem of the child's internalization is very complex, but it may be more usefully studied by looking at the child's linguistic controls, as Brown (1965) has suggested:

> Learning by identification is certainly a complex geometry ... with two parents to manifest power and administer direct reward and punishment there are many possible kinds of family pattern, many kinds of learning problems presented to children. For some kinds of behaviour, for example speaking the local language, all forces work in the same direction, both parents model English and both parents reward it.

In general, although the social learning approach has not regarded language as semantically important for the child's acquisition of understanding, it has focused on some critical questions.

The cognitive-developmental perspective

This approach has developed around the theory of the child's moral judgment developed by Piaget (1933). It has indirectly been influential in increasing concern with cognitive socialization, but it has not as yet been used specifically in child-rearing studies. The research on cognitive development has been influenced by Piaget's and Kohlberg's inquiries into moral development. The problems of developmental constraints in the study of child rearing require consideration in any theory of socialization. The focus of Piaget's theory, which has been open to critical consideration, is the equation of moral development, the acquisition of internal moral standards with the child's development of moral thought and judgment (see Kohlberg, 1969). Piaget suggests that the child's internal standards are a set of transformations of primitive conceptions which accompany the child's cognitive growth and the development of his perceptual ordering of the social world. The child moves from having an innate sense of justice, as retribution, from seeing acts of justice as either the experiencing of expiative punishment or immanent 'natural' justice which rights the situation, to a sense of justice concerned with equity, *distributive* justice. The child's perception of the social world changes as he grows up and moves from a focus on unilateral authority relationships, a parent dominated world view, to participate in and control reciprocal peer relationships in co-operation. For the child to develop internalized moral standards it is necessary for these socio-developmental changes to be accompanied by cognitive growth. The child, through the development of cognitive judgment, changes from a perspective of moral realism and constraint to one of intellectual realism; thus the child develops a morality of co-operation and equity, in which he will use abstract principles of justice. Piaget sees this process as occurring in two stages, which can broadly be associated with the following age-ranges. The stage of moral realism begins about six, and by nine years is gradually changing toward the morality of co-operation. By the age of thirteen to fourteen the child can begin to understand and to operate distributive justice of equity.

This theory has been criticized on several points. The age 'stages' are often disputed and research has shown that a more complex gradient of stages is required (see Kohlberg, 1964). The simplicity of the child's social relationships has also been strongly criticized, both from the view that the child experiences more varied and complex social inter-action with significant others, and from the perspective of the social class differences in experiences. This theory is seen as too dependent on the child's intellectual development and judgment for its view on internalized standards. Some critics have suggested that it requires the individual to reach a 'high' standard of intellectual development to be considered as having an adequate set of internalized standards.

The main problem that Piaget's work raises, both in theory and in research, is the problem of the difference between the child's ability to understand behaviour, rules and principles while not being able to reproduce them. This is particularly so in any research situation, such as those of Piaget and his followers. Kohlberg (1963) has noted that it is possible for the child to have the rule but not to be able to express it. This raises the important, and increasingly critical question for research in child socialization.

Research following from Piaget's theory has focused on two aspects: the testing of the stages of moral development with different populations; and the examination of different and more complex social relationships for morality. Although this work has mainly concentrated on demographic variables (social class and sex), researches by Boehm (1962), Boehm and Nass (1962), and Johnson (1962) have shown that differences in the child's social class will influence the level of attaining moral maturity of judgment, and that there will be some relationship with measured IQ. MacRae (1954) suggested that middle-class children depended for longer on adult rules and authority, yet at the same time were able to offer more mature moral judgments. This suggested that there was possibly a 'hidden' social class IQ relation, or, as Bernstein (1970) has suggested, that the role-relationships of child control associated with social class, encourage different socio-linguistic abilities which are reflected in judgmental maturity and approach to linguistically based (reasoning) tests. Both Boehm and Durkin (1959, 1961) have shown that children do not break with adult authority directly and that there is a variation in the specificity of the child's judgments which does not directly correspond to levels of maturity. On some problems children were able to produce morally mature judgments, that is they were able to use 'abstract' principles earlier than expected; on other problems it was later. MacRae (1954) has suggesed that moral judgments should not be considered as uni-dimensional. He suggests that there are two elements, the cognitive learning of rules and emotional learning, which enables the individual child to apply these rules to his own behaviour. This suggestion again indicates that there may be two different operations—the child's ability to acquire rules *and* his ability to use them in performance. Kohlberg has considered this point in his review (1969). This may be an important distinction to make in socialization theory.

Kohlberg's research has focused on the way in which the age schemata described by Piaget need to be altered and made more complex. In his research (1963, 1964) he proposes a six-stage developmental sequence. His work supports Piaget's sequences, but he thinks that the developmental influences on the child are more varied and do not have universal similarity. He states his position as follows: the study provides clear support for the general developmental view of morality underlying Piaget. The development of moral judgment cannot be explained by a 'non-developmental' view of moral learning as simply the 'internalization' of cultural rules through verbal learning, reinforcement or identification. The findings, however, are not entirely consistent with Piaget's specific theory; the data suggest that the 'natural' aspects of moral development are continuously a reaction to the whole social world rather than a product of a certain stage, a certain concept (reciprocity), and a certain type of social relation (peer relation). The development of a morality of identification with authority is dependent upon social role-taking and the development of concepts of reciprocity, justice and group welfare through the childhood years.

This perspective of Piaget's theory has been important, both in focusing research attention on cognitive developmental constraints in socialization, and in raising problems about the ways in which children learn rules. The research has shown that there are problems in how rules are formulated and in how they are acquired. Piaget himself has expressed dissatisfaction at the fact that research has focused on verbal methods (see introduction to Flavell, 1963). Children learn many (possibly most) social rules through verbal means. This raises two queries: one, is the child's rule-learning strongly context-dependent? The research on the varying specificity of moral judgments would seem to suggest this. Second, is it possible that the child can acquire and understand statements of moral judgments without being able to reproduce linguistically appropriate responses, or without being able to incorporate these rules into his performances? This suggests both the need to consider a possible competence-performance distinction in moral learning; it also raises doubts about the accepted view of 'internalized rules', which considers them to be rules which once adequately learnt will guide all performance. Or it possibly only raises queries about the way research examines the existence of the rules. As Brown has commented, 'Students of language know that children utilize a grammar long before they have any explicit knowledge of grammar. In the sphere of morality is it reasonable to suppose that we respond to the promptings of an inner voice before we explain our actions in terms of that inner voice?'

The social competence (role theory) perspective

The role-theory perspective on social control differs from other theories in that it focuses directly on the child's ability to perform his social roles with approval. It concentrates on the child's acquisition of social competence, in other words internalization of the role is assumed. Mead (in Strauss (1956)) suggested that the child acquires the values of the society through acquiring the shared, communal symbol system which is contained in the language. What is important, therefore, is the process by which the child learns the symbolic requirements of the actions which he must perform to gain social approval, but it does not assume that there will be any natural conflict between the individual and the roles once the child has acquired the symbolic-cognitive ability given by language. As Swanson (1961) puts it in comparing Freudian and Meadian view:

> like Mead, Freud wanted to account for rationality. Whereas Mead was concerned with the irrationality which appears because the environment does not respond properly to the individual's inner life, Freud sought to understand the irrationality produced by subjective conditions which prevent the individual from interpreting the world around him . . . Mead sought the conditions of valid knowledge as the appropriate alignment of means and ends, the alignment of the act in its covert and overt aspects with the environment . . . Mead takes it as objectively problematic that acts and objects can be aligned but assumes that gratification will follow if they are.

The covert aspects of social acts can be brought out by verbal inquiry and cognitive reflection. The child becomes aware of others' expectations of him and of others' responses to his acts. From these experiences he develops a sense of the requirements of 'the society', a *generalized other* which the child can use to 'guide' and effectively control his own and others' behaviour (see Elkin, 1960).

Social role theory takes man's desire to be social for granted. It focuses instead upon the way in which members can behave in socially patterned and ordered ways to give approved performances, which we refer to analytically as their social 'role'. The child's acquisition of his social roles consists of getting to know both the details of what behaviours are appropriate to a social position and situation, how to recognize these and how to perform them.

Although Mead's concept of 'social role', variously defined, has become a part of all social psychological theories and has been very influential in all child-rearing studies, Mead's actual premises have never been empirically investigated. Mead's theory, with its emphasis on rational-cognitive processes of learning and on the importance of language and the reflective process that this makes possible, had not been a subject of direct empirical research until quite recently. Research (Brim, 1960; Elder and Bowerman, 1963; Emmerich and Smoller, 1964; Koch, 1955) has focused upon the child's acquisition of roles in childhood, especially the 'structural' roles of sex- and age-related behaviours as well as specific (local) roles that the child learns from significant others in his family.

Emmerich and Smoller (1964) looked at the 'significant others' influencing the child's early role-learning. They found few sex differences in adult's expectations, but a difference in the range of expectations between parents, teachers and older siblings. They suggested that through contact, both with older siblings or friends and with adults outside of the home, the child is able to develop a 'universal' basis for his/her role-expectations. Brim (1960) has suggested that there are two aspects to the child's role-learning: (1) he must understand the 'focal' statuses of the society so that he can understand his position and that of important others; (2) the child must learn how to perform his own roles, both with knowledge of the appropriate actions and feelings. From this perspective the child's 'learning task' appears almost formidable in its complexity. Most of the research in this area has looked at roles in terms of 'expectations' reported by parents, or older children, in questionnaires; there has been little observational work or detailed work on how the parents 'define' their own and their child's roles in a free, unstructured setting. Yet the problem of role-acquisition presents the most difficult research questions. For the problem of 'defining' a particular role is *prior* to research on whether it is either made available by the parents or has been acquired by the child. Most of the work has assumed that social roles are more clearly describable and agreed than they probably are. The work on the parents' control with children of differing sex (for example, see Maccoby, 1961a; Rothbart and Maccoby, 1966) assumes that for both parents and researchers 'sex' is a 'clear', and non-controversial social category, so that the 'rules' of appropriate behaviours can be seen and applied. Bernstein's theory (1964, 1970), in emphasizing the close affinity between roles and socio-linguistic codes, makes a critical departure from other work in the role theory tradition. In this theory it is suggested that the mothers' speech reflects some of the basic underlying social assumptions of the family group. The child acquires these social principles as he acquires his knowledge of language. Bernstein describes this process as follows: 'the experience of the child is transformed by the learning generated by his own apparently voluntary acts of speech. The social structure becomes, in this way, the sub-stratum of the child's experience through the manifold consequences of the linguistic process.' It can be seen from this very brief description that Bernstein's work is an exception to the tradition of child-rearing studies.

The transmission of the socio-moral order: social influences on the parents as socializers

In this section we will focus specifically on the parents' role in the child's acquisition of social control. The child is born into a social world which is already structured for his inclusion. The child will have a described social position from his birth, and family and other members will expect certain behaviour of the child. Many studies of the child's socialization do not seem aware of how the child is a part of an already constituted social scene. In this section we will focus on these expectations and on the practices that the parents use to bring up their child as they think 'right' or 'desirable'. These expectations and goals are shaped by the parents' own experience of their social world—their own childhood, education and occupational experience, which decide the parents' place in the stratificational structure of modern industrial society, and which are described as their social class. The studies we review here have examined how this stratificational structure is continued through the influence of different social class experiences on the parents' practices and goals of child-rearing. The social world and the knowledge of how it works is given to the child from the parent's own perspective. For the child the parents and the family organization provide his whole sense of the 'social world', which is as Parsons (1956) suggests the wider social world 'in microcosm'. The world is mediated to the child by the family. The child learns how to manage his social relationships through the appropriate and approved behaviour in the family. How enduring this influence may be has been a critical problem to be studied in child socialization and has raised questions of continuity and change of the society. The social class differences in child-rearing practices make for the child different learning situations and transmit different understandings of the social structure. Allison Davis (1941), in one of the most influential papers in this field, described the situation as 'the pivotal meaning of social class, to students of human development is that it defines and systematises different learning environments for children of each social class.'

Social class differences in parental practices

This is one of the oldest traditions in the study of child socialization. The early work was initially influenced by Freudian social anthropological theories (culture-personality theories). The work in the forties and fifties specifically tested the idea that social class distinctions were maintained by personality differences which were attributable to differing parental practices. Both social class differences in personality and in practices were examined. Sewell (1952, 1961) found little evidence of the expected social class differences in personality. Brown (1965) has commented, 'The reviews of the literature show that weaning and toilet training are not known to have any consequences for the personality.' But differences in the practices of child rearing in different social classes were established by this work. This led, as we have described above, to different theories and explanations about the acquisition process, especially to a new focus on *cognitive* consequences of the parents' actions. The quotation from Allison Davis on the previous page, suggests the new move to look at the parent's behaviour as creating a 'learning environment' for the child. The work of Davis and Havighurst (1946) and Ericson (1946) showed that there were differences in the techniques of child-rearing between social classes, and Davis and Havighurst showed that these differences were far stronger than ethnic differences between black and white groups. Using a Freudian influenced perspective to select the critical areas of interest in child-rearing, they showed that mothers were more *permissive* in their baby-rearing in the lower class, and more *severe* in the middle class. By permissive, Davis and Havighurst meant that the child was not required to keep to parental demands and schedules, but appeared to have some influence on the parents' requirements. The middle-class child was more rigidly trained and was required to keep to the parents' goals. This view was supported by Green (1945), with his suggestions that the middle-class child was frustrated and neurotic, but dismissed by Orlansky (1949), who disagreed with the Freudian view of personality and the effect of the parents' practices. In the long-term, the importance of this work did not rest with its considerations of personality differences, but with the way in which the parents' techniques of discipline were examined and categorized, especially the idea of permissive techniques. Sears, Maccoby and Levin in 1952 (published 1957) looked at similar social class groups, but they found contradictory evidence: the lower-class parents were more rigid, the middle-class more flexible in requirements, both of the baby and of the young child. This study contrasted the idea of permissive techniques with that of 'psychological' discipline, (which was an extension of the categorization used by MacKinnon (1938)). Psychological techniques involved the use of reasoning with the child and the 'withdrawal of love'. Sears, Maccoby and Levin found that the middle-class mothers used more of these techniques. Two further studies (White, 1957; Littman, Moore and Pierce-Jones, 1957), using similar social class groups from different geographic areas, found a lesser but still notable difference between the classes. The study of Littman, Moore and Pierce-Jones raised several interesting queries about the findings of these child-rearing studies. They queried whether a single criterion of socialization indulgence (or permissiveness) could possibly be constructed from the varieties of behaviours reported, and whether there could be an intertwining effect between the practices. They suggested that a general 'theme' of permissiveness might be seen in all the practices of parents. These queries seem to suggest a need, for more detailed investigation of practices and place in doubt correlational studies of child-rearing which use rating-scales and 'globally' descriptive categories. Other criticisms of these studies (for example, Maccoby, 1968), pointed to the lack of comparability of the data in the different studies and to the problems of different categorizations of behaviour. Davis and Havighurst (1955) reorganized and measured some of their data to make them more comparable with the Boston study, but still found the same divergent pattern.

The most comprehensive review article which brings together the whole area of parental practices studies is that by Bronfenbrenner (1958). Bronfenbrenner has noted that, in spite of measurement differences, the trend of social class differences was maintained, although the differences were over varying practices, and he has suggested the 'cultural lag' hypothesis, that the working class take up the practices discarded by the middle class, and that this would account for the switch in findings between the Chicago and Boston studies. Wolfenstein (1951), in the paper, 'Towards a fun morality' has shown the enormous changes in the advice available to parents, from rigidity of training to the idea that the mother and child should co-operate and enjoy the experiences of childhood. This work supports Bronfenbrenner's suggestion as it appears to contain views similar to those expressed by middle-class parents. Walters and Crandall (1960), in a more detailed analysis which used both observational and questionnaire materials, showed a curvilinear trend of social class difference from 1940 to 1960; the period of greatest difference being the 1950s, when they suggest the middle class were most permissive. It appears from these studies that differences between social class groups can be located, in spite of discrepancies in the measurement of social class and in data collection and comparison (see, for example, the criticisms of Yarrow (1963) about the use of retrospective experience in child-rearing questionnaires).

It seems in retrospect that these studies were attempting too much. They attempted to outline the practices used in different classes, describe the critical areas of difference between the classes for predictive purposes and to consider the consequences of these differences for the child; while implicitly attempting to describe or suggest what the accepted or 'normative' practice of child-rearing should be. For to describe a practice as 'indulgent' or permissive means that the researcher has some theory which suggests what non-indulgent behaviour would be like. In order to see how the parents teach their children the 'social rules' it is probably necessary to consider what these rules may be.

The more recent work in child-rearing has attempted to remedy these criticisms by looking in more detail at either social class and its influence on the parents, or in more detail at parental practices.

Miller and Swanson (1958), in their study *The Changing American Parent*, have taken a different approach to the examination of social class. They looked at the parents' occupations, focusing on the father, in terms of a bureaucratic or entrepreneurial distinction. Bureaucratic meant that the job involved low risk-taking, but a high amount of inter-personal inter-action; entrepreneurial indicated that the job involved high risk and low inter-personal inter-action. This was a new look at social class, for it suggested the importance of the parents' opportunity to experience symbolic and verbally mediated work relationships, for the kinds of values and goals that the parents would develop for child-rearing. It suggested that social class could be examined in a more dynamic way by looking at the effects of the personal experiences of parents which continuously shape and influence the parents' goals. Although Miller and Swanson did not find any differences in practices between the two occupational groups, research by Slater and Gold (1958) did find family role structure difference using a similar class categorization. This suggests that if the family role structure were related to the child-rearing practices, a difference might have been found. Bronfenbrenner (1960) has also noted that the middle class make more discrimination in the sex roles than do the lower class. He suggests that this is the result of a situation where the boys do not receive sufficient control or limit-setting. These studies indicate the importance in any evaluation of control in child-rearing to take the family context, as well as the social class into account.

The other response to the criticisms of the earlier child-rearing studies was to make more detailed examinations of the parents' practices. Hoffman (1963), in a detailed study of the parents' use of power assertion, showed that the middle-class parents were low on any expression of power with the child, either through verbal or physical means. He found lower-class parents predictably higher in power assertion, although the power structure of the family, whether of equal or unequal dominance, significantly affected the degree of power assertion. Hoffman's study is especially interesting for the amount of detailed measures obtained from direct observation *and* from questionnaires. He suggests that the main feature of power assertion by the parent is a refusal to discuss alternatives or to offer any explanation of the requests for obedience. The work shows that if a lower-class family has parental role-sharing the amount of power assertion by the parents will be lower. Some of the British child-rearing studies discussed by Klein (1965) have shown a similar decrease in use of physical punishment as the parental roles are more egalitarian (see, for example, Klein's discussion of Bott's work). Kohn (1958, 1959), in studies of parental authority and discipline techniques, showed that the middle class is more likely to punish the child for the intentions of his acts, whereas the lower class will punish for the consequences. The implications of Kohn's work are important, for it suggests the need to look not only at the type of technique used by the parent and rated (or evaluated) by the researcher but the need to consider the parent's *own* definition of the child's acts. Further, it suggests that the mother may reason with herself before acting. This indicates that although the amount of social class difference in techniques was decreasing, especially the use of physical punishment (see Becker, 1964) the reasoning behind these practices may have remained different. Becker summarized the social class differences as follows:

> Generally the research has shown that middle class parents provide more warmth and are more likely to use reasoning, isolation, show of disappointment, or guilt-evoking appeals in disciplining the child. They are also likely to be more permissive about demands for attention from the child, sex behaviour, aggression to parent. table manners, neatness, bedtime rules and general obedience. Working class parents are more likely to use ridicule, shouting or physical punishment in disciplining the child and to be generally more restrictive.

One of the most important questions to be asked of this whole area of study is raised by Kohn (1963) when he asks how important are the differences described by the researcher for the parents themselves and for their children? The researcher may categorize the behaviour as 'permissive', but it may not appear so to the mother and child who know this behaviour in the context of their daily lives. Kohn has commented, 'when we generalize from specifics to talk of a change from restrictive to permissive practices or worse yet, of a change from restrictive to permissive parent-child relations we impute to them [the practices] a far greater importance than they probably have, either to parents or to children.' The parents and children are acting and making judgments within an on-going scene of which they are a part; the researchers' categorizations seem to be made from some external, Archimedean point outside of the actual scene. Kohn's solution to this problem was to study not the reported (or even observed) behaviours of the parents, but to look at their reported values. He has suggested that a study of values as 'the goals or aims of child-rearing is a more useful approach than a study of practices'. Kohn's study with Carroll (1960) followed from the early work of Duvall (1946), who found in a study of white and black parents and children that there was a social class difference in their ideas about what a good mother should be. Duvall suggested that the middle-class mother had values that were concerned with developmental goals, expectations about the way a child should develop, that looked to the future, while working-class parents looked to the immediate present and were concerned with goals of conformity and obedience. Kohn and Carroll found similar values expressed. They suggested that the middle class may take for granted the values of cleanliness, obedience, that are seen as important by the working class, and that there may be a difference in the parents' explanation of their concerns in that 'honesty' may mean 'truthfulness' to the working class although expressed as the former. Kohn suggests that what is important is what the parents find 'problematic' in child-rearing, however this is expressed.

While the more detailed studies of Hoffman and Kohn look at the kinds of explanations offered by the parents, whether these focus on the intentions or consequences of the child's actions, their research does not describe the *linguistic form* of the explanations. The importance of reasoning as a technique of control was recognized in the work of Sears, Maccoby and Levin but they included reasoning with other techniques which they considered to be 'psychological'. The previous section on the child's processes of acquisition shows the different interpretations that 'use of reasoning' can have, and the different consequences for the child according to the researcher's theory. Becker's view of language suggests that explanations provide the child with a more complex system of 'cues' by which to regulate his behaviour. The child who is reasoned with knows in some detail *how* his behaviour is not right. He will be able to develop cognitive guides for future actions. The cognitive-developmental approach goes much further and suggests that the child develops conceptual control over his behaviour. The child who receives explanations, rather than actions as control, is likely to develop conceptually both more quickly, and to acquire more abstract concepts, (see, for example, the research of Hess and Shipman 1965) and to 'test out' hypothetically possible alternative actions. Klein (1965) suggests that this experience will result in the child developing an ability to plan ahead, to become oriented to future actions and possibilities and to be less dominated by the immediate situation. The literature on child-rearing also seems to suggest that the child can only learn the ability to 'reason' from explicitly, *logically reasoned* talk, which only some parents offer the child. Quoting from Isaacs (1929), Klein suggests that this ability is more general: 'it is in his make believe play that the child first glimpses the possibility of hypothesis, "as-ifness", without which no science is possible, no reasoning can be sustained . . . yet to hold such a notion in his mind and develop its implications, if so-and-so, then so-and-so, is an ability necessary for his logical development.' Since *all* children appear to develop their own make-believe play, it could be suggested that all children develop the ability to use everyday reasoning about their own life and affairs. What some children do not seem to develop is the ability to produce 'logically' (or formal) *verbally explicit* arguments about their actions, which is only *one* kind of reasoning ability.

How much the child takes over the parents' concepts and reasons and how much the child is able to develop a reasoning ability and conceptual system of his own still needs to be fully researched.

The child's experience of language may shape his cognitive and other behavioural preferences without giving any explicit content to these. It is possible that the details of the parents' reasons and explanations and the control situations in which these are given, need to be looked at before these questions can be answered. One of the problems of much of the work on parental practices has been the lack of detail of the categorizations. *A single category 'reasoning' may include many different sorts of behaviour.*

Clearly the amount and, even more, the kind of talk that passes between mother and child is very important, but a distinction will need to be made between the mother's use of talk and explanation in a general, undetailed categorization, and the child's ability to develop certain kinds of reasoning. As Bernstein (1971) has suggested, 'It is not just a question of more talk but of a particular kind. Judgements, their bases and consequences would be a marked content of the communication.' This suggests that we need to study the content, the context *and* the linguistic 'shape' of the explanations between mother and child in order to begin to consider the socio-cognitive implications for the child. In his theory Bernstein suggests that the child acquires his knowledge of the social structure through his experiences of the parents' socio-linguistic code which realizes the parents' differing orientation to control. He proposes two basic *modes of control*, positional and personal. In the positional control mode children are given few or rule-bounded explanations for their actions, whilst in the personal control mode parents act in terms of explicitly stated goals and explanations, which are focused on their particular child. Thus in personal control children experience detailed explanations provided for them about their own and their parents' actions and are more likely to be able to understand how the general social rules work and are realized in their own daily lives.

In conclusion it seems from this review that the literature on child-rearing often assumes that parents and children have only a pedagogical intent in pursuing their daily lives. This gives a rather distorted view of the socialization process. The activity of child-rearing does not consist only in following the rules, but also in making the rules fit the activity already performed, or decided upon. The need in socialization research is to look for these organizing principles as the parents define them *and* as the child perceives them. It is possible that what the child acquires from the parent are these general principles *which he can use to generate his own behaviour*. The way the child learns language should give us examples of particularly detailed studies of this learning process. Language acquisition may show us in some detail how the mother and child are able reciprocally to negotiate a (non-pedagogical) learning situation, for parents are not in doubt that the child needs to learn language. The child's need for this skill is taken for granted and most parents are able, when necessary, to point to the rules of language (its grammar) as all are competent speakers of *their* native language. The way parents help the child to gain this essential skill shows us something of their ability to socialize the child into other taken-for-granted competencies. For we suggest that parents do not *explicitly* formulate the learning tasks of child-rearing but use their own daily lives as an implicit model of social competency for their children. We suggest that a special characteristic of the 'rules' of child-rearing is that they are only brought into being explicitly, after the fact. After the child had done something the parent thinks is 'not right' a rule is seen to be infringed and is given or explained by the parent, but for most of the child's daily life the 'rules' remain implicit in the activities. Garfinkel (1967) has suggested that it is the nature of 'everyday reasoning' to be guided by general rather than detailed principles. It is often only in recollection that a person 'gives a reason' for an action, and this 'reason' may not have been the original instigation for the action. We act and reason in everyday life pragmatically to give solutions to practical problems which are sufficient, for the while, to guide our further actions. So far the research on child-rearing does not seem to have suggested that the child acquires his knowledge of the social structure in a similar way.

The child's acquisition of language

In the previous section we considered how the studies of child socialization had neglected the linguistic transmission of cultural knowledge; language was regarded as a transparent medium in which information was given both to the child and to the interviewer, but the way in which the form of the language shapes the information was not entertained. It is in the area of language learning that theories of the child's acquisition of the rule-governed behaviour is being shaped. Theories of the acquisition of syntactic rules may provide a parallel model for the child's acquisition of the 'rules' of social structure. We suggest that a study of the way language is used in giving social rules to children and in conducting actual social scenes would give us more information *about the rules themselves*, and the study of the speech in inter-action settings with mothers and children can show us how rules guide and constrain actual social performances. For this study we need to know something of the way the child learns language, and the various ways of talking in different social situations, which have been described as the linguistic repertoire of communicative economy of the society (see Gumperz, 1964; Hymes, 1964). Until recently the child's developing linguistic competence has been evaluated apart from the occasions that give rise to the child's communications. The need for alternative approaches for the study of this and other aspects of the child's social learning is being increasingly raised (see Cazden, 1966; Cicourel, 1968, 1970; Hymes, 1968; Slobin *et al.*, 1967). In this section we will review some of the studies of the child's acquisition and use of language.

Two approaches to language development have developed in the last few years: (1) the study of grammatical development of linguistic competence; (2) the study of linguistic usage rules, or communicative competence. In the former approach the investigator focuses on the child's control of the linguistic rules proper, regardless of context; and in the latter the investigator looks at linguistic rules in relation to how they are used in particular communication settings, along with other communication skills (e.g. rules of etiquette, rules of appropriate usage, etc.). By far the greatest amount of work has been concentrated in the area of linguistic rules and has focused largely on the work in Western, middle-class communities. The study of communicative competence is only just beginning and will be reviewed briefly at the end of this section.

The literature on the study of linguistic competence has grown to enormous proportions in recent years; a complete review is outside the scope of this paper (an excellent introductory discussion can be found in Slobin, 1971; for other reviews see Brown, Cazden and Bellugi 1969; Ervin-Tripp, 1970), therefore we will focus on some of the main issues emerging from this research which are of special interest to sociologists. These issues can be discussed from two perspectives: (1) by focusing on stages of the development of language; (2) by looking at the nature of the linguistic rules acquired. Early grammatical development can be divided into the following stages: a babbling stage when the child exercises his voice in almost random fashion, producing an amazing variety of apparently meaningless sounds or syllables (Weir, 1962); the one-word stage when the child learns to name structurally similar individual words, whether referring to actions, requests or objects. The development of grammar proper begins with the two-word or pivot-word stage (Braine, 1963). Following this early grammatical stage the child begins to develop the ability to form hierarchically organized constructions and the ability to perform transformations of the type postulated by generative grammarians (Slobin, 1971). While there are wide differences in individual learning and in the age at which a particular stage is reached, the sequence of the stages is *universal* and the average age at which these stages emerge is also universally similar (Slobin, 1970). There is no evidence to show that social class or cultural differences in any way affect the child's learning of these basic grammatical patterns. It seems that all children by the age of four or five, regardless of how they have been reared, have gained control of the grammatical system of their own native language.

These universal aspects of language-learning processes, when viewed along with other linguistic findings on the universality of grammatical structure, have given rise to the claim by Chomsky and his followers (Chomsky, 1968) that linguistic competence, that is the child's knowledge of grammatical rules, is innate; that, in a sense, a child is born with a latent knowledge of grammatical rules and that the socialization process activates this knowledge and gives it cultural substance. This view of the innateness of grammar brings the generative grammarian into direct conflict with followers of the earlier imitative-practice model of language learning. In this latter view the new-born child was seen as a *tabula rasa* who acquired language only by direct imitation of the speech models provided by his family. The search for solutions to this issue has for the first time lead to direct psycho-linguistic inquiries into the nature of linguistic rules.

Ervin-Tripp (1964) has examined the research on the imitative models and has shown that there is little evidence that the child directly imitates its parents. Braine (1969) and Ervin-Tripp give the example of children being incapable of correctly repeating an inflectional change and correction after the parent. The child will appear to keep to his 'own' rule while at the time adding the parent's version to please the parent.[1] Also, as Cazden (1966) has noted, evidence for the practice model is hard to find because children make mistakes that pass unperceived by the parents. The apparent 'randomness' of the parents' correction of the child's speech has often been cited as evidence that the behaviourist view of language learning by imitation alone cannot be an adequate explanation. It has also been noted that children repeatedly hear ungrammatical remarks from their parents but do not appear to imitate these.

A more plausible explanation is that the child employs a *generative model*; that is, from the performances that he experiences he is able to develop a set of rules about language for himself, from which he can produce his own varied, linguistic performances.

These rules are adapted and expanded by the child until most of the utterances the child produces are grammatically acceptable to adults. No research has yet shown how long this process might continue; possibly with considerable slow-down after the age of five–seven, it might continue into adulthood. Considerable research has shown the usefulness of this model (for example, Menyuk, 1964; Brown and Frazer, 1964; Slobin, 1966). There is a great deal of evidence available for, as McNeill (1966) has said, 'Sentences that cannot be accounted for as adult sentences provide the best evidence that the child knows productive rules.' Some research has focused on the way in which the child appears, from his performances, to construct his own rules. Braine (1963) has suggested that the child's basic generative rule might be S – P + O, (where P is a pivot class and O is an open class). These classes in the child's speech contain items which are heterogeneous in adult grammars. The *pivot* word always remains in the same position and can be variously combined to make complete utterances. Weir (1962) gives good examples of this in her research of the 'overhead' speech of her two-and-a-half-year-old son. McNeill has shown how Braine's findings can be substantiated in the research of Ervin-Tripp, and Brown and Bellugi. This seems to give some strong evidence for the child's generative-productive capacity.

Other research (for example, see Chomsky, 1969; Menyuk, 1964; Slobin, 1966) has focused on examining in detail how the rules which can be written by the researcher from children's performances can be compared with adult rules, and so how judgments of the child's linguistic competence can be made. The way the child acquires language is assumed to be expressed by the generative model if the rules and the child's performances match. Menyuk (1964) has described the acquisition process as follows: 'With a generative model of grammar, it is hypothesized, that the perceiver or child has incorporated both the generative rules of the grammar and a heuristic component, that samples an input sentence and by a series of successive approximations determine which rules were used to generate the sentence.' In short, studies of the child's growing linguistic competence look at the child's performance as though the child could select from all possible examples without other (performance, situational) criteria influencing his judgment. Rules are written from the assumption of situationally 'unembedded' or context-free performances, and it is assumed that 'something like' the rules the linguists write exist 'in the head' of the child. These rules can then be used by the child to generate the 'infinite' set of possibilities which is linguistic performance. As Menyuk has described 'the child uses his set of rules to generate not only the sentences he has heard but all possible examples. In addition his linguistic knowledge is systematically extended without further instruction.' The earlier transformationalist arguments have been weakened somewhat by the observation of more recent researchers that although some of the child's sentences may look like adult grammar, their usage is sufficiently limited or context-bound that these rules may not be needed to account for what the child does (Kernan, 1969; Bloom, 1969). There are indications that Fillmore's case grammar or similar generative semantic approaches to the study of grammar may more efficiently account for the differences between child grammar and adult grammar (Fillmore, 1968), than simply matching the child rules to adult rules.

The work on grammatical rules reveals another important issue in language acquisition, that the child may be able to comprehend more than he can produce, and thus not reveal his competence by his performance. Frazer, Bellugi and Brown (1963) examined this problem experimentally. They found that children's ability to comprehend and to distinguish between different grammatical statements for similar pictures, an ability to distinguish tense and other inflectional differences, was in advance of their ability to *produce* similar distinctions. McNeill points to the young child's 'holophrasistic' speech where single words 'stand for' a whole utterance, the meaning of which (or rather the communicative intent) the child knows when an adult misinterprets, but which he is not able to produce linguistically. Brown and Bellugi (1964) point to the problems parents have in deciding which of several alternatives can be the appropriate expansion of the child's 'telegram'. It appears that along with the child's performance it is necessary to take other features of the speech setting into account. The search for the child's competence in his performance depends upon the researcher's ability to decide upon the 'meaning' of the speech. This will probably entail the assumption that the same or similar 'ideas' are in the mind of the child as in the mind of the interpreting adult. Slobin (1966) has described the problem of attempting to write a grammar of children's speech:

> Linguistic competence is a model of what is assumed to exist in the mind of the speaker, a model built by the linguist on the basis of his intuitive ability to discriminate well-formed from ill-formed utterances. The plausibility of its existence can only be ascertained by careful study of the actual performance which it is believed to determine.

It may be necessary for the researcher to make assumptions about the child's speech as the parent does, for it may be necessary to consider the meaning of the utterance in order to assess its grammatical acceptability. Thus, in order to write the 'rules' of a generative grammar for children's speech the researcher may have to consider the performance as part of a communicative event, but the description of this event will not eventually be a part of the rules or of the theory. The situated dependence of children's speech is shown in Brown and Bellugi's work—the child's telegraphic speech. Parents find many utterances ambiguous or open to several interpretations and so have to turn to the context of the event and personal knowledge of the child to 'know what he means'. Cazden (1966) suggests that the 'everyday' way in which we 'work out' what the child means often passes without notice. She says 'in discussing optimal sequencing of stimuli, I suggest that if it does occur . . . it must be fortuitously. Expansions by their very nature, provide such sequencing. No one has suggested that the parents expand with any conscious tutorial intention. *It seems simply to be one way of keeping a conversation with a young child going.*' It seems that in order to develop rules for the child's speech competence in terms of its grammaticality, researchers may have to take into account what they know of the language, of the speech situation, of the topic and of the child. This suggests that the rules which are deduced and written for the child's performance may not be as independent of contextual assumptions as the generative model supposes. Several recent experimental investigations in the areas of phonological and semantic development also point to the context-embeddedness of children's speech. Moskowitz (1970), in a review dealing with the acquisition of syllables structure, has shown that when the child first learns sounds these are not learnt in isolation but in syllable sequences, e.g. consonant vowel sequences. The ability to separate particular sounds from surrounding sequences is acquired only at a later stage. Similarly, Stross (1970) demonstrates that children can make what seem to be highly complex semantic distinctions among variants of the same activity, but that such distinctions are always learnt in the context of particular sentences and not in isolation.

Thus it seems that in order to write competence rules the researcher has to make assumptions and trade upon his own knowledge of 'social appropriateness'. The researcher cannot write rules for a child's grammar unless the 'meaning' of the child's utterance is taken into account, and this meaning will be context-dependent. Part of this context-dependent knowledge will be the adult's own conception of the language. As Klima and Bellugi (1966) have commented, 'It shall be understood that when we write rules for the children's grammar it is just a rough attempt to give substance to our feelings about, and general observations demonstrating, the regularity in the syntax of children's speech.'

We have noted that no matter how 'clear' and context-unspecific grammatical descriptive rules appear they will have relied upon, in their construction, features and details which are not now a part of the rules or the theory. Therefore, no matter how detailed these rules are they will not be sufficient for the generation of adequate social performances of appropriate speech acts. An alternative approach has developed using the notion of communicative competence (Gumperz and Hymes, 1964). This concept was advanced to deal with some of the objections raised against the type of linguistic research that separates grammar from context and from rules of usage. Although studies of communicative competence may deal with rules of phonology and grammar, they see the acquisition of these features as dependent on, or as developing in response to, the type of communicative tasks that the child's life-style requires. Whereas psycho-linguistic analysis concentrates on the analysis of words and sentences, the studies of communicative competence focus on inter-action sequences seen as exchanges between speakers, i.e. mother–child, child–child, etc. If we look at the inter-action sequences rather than mere sentences we have to take account of a number of additional linguistic features of what Hymes has called speech acts (Hymes, 1962; Gumperz and Hymes, 1972); for example; it becomes necessary to account for intonation contours, para-linguistic features of speech, variations in style etc. Other discourse features to be accounted for are: the child's ability to select words appropriate to his intent or to choose appropriate styles or codes, his control over sequencing rules, that is the rules which govern the assignment of right to speaking (Sacks, 1972) and the selection of appropriate content. The study of these features of speaking is still in its beginning but it is clear these features are regulated by 'rules' which, like grammatical rules, are not consciously explicit (Gumperz, 1970). There is also some evidence to show that acquisition of these socio-linguistic rules is subject to the same problems of over-generalizations and the generation of structures different from those of adults as syntactic rules.

The studies of communicative competence have gone some way towards remedying the neglect of context in the earlier linguistic studies. Yet, although they have explored the nature of speech events and the regulation of these by socio-linguistic rules, they have not approached the critical question raised in this review, that of the nature of social rules. In the following section we will briefly explore this question.

Suggestions for an alternative approach

In this section we would like to suggest the direction that an alternative approach should take, towards more contextually specific and detailed studies, which will attempt to show how the 'rules' of the society are put into practice in child-rearing situations. We shall look briefly at some of the ethnographic studies which take this kind of approach. The problems that these studies have encountered in giving detailed descriptions of the 'rules' of everyday life suggest some of the characteristics of social rules which need to be taken into account. Just as the study of language acquisition provides an insight into the nature of grammatical rules, the study of how the child acquires an understanding of what is necessary for competent membership of a social group can elucidate the nature of social rules. The parents' need to make clear and available to the child the conditions of membership and also provide additional information on these rules, as Cicourel (1968) suggests: 'Adult descriptions of the "why" of everyday life to children provide a rich source of information on adult notions of simplified social structures.' Further, the researchers' attempts to discover this information will, as we have already indicated, reveal something of the implicit assumptions and knowledge that the researcher has about the 'working' of the social structure, and on which he/she must necessarily rely to make sense of the available information. In this way the researcher can be seen to be in a similar position to the child in having to uncover the 'rules' regulating social scenes while also being a practising member of them.

There exists a large body of literature which has made detailed, descriptive studies of child-rearing practices—the ethnographic studies of anthropology which have studied foreign cultures and the social anthropological and ecological studies that have been made in our own society. We will very briefly comment upon a few of these studies in order to see what problems they may have encountered in making detailed descriptions of socialization practices. The best examples of the social anthropological studies are represented by the work of Beatrice Whiting and colleagues on the 'Six cultures' project (1963) and by the British tradition of community studies reviewed in detail by Klein (1965) as *Samples from English Cultures*. The six cultures project attempted to give detailed and comparable accounts of child-rearing practices in six different societies (both rural and urban), in India, Kenya, Japan, the Philippines, Mexico and the USA. The English studies were made for various purposes, but all were concerned with giving detailed accounts of what it would be like to live as a participant, in a mining village, a northern industrial town, as an industrial worker, and in a London single-class (working-class) community. Both sets of studies implicitly contain a theory of the relationship of the individual and his personality to the social system. The explicit aim of the Whiting studies was to explore this relationship through making comparable descriptions of the societies.

Psychological-ecological studies made by Barker and Wright (for example, *One Boy's Day*, 1951) represent a rather different tradition of studies which has not been extended much beyond their own work. Barker and Wright attempted to describe in detail the ongoing behaviour in a community (as in *The Mid-West and its Children*, 1955) *in the process of its occurrence*. Earlier Bossard (1943, 1945) had suggested a similar attempt could be made from a sociological viewpoint in studying family conversations, but this work also has not been extended much beyond Bossard and Boll's (1950) studies of family rituals. We will look at some problems that these researchers met in making their descriptions. Their experience will show us how difficult it is to observe social rules in practice, and also to write rules for everyday practices.

We will look at three problems that these studies have raised. *First*, there is the problem of the immense amount of detail that any direct observation of actual situated behaviour presents to the researcher. Barker (1963) and colleagues have described the process as the need to select from a continuous 'stream of behaviour'. The studies made by Barker and Wright were attempts to code all the details of any action sequence within different units of behaviour. The descriptions that they gave of even a simple sequence, such as a child pulling off his coat and speaking with his mother at the same time, show how complicated is the seemingly simplest action sequence. Anyone familiar with participant observation coding will know that the details available at any moment seem to be 'infinite'. In a recent paper Gumperz (1970) has discussed some of the difficulties of assigning meanings to conversational data under these conditions where the investigator does not share the speaker's background assumptions. Yet Barker and Wright's work shows, through just a glance at any page of analysis, how mutually *embedded* actions or events are. Talk is embedded in sequences of actions, some of which may need to be known in order to understand the talk itself. The actions may also depend on the accompanying talk for their relevance. The ethnographic researcher is presented with the task of 'making sense' and interpreting these contingent events. It has sometimes been noted in ethnographic work that the problem of selection is easier if the researcher is 'foreign' to the scene. Whiting commented, in describing the difficulties of an American ethnographer in an American community, 'It is difficult for "natives" to collect ethnographic data which is comparable to that collected by an individual of a different culture'. The reason for the value of 'strangers' is two-fold. A stranger who is not involved in the culture himself is likely to perceive events that are 'taken-for-granted' by the native of the culture. But at the same time a stranger is less likely to be aware of the possible 'infinite', or at least the multiplicity of meanings that an action can have for a native, and so he is less likely to be overwhelmed by the immensity of detail that a description might need. In this way, by being or attempting to be a stranger to a culture, the ethnographer solves the problem of selection of detail.

The *second* problem raised by these studies is how can the

researcher uncover the relevant regularities of rules to which his theoretical perspective guides him? The ethnographer has to give some 'shape' to the events which he observes and records in order to be able to find the regularities or details for which he is looking. Dollard (1935), in proposing that socialization studies should use the information contained in life histories as accounts of how a new person is added to the group and becomes an adult through the traditional experiences of 'his society', suggests how important is this theoretical 'shaping'.

> We propose a common sense definition of the life history as a deliberate attempt to define the growth of a person in a cultural milieu and to make theoretical sense of it . . . it is not just an account of a life with events separately identified like beads on a string, although this is the form in which naïve attempts to present a life history usually meet us; if this were true, every man would be a psychologist, because every person can give us data of this type. The material must, in addition be worked up and mastered from some systematic viewpoint.

Dollard's view points out that the researcher uses his theoretical perspective to know what to look for in the field. But members of Whiting's project found that theoretical agreement did not solve the problem of agreement at the level of description of events in the various cultures, as Whiting comments in the introduction to the study, 'In spite of the research design, the data are not always comparable, that in the different areas studied some monographs have better coverage than others.' In spite of a common theoretical perspective the selection of details from the cultural scenes remained difficult and a matter of each ethnographer's negotiation between the theoretically governed category and the actual, observed events.

This reveals the *third* problem of these studies. Once the researcher becomes aware of his own perspective, of how his categorization acts as a grid or filter through which the data are sifted, this perspective can appear to 'get in the way'. The researcher becomes aware of the fact that the way in which he fits his observations into the categories is itself a problem. Douglas (1970) touches upon this issue when she points out the difficulty of not finding instances of the expected rituals in culture. She suggests that an ethnographer is tempted to press his data further to find instances that might fit. Once the ethnographer is alerted to his own interpretations, he may also consider how the events can be classified and variously perceived by members. The ethnographer, in spite of his 'strangeness' becomes aware of some of the implicit assumptions which he makes in order to achieve his classifications. As

Cicourel (1968) suggests, 'The researcher has to 'work' to achieve a fit—the source of structural descriptions of members' behaviour by the researcher, is through misleading but self-contained packages of meaning or blue-prints for behaviour. Situational constraints and unfolding contingencies are eliminated or minimized, and normative structure becomes the ethnographic focus.' The researcher, in looking for the 'clear' or rule-like structure of everyday behaviour which the ethnographer observes, may leave aside much of the 'confusing' detail that members actually rely upon to make the rules work. As we noted in the case of writing linguistic rules, researchers 'traded upon' details which were neither written into the theory nor the rules of the grammar. In such instances it would not be possible to work back from the descriptive rules to the actual behavioural events. That is what we take Cicourel to mean when he speaks of 'misleading but self-contained packages of meaning or blue-prints for behaviour'.

It seems that these detailed descriptions of activities may not be used, without controversy, to locate the 'social rules', for such rules are not visible without the researchers' interpretation. In order to see how rules are put into practice in everyday settings, it becomes necessary to look at what constitutes the 'rule' for members of the society. It is not enough to rely on our observer's judgment. We suggest that it might be necessary to do the reverse of Dollard's directions and look at 'every man as a psychologist' and at his own 'interpretation or even description of his actions'. This is, in fact, what the linguist theoretically attempts to do with the notion of competence. It is noticeable that ethnographic studies which rely strongly on verbal reportage do not consider members' descriptions from what Dollard calls their 'naïve standpoint' at face value. If this were done the ethnographer, in having to 'work' to negotiate a fit between the social rules and the behaviour which is said to come under the rules, would discover that members are in fact in a similar position to the ethnographer himself. One ethnographer, Moerman (1970), has described this experience in looking at the working of the marriage and divorce rules in Lue society:

> The proposition that three divorces damage a reputation and that marriage ends gossip are both 'true as a rule' in two senses characteristic of social rules. First, counter instances do not disprove them (Helmer and Resher, 1960). Second, a member can use the rules to argue but not, to clinch, the correctness of his judgements about actions, events, and persons . . . To phrase it somewhat differently, in addition to their 'et cetera clause' (Garfinkel, 1964) social rules, and members' procedures for

> subsuming cases under them, have an 'unless clause' which members can cite in order to classify a case or to explain their having, 'as it turned out' retrospectively, misclassified it.

If we accept Moerman's two principles of social rules it appears that members, ethnographers, and linguists are in the same position of using rules to 'account for' behaviours and events, while at the same time adjusting the accounts of the behaviours or the rules to fit the case at hand.

Rule-following as a situated accomplishment

If it is the case that we are compelled to negotiate the fit of social rules to social events, then rule-following becomes a 'situated accomplishment'. Rule-following is not simply a matter of applying a rule which is sufficiently detailed to cover all cases, and so independent of the context in which it is used. How is it we make social rules work? Previous comments from Clausen (1968) suggest an answer. He has said, 'Most parents do not explicitly formulate the various aims . . . in child-rearing some of these are so completely taken-for-granted they need not be formulated, others become formulated when what is taken-for-granted proves to be problematic.' If we shift Clausen's perspective slightly and look, not only at the parents' statements of problems, their statements of 'social rules', but also at what they 'take-for-granted', we will see something of the 'background expectancies' that make the rule-like statements workable (Garfinkel, 1967). What kind of taken-for-granted information do members and researchers use? Brown (1965) has suggested one possibility when he describes how child-rearing researchers make the category 'withdrawal of love' fit the data that they are coding, as follows:

> 'Withdrawal of love' is a psychologist's phrase. Mothers do not spontaneously report using it and interviewers do not even ask about it. The rating had to be made by inference from certain kinds of reported behaviour. Do we know what withdrawal of love is like? Mother looks hurt or her voice quivers a little. She has less to say than usual, her movements are brusque, her jawline shows a certain tension. If something slightly disagreeable happens—a cup breaks or the cat gets in her way—she over reacts, bursting into tears or a temper. Perhaps you recognize it, not only mothers practice it but husbands and wives, sisters and brothers.

What Brown is suggesting is that researchers use their *own* knowledge of everyday activities to interpret and fill out the member's descriptions. What he seems to overlook is that we all, as members, trade upon certain taken-for-granted features of social actions, and that filling out and interpreting other's 'accounts' is a member's problem too. We all solve this problem, for the while and for practical purposes, by our talk. We ask, probe and reflect during the on-going social action through talk, which enables us to make our social accounts and inflections visible to the other participants. We generate social inter-action through talk. Cicourel (1968) has described this process as follows:

> Members use the interpretive procedures and their reflexive features as instructions for negotiating social scenes over time. Members are continually giving each other instructions (verbal and non-verbal cues and content) as to their intentions, their social character, their biographies and the like . . . [these] features provide continuous instructions to participants such that members can be said to be programming each other's actions as the scene unfolds.

What this perspective is suggesting is that researchers can see how members make the social rules 'work' for themselves by looking *at*, not beyond, the talk that members offer. Although interpretation of this talk will rely upon certain 'interpretive procedures' or 'background expectancies' which we all share, we will see something of *the procedure of practising social rules in members talk.*

From this perspective we see that social rules can never be *self-explicating*, No matter how much detail they contain, they need to be made to fit the particular circumstances of the activities. Socialization is not a matter of learning the 'rules' and applying them, but of developing a set of 'interpretive procedures', a set of taken-for-granted assumptions that enables the member to see the rules in the first place. This view is rather different from that proposed in most studies of socialization, where the ability to behave in socially acceptable ways is equated with the ability to 'follow the rules', as in this description by Strauss (1953):

> Conceptions of roles and conceptions of rules grow *pari passu.* Built into role conceptions are justifications of motivations for behaviour appropriate or inappropriate for enactment of roles . . . To talk of rules and punishment for rule infraction is just another way of stating role relationships. The young child's inability to grasp the nature or full extent of adult rules means that he is unable to make proper conceptual distinctions, likewise he is unable to grasp the consequences for certain roleplayers of certain acts committed by certain other role players.

We are suggesting here an opposing view to that of Strauss, which Cicourel (1970) has described as:

> The members of a group or tribe or society do not live by social rules or norms or laws that are self-explicative, but must acquire (psychological and) sociological cognitive properties that generate and provide the basis for interpreting rules as guides to social conduct . . . these sociological cognitive properties are essential presuppositions or 'interpretive procedures' necessary for the speaker-hearer to make sense of his environment as an emergent, temporally constituted scene.

Cicourel is suggesting that what the child acquires from his socialization experience is a developmental *generative* understanding of the social structure and other activities which enables him to 'see' and to take-for-granted what others do. From this generative basis the child can produce his own varied social performances (Cicourel, 1968):

> The child cannot be taught to understand and use surface rules unless, like language, he acquires a basis for assigning meaning to his environment; a sense of social structure . . . there are no surface rules for instructing the child on how articulation is to be made . . . Surface rules always require some specification of the particulars which would render rules as appropriate and useful for dealing with actual behavioural displays.

Parents cannot explicitly teach the child how to acquire the generative interpretive procedures, but through showing the child how, for all practical purposes, 'surface rules' can be understood and made to work in the child's daily life. The parent is helping the child to develop a 'sense of the social structure', of what can be taken-for-granted and what can be discussed and questioned. Therein lies the importance of Bernstein's theory of the parent's explanations and the different modes of social control. Thus, in acquiring the ways of talk of his social group, the child is acquiring, 'for all practical purposes', a way of producing and recognizing 'perceivedly normal' or routine behaviour in himself and others. Through learning to talk and negotiate social inter-action with others the child is learning to apply and to follow rules as a 'situated accomplishment'.

Acknowledgments

Work on this paper was completed under a post-doctoral fellowship at the University of California. Thanks are due to the Ford

Foundation for support and to Professors Basil Bernstein, Aaron Cicourel and John J. Gumperz for help and criticism.

Notes

1 The example cited above is also illustrative of the child having his own language rules. The child says, 'nobody don't like me'; the mother replies, 'No, say nobody likes me.' The child replies with his version. This dialogue is repeated eight times until the child says in exasperation 'all right, nobody don't likes me.'

References

ALLINSMITH, W. (1957), 'Conscience and conflict: the moral force in personality', *Child Development*, 28, pp. 469–76.

ARONFREED, J. (1961), 'The nature, variety and social patterning of moral response to transgression', *J.Ab. and Soc. Psych.*, 63, pp. 223–40.

ARONFREED, J. (1963), 'The effects of two socialization paradigms on two moral responses to transgression', *J.Ab. and Soc. Psych.*, 66, pp. 437–48.

ARONFREED, J. (1964), 'The origins of self-criticism', *Psych. Rev.*, 71, pp. 193–218.

ARONFREED, J. (1965), 'Internalized behavioural suppression and the timing of social punishment', *J. Personality and Soc. Psych.*, pp. 3–16.

ARONFREED, J. (1968), *Conduct and Conscience*. New York: Academic Press.

ARONFREED, J. (1969), 'The concept of internalization', in *The Handbook of Socialization Theory and Research* (ed.) D. Goslin. Chicago: Rand McNally.

ARONFREED, J., CUTTICK, R. A. and FAGAN, S. A. (1963), 'Cognitive structure, nurturance and punishment in the experimental induction of self-criticism', *Child Development*, 34, pp. 281–94.

BANDURA, A. (1969), 'Social-learning theory of identificatory processes', *The Handbook of Socialization Theory and Research* (ed.) D. Goslin, op. cit.

BANDURA, A. and HUSTON, A. C. (1961), 'Identification as a process of incidental learning', *J.Ab. and Soc. Psych.*, 59, pp. 311–19.

BANDURA, A. and MACDONALD, F. (1963), 'The influence of social reinforcements and behaviour models in shaping children's moral judgements', *J.Ab. and Soc. Psych.*, 66, pp. 274–81.

BANDURA, A., ROSS, D. and ROSS, S. A. (1963), 'A test of status envy, social power, and secondary reinforcement theories of identificatory learning', *J.Ab. and Soc. Psych.*, 66, pp. 527–34.

BARKER, R. (1963), *The Stream of Behaviour*. New York: Appleton-Century-Crofts.

BARKER, R. and WRIGHT, H. (1951), *One Boy's Day*. New York: Harper & Row.

BARKER, R. and WRIGHT, H. (1955), *The Mid-West and its Children.* New York: Harper & Row.

BECKER, W. (1964), 'Consequences of different kinds of parental discipline', in *Review of Child Development Research* (ed.) L. Hoffman and M. Hoffman. New York: Russell Sage Foundation.

BERNSTEIN, B. (1964), 'Elaborated and restricted codes: their social origins and some consequences', *Ethnography of Communication* (ed.) D. Hymes and J. J. Gumperz, special issue, *American Anthropologist*, 66, no. 2.

BERNSTEIN, B. (1965), 'A socio-linguistic approach to social learning', *Survey of the Social Sciences* (ed.) J. Gould. London: Penguin.

BERNSTEIN, B. (1970), 'Social class, language and socialization', *Current Trends in Linguistics*, 12, A. Abramson *et al.* (eds). The Hague: Mouton.

BERNSTEIN, B. (1971), 'A socio-linguistic approach to socialization: with some reference to educability', *Directions in Sociolinguistics* (ed.) J. J. Gumperz and D. Hymes. New York: Holt, Rinehart & Winston.

BLOOM, L. (1969), *Language Development: Form and Function in Emerging Grammars.* Cambridge, Mass.: M.I.T. Press.

BOEHM, L. (1962), *Child Development*, 33, pp. 575–89.

BOEHM, L. and NASS, M. (1962), 'Social class differences in conscience development', *Child Development*, 33, pp. 565–74.

BOSSARD, J. (1943), 'Family table talk—an area for sociological study', *Am. Soc. Rev.*, pp. 295–301.

BOSSARD, J. (1945), 'Family modes of expression', *Am. Soc. Rev.*, pp. 226–37.

BOSSARD, J. and BOLL, E. (1950), *Ritual in Family Living.* Philadelphia: University of Pennsylvania Press.

BRAINE, M. D. S. (1963), 'The ontogeny of English phrase structure: the first phase', *Language*, 39, pp. 1–13.

BRAINE, M. D. S. (1969), 'On two types of models of the internalization of grammar', *The ontogenesis of grammar: some facts and several theories* (ed.) D. Slobin (in press).

BRIM, O. (1957), 'The parent-child relation as a social system: (1) parent-child roles', *Child Development*, 28, pp. 343–64.

BRIM, O. (1958), 'Family structure and sex role learning by children—a further analysis of Helen Koch's data', *Sociometry*, 21, pp. 1–16.

BRIM, O. (1960), 'Personality development as role learning', *Personality Development in Children* (ed.) I. Iscoe and H. Stevenson. University of Texas Press.

BRIM, O. (1966), 'Socialization through the life cycle', *Socialization After Childhood* (ed.) O. Brim and S. Wheeler. New York: John Wiley.

BRONFENBRENNER, U. (1958), 'Socialization through time and space', *Readings in Social Psychology* (ed.) T. Newcomb and E. L. Hartley, 3rd ed. New York: Holt, Rinehart & Winston.

BRONFENBRENNER, U. (1960), 'Freudian theories of identification and their derivatives', *Child Development*, 31, pp. 15–40.

BRONFENBRENNER, U. (1961), 'The changing American child', *Merrill Palmer Quarterly*, 7, pp. 73–165.

BRONFENBRENNER, U. (1961), 'Toward a theoretical model for the analysis of parent-child relationships in a social context', *Parental Attitudes and Child Behaviour* (ed.) J. Glidewell. Springfield, Ill.: Charles Thomas.

BROWN, R. (1965), 'The child's acquisition of morality', *Social Psychology*. New York: Free Press.

BROWN, R. and BELLUGI, U. (1964), 'The processes in the acquisition of syntax', *New Directions in the Study of Language* (ed.) E. Lenneberg. Cambridge, Mass.: M.I.T. Press.

BROWN, R., CAZDEN, C. and BELLUGI, U. (1969), 'The child's grammar from 1 to 11', *Minnesota Symposia on Child Psychology*, vol. 2 (ed.) J. P. Hill. Minneapolis: University of Minnesota Press.

BROWN, R. and FRAZER, C. (1964), 'The acquisition of syntax', *Child Development Monographs: The Acquisition of Language* (ed.) R. Brown and U. Bellugi, 29, pp. 43–79.

BURTON, R., MACCOBY, E. and ALLINSMITH, W. (1961), 'Antecedents of resistance to temptation in four-year-old children', *Child Development*, 32, pp. 689–710.

CAZDEN, C. (1966), 'Sub-cultural differences in child language: an inter-disciplinary review', *Merrill Palmer Quarterly*, 12, pp. 185–219.

CHILD, I. and ZEIGLER, F. (1967), 'Child Socialization'. *The Handbook of Social Psychology* (ed.) G. Lindzey and E. Anderson, 2nd ed. Mass.: Addison-Wesley.

CHOMSKY, N. (1965), *Aspects of a Theory of Syntax*. Cambridge, Mass.: M.I.T. Press.

CHOMSKY, N. (1968), *Language and Mind*. New York: Harcourt, Brace, Jovanovich.

CHOMSKY, C. (1969), *The Acquisition of Syntax in Children from 5 to 10*. Cambridge, Mass.: M.I.T. Press.

CICOUREL, A. V. (1968), 'The acquisition of social structure: towards a developmental sociology of language and meaning', *Understanding Everyday Life* (ed.) J. Douglas. London: Routledge & Kegan Paul.

CICOUREL, A. V. (1970), 'Generative Semantics and the structure of social interaction'. International Days of Sociolinguistics, Lugi Struzo Institute, Rome. To be published in *Current Trends in Linguistics*, vol. 12, (ed.) A. Abramson *et al*. The Hague: Mouton.

CICOUREL, A. V. and BOESE, R. (1970), 'Sign language acquisition and the teaching of deaf children', *The Functions of Language: an anthropological and psychological approach* (ed.) D. Hymes, C. Cazden and V. John.

CLAUSEN, J. (1968), 'The history of socialization studies', *Socialization and Society* (ed.) J. Clausen. New York: Little, Brown.

CLAUSEN, J. and WILLIAMS, S. (1963), 'Sociological correlates of child behaviour', N.S.S.E. 62nd yearbook, *Child Psychology* (ed.) H. Stevenson. University of Chicago Press.

COSER, L. and ROSENBERG, B. (1955), 'Social Control', *Sociological Theory: A Book of Readings*, 2nd ed. New York: Collier-Macmillan.

DAVIS, A. (1941), 'American status system and the socialization of the child', *Am. Sociological Rev.*, 6, pp. 345–54.

DAVIS, A. and HAVIGHURST, R. (1946), 'Social class and colour differences in child-rearing', *Am. Soc. Rev.*, 1, pp. 698–710.

DAVIS, A. and HAVIGHURST, R. (1955), 'A comparison of the Chicago and Harvard studies', *Am. Soc. Rev.*, 20, pp. 438–42.

DOLLARD, J. (1935), *Criteria for the Life History*, Yale University Press.

DOUGLAS, M. (1970), *Natural Symbols: Explorations in Cosmology*. London: Cresset Press.

DURKHEIM, E. (1953), *Sociology and Philosophy*, translated with introduction by J. G. Peristany. Chicago: Free Press.

DURKIN, D. (1959), 'Child's conception of justice—comparison with Piaget's data', *Child Development*, 30, pp. 59–67.

DURKIN, D. (1959), 'Child's acceptance of reciprocity as a justice principle', *Child Development*, 30, pp. 289–96.

DURKIN, D. (1960), 'Sex differences in children's concept of justice', *Child Development*, 31, pp. 361–8.

DURKIN, D. (1961), 'The specificity of children's moral judgements', *Journal of Genetic Psychology*, 98, pp. 3–13.

DUVALL, E. M. (1946), 'Conceptions of parenthood', *Am. J. of Soc.*, 52, pp. 193–203.

ELDER, C. and BOWERMAN, C. (1963), 'Family structure and child rearing: the effect of family size and sex composition', *Am. Soc. Rev.*, 28, pp. 891–905.

ELKIN, F. (1960), *The Child and Society*. New York: Random House.

EMMERICH, W. and SMOLLER, F. (1964), 'The role patterning of parental norms', *Sociometry*, 27, pp. 382–96.

ERICSON, M. (1946), 'Child-rearing and social status', *Am. J. of Soc.*, 53, pp. 190–2.

ERVIN-TRIPP, S. (1964), 'Imitation and structural change in children's language', *New Directions in the Study of Language* (ed.) E. Lenneberg.

ERVIN-TRIPP, S. and MILLER, W. (1964), 'The development of grammar in child language', *Child Development Monographs: The Acquisition of Language* (ed.) R. Brown and U. Bellugi, 29, pp. 9–34.

ERVIN-TRIPP, S. (1970), 'Structure and process in language acquisition', 21st Annual Round Table: Monograph Series on *Language and Linguistics* (ed.) J. Alatis, Georgetown University, Washington D.C.

FARIS, E. (1937), 'The social psychology of George Herbert Mead', *Am. J. of Soc.*, 43, pp. 391–403.

FILLMORE, C. J. (1968), 'The case for case', *Universals in Linguistic Theory* (ed.) E. Bach and R. T. Harms. New York: Holt Rinehart & Winston.

KOHN, M. and CARROLL, E. (1960), 'Social class and the allocation of parental responsibilities', *Sociometry*, 23, pp. 372–92.

LENNEBERG, E. H. (1967), *Biological Foundation of Language*. New York: Wiley.

LITTMAN, R., MOORE, R. and PIERCE-JONES, J. (1957), 'Social class differences in child rearing: a third community for comparison with Chicago and Newton (Boston)'. *Am. Soc. Rev.*, 22, pp. 694–712.

LOEVINGER, J. (1959), 'Patterns of parenthood and theories of learning', *J. Ab. and Soc. Psych.*, 59, pp. 148–50.

LURIA, A. R. and YUDOVITCH, F. (1959), *Speech and the Development of Mental Processes*. London: Staples Press.

MACCOBY, E. E. (1959), 'Role taking and its consequences for social learning', *Child Development*, 30, pp. 239–52.

MACCOBY, E. E. (1961a), 'The taking of adult roles in middle childhood', *J. Ab. and Soc. Psych.*, 63, pp. 493–503.

MACCOBY, E. E. (1961b), 'The choice of variables in the study of socialization', *Sociometry*, 24.

MACCOBY, E. E. (1968), 'The development of moral values and behaviour in childhood', *Socialization and Society* (ed.) J. Clausen, op. cit.

MACRAE, D. (1954), 'A test of Piaget's theories of moral development', *J. of Ab. and Soc. Psych.*, 49, pp. 14–18.

MacKINNON, D. W. (1938), 'Violation and prohibitions', *Explorations in Personality*, (ed.) H. A. Murray. Oxford University Press.

MAIER, H. W. (1965), *Three Theories of Child Development*. New York: Harper Row.

MCNEILL, D. (1966), 'Developmental psycholinguistics', in *The Genesis of Language* (ed.) F. Smith and G. Miller. Cambridge, Mass.: M.I.T. Press.

MCCARTHY, D. (1960), 'Language development', *Child Development Monographs,* 25, no. 3, pp. 5–14.

MENYUK, P. (1964), 'Alteration of rules in children's grammar', *Journal of Verbal Learning and Verbal Behaviour*, 3, pp. 486–8.

MERLEAU-PONTY, M. (1964), 'Man and adversity', *Signs*, trans. Richard McCleary. Northwestern University Press.

MILLER, D. (1969), 'Psychoanalytic theories of development', *Handbook of Socialization Theory and Research*, ed. D. Goslin, op. cit.

MILLER, D. and SWANSON, C. (1958), *The Changing American Parent*. New York: Wiley.

MILLER, D. and SWANSON, C. (1960), *Inner Conflict and Defence*. New York: Holt, Rinehart & Winston.

MILLER, N. and DOLLARD, J. (1940), *Frustration and Aggression*. Yale University Press.

MOERMAN, M. (1970), 'A little knowledge', *Cognitive Anthropology* (ed.) S. Tyler. New York: Holt, Rinehart & Winston.

MOSKOWITZ, A. (1970), 'The acquisition of phonology', Working Paper 34, Language Behaviour Research Laboratory, University of California, Berkeley.

MURDOCK, G. (1957), 'World ethnographic sample', *American Anthropologist*, 59, pp. 664–87.

ORLANSKY, H. (1949), 'Infant care and personality', *Psychological Bulletin*, 46, pp. 1–48.

PARSONS, T. (1964), *Social Structure and Personality*. Chicago: Free Press.

PARSONS, T. and BALES, R. F. (1956), *Family, Socialization and Interaction Process*. Chicago: Free Press.

PEARLIN, L. and KOHN, M. (1966), 'Social class, occupation and parental values: a cross-national study', *Am. Soc. Rev.*, 31, pp. 466–79.

PIAGET, J. (1933), *The Moral Judgement of the Child*, 1962 edn. New York: Collier Books.

REX, J. (1963), *Key Problems in Sociological Theory*. London: Routledge & Kegan Paul.

RIEFF, P. (1959), *Freud: The Mind of a Moralist*. New York: Viking Press.

ROTHBART, M. and MACCOBY, E. E. (1966), 'Parents' differential reactions to sons and daughters', *J. of Personality and Soc. Psych.*, 4, pp. 237–43.

SACKS, H. (1972), 'The analysability of children's stories', in *Directions in Sociolinguistics*, (ed.) J. J. Gumperz and D. Hymes, op. cit.

SANFORD, N. (1955), 'The dynamics of identification', *Psych. Rev.*, 62, pp. 106–17.

SCHUTZ, A. (1962), *Collected Papers:* vol. I. *The Problem of Social Reality* (ed.) M. Nantnason. The Hague: Martinus Nijhoff.

SCHUTZ, A. (1964), *Collected Papers:* vol. II. *Studies in Social Theory* (ed.) A. Brodensen. The Hague: Martinus Nijhoff.

SEARS, R. (1960), 'The growth of conscience', *Personality and Child Development*, (ed.) I. Iscoe and H. Stevenson, op. cit.

SEARS, R. (1961), 'Relation of early aggression experiences to aggression in middle childhood', *J. of Ab. and Soc. Psych.*, 63, pp. 466–92.

SEARS, R., MACCOBY, E. E. and LEVIN, H. (1957), *Patterns of Childrearing*. Chicago: Row Patterson.

SEARS, R., RAU, L. and ALPERT, R. (1965), *Identification and Child Rearing*. Stanford University Press.

SEWELL, W. (1952), 'Infant training and the personality of the child', *Am. J. of Soc.*, 58, pp. 150–9.

SEWELL, W. (1961), 'Social class and childhood personality', *Sociometry*, 24, pp. 340–56.

SEWELL, W. (1963), 'Some recent developments in socialization theory and research', *The Annals of the American Academy of Political and Social Science*, 349.

SLATER, C. and GOLD, M. (1958), 'Office, factory, store . . . and family: a study of integration setting', *Am. Soc. Rev.*, 23. pp. 64–74.

SLOBIN, D. (1966), 'Grammatical transformations and sentence comprehension in childhood and adulthood', *Journal of Verbal Learning and Verbal Behaviour*, 5, pp. 219–27.

SLOBIN, D. (1970). 'Suggested universals in the ontogenesis of grammar', Working Paper 32, Language Behaviour Research Laboratory, University of California, Berkeley.

SLOBIN, D. (1971), *Psycholinguistics*. Glenview, Illinois: Scott, Foresman.

SLOBIN, D., ERVIN-TRIPP, S. *et al.* (1967), 'A field manual for cross-cultural study of communicative competence', Language Behaviour Research Laboratory, University of California, Berkeley.

SPIRO, M. (1959), 'Culture and personality: the natural history of a false dichotomy', *Psychiatry*, 14, pp. 19–41.

STRAUSS, A. (1953), 'The development of conceptions of rules in children', *Child Development*, 25, pp. 193–208.

STRAUSS, A. (1956), *The Social Psychology of George Herbert Mead*, ed. writings of G. H. Mead, Phoenix Books, University of Chicago Press.

STROSS, B. (1970), 'Language acquisition in Tenejapa Tzeltal children', Working Paper 20, Language Behaviour Research Laboratory, University of California, Berkeley.

SWANSON, C. (1961), 'Mead and Freud: their relevance for social psychology', *Sociometry*, 23, pp. 319–39.

VYGOTSKY, L. V. (1962), *Thought and Language*, trans. E. Hauffman and G. Vakar. Cambridge, Mass.: M.I.T. Press.

WALTERS, E. and CRANDALL, V. (1960), 'Social class and observed maternal behaviour', *Child Development*, 35, pp. 1021–32.

WEIR, R. (1962), *Language in the Crib*. The Hague: Mouton.

WHITE, M. S. (1957), 'Social class, childrearing practices and child behaviour', *Am. Soc. Rev.*, 22, pp. 704–12.

WHITING, B. (1963), *Six Cultures: Studies in Childrearing*. New York: Wiley.

WHITING, J. (1959), 'Sorcery, sin and superego: some cross-cultural mechanisms of social control', *Nebraska Symposium on Motivation*, (ed.) G. Jones. University of Nebraska Press.

WHITING, J. (1960), 'Resource mediation and learning by identification', *Personality and Child Development*, (ed.) I. Iscoe and H. Stevenson, op. cit.

WHITING, J. and CHILD, I. (1953), *Child Training and Personality*. Yale University Press.

WOLFENSTEIN, M. (1951), 'Towards a fun morality', *Journal of Social Issues*, 4, pp. 15–25.

WRONG, D. (1961), 'The oversocialized concept of man in sociology', *Am. Soc. Rev.*, 26, pp. 184–93.

YARROW, M. R. (1963), 'Problems of methods in parent-child research', *Child Development*, 34, pp. 215–26.

Appendix The functional basis of language

M. A. K. Halliday

What do we understand by a 'functional approach' to the study of language? Investigations into 'the functions of language' have often figured prominently in linguistic research; there are several possible reasons for wanting to gain some insight into how language is used. Among other things, it would be helpful to be able to establish some general principles relating to the use of language; and this is perhaps the most usual interpretation of the concept of a functional approach.

But another question, no less significant, is that of the relation between the functions of language and language itself. If language has evolved in the service of certain functions that may in the broadest sense be called 'social' functions, has this left its mark? Has the character of language been shaped and determined by what we use it for? There are a number of reasons for suggesting that it has; and if this is true, then it may be an important factor in any discussion of language and society.

There is one aspect of the relation between language and its use which immediately springs to mind, but which is not the one we are concerned with here. The social functions of language clearly determine the pattern of language *varieties*, in the sense of what have been called 'diatypic' varieties, or 'registers'; the register range, or linguistic repertoire, of a community or of an individual is derived from the range of uses that language is put to in that particular culture or sub-culture. There will probably be no bureaucratic mode of discourse in a society without a bureaucracy. The concept 'range of uses' has to be understood carefully and with common sense: there might well, for example, be a register of military diction in a hypothetical society that does not make war—because it observes and records the exploits of others that do. Its uses of language do not include fighting, but they do include historiography and news reporting. This is not a departure from the principle, merely an indication that it must be thoughtfully applied.[1]

But diatypic variation in language, the existence of different fields and modes and tenors of discourse, is part of the resources of the linguistic system; and the system has to be able to accommodate it. If we are able to vary our level of formality in talking or writing, or to switch freely between one type of context and another, using language now to plan some organized activity, now to deliver a public lecture, now to keep the children in order, this is because the nature of language is such that it has all these functions built in to its total capacity. So even if we start from a consideration of how language varies—how we make different selections in meaning, and therefore in grammar and vocabulary, according to the context of use—we are led into the more fundamental question of the relation between the functions of language and the nature of the linguistic system.

Hence the interpretation of our original question which concerns us here is this: is the social functioning of language reflected in linguistic structure—that is, in the internal organization of language as a system? It is not unreasonable to expect that it will be. It was said to be, in fact, by Malinowski, who wrote in 1923 that 'language in its structure mirrors the real categories derived from the practical attitudes of the child . . .'[2] In Malinowski's view all uses of language, throughout all stages of cultural evolution, had left their imprint on linguistic structure, although 'if our theory is right, the fundamental outlines of grammar are due mainly to the most primitive uses of language.'

It was in the language of young children that Malinowski saw most clearly the functional origins of the language system. His formulation was, actually, 'the practical attitudes of the child, and of primitive or natural man'; but he later modified this view, realizing that linguistic research had demonstrated that there was no such thing as a 'primitive language'—all adult speech represented the same highly sophisticated level of linguistic evolution. Similarly all uses of language, however abstract, and however complex the social structure with which they were associated, were to be explained in terms of certain very elementary functions. It may be true that the developing language system of the child in some sense traverses, or at least provides an analogy for, the stages through which language itself has evolved; but there are no living specimens of its ancestral types, so that any evidence can only come from within, from studying the language system and how it is learnt by a child.

Malinowski's ideas were rather ahead of his time, and they were not yet backed up by adequate investigations of language development. Not that there was no important work available in this field at the time Malinowski was writing; there was, although the first great expansion of interest came shortly afterwards. But most of the work—and this remained true until very recently, right throughout the second wave of expansion, the psycholinguistic movement of the 1960s—was concerned primarily with the mechanism of language rather than with its meaning and function. On the one hand, the interest lay in the acquisition of sounds—in the control of the means of articulation and, later on, in the mastery of the sound system, the phonology, of the language in question. On the other hand, attention was focused on the acquisition of linguistic forms—the vocabulary and the grammar of the mother tongue. The earlier studies along these lines were mainly concerned with the learning of words and word-grammar—the size of the child's vocabulary month by month, and the relative frequency of the different parts of speech—backed up by investigations of his control of sentence syntax in the written medium.[3] More recently the emphasis has tended to shift towards the acquisition of linguistic structures, seen in terms of a particular psycholinguistic view (the so-called 'nativist' view) of the language-learning faculty.

These represent different models of, or orientations towards, the language-learning process. They are not, however, either singly or collectively, adequate or particularly relevant to our present perspective. For this purpose, language acquisition—or rather language development, to revert to the earlier term; 'acquisition' is a rather misleading metaphor, suggesting that language is some sort of property to be owned—needs to be seen as the mastery of linguistic functions. Learning one's mother tongue is learning the uses of language, and the meanings, or rather the meaning potential, associated with them. The structures, the words and the sounds are the realization of this meaning potential. Learning language is learning how to mean.

If language development is regarded as the development of a meaning potential it becomes possible to consider the Malinowskian thesis seriously, since we can begin by looking at the relation between the child's linguistic structures and the uses he is putting language to. Let us do so in a moment. First, however, we should raise the question of what we mean by putting language to this or that use, what the notion of language as serving certain functions really implies. What are 'social functions of language', in the life of *homo grammaticus*, the talking ape?

One way of leading into this question is to consider certain very specialized uses of language. The languages of games furnish many such instances; for example, the bidding system of contract bridge. The language of bidding may be thought of as a system of meaning potential, a range of options that are open to the player as performer (speaker) and as receiver (addressee). The potential is shared; it is neutral as between speaker and hearer, but it presupposes speaker, hearer, and situation. It is a linguistic system: there is a set of opinions, and this provides an environment for each option in terms of the others—the system includes not merely the option of saying 'four hearts' but also the specification of when it is appropriate. The ability to say 'four hearts' in the right place, which is an instance, albeit a trivial one, of what Hymes explains as 'communicative competence', is sometimes thought of as if it was something quite separate from the ability to say 'four hearts' at all; but this is an artificial distinction: there are merely different contexts, and the meaning of four hearts within the context of the bidding stage of a game of contract bridge is different from its meaning elsewhere. (We are not concerned, of course, with whether four hearts is 'a good bid' in the circumstances or not, since this cannot be expressed in terms of the system. We are concerned, however, with the fact that 'four hearts' is meaningful in the game following 'three no trumps' or 'four diamonds' but not following 'four spades'.) We are likely to find ourselves entangled in this problem, of trying to force a distinction between meaning and function, if we insist on characterizing language subjectively as the ability, or competence, of the speaker, instead of objectively as a potential, a set of alternatives. Hence my preference for the concept of 'meaning potential', which is what the speaker/hearer *can* (what he can mean, if you like), not what he knows. The two are, to an extent, different ways of looking at the same thing; but the former, 'inter-organism' perspective has different implications from the latter, 'intra-organism' one.

There are many 'restricted languages' of this kind, in games, systems of greetings, musical scores, weather reports, recipes and numerous other such generalized contexts. The simplest instance is one in which the text consists of only one message unit, or a string of message units linked by 'and'; a well-known example is the set of a hundred or so cabled messages that one was permitted to send home at one time while on active service, a typical expression being *61 and 92*, decoded perhaps as 'happy birthday and please send DDT'. Here the meaning potential is simply the list of possible messages, as a set of options, together with the option of choosing more than once, perhaps with some specified maximum length.

The daily life of the individual talking ape does not revolve around options like these, although much of his speech does take place in fairly restricted contexts where the options are limited and the meaning potential is, in fact, rather closely specifiable. Buying and selling in a shop, going to the doctor, and many of the routines of the working day all represent situation types in which the language is by no means restricted as a whole, the transactional meanings are not closed, but nevertheless there are certain definable patterns, certain options which typically come into play. Of course one can indulge in small talk with the doctor, just as one can chatter idly while bidding at bridge; these non-transactional instances of language use (or, better, 'extra-contextual', since 'transactional' is too narrow—the talk about the weather which accompanies certain social activities is not strictly transactional, but it is clearly functional within the context) do not at all disturb the point. To say this is no more than to point out that the fact that a teacher can behave with his students otherwise than in his contextual role as a teacher does not contradict the existence of a teacher–student relationship in the social structure. Conversation on the telephone does not constitute a social context, but the entry and the closure both do: there are prescribed ways of beginning and ending the conversation.[4] All these examples relate to delimitable contexts, to social functions of language; they illustrate what we use language for, and what we expect to achieve by means of language that we should not achieve without it. It is instructive here to think of various more or less everyday tasks and ask oneself how much more complicated they would be to carry out if we had to do so without the aid of language.[5]

We could try to write a list of 'uses of language' that we would expect to be typical of an educated adult member of society. But such a list could be indefinitely prolonged, and would not by itself tell us very much. When we talk of 'social functions of language', we mean those contexts which are significant in that we are able to specify some of the meaning potential that is characteristically, and explainably, associated with them. And we shall be particularly interested if we find that in doing so we can throw light on certain features in the internal organization of language.

With this in mind, let us now go on to consider the language of the child, and in particular the relation between the child's linguistic structures and the uses to which he puts his language. The language system of the very young child is, effectively, a set of restricted language varieties; and it is characteristic of young children's language that its internal form reflects rather directly the function that it is being used to serve. What the child does with language tends to determine its structure. This relatively close match between structure and function can be brought out by a functional analysis of the system, in terms of its meaning potential. We can see from this how the structures that the child has mastered are direct reflections of the functions that language serves for him.

Figures 1–3 give an actual example of the language system of a small child. They are taken from the description of Nigel's language at age nineteen months; and each represents one functional component of the system—or rather, each one represents just a part of one such component, to keep the illustration down to a reasonable size. The total system is made up of five or six functional components of this kind.[6] Figure 1 shows the system Nigel has developed for the instrumental function of language. This refers to the use of language for the purpose of satisfying material needs:

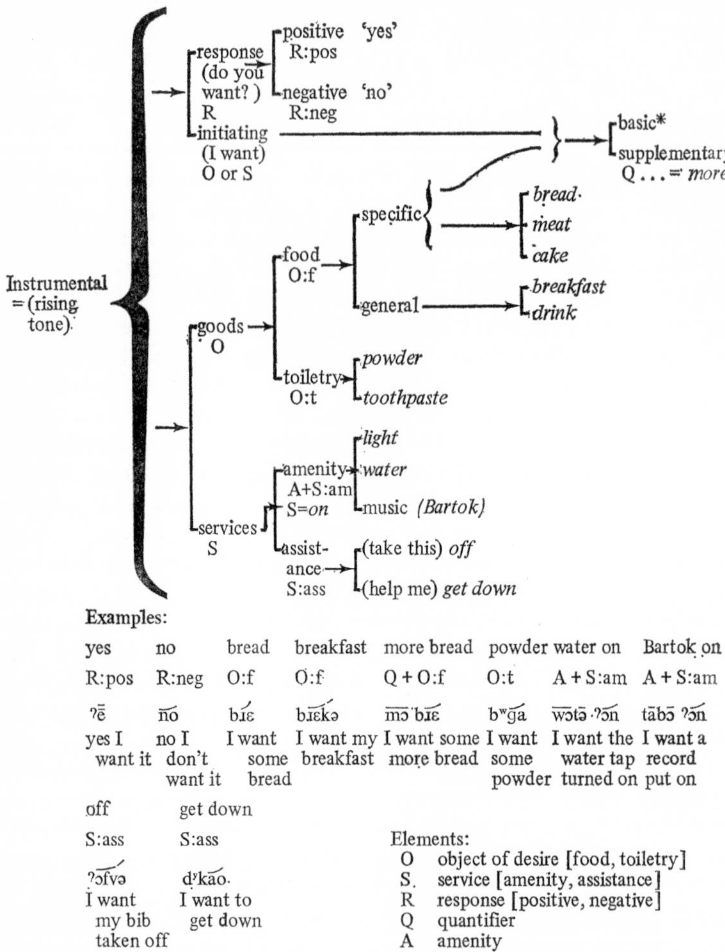

Figure 1 Nigel at nineteen months: part of the instrumental component

it is the 'I want' function, including of course 'I don't want'. Here the child has developed a meaning potential in which he can request either goods or services, the latter in the form either of physical assistance or of having something made available to him. We show some examples of these requests. In addition his demand may be in response to a question 'do you want . . . ?', in which case the answer may be positive or negative; or it may be initiated by himself, in which case it is always positive. Furthermore, under one set of conditions, namely where the demand is initiated by himself and it is a demand for a specific item of food, there is a further option in the meaning potential since he has learnt that he can demand not only a first instalment but also a supplementary one, 'more'. (This does not correspond to the adult interpretation; he may ask for more bread when he has not yet had any bread but has had something else. Note that he has not yet learnt the meaning 'no more'.) With toiletry, and with general demands for food, this option does not arise. In the system of 'basic' versus 'supplementary', therefore, the term 'basic' is the unmarked one (indicated by the asterisk), where 'unmarked' is defined as that which must be selected if the conditions permitting a choice are not satisfied.

Each option in the meaning potential is expressed, or 'realized', by some structure-forming element. In the instrumental component there are just five of these: the response element, the object of desire, the service desired, the amenity, and the quantifier. The selection which the child makes of a particular configuration of options within his meaning potential is organized as a structure; but it is a structure in which the elements are very clearly related to the type of function which the language is being made to serve for him. For example, there is obviously a connection between the 'instrumental' function of language and the presence, in the structures derived from it, of an element having the structural function 'object of desire'. What is significant is not, of course, the label we put on it, but the fact that we are led to identify a particular category, to which a label such as this then turns out to be appropriate.

The analysis that we have offered is a functional one in the two distinct but related senses in which the term 'functional' is used in linguistics. It is an account of the functions of language; and at the same time the structures are expressed in terms of functional elements (and not of classes, such as noun and verb). It could be thought of as a kind of 'case grammar', although the structural parts are strictly speaking 'elements of structure' (as in system-structure theory) rather than 'cases'; they are specific to the context (i.e. to the particular function of language, in this instance), and they account for the entire structure, whereas cases are contextually undifferentiated and also restricted to elements that are syntactically dependent on a verb.

We have assumed for purposes of illustration a relatively early stage of language learning; at this stage Nigel has only one- and two-element structures. But it does not matter much which stage was chosen; the emphasis is here on the form of the language system. This consists of a meaning potential, represented as a network of options, which are derived from a particular social function and are realized, in their turn, by structures whose elements relate directly to the meanings that are being expressed. These elements seem to be more appropriately described in terms such as 'object of desire', which clearly derives from the 'I want' function of language, than in any 'purely' grammatical terms, whether these are drawn from the grammar of the adult language (like 'subject') or introduced especially to account for the linguistic structures of the child (like 'pivot'). I shall suggest, however, that in principle the same is true of the elements of structure of the adult language: that these also have their origin in the social functions of language, though in a way that is less direct and therefore less immediately apparent. Even such a 'purely grammatical' function as 'subject' is derivable from language in use; in fact, the notion that there are 'purely grammatical' elements of structure is really self-contradictory.

The same principle is noticeable in the other two functions which we are illustrating here, again in a simplified form. One of these is the 'regulatory' function of language (Figure 2). This is the use of language to control the behaviour of others, to manipulate the persons in the environment—the 'do as I tell you' function. Here we find a basic distinction into a demand for the other person's company and a demand for a specific action on his or her part. The demand for company may be a general request to 'come with me', or refer to a particular location 'over there', 'down here', 'in the (other) room'; and it may be marked for urgency. The performance requested may be drawing a picture or singing a song; if it is a song, it may be new (for the occasion) or a repeat performance. It is interesting to note that there is no negative in the regulatory function at this stage; the meaning 'prohibition' is not among the options in the child's potential.

The third example is of the 'interactional' function (Figure 3). This is the child's use of language as a means of personal interaction with those around him—the 'me and you' function of language. Here the child is either interacting with someone who is present ('greeting') or seeking to interact with someone who is

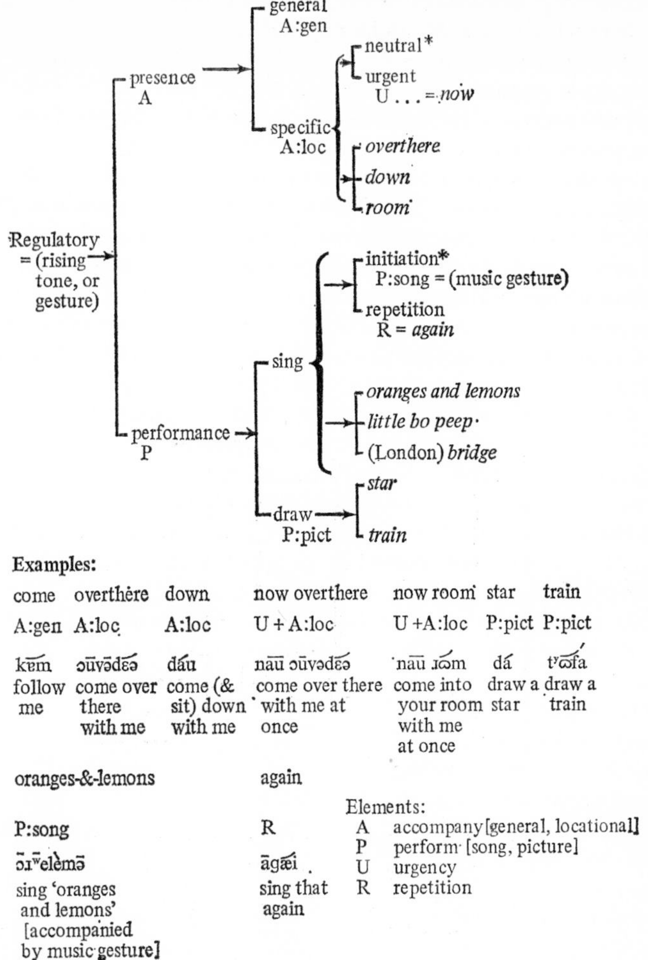

Figure 2 Nigel at nineteen months: part of the regulatory component

absent ('calling'). That someone may either be generalized, with *hullo* used (i) in narrow tone accompanied by a smile, to commune with an intimate or greet a stranger, or (ii) in wide tone, loud, to summon company; or it may be personalized, in which case it is either a statement of the need for interaction, . . . *come!*, or a search, *where . . . ?* And there is here a further choice in meaning, realized by intonation. All utterances in the instrumental and regulatory functions end on a high rising tone, unless this is replaced by a gesture, as in the demand for music; this is the tone which is used when the child requires a response of any kind. In the interactional function there are two types of utterance, those requiring a response and those not; the former have the final rise, the latter end on a falling tone (as do utterances in the other functions which we have not illustrated here).

It would be wrong to draw too sharp a line between the different functions in the child's linguistic system. There is a clear connection between the instrumental and the regulatory functions, in that both represent types of demand to be met by some action on the part of the addressee; and between the regulatory and the interactional, in that both involve the assumption of an interpersonal relationship. Nevertheless, the functions we have suggested are distinguish-

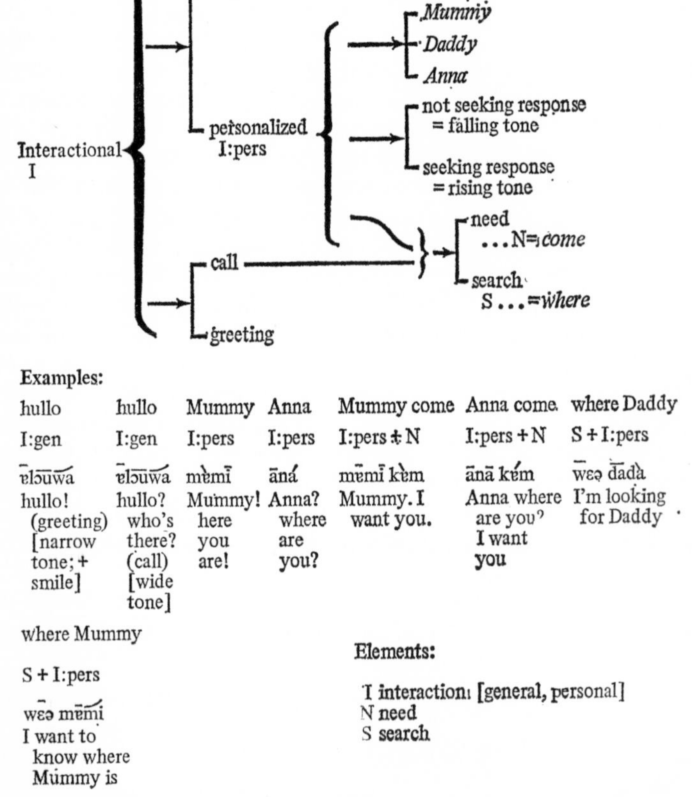

Figure 3 Nigel at nineteen months: part of the interactional component

able from one another; and this is important, because it is through the gradual extension of his meaning potential into new functions that the child's linguistic horizons become enlarged. In the instrumental function, it does not matter who provides the bread or turns the tap on; the intention is satisfied by the provision of the object or service in question. In the regulatory function on the other hand the request involves a specific person; it is he and no one else who must respond, by his behaviour. The interactional also involves a specific person; but he is not being required to do anything, merely to be there and in touch. There are, to be sure, borderline cases, and there are overlaps in the realization (e.g. *come* is sometimes regulatory, sometimes interactional in meaning); but such indeterminacy will be found in any system of this kind.

These extracts from the account of Nigel's developing linguistic system will serve to illustrate the types of structure that are encountered in the language of the very young child, and how they relate directly to the options that he has in his meaning potential. The networks show what the child can do, in the sense of what he can mean; the structural interpretations show the mechanism by which he does it—how the meanings are expressed, through configurations of elementary functions.

In another paper[7] I have suggested what seem to me to be the basic functions that language comes to fulfil in the early life of the child, listing the instrumental, the regulatory, the interactional, the personal, the heuristic, the imaginative and the representational. (The last was badly named; it would have been better called 'informative', since it referred specifically to the use of language for transmitting information.) These are the generalized social functions of language in the context of the young child's life. When the child has learnt to use language to some extent in any of these functions, however limited the grammatical and lexical resources he can bring to bear, then he has built up a meaning potential for that function and has mastered at least a minimal structural requirement—it may be a 'configuration' of only one element—for purposes of expressing it.

The social functions which language is serving in the life of the child determine both the options which he creates for himself and their realizations in structure. We see this clearly in the language of young children, once we begin to think of language development as the development of the social functions of language and of a meaning potential associated with them. However, although this connection between the functions of language and the linguistic system is clearest in the case of the language of very young children, it is essentially, I think, a feature of language as a whole. The internal organization of natural language can best be explained in the light of the social functions which language has evolved to serve. Language is as it is because of what is has to do. Only, the relation between language function and language structure will appear less directly, and in more complex ways, in the fully developed adult system than in children's language.

To say this is in effect to claim, with Malinowski, that ontogeny does in some respect provide a model for phylogeny. We cannot examine the origins of language. But if we can relate the form of the adult language system to its social functions, and at the same time show that the language of the child, in its various stages, is explainable in terms of the uses that he has mastered up to the particular stage, then we have at least opened up the possibility of interesting discussion about the nature and social origins of language.

It is characteristic, it seems, of the utterances of the very young child that they are functionally simple; each utterance serves just one function. If an utterance is instrumental in function, seeking the satisfaction of some material desire, then it is just instrumental and nothing else. This represents a very early stage of language development. It is shown in our illustrations by the fact that each utterance is totally specified by just one network: to derive *more bread!* we need only the instrumental system network, which fully describes its structure.

The adult language bears the marks of its humble origins in systems like these. But it differs in fundamental ways; and perhaps the most fundamental—because this is what makes it necessary to develop a level of linguistic form (grammar and vocabulary) intermediate between meanings and sounds—is the fact that utterances in the adult language are functionally complex. Every adult linguistic act, with a few broadly specifiable exceptions, is serving more than one function at once.

One very familiar type of phenomenon which illustrates this fact is that of denotation and connotation in word meanings. For example, after the F.A. Cup Final match between Leeds and Chelsea a friend of mine who is a Londoner greeted me with *I see Chelsea trounced Leeds again*, using the word *trounce* which means 'defeat' plus 'I am pleased'. But the functional multivalence of this utterance goes much further than is signalled by the word-meaning of *trounce.* The speaker was conveying a piece of information, which he suspected I already possessed, together with the further information (which I did not possess) that he also possessed it; he was referring it to our shared experience; expressing his triumph over me (I am a Leeds supporter and he knows it); and relating back to some previous exchanges between us. There is no simple functional category from which we can derive this utterance, corresponding to categories such as regulatory or instrumental in the linguistic system of the young child.

The problem for a socio-linguistic theory is: what is there in the adult language which corresponds to the functional components, the systems of meaning potential, that make up the early stages in the child's language development? Or, since that is a rather slanted way of asking the question, what is the relation of the fully developed language system to the social functions of the adult language? And can we explain something of the form that languages take by examining this relation?

In one sense, the variety of social functions of language is, obviously, much greater in the adult. The adult does more different things than the child; and in a great many of his activities, he uses language. He has a very broad diatypic spectrum. Yet there is another sense in which the adult's range of functional variation may be poorer, and we can best appreciate this if we take the child as our point of departure. Among the child's uses of language there appears, after a time, the use of language to convey new information: to communicate a content that is (regarded by the speaker as) unknown to the addressee. I had referred to this in a general way as the 'representational' function; but it would be better (as I suggested above) if one were to use a more specific term, such as 'informative', since this makes it easier to interpret subsequent developments. In the course of maturation this function is increasingly emphasized, until eventually it comes to dominate, if not the adult's use of language, at least his conception of the use of language. The adult tends to be sceptical if it is suggested to him that language has other uses than that of conveying information; and he will usually think next of the use of language to *mis*inform—which is simply a variant of the informative function. Yet for the young child the informative is a rather minor function, relatively late to emerge. Many problems of communication between adult and child, for example in the infant school, arise from the adults' failure to grasp this fact. This can be seen in some adult renderings of children's rhymes and songs, which are often very dramatic, with an intonation and rhythm appropriate to the content; whereas for the child the language is not primarily content—it is language in its imaginative function, and needs to be expressed as pattern, patterns of meaning and structure and vocabulary and sound. Similarly, failures have been reported when actors have recorded foreign language courses; their renderings focus attention only on the use of language to convey information, and it seems that when learning a foreign language, as when learning the mother tongue, it is necessary to take other uses of language into account, especially in the beginning stages.

What happens in the course of maturation is a process that we might from one point of view call 'functional reduction', whereby the original functional range of the child's language—a set of fairly discrete functional components each with its own meaning potential—is gradually replaced by a more highly coded and more abstract, but also simpler, functional system. There is an immense functional diversity in the adult's use of language; immense, that is, if we simply ask 'in what kinds of activity does language play a part for him?' But this diversity of usage is reduced in the internal organization of the adult language system—in the grammar, in other words—to a very small set of functional components. Let us call these for the moment 'macro-functions' to distinguish them from the functions of the child's emergent language system, the instrumental, the regulatory and so on. These 'macro-functions' are the highly abstract linguistic reflexes of the multiplicity of social uses of language.

The innumerable social purposes for which adults use language are not represented directly, one by one, in the form of functional components in the language system, as are those of the child. With the very young child, 'function' equals 'use'; and there is no grammar, no intermediate level of internal organization in language, only a content and an expression. With the adult, there are indefinitely many uses, but only three or four functions, or 'macro-functions' as we are calling them; and these macro-functions appear at a new level in the linguistic system—they take the form of 'grammar'. The grammatical system has as it were a functional input and a structural output; it provides the mechanism for different functions to be combined in one utterance in the way the adult requires. But these macro-functions, although they are only indirectly related to specific uses of language, are still recognizable as abstract representations of the basic functions which language is made to serve.

One of these macro-functions is what is sometimes called the representational one. But just as earlier, in talking of the use of language to convey information, I preferred the more specific term 'informative', so here I shall also prefer another term—but this time a different one, because this is a very distinct concept. Here we are referring to the linguistic expression of ideational content; let us call this macro-function of the adult language system the 'ideational' function. For the child, the use of language to inform is just one instance of language use, one function among many. But with the adult, the ideational element in language is present in all its uses; no matter what he is doing with language he will find himself exploiting its ideational resources, its potential for expressing a content in terms of the speaker's experience and that of the speech community. There are exceptions, types of utterance like *how do you do?* and *no wonder!* which have no ideational content in them; but otherwise there is some ideational component involved, however small, in all the specific uses of language in which the adult typically engages.

This no doubt is why the adult tends to think of language primarily in terms of its capacity to inform. But where is the origin of this ideational element to be sought within the linguistic repertoire of the very young child? Not, I think, in the informative function, which seems to be in some sense secondary, derived from others that have already appeared. It is to be sought rather in the combination of the personal and the heuristic, in that phase of linguistic development which becomes crucial at a particular time, probably (as in Nigel's case) shortly after the emergence of the more directly pragmatic functions which we illustrated in Figures 1–3. At the age from which these examples were taken, nineteen months, Nigel had already begun to use language also in the personal, the heuristic and the imaginative functions; it was noticeable that language was becoming, for him, a means of organizing and storing his experience. Here we saw the beginnings of a 'grammar'—that is, a level of lexico-grammatical organization, or linguistic 'form'; and of utterances having more than one function. The words and structures learnt in these new functions were soon turned also to pragmatic use, as in some of the examples quoted of the instrumental and regulatory functions. But it appears that much of the initial impetus to the learning of the formal patterns (as distinct from the spontaneous modes of expression characteristic of the first few months of speech) was the need to impose order on the environment and to define his own person in relation to and in distinction from it. Hence—to illustrate just from vocabulary—we find the word *bus*, though it is RECOGNIZED as the name of a toy bus as well as of full-sized specimens, being used at first exclusively to comment on the sight or sound of buses in the street and only later as a demand for the toy; and the one or two exceptions to this, e.g. *bird* which was at first used ONLY in the instrumental sense of 'I want my toy bird', tend to drop out of the system altogether and are relearnt in a personal-heuristic context later.

It seems therefore that the personal-heuristic function is a major impetus to the enlarging of the ideational element in the child's linguistic system. We should not however exaggerate its role *vis-à-vis* that of the earlier pragmatic functions; the period fifteen to twenty-one months was in Nigel's case characterized by a rapid development of grammatical and lexical resources which were (as a whole) exploited in all the functional contexts that he had mastered so far. The one function that had not yet emerged was the informative; even when pressed—as he frequently was—to 'tell Mummy where you went' or 'tell Daddy what you saw', he was incapable of doing so, although in many instances he had previously used the required sentences quite appropriately in a different function. It was clear that he had not internalized the fact that language could be used to tell people things they did not know, to communicate experience that had NOT been shared. But this was no barrier to the development of an ideational component in his linguistic system. The ideational element, as it evolves, becomes crucial to the use of language in all the functions that the child has learnt to control; and this gives the clue to its status as a 'macro-function'. Whatever specific use one is making of language, one will sooner or later find it necessary to refer explicitly to the categories of one's experience of the world. All, or nearly all, utterances come to have an ideational component in them. But, at the same time, they all have something else besides.

When we talk of the ideational function of the adult language, therefore, we are using 'function' in a more generalized sense (as indicated by our term 'macro-function') than when we refer to the specific functions that make up the language of the young child. Functions such as 'instrumental' and 'regulatory' are really the same thing as 'uses of language'. The ideational function, on the other hand, is a major component of meaning in the language system that is basic to more or less all uses of language. It is still a 'meaning potential', although the potential is very vast and complex; for example, the whole of the transitivity system in language—the interpretation and expression in language of the different types of process of the external world, including material, mental and abstract processes of every kind—is part of the ideational component of the grammar. And the structures that express these ideational meanings are still recognizably derived from the meanings themselves; their elements are in this respect not essentially different from those such as 'object of desire' that we saw in Figures 1–3. They represent the categories of our interpretation of experience. So for example a clause such as *Sir Christopher Wren built this gazebo* may be analysed as a configuration of the functions 'agent' *Sir Christopher Wren*, 'process: material: creation' *built*, 'goal: effected' *this gazebo*, where 'agent', 'process', 'goal' and their sub-categories reflect our understanding of phenomena that come within our experience. Hence this function of language, which is that of encoding our experience in the form of an ideational content, not only specifies the available options in meaning but also determines the nature of their structural realizations. The notions of agent, process and the like make sense only if we assume an ideational function in the adult language, just as 'object of desire' and 'service' make sense only if we assume an instrumental function in the emergent language of the child. But this analysis is not imposed from outside in order to satisfy some theory of linguistic functions; an analysis in something like these terms is necessary (whatever form it finally takes for the language in question) if we are to explain the structure of clauses. The clause is a structural unit, and it is the one by which we express a particular range of ideational meanings, our experience of processes—the processes of the external world, both concrete and abstract, and the processes of our own consciousness, seeing, liking, thinking, talking and so on. Transitivity is simply the grammar of the clause in its ideational aspect.

Figure 4 sets out the principal options in the transitivity system of English, showing how these are realized in the form of structures. It can be seen that the structure-forming elements—agent, process, phenomenon etc.—are all related to the general function of expressing processes. The labels that we give to them describe their specific roles in the encoding of these meanings, but the elements themselves are identified syntactically. Thus, in the English clause there is a distinct element of structure which expresses the cause of a process when that process is brought about by something other than the entity that is primarily affected by it (e.g. *the storm* in *the storm shook the house*); we can reasonably label this the 'agent', but whether we do so or not it is present in the grammar as an element deriving from the ideational function of language.

The clause, however, is not confined to the expression of transitivity; it has other functions besides. There are non-ideational elements in the adult language system, even though the adult speaker is often reluctant to recognize them. Again, however, they are grouped together as a single 'macro-function' in the grammar, covering a whole range of particular uses of language. This is the macro-function that we shall refer to as the 'interpersonal'; it embodies all use of language to express social and personal relations, including all forms of the speaker's intrusion into the speech situation and the speech act. The young child also uses language interpersonally, as we have seen, interacting with other people, controlling their behaviour, and also expressing his own personality

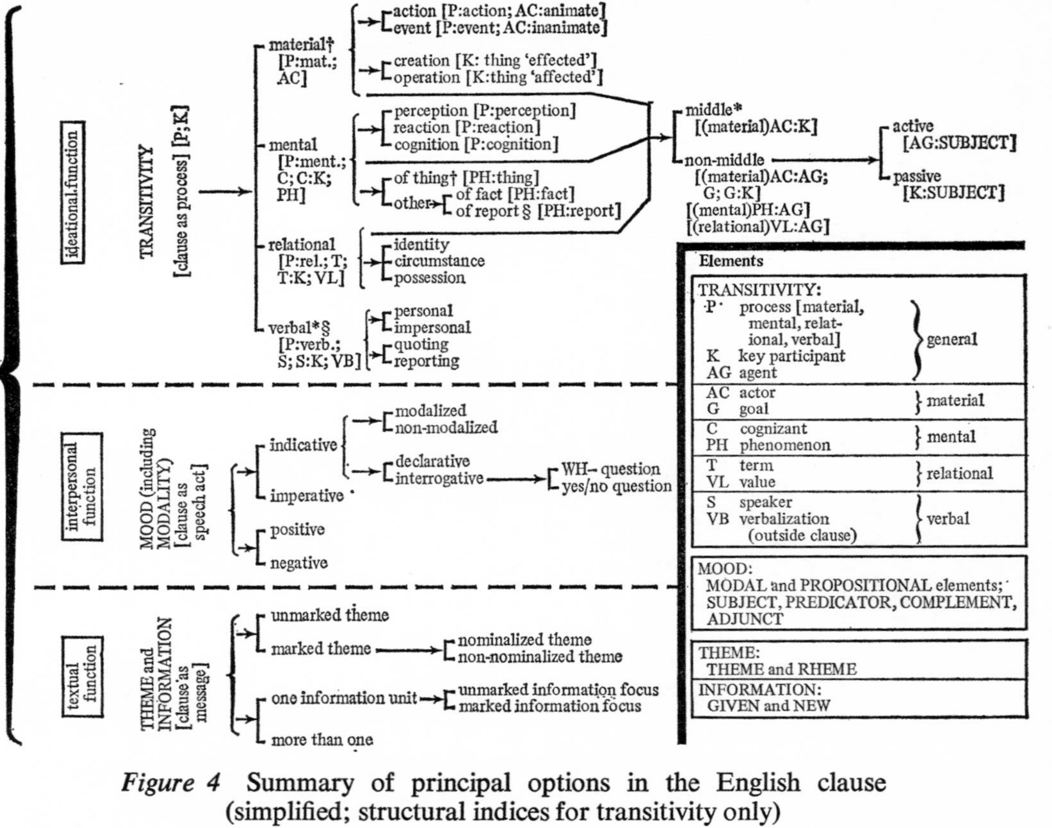

Figure 4 Summary of principal options in the English clause (simplified; structural indices for transitivity only)

and his own attitudes and feelings; but these uses are specific and differentiated. Later on they become generalized in a single functional component of the grammatical system, at this more abstract level. In the clause, the interpersonal element is represented by mood and modality—the selection by the speaker of a particular role in the speech situation, and his determination of the choice of roles for the addressee (mood), and the expression of his judgments and predictions (modality).

We are not suggesting that one cannot distinguish, in the adult language, specific uses of language of a socio-personal kind; on the contrary, we can recognize an unlimited number. We use language to approve and disapprove; to express belief, opinion, doubt; to include in the social group, or exclude from it; to ask and answer; to express personal feelings; to achieve intimacy; to greet, chat up, take leave of; in all these and many other ways. But in the structure of the adult language there is an integrated 'interpersonal' component, which provides the meaning potential for this element as it is present in all uses of language, just as the 'ideational' component provides the resources for the representation of experience that is also an essential element whatever the specific type of language use.

These two macro-functions, the ideational and the interpersonal, together determine a large part of the meaning potential that is incorporated in the grammar of every language. This can be seen very clearly in the grammar of the clause, which has its ideational aspect, transitivity, and its interpersonal aspect, mood (including modality). There is also a third macro-function, the 'textual', which fills the requirement that language should be operationally relevant —that it should have a texture, in real contexts of situation, that distinguishes a living message from a mere entry in a grammar or a dictionary. This third component provides the remaining strands of meaning potential to be woven into the fabric of linguistic structure.

We shall not attempt to illustrate in detail the interpersonal and the textual functions. Included in Figure 4 are a few of the principal options which make up these components in the English clause; their structural realizations are not shown, but the same principle holds, whereby the structural mechanism reflects the generalized meanings that are being expressed. The intention here is simply to bring out the fact that a linguistic structure—of which the clause is the best example—serves as a means for the integrated expression of all the functionally distinct components of meaning in language. Some simple clauses are analysed along these lines in Figure 5.

	this gazebo	was	built	by Sir Christopher Wren
IDEATIONAL material:(action/ creation/(non-middle:passive))	G:K: effected	P:material/ action		AC:AG: animate
INTERPERSONAL. declarative/non-modalized	Modal		Propositional	
	Subject	Predicator		Adjunct
TEXTUAL unmarked theme one information unit: unmarked	Theme	Rheme		
	Given			New

	I	had		a cat...
IDEATIONAL relational: (possession/middle)	T:K	P:rel- ational		VL
INTERPERSONAL declarative/non-modalized	Modal	=did	have Propositional	
	Subject	Predicator		Complement
TEXTUAL unmarked theme one information unit: unmarked	Theme	Rheme		
	Given	New		

	...the cat	pleased		me
ID. mental:(reaction/ fact/(non-middle: active)	PH:AG: thing	P:mental: reaction		C:K
INT. declarative/ non-modalized	Modal	=did	please	Propositional
	Subject	Predicator		Complement
TEXT. unmarked theme one information unit: unmarked	Theme	Rheme		
	Given	New		

	such a tale	you	would	never believe
ID. mental:(cognition/ report/middle)	PH: report	C:K	P:mental: cognition	
INT.declarative/ modalized negative	Propo-.	Modal		-sitional
	Complement	Subject	Predicator	
TEXT. marked theme: non-nominalized two information units	Theme	Rheme		
	New ‖	Given	New	

Figure 5 Analysis of clauses, showing simultaneous structures

What we know as 'grammar' is the linguistic device for hooking up together the selections in meaning which are derived from the various functions of language, and realizing them in a unified structural form. Whereas with the child, in the first beginnings of the system, the functions remain unintegrated, being in effect functional varieties of speech act, with one utterance having just one function, the linguistic units of the adult language serve all (macro-) functions at once. A clause in English is the simultaneous realization of ideational, interpersonal and textual meanings. But these components are not put together in discrete fashion such that we can point to one segment of the clause as expressing one type of meaning and another segment as expressing another. The choice of a word may express one type of meaning, its morphology another, and its position in sequence another; and any element is likely to have more than one structural role, like a chord in a polyphonic structure which participates simultaneously in a number of melodic lines. This last point is illustrated by the analyses in Figure 5.

We hope to have made it clear in what sense it is being said that the concept of the social function of language is central to the interpretation of language as a system. The internal organization of language is not accidental; it embodies the functions that language has evolved to serve in the life of social man. This essentially was Malinowski's claim; and, as Malinowski suggested, we can see it most clearly in the linguistic system of the young child. There, the utterance has in principle just one structure; each element in it has therefore just one structural function, and that function is related to the meaning potential—to the set of options available to the child in that particular social function.

In the developed linguistic system of the adult, the functional origins are still discernible. Here, however, each utterance has a number of structures simultaneously—we have used the analogy of polyphony. Each element is a complex of roles, and enters into more than one structure (indeed the concept 'element of structure' is a purely abstract concept; it is merely a role set, which is then realized by some item in the language). The structure of the adult language still represents the functional meaning potential; but because of the variety of social uses of language, a 'grammar' has emerged whereby the options are organized into a few large sets in which the speaker selects simultaneously whatever the specific use he is making of language. These sets of options, which are recognizable empirically in the grammar, correspond to the few highly generalized realms of meaning that are essential to the social functioning of language—and hence are intrinsic to language as a system. Because language serves a generalized 'ideational' function, we are able to use it for all the specific purposes and types of context which involve the communication of experience. Because it serves a generalized 'interpersonal' function, we are able to use it for all the specific forms of personal expression and social interaction. And a prerequisite to its effective operation under both these headings is what we have referred to as the 'textual' function, whereby language becomes text, is related to itself and to its contexts of use. Without the textual component of meaning, we should be unable to make any use of language at all.

If we want to pursue this line of interpretation further, we shall have to go outside language to some theory of social meanings. From the point of view of a linguist the most important work in this field is that of Bernstein, whose theories of cultural transmission and social change are unique in this respect, that language is built into them as an essential element in social processes. Although Bernstein is primarily investigating social and not linguistic phenomena, his ideas shed very considerable light on language; in particular, in relation to the concept of language as meaning potential, he has been able to define certain contexts which are crucial to the socialization of the child and to identify the significant

I SYSTEMS

a → [x / y]	there is a system *x*/*y* with entry condition *a* [if *a*, then either *x* or *y*]
a { → [x / y] ; → [m / n] }	there are two simultaneous systems *x*/*y* and *m*/*n*, both having entry condition *a* [if *a*, then both either *x* or *y* and, independently, either *m* or *n*]
a → [x → [m / n] ; y]	there are two systems *x*/*y* and *m*/*n*, ordered in dependence such that *m*/*n* has entry condition *x* and *x*/*y* has entry condition *a* [if *a* then either *x* or *y*, and if *x*, then either *m* or *n*]
a } b } → [x / y]	there is a system *x*/*y* with compound entry condition, conjunction of *a* and *b* [if both *a* and *b*, then either *x* or *y*]
a] c] → [m / n]	there is a system *m*/*n* with two possible entry conditions, disjunction of *a* and *c* [if either *a* or *c*, or both, then either *m* or *n*]
a* ... x*	[or any paired symbol] *x* is unmarked with respect to *a* [if *a*, then always *x*]
x*	*x* is unmarked with respect to all environments [if any tangential feature, then always *x*]. Note: a tangential feature is the oblique term in a superordinate system, e.g. *a* in → [a / b → [x* / y]]

II STRUCTURES

X	X is added
X...	X precedes (occurs initially)
...X	X follows (occurs finally)
X+Y	Y follows X
X:z	X is (further specified as) z
X:Y	X is (combined into one element with) Y
X=*a*	X is (realized as) *a*
[X]	X is optional

Figure 6 Summary of notational conventions

Index